MENTAL PHILOSOPHY:

INCLUDING THE

INTELLECT, SENSIBILITIES, AND WILL.

BY

JOSEPH HAVEN,

PROFESSOR OF INTELLECTUAL AND MORAL PHILOSOPHY
IN AMHERST COLLEGE.

BOSTON:
GOULD AND LINCOLN,
59 WASHINGTON STREET.
NEW YORK: SHELDON AND COMPANY.
CINCINNATI: GEORGE S. BLANCHARD.
1862.

PREFACE.

If any apology were necessary for adding yet another to the numerous works on Mental Philosophy which have recently appeared, the circumstances that led to the preparation of the present volume may, perhaps, constitute that apology.

When called, several years since, to the chair of Mental and Moral Philosophy, in this Institution, the text-books, then in use, seemed to me not well adapted to the wants of College students. Nor was it easy to make a change for the better. Of the works in this department, then generally in use in our Colleges, some presumed on a more extensive acquaintance with the science than most young men at this stage of education are likely to possess; others, again, erring on the opposite extreme, were deficient in thorough and scientific treatment; while most, if not all, were, at the best, incomplete, presenting but a partial survey of the entire field. In none of them was the science of mind presented in its completeness and symmetry, in a manner at once simple, yet scientific; in none of them, moreover, was it brought down to the present time. Something more complete, more simple, more thorough, seemed desirable.

Every year of subsequent experience as a teacher has but confirmed this impression, and made the want of a book better adapted to the purposes of instruction, in our American Colleges, more deeply felt. The works on mental science, which have recently appeared in this country, while they are certainly a valuable contribution to the department of philosophy, seem to meet this deficiency in part, but *only* in part. They traverse usually but a portion of the ground which Psychology legitimately occupies, confining their attention, for the most part, to the *Intellectual* Faculties, to the exclusion of the *Sensibilities*, and the *Will*.

Feeling deeply the want which has been spoken of, it seemed to me, early in my course, that something might be done toward remedying the deficiency, by preparing with care, and delivering to the classes, lectures upon the topics presented in the books, as they passed along. This course was adopted — a method devolving much labor upon the instructor, but rewarding him by the increased interest and more rapid progress of the pupils. Little by little the present work thus grew up, as the result of my studies, in connection with my classes, and of my experience in the daily routine of the recitation and lecture room. Gradually the lectures, thus prepared, came to take the place more and more of a text-book, until there seemed to be no longer any reason why they should not be put into the hands of the student as such.

It is much easier to decide what a work on mental science ought to be, than to produce such a work. It should be comprehensive and complete, treating of all that properly pertains to Psychology, giving to every part its due proportion and development. It should treat the various topics presented, in a thorough and scientific manner. It should be conversant with the literature of the department, placing the student in possession, not only of the true doctrines, but, to some extent also, of the *history* of those doctrines, showing him what has been held and taught by others upon the points in question. In style it should be clear, perspicuous, concise, yet not so barren of ornament as to be destitute of interest to the reader.

At these qualities the writer has aimed in the present treatise; with what success, others must determine.

All science, in proportion as it is complete and true, becomes simple. In proportion as this result is attained, the labor bestowed upon it disappears from view, and the writer seems, perhaps, to others, to have said but a very plain and common thing. This is peculiarly the case with mental science. The difficulty of discussing with clearness and simplicity, and, at the same time, in a complete and thorough manner, the difficult problems of Psychology, will be understood only by those who make the attempt.

J. H.

AMHERST COLLEGE, September, 1857.

CONTENTS.

INTRODUCTION.

CHAPTER I.

CHAPTER II.

DIVISION FIRST.

THE INTELLECTUAL FACULTIES.

PRELIMINARY TOPICS.

CHAPTER I.

CHAPTER II.

CHAPTER III.

PART FIRST.

THE PRESENTATIVE POWER.

PART SECOND.

THE REPRESENTATIVE POWER.

CHAPTER I.

CHAPTER II.

PART THIRD.

THE REFLECTIVE POWER.

CHAPTER I.

CHAPTER II.

PART FOURTH.

INTUITIVE POWER.

CHAPTER I.

CHAPTER II.

CHAPTER III.

CHAPTER IV.

SUPPLEMENTARY TOPICS.

CHAPTER I.

CHAPTER II.

DIVISION SECOND.

THE SENSIBILITIES.

PRELIMINARY TOPICS.

CHAPTER I.

CHAPTER II.

PART FIRST.

SIMPLE EMOTIONS.

CHAPTER I.

CHAPTER II.

PART SECOND.

THE AFFECTIONS.

CHAPTER I.

CHAPTER II.

PART THIRD.

THE DESIRES.

CHAPTER I.

CHAPTER II.

CHAPTER III.

CHAPTER IV.

DIVISION THIRD.

THE WILL.

PRELIMINARY OBSERVATIONS.

CHAPTER I.

CHAPTER II.

CHAPTER III.

CHAPTER IV.

CHAPTER V.

CHAPTER VI.

CHAPTER VII.

INTRODUCTION.

CHAPTER I.

ON THE NATURE AND IMPORTANCE OF MENTAL SCIENCE.

§ I.—NATURE OF THE SCIENCE.

Mental Philosophy, what.—What is Mental Philosophy, as distinguished from other branches of science?

Philosophy, in the wide sense usually given it, denotes the investigation and explanation of the causes of things; it seeks to discover, and scientifically to state, the general laws both of matter and mind; its object is to ascertain facts, and their relation to each other. Mental Philosophy has for its object to ascertain the facts and laws of mental operation.

Metaphysics, what.—Of the two grand departments of human knowledge—the science of matter and the science of mind—the former, comprising whatever relates to material phenomena, the science of nature, is known under the general name of *Physics;* the latter, the science of mind, is often designated by the corresponding term, neither very correct nor very fortunate, *Metaphysics.* This term is often used to include whatever does not properly fall under the class of Physics. In its strict sense, it does not include so much, but denotes properly the science of abstract truth; the science of being, in itself considered—apart from its particular accidents and properties—that which we now call Ontology. The term is commonly ascribed to Aristotle, but incorrectly. It originated with his followers. Several treatises of his relating to natural science having been collected and published, under the title τα φυσικα, other treatises on philosophical subjects were afterward arranged, under the title τα μετα φυσικα, indicating their relation to the former, as proper to be read after the perusal of those. Hence the term came into use in the general sense, already spoken of, to denote whatever is not included under physics, although originally employed with a much more limited meaning.

Mental Philosophy not properly Metaphysics.—Neither in its wider nor in its stricter sense does this term properly designate the science of mind. Mental Philosophy neither embraces every thing not included under physics, nor is it the science of abstract being. As one of the intellectual, in distinction from the physical sciences, it holds a place along with Logic—the science of the laws of human thought and reasoning; Ethics—the science of morals; Politics—the science of human organization and government; to which should be added Ontology—the science of pure being; all which are properly embraced under the term Metaphysics, in its wider and popular sense. To designate the science of mind in distinction from these other sciences, some more definite term is required. The word *Psychology* is now coming into use as such a term.

Mental Philosophy a Natural Science.—The science of mind, indeed, deserves in one aspect to be ranked among the *natural* sciences. It is a science resting on experience, observation, and induction—a science of facts, phenomena, and laws which regulate the same. That which is specifically its object of investigation—the human mind—is strictly a part, and most important part of *nature*, unless we exclude man himself from the world to which he belongs, and of which he is lord.

Possibility of such a Science.—The possibility of the science of the human mind has been denied by some; but without good reason. If we can observe and classify the phenomena of nature, in her varied forms, animate and inanimate, and ascertain in this way the laws to which she is subject; if it is possible thus to construct a science of plants, of animals, of the elements that compose the substance of the earth, of the strata that lie arranged beneath its surface, of the forces and agencies that at any time, recent or remote, have been at work to produce the changes which have taken place upon and within our globe—nay, more, if leaving our own planet we may, by careful observation of the heavenly bodies, learn their places, movements, distances, estimate their magnitude and density, measure their speed, and thus construct a science of the stars, surely the phenomena of our own minds, the data of our own consciousness, must be at least equally within our reach, and equally capable of observation, classification, and scientific statement. If we can observe the habits of animals and plants, we can observe also the habits of men, and the phenomena of human thought and passion. If the careful induction of general truths and principles from observed facts form the basis and method of true science in the one case, so in the other.

Science of Matter and of Mind analogous.—The science of matter, and the science of mind agree perfectly in this, that all we know of either is simply the phenomena which they exhibit. We know not matter as it is in itself, but only as it affects our senses. We perceive certain qualities or properties of it, and these we embody in our definition, and beyond these we say nothing, because we know nothing. Equally relative is our knowledge of mind. What it is in itself we know not, but only its phenomena as presented to our observation and consciousness. It thinks and feels, it perceives, remembers, reasons, it loves, hates, desires, determines; these exercises are matter of experience and observation; they constitute our knowledge and our definition of mind, and beyond we cannot go.

Modes and Sources of Information the same in both.— This being the case, it is evident that both our sources of information, and our mode of investigation, must be essentially the same in the two departments of science. In either case our knowledge must be limited to phenomena merely, and these must be learned by observation and experience. A careful induction of particulars will place us in possession of general principles, or laws, and these, correctly ascertained and stated, will constitute our science, whether of matter or mind.

They differ in one Respect.— In one respect, indeed, our means of information with regard to the two branches of science differ. While both matter and mind can be known only by the observation of the phenomena which they present, in mental science the field of such observation lies in great part within ourselves—the phenomena are those of our own present or former consciousness—the mind is at once both the observer and the object observed. This circumstance, which at first seems to present a difficulty, is in reality a great advantage which this science possesses over all others.

Apparent Difficulty.—The difficulty which it seems to present is this: How can the eye perceive itself? How can the mind, as employed, for example, in remembering, or judging, or willing, inspect its own operations, since the moment its attention is turned to itself it is no longer engaged in that operation which it seeks to inspect—is no longer remembering, or judging, or willing, but is employed only in self-observation? We admit that the mind, in the very instant of its exercising any given faculty, cannot make itself, as thus engaged, the object of attention. But the operations of the mind, as given in consciousness, at any moment, may be retained or replaced by memory the next moment, and as thus replaced and attested, may stand before us the proper objects of our investigation, so long as we please. This puts it in the power of the mind to observe and to know itself.

Real Advantage. — The advantage accruing from the circumstance that the phenomena to be observed are those of our own present or former consciousness, is this: that those phenomena are fully within our reach, and also are capable of being known with greater certainty. In physical science the facts may be scattered over the globe, and over centuries of time, not personally accessible to any one observer in their completeness, and yet that completeness of observation may be essential to correct science. In psychology, the observer has within himself the essential elements of the science which he explores; the data which he seeks, are the data of his own consciousness; the science which he constructs is the science of himself.

Comparative Value of this kind of Knowledge. — The knowledge thus given in conscious experience is more correct and reliable than any other. It has this peculiarity, that it cannot be disputed. I may be mistaken in regard to the properties of a piece of matter which I hold in my hand, and which seems to me to be square or round, of such or such a color, and of such or such figure, size, and density; but I cannot be mistaken as to the fact, that it *seems* to me to be of such color, figure, etc. The former are results of perception and judgment; the latter is an immediate datum of consciousness, and cannot be called in question. To doubt our own consciousness is to call in question our very doubt, since the only evidence of our doubting is the consciousness that we doubt. As to the phenomena of the external world — the things that are passing without — I may be mistaken; as to what is passing in my own mind — the thoughts, feelings, volitions of my own conscious self — there is no room for doubt or mistake.

Not limited to Consciousness. — I do not mean, by what has been said, to imply that in our own observation of mental phenomena we are limited to the experience of our own minds, but only that this is the principal source of our information. The mental operations of others, so far as we have access to their minds, are also legitimate data. These we may observe for ourselves in the daily intercourse of life, may notice how, under given circumstances, men will think, feel, and act, and the knowledge thus acquired will constitute a valuable addition to our self-knowledge. We may receive also, in this science, as in any other, the testimony of others as to their own mental states and operations. In so far as psychology relies upon these sources, it stands on a footing with other sciences.

§ II. — Importance of Mental Science.

Comparative Neglect. — That the science of the mind has not hitherto held that high place in the public regard and estimation, at least in our own country, to which it is justly entitled, as compared with other branches of knowledge, can hardly be denied. The cause of this comparative neglect is to be found partly in the nature of the science itself, partly in the exclusively practical tendencies of the age.

The first Cause considered. — The *nature of the science* is such that its benefits are not immediately apparent. The dullest mind can perceive some use in chemistry, or botany, or natural philosophy. They are of service in the analysis of soils, the rotation of crops, the comprehension of the laws of mechanical and chemical forces. But mental science has no such application, no such practical results patent and obvious to the careless eye. Its dwelling-place and sphere of action lie removed somewhat from the observations of men. It has no splendid cabinets or museums to throw open to the gaze of the multitude. It cannot arrange in magnificent collection all the varieties of mental action, all the complications of thought and feeling as yet observed, nor illustrate by curious instruments, and nice experiments, the wonderful laws of association, the subtle changes and swift flashes of wit and fancy, and quick strong emotion, the impulses of desire, the curious play of volition, the unexplained mystery of thought, the lights and shadows that come and go upon the field of consciousness. For these curious and wonderful phenomena of the inner life there are no philosophic instruments or experiments, no charts or diagrams. Nor are there yet brilliant discoveries to be made, nor splendid rewards to be gained by the votaries of this science. "Four or five new metals," says Sydney Smith, "have been discovered within as many years, of the existence of which no human being could have had any suspicion; but no man that I know of pretends to discover four or five new passions."

The second Cause. — But the chief obstacle, as I suppose, to the more general cultivation of mental science is to be found in the exclusively practical tendencies of the age. We are a people given more to action than to thought, to enterprise than to speculation. This is perhaps inseparable from the condition of a new state. An age of action is seldom an age of reflection. External life demands the energies of a new people. The elements are to be subdued, mountains levelled, graded, tunnelled, roads constructed, cities built, and many useful, necessary works to be wrought with toil and cost, before that period comes of golden affluence, and leisure, and genial taste, and elegant culture, that can at once appreciate and reward the higher efforts of philosophic investigation.

Relation to other Sciences. — The *importance* of mental science appears from its relation to other sciences. We find in nature a gradually ascending series. As we pass from the observation and study of the mineral to the forms of vegetable life, from the plant to the insect — and thence to the animal, and from the animal, in his various orders and classes, to man, the highest type of animated existence on the earth, we are conscious of a progression in the rank and dignity of that which we contemplate. But it is only when we turn our attention from all these to the intelligence that dwells within the man, and makes him master and lord of this lower world, that we stand upon the summit of elevation and overlook the wide field of previous inquiry. Toward this all other sciences lead, as paths along the mountain side, starting from different points, and running in different directions, converge toward a common terminus at the summit. As the mineral, the plant, the insect, the animal, in all their curious and wonderful organizations, are necessarily inferior to man, so is the science of them, however important and useful, subordinate to the science of man himself; and as the human body, curious and wonderful in its organism and its laws, is nevertheless inferior in dignity and worth to the spirit that dwells within, and is the true lord of this fair castle and this wide and beautiful domain, so is the science of the body, its mechanism, its chemistry, its anatomy, its laws, inferior to the science of the mind, the divinity within.

Other Sciences Creations of the Mind.—Many of the sciences justly regarded as the most noble, are themselves the creations of the mind. Such, for example, is the science of number and quantity—a science leading to the most sublime results, as in the calculations of the astronomer, yet a pure product of the human intellect. Indeed what is all science but the work of mind? The creations of art are wonderful, but the mind that can conceive and execute those creations is still more to be admired. Language is wonderful, but chiefly as a production and expression of mind. The richness, the affluence, the eloquence, the exactness, the beauty, for example, of the Greek tongue, of what are these the qualities, and where did they dwell—in the Greek language, or in the Greek mind? Which is really the more noble and wonderful then, the language itself, or the mind that called into being such a language, and employed it as an instrument of expression; and of which is the science most noble and worthy of regard?

We admire the genius of a Kepler and a Copernicus, we sympathize with their enthusiasm as they observe the movements and develop the laws of the heavenly bodies; we look through the telescope, not without a feeling of awe, as it seems to lift us up, and bear us away into the unknown and the infinite, revealing to us what it would almost seem had never been intended for the human eye to see; but one thing is even more wonderful than the telescope — that is the mind that contrived it. One thing is more awe-inspiring than the stars, and that is the mind that discovers their hidden laws, and unlocks their complicated movements; and when we would observe the most curious and wonderful thing of all, we must leave the tubes and the tables, the calculations and the diagrams with which the man works, and study the man himself, the workman.

Relation of this Science to the practical Arts and Sciences. — But aside from the view now presented, the connection of mental science with other and practical arts and sciences is much more intimate than is usually supposed. Take for example the very noblest of all sciences — theology; we find it, in an important sense, based upon and receiving its shape and character from the views which we entertain, and the philosophy which we adopt of the human mind. Our philosophy underlies our theology, even as the solid strata that lie unseen beneath the surface give shape and contour and direction to the lofty mountain range.

Psychology as related to Theology. — Not to speak of the very idea which we form of the divine Being, borrowed as it must be, in a sense, from our previous conception of the human mind, and our own spiritual existence, not to speak of the arguments by which we seek to establish the existence of the divine Being, involving as they do some of the nicest and most important of the laws of human thought, what problems, we may ask, go deeper into the groundwork of any theological system than those pertaining to human ability, and the freedom of the will — the government of the affections and desires — the power of a man over himself, to be other and better than he is, and to do what God requires. But these are questions purely psychological. You cannot stir a step in the application of theology to practical life, till you have settled in some way these questions, and that view, whatever it be, crude or profound, intelligible or absurd, is, for the time, your science, your philosophy of the mind.

Psychology as related to the healing Art. — Scarcely less intimate is the connection of psychology with the science of life. The physician finds in the practice of his profession, that in order to success, the laws of the human mind must constitute an important part of his study — how to avoid, and how to touch, the secret springs of human action. A word rightly spoken is often better than a medicine. In order to comprehend the nature of disease he must understand the effect on the bodily organization of the due, and also of the undue, exertion of each of the mental faculties; in fine, the whole relation of the mind to the bodily functions, and its influence over them — a field of inquiry as yet but imperfectly understood, if indeed adequately appreciated by the medical profession.

As related to Oratory. — To the public speaker, whether at the bar, in the public assembly, in the halls of legislation, or in the pulpit, it need hardly be said that a knowledge of this science, and the ability to make practical use of it, is indispensable. Success in oratory depends, doubtless, in a measure, upon other things; but he who best understands the laws and operations of the human mind, how to touch the sensibilities, how to awaken the passions, how to excite the fears and the hopes, how to rouse the resentment of his hearers, how to soothe the troubled spirits, and allay the excitement of feeling, and disarm prejudice, and call into play the sober reason and calm judgment of man, will best be able to accomplish his purpose. He will be able to turn to his own account the circumstances of the occasion, and like a skilful organist, touch with ease, yet with precision and effect, what key he will. No man can do this who does not well understand the instrument.

As related to the Art of Education. — Especially is this science of use to the *teacher* in the knowledge which it gives him of the mind of his pupil, and the skill in dealing with that mind. The mind of the pupil is to him the instrument on which he is required to play — a curious instrument of many and strange keys and stops — capable of being touched to wonderful harmony, and to fearful discord; — and to handle this instrument well is no ordinary acquirement. What shall we say of the man who knows nothing of the instrument, but only the music to be performed, nothing of the mind to be taught, but only the knowledge to be communicated? To know the mind that is to be taught, how to stimulate, how to control, how to encourage, how to restrain, how to guide and direct its every movement and impulse, is not this the very first and chief thing to be known?

Connection of this Science with our own personal Interests. — The importance of mental science is evident not only from its relation to other sciences, but from the relation it sustains to man and his higher interests. Some sciences interest us as abstractions — merely speculative systems of truth; others as realities, but of such a nature, and so remote from the personal interests and wants of the race to which we belong, that they make little appeal to our sensi bilities. Thus it is with mathematical and astronomica truth. The heavenly bodies, whose movements we observe, hold on their swift silent way, in the calmness of their own eternity, regardless of man and his destiny, even as they rolled ages ago, and as they will ages hence. What have we to do with them or they with us? We watch them as they hold their course through the deep firmament, as children, standing on the sea-side, watch the distant snowy sail that glides silently along the horizon, afar off, beautiful, unknown. So sail those swift ships of the firmament, and only he who made them knows their history.

Psychology in contrast with other Sciences in this respect. — But when we come to the study of ourselves, and the laws of our own intelligence, our inquiries assume a practical importance which attaches to no other departments of truth. It is no longer the sail dimly visible on the far horizon, but our own conscious being that is the object of thought. The question no longer is, Whence comes that swift ship, and whither goes it, but, What am I, and whither going; what my history, and my destiny? This mysterious soul which animates me, and is the presiding divinity over all my actions, what is it, with all its wondrous faculties — sense, imagination, reason, will — those powers of my being? What is that change which passes upon me, which men call sleep, and that more mysterious and fearful change that must soon pass upon me, and that men call death? How is it that events of former years come back to mind, with all the freshness and reality of passing scenes? What is that principle of my nature that ever assumes to itself the right of command, saying to all my inclinations and passions, thou shalt, and thou shalt not, and when I disobey that mandate, filling my whole soul with misery, my whole future existence with remorse? And what and whence that word *ought*, that has so much to do with me and my pursuits: ought what, and why ought, and to whom? — Am I free, or am I subject to inevitable necessity; if free, then how are all my actions controlled, and predetermined by a divine Providence? If not free, then how am I responsible? Who shall solve this problem; who shall read me this strange inexplicable riddle of human life? Such are the questions and themes which mental philosophy discusses, and we perceive at a glance their intimate connection with the highest interests and personal wants of man as an individual.

Connection of this Science with mental Discipline. — The

importance of mental science may be further apparent in its effect on the culture and discipline of the mind. It is the peculiar effect of this science to sharpen and quicken the mental powers, to teach precision and exactness of thought and expression, to train the mind to habits of close attention and concentration of thought, to lead it to inquire into the causes and relations of things; in a word, to render it familiar with the great art of distinguishing things that differ. It would hardly be possible to name another branch of study that tends so directly to produce these results in the cultivation of the mind.

CHAPTER II.

ANALYSIS AND CLASSIFICATION OF THE MENTAL POWERS.

Importance of such a preliminary Investigation. — It is of the highest importance, as we approach a science like the one before us, to obtain, if possible, at the outset, a clear and comprehensive view of the field about to be explored. It is desirable that the traveller, before entering a new country, should learn something respecting its extent, its political and geographical divisions, its manners, its laws, its history. Even more necessary is it, in entering upon a new science, to know its boundaries and divisions, to obtain clear idea, at the very commencement of our inquiries, of the number, nature, extent, and arrangement of the subjects we are about to investigate. Otherwise we shall be liable to confusion and error, shall not know where, at any moment, in the wide field of investigation, we may chance to be, or what relation the topic of our immediate inquiry holds to the whole science before us; as a ship on the ocean, without observation and reckoning, loses her latitude and longitude. We shall be liable to confound those distinctions which are of less, with those which are of more importance, and to mistake the relation which the several topics of inquiry bear to each other. Especially is this previous survey and comprehension of the subject essential in a science like this, where so much depends on the clearness and accuracy with which we distinguish differences often minute, and on the definiteness with which we mark off and lay out the several divisions of our work. A thorough analysis and classification of the various faculties of the mind, is necessary, in the first place, before we enter upon the special investigation of any one of them. Such a classification must serve as our guide-book and chart in all further inquiries.

Difficulty of such an Investigation.—The importance of such a preliminary investigation is scarcely greater than its difficulty. It would be easy, indeed, to mention, almost at random, a considerable number of mental operations, with whose names we are familiar; and a little thought would enable us to enlarge the list almost indefinitely. But such a list, even though it might chance to be complete, would be neither an analysis nor a classification of these several powers. It would neither teach us their relations to each other and to the whole, nor enable us to understand the precise nature and office of each faculty. We could not be sure that we had not included under a common name operations essentially different, or assigned distinct places and offices to powers essentially the same. Much depends, moreover, on the order in which we take up the several faculties.

It is evident at a glance that to form a clear, correct, and comprehensive arrangement of the powers of the mind, is no slight undertaking. A complete understanding of the whole science of the mind is requisite. It is one of the last things which the student is prepared to undertake, yet one of the first which he requires to know. Unfortunately for the science, perhaps no topic in the whole circle of intellectual investigation has been more generally neglected, by those who have undertaken to unfold the philosophy of the mind, than the one now under consideration.

§ I. — General Analysis.

A mental Faculty, what. — In making out any scheme of classification, the question at once arises, how are we to know what are, and what are not distinct faculties? In order to this, we must first determine what constitutes a mental faculty.

What, then, is a faculty of the mind? I understand by this term simply the mind's power of acting, of doing something, of putting forth some energy, and performing some operation. The mind has as many distinct faculties, as it has distinct powers of action, distinct functions, distinct modes and spheres of activity. As its capabilities of action and operation differ, so its faculties differ.

The Mind not complex. — Now mental activity is, strictly speaking, one and indivisible. The mind is not a complex substance, composed of parts, but single and one. Its activity may, however, be exercised in various ways, and upon widely different classes of objects; and as these modes of action vary, we may assign them different names, and treat of them in distinction from each other. So distinguished and named, they present themselves to us as so many distinct powers or faculties of the mind. But when this is done, and we make out, for purposes of science, our complete list and classification of these powers, we are not to forget that it is, after all, one and the same indivisible spiritual principle that is putting forth its activity under these diverse forms, one and the same force exerting itself — whether as thinking, feeling, or acting — whether as remembering, imagining, judging, perceiving, reasoning, loving, fearing, hating, desiring, choosing. And while we may designate these as so many faculties of the mind, we are not to conceive of them as so many constituent parts of a complex whole, which, taken together, compose this mysterious entity called the mind, as the different limbs and organs of the physical frame compose the structure called the body. Such is not the nature of the mind, nor of its faculties.

The Question before us.—In inquiring, then, what are the faculties of the mind, we have simply to inquire what are the distinct modes of its activity, what states and operations of the mind so far resemble each other as to admit of being classed together under the same general description and name. Our work, thus understood, becomes in reality a very simple one.

The more important Distinctions to be first ascertained.—What, then, are the clearly distinct modes of mental activity? And first let us endeavor to ascertain the wider and more important distinctions. We shall find that, innumerable as the forms of mental activity may at first sight appear, they are all capable of being reduced to a few general and comprehensive classes.

The first Form of mental Activity.—I sit at my table. Books are before me. I open a volume, and peruse its pages. My mind is occupied, its activity is awakened; the thoughts of the author are transferred to my mind, and engage my thoughts. Here, then, is one form of mental activity. This one thing I can do; this one power I have—the faculty of thought.

The second Form.—But not this alone: I am presently conscious of something beside simple thought. The writer, whose pages I peruse, interests me, excites me; I am amused by his wit, moved by his eloquence, affected by his pathos; I become indignant at the scenes and characters which he portrays, or, on the contrary, they command my admiration. All this by turns passes over me, as the fitful shadows play upon the waters, coming and going with the changing cloud. This is not pure thought. It is thought, accompanied with another and quite distinct element, that is, *feeling*. This power also I have ; — I can feel.

A third Form. — And not this alone. The process does not end here. Thought and feeling lead to action. I resolve what to do. I lay down my book, and go forth tc perform some act prompted by the emotion awakened within me. This power also I have ; — the faculty of voluntary action, or volition.

These three Forms comprehensive. — Here, then, are three grand divisions or forms of mental activity — thought, feeling, volition. These powers we are constantly exerting. Every moment of my intelligent existence I am exercising one or another, or all of these faculties. And, what is more, of all the forms of mental activity, there is not one which does not fall under one or another of these three divisions — thought — feeling — volition. Every possible mental operation may be reduced to one of these three things.

We have, then, these grand departments or modes of mental activity, comprehensive of all others : Intellect, or the faculty of simple thought ; Sensibility, or the faculty of feeling ; Will, or the faculty of voluntary action.

Under these leading powers are comprehended subordinate modes of mental activity, known as faculties of the Intellect, or of the Sensibility, or of the Will.

We have at present to do only with those of the Intellect.

§ II. — Analysis of Intellectual Powers.

Sense-perception. — Observing closely the intellectual operations of the mind, we find a large class of them relating to objects within the sphere of sense, external objects, as perceived by the senses. The mind, through the medium of sense, takes direct cognizance of these objects. This class of operations we may call Sense-perception, and the faculty thus employed, in distinction from other leading divisions of the intellectual powers, we may call *Sense*, or the *Presentative* faculty. Its distinctive office is to *present* to the mind, through the senses, objects external, sensible, as now and here present.

The Representative Power.—But the mind not only receives impressions of external objects, as present, and acting on the organs of sense; it has also the faculty of *conceiving* of them in their *absence*, and *representing* them to itself. This faculty, as distinguished from the receptive power, or sense, we may call the *Representative* Power.

Mental Reproduction, and mental Recognition as distinguished.—This power operates in various forms. There may be the simple representation of the absent object, without reference to the act of former perception, as when I think of the Strasburg tower, without recalling any particular instance of its perception. Or there may be such recalling of the former act and instance of perception. The thought of the tower, as it presents itself to my mind, may stand connected definitely with the idea of the time, and place, and attending circumstances in which, on some occasion, I saw that object. It is then *recognized* as the object which was seen at such or such a time. The former is an instance of *mental reproduction* simply—the latter, of *mental recognition.* We have in common language but one name for the two—although the term more strictly belongs only to the latter—and that is, *Memory.*

Representation of the Ideal in distinction from the Actual.—Again, unlike either of these, there may be a conception and representation of the object, not at all as it is in reality, and as it was perceived, but varied in essential particulars, to suit our own taste and fancy—a tower not of ordinary stone, but of some rare and costly marble—not of ordinary height, but reaching to the skies, etc., etc. In the former cases we conceived only of the *actual*, now of the *ideal.* This faculty is called *Imagination.* Both are forms of the representative power, not *presenting*, but only *representing* objects.

Conception of the Abstract.—The Discursive or Reflective Power.—In the cases thus far described we have conceived of some sensible object, considered in and by itself, capable of being represented to thought. We may, however, conceive not of an object in itself considered, but of the properties and relations of objects in the abstract. Thus we compare and class together those objects which we perceive to possess certain properties in common; as books bound in cloth, or in leather, octavos, or duodecimos. In so doing we exercise the faculty of *generalization*, which involves comparison, and also what is usually termed abstraction. Or we may reverse the process, and instead of classing together objects possessing certain elements in common, we may analyze a complex idea, or a comprehensive term, in order to derive from it whatever is specifically included in it. Thus from the general proposition, "All men are mortal," inasmuch as the term "all men" includes Socrates, I infer that Socrates is mortal. The process last named is called *reasoning*.

In either case, both in the synthetic and the analytic process now described, we are dealing not with the *concrete* but the *abstract*. The properties and relations of things, rather than things themselves, are the objects of our thoughts. Still they are the properties and relations primarily of *sensible objects*, and of these objects as *conceived*, and not as presented to sense. To distinguish this class of conceptions from those previously considered, and also from that presently to be noticed, we may designate this power of the mind as the *Discursive* or *Reflective* Power. Its results are notions of the *understanding* rather than impressions of sense, or ideas of reason.

Conceptions not furnished by Sense.—The Intuitive Power.—We have considered thus far those intellectual operations which fall within three leading departments of mental activity; — the Presentative, Representative, and Discursive Powers. These operations all have reference directly or indirectly to *sensible* objects. The first regards them as *present;* the second represents them as *absent;* the third considers their properties and relations in the *abstract.*

But the mind has also the faculty of forming ideas and conceptions not furnished by the senses. It departs from the sphere of sense, and deals with the *super*-sensible, with those primary ideas and first principles presupposed in all knowledge of the sensible. Such are the ideas of time, space, cause, the right, the beautiful. These are suggested by the objects of sense, but not directly derived from nor given by those objects. They are *ideas* of *reason*, rather than notions of understanding. They are awakened in the mind on occasions of sensible perception, but not conveyed to the mind through the senses, as in perception, nor directly derived from the object as in the case of the representative and discursive powers. This faculty we may call the *Originative* or *Intuitive* Power, in distinction from those previously considered.

Summary of leading Divisions. — We have then four grand divisions of intellectual operations, under which the several specific faculties arrange themselves; viz., the Presentative, the Representative, the Discursive, and the Originative or Intuitive faculty. The first has to do with sensible objects, as present; the second has to do with the same class of objects as absent; the third deals with their abstract properties and relations; and the fourth has to do not with the sensible, in any form, but with the super-sensible.

I believe the faculties of the intellect, in pure thinking, may all be reduced to those forms now specified, under these four leading divisions

RESULTS OF THE PRECEDING ANALYSIS IN A TABULAR FORM:

POWERS OF THE INTELLECT.

I. PRESENTATIVE,		*Perception.*
II. REPRESENTATIVE,	1. Of the Actual,	*Memory.*
	2. Of the Ideal,	*Imagination.*
III. REFLECTIVE,	1. Synthetic,	*Generalization.*
	2. Analytic,	*Reasoning.*
IV. INTUITIVE,		*Original Conception.*

§ III. — HISTORICAL SKETCH — VARIOUS DIVISIONS OF THE MENTAL FACULTIES.

The earlier Division. — The general division of the powers of the mind, for a long time prevalent among the earlier modern philosophers, was into *two* chief departments, known under different names, but including under the one what we now term the intellect, under the other what we designate as the sensibilities and the will, which were not then, as now, distinguished from each other in the general division, but thrown into one department. Under the first of these departments, they included the thinking and reasoning powers, the strictly intellectual part of our nature; under the second, whatever brings the mind into action — the impelling and controlling power or principle — the affections, emotions, desires, volitions, etc. The names given to these two divisions varied with different writers, but the difference was chiefly in the name, the principle of division being the same. By some authors they were designated as the *contemplative* and the *active* powers, by others *cognitive* and *motive.* The latter was the nomenclature proposed by Hobbes. Others again adopted the terms understanding and will, by which to mark the two divisions; Locke, Reid, some of the French philosophers, and, in our own country, Edwards, followed this division. Stewart designates them, the one class as the *intellectual,* and the other as the *active* and *moral* powers. Brown objects to this phraseology on the ground that the intellectual powers are no less active than the other. He divides the mental powers or states primarily into what he calls *external* and *internal* affections of the mind, comprehending under the former all those mental states which are immediately preceded by and connected with the presence of some external object; under the latter, those states which are not thus immediately preceded. The latter class he divides into intellectual states and emotions, a division corresponding essentially to those of the authors previously mentioned, the emotions of Brown comprehending essentially the powers which others had termed motive, or active and moral.

Prevalence of this Method. — This twofold division of the mental powers, under different names, as now stated, has been the one generally prevalent until a comparatively recent date. It may doubtless be traced, as Sir William Hamilton suggests, to a distinction made by Aristotle, into *cognitive* and *appetent* powers.

The more recent Method. — The threefold division of the mental faculties very early came into use among philosophical and theological writers in this country, and is now very generally adopted by the more recent European writers of note, especially in France and Germany. According to this division the various affections and emotions constitute a department by themselves, distinct from the will or the voluntary principle. There are many reasons for such a distinction; they have been well stated by Professor Upham Cousin adopts and defends the threefold division, and pre viously still, Kant, in Germany, had distinguished the mental powers under the leading divisions of intelligence, sensibility, and desire.

MENTAL PHILOSOPHY.

DIVISION FIRST.

THE INTELLECTUAL FACULTIES.

PRELIMINARY TOPICS.

CHAPTER I.

CONSCIOUSNESS.

General Statement. — Before proceeding to investigate the several specific faculties of the intellect, as already classified, there are certain preliminary topics to be considered, certain mental phenomena, or mental states, involved more or less fully in all mental activity, and on that account hardly to be classed as specific faculties, yet requiring distinct consideration. Such are the mental states which we denominate as *consciousness* and *attention.*

Definitions. — Consciousness is defined by Webster as the knowledge of sensations and mental operations, or of what passes in our own minds; by Wayland, as that condition of the mind in which it is cognizant of its own operations; by Cousin, as that function of the intelligence which gives us information of every thing which takes place in the interior of our minds; by Dr. Henry, translator of Cousin, as the being aware of the phenomena of the mind — of that which is present to the mind; by Professor Tappan, as the necessary knowledge which the mind has of its own operations. These general definitions substantially agree. The mind is aware of its own operations, its sensations, perceptions, emotions, choices, etc., and the state or act of being thus cognizant of its own phenomena we designate by the general term *Consciousness.*

Reasons for regarding Consciousness as not a distinct Faculty. — Is this, however, a distinct faculty of the mind? The mind, it is said, is always cognizant of its own operations: when it perceives, it is conscious of perceiving; when it reasons, it is conscious of reasoning; when it feels, it is conscious of feeling; and not to be conscious of any particular mental act, is not to perform that act. To have a sensation, and to be conscious of that sensation, it is said, are not two things, but one and the same, the difference being only in name. A perception is indivisible, cannot be analyzed into a fact, and the consciousness of the fact, for the perception is an act of knowing, and does not take place if it be not known to take place. This is the view taken by Sir William Hamilton, Professor Bowen, and others of high authority. It was maintained by Dr. Brown with much force as an objection to the doctrine of Reid, who had recognized consciousness as a distinct faculty.

Reasons for the opposite View. — On the other hand, the claims of this form of mental activity to be regarded as a faculty of the mind, distinct from and coördinate with the other mental powers, are admitted and maintained by writers of authority, among whom are Dr. Wayland and President Mahan. They maintain that the office of consciousness being to give us knowledge of our own mental states, and this function being quite distinct from that of any other mental faculty, the capacity or power of performing this function deserves to be regarded as itself a faculty of the mind. It is maintained also by Dr. Wayland that consciousness does not necessarily invariably accompany all mental action, but that there may be, and are, acts of which we are not at the time conscious.

Instances in proof of this Position. — In support of this position he refers to certain cases as instances of unconscious perception; as when, for example, a clock strikes within a few feet of us, while we are busily engaged, and we do not notice it, or know that it has struck, yet if questioned afterward, are conscious of an impression that we have heard it; as when also while reading aloud to another person, some thought arrests our attention, and yet by a sort of mechanical process, we continue the reading, our mind, meanwhile, wholly occupied with another subject, until presently we are startled to find that we have not the remotest conception of what we have just been reading; yet we read every word correctly, and must, it would seem, have perceived every word and letter. He refers also to the case of the short-hand writer to the House of Lords in England, who, on a certain occasion, while engaged in taking the depositions of witnesses in an important case, after many hours of continued exertion and fatigue, fell, for a few moments, into a state of entire unconsciousness, yet kept on writing down, and that with perfect accuracy, the depositions of the witness. Of the last few lines, when he came to read them, he had no recollection whatever, yet they were written as legibly and accurately as the rest. From these and similar cases it is inferred that there may be mental activity of which we have at the time no consciousness.

The Evidence examined. — With regard to the cases now cited, it seems to me that they do not fully establish the point in question. For in the first place, it may be doubted whether they really involve any mental activity — whether they are properly mental acts, and not merely mechanical or automatic. It is well known that many processes which ordinarily require more or less attention may, when they have become perfectly familiar, be carried on for a time almost without thought. The senses, so far as they are required to act at all, seem in such cases to act mechanically, or automatically, somewhat as a wheel when once set in motion continues for a time to revolve by its own momentum, after the propelling force is withdrawn. The mental activity exerted in such cases, if there be any, is so very slight as to escape attention, and we are unconscious of it simply because there was little or nothing to be conscious of. We have an illustration of this in the act of walking, while busily engaged in conversation with a friend, or in our own meditations. We are not conscious of any mental act preceding or directing each step and movement of the limbs, but having at the outset decided what direction to take, the mind gives itself to other matters, while the process of walking goes on by a sort of mechanical impulse, until presently something occurs to arrest our attention and direct it to the physical movement in which we are engaged. The muscular contractions tend to follow each other in a certain regular succession; a certain law of association seems to govern their movements, as is seen in the rapid motions of the pianist, the flute player, the type distributor, and in many similar cases; and so long as the regular succession, and accustomed order of movement, is undisturbed, the process goes on with little or no interference of the intellectual principle. In such cases the act can hardly be said to involve mental activity.

A further Question. — But aside from this, even admitting that the acts under consideration are such as to involve mental activity, what evidence is there, it may still be asked, that there was at the moment no consciousness of that activity? That there was *subsequently* no consciousness of it, does not make it certain that there was none at the time. The subsequent consciousness of an act is neither more nor less than memory, and is not properly consciousness at all. Consciousness takes cognizance, properly speaking, only of the present, not of the past. The absence of subsequent consciousness is simply absence of memory, and this may be accounted for in other ways than by supposing a total absence of consciousness in the first instance. Whatever mental activity was really exerted by the short-hand reporter in the case referred to, he was, doubtless, conscious of exerting at the time, but it may have been so slight, and the mind so little impressed by it, in the state of physical weariness and prostration, that it was not remembered a moment afterward. We remember not every thing that occurs, but only that to which we attend, and which makes some impression upon us.

The true Explanation.—In the other cases referred to, the explanation now given is still more evidently the true one. What is called an absence of consciousness is simply an absence of attention at the time, and consequently of memory afterward. The person who is reading aloud, in the case supposed, is mentally occupied with something else than the sentiments of the author, is not attending, in a word, to what he is reading, and hence does not, a moment after, remember what it was that he read. So of the striking of the clock. The sound fell upon the ear, the auditory nerve performed its office, the usual change, whatever it may be, was produced in the brain, but the process of hearing went no further; either no mental activity was awakened by that sound, or, if any, but the slightest, for the mind was otherwise occupied, in a word, did not attend to the summons of the messenger that waited at the portal, and hence there was no subsequent remembrance of the message, or at most a vague impression that something of the kind was heard.

On the whole, it does not appear from the cases cited, that mental activity is ever, at the moment of its exertion, unaccompanied with consciousness.

Summary of the Argument.—I hesitate then to assign consciousness a place among the faculties of the mind, as distinct from and coördinate with them, for the following reasons:

1. It seems to me to be involved in all mental acts. We cannot, as it has been already said, suppose an act of perception, for example, or of sensation, without the consciousness of that perception or sensation. Whatever the mind does, it knows that it does, and the knowing is involved in, and given along with the doing. Not to know that I see a book, or hear a sound, is in reality not to see and not to

hear it. Not to know that I have a sensation is not to have it. But what is involved in all mental action cannot be set down by itself as a specific mental act. This were much the same as to reckon the whole among the parts.

2. Consciousness, while involved in, cannot be, either psychologically or chronologically, distinguished from the mental acts which it accompanies. The act and the consciousness of the act are inseparable in time, and they are incapable of being distinguished as distinct states of mind. We cannot break up the sensation or perception into a fact, and the consciousness of that fact. Logically we may distinguish them as different objects of thought and attention, but not psychologically as distinct acts of mind.

3. Consciousness is not under the control of the will, and is not therefore a faculty of the mind. It is not a power of doing something, but an inseparable concomitant of all doing. What has been termed by some writers voluntary consciousness, or *reflection*, is simply attention directed to our own mental acts.

Distinction of Consciousness and Self-Consciousness.— Others again distinguish between consciousness and self-consciousness; but all consciousness, properly so called, involves the idea of self, or the subjective element. To know that I have a sensation, is virtually to know myself as having it.

Cases of abnormal or suspended Consciousness.—In certain disordered and abnormal states of the nervous organism, the knowledge of what has transpired previously to that state seems to be lost; and then again, on passing out of that condition into the normal one, all knowledge of what took place while in the abnormal state is wanting. Instances are on record where persons have alternated in this manner from one to the other condition, carrying on, as it were, by turns, two separate and independent lines of mental activity. An instance of this nature is related by Dr. Wayland. It has been usual to speak of these as instances of disordered or suspended consciousness. Strictly speaking, however, it is not consciousness but memory that is in such cases disordered. It is not the knowledge of the present, but of the *past*, that is disturbed and deficient. While the abnormal state continues, the individual is conscious of what transpires in that state. When it ceases, the patient wakes as from a reverie or dream, and retains no *recollection* of any thing that took place during its continuance. It is the *memory* that fails, and not the consciousness. We are never *conscious* of the *past*.

Objects of Consciousness.—1. Consciousness deals only with reality. We are conscious only of that which is, not of that which may be. The poet is conscious indeed of his fiction, the builder of air-castles is conscious of his reverie, but the fiction and the reverie, regarded as mental acts, are *realities*, and it is only as mental acts that they are objects of consciousness.

2. Not every thing real is an object of consciousness, but only that which is *present* and in *immediate relation* to us. The destruction of Pompeii, and the existence of an Antarctic continent are realities, but not objects of my consciousness.

3. Primarily and directly we are conscious of our own mental states and operations; of whatever passes over the field of our mental vision, our thoughts, feelings, actions, physical sensations, moral sentiments and purposes: mediately and indirectly we are conscious of whatever, through the medium of sense, comes into direct relation to us. For instance, when I put forth my hand and it strikes this table, I am conscious not only of the movement, and the effort to move, but of the sensation of resistance also, and indirectly I may be said to be conscious not of the resistance only, but of something — to wit, the table — as resisting. This something I know, as really as I know the sensation and the fact of resistance. To this immediate perception of the external world in direct relation to our physical organism, Sir W. Hamilton would extend the sphere of consciousness. Usual-

ly, however, the term has been employed in a more restricted sense — to denote the knowledge of what passes within, rather than of what lies without the mind itself.

CHAPTER II.

ATTENTION.

General Character of this Power. — It has not been usual to treat of Attention as one of the distinct faculties of the mind. It is doubtless a power which the mind possesses, but like the power of conception, or more generally the power of thought and mental apprehension, it is involved in and underlies the exercise of all the specific mental faculties. Nor is it, like consciousness, confined to a distinct department of knowledge, viz., the knowledge of our own mental states. It is subsidiary to the other mental powers, rather than a faculty of original and independent knowledge. It originates nothing — teaches nothing — puts us in possession of no new truth — has no distinct field and province of its own. And yet without it other faculties would be of little avail.

Definitions. — If it were necessary to define a term so well understood, we might describe it as the power which the mind has of directing its thoughts, purposely and voluntarily, to some one object, to the exclusion of others. It is described by Dr. Wayland as a sort of voluntary consciousness, a condition of mind in which our consciousness is excited and directed by an act of the will. He speaks also of an involuntary attention, a state of mind in which our thoughts, without effort or purpose of our own, are engrossed by objects of an exciting nature. It may be questioned, perhaps, whether this is properly attention. Only in so far as attention is a voluntary act is it properly a power of the mind, and only in so far does it differ from the simple activity of thought, or of consciousness. The latter is always involuntary, and in this it differs from attention.

Instances in Illustration. — It can hardly be necessary to illustrate by example the nature of a faculty so constantly in exercise. Every one perceives, for instance, the difference between the careless perusal of an author — the eye passing listlessly over the pages, and the mind receiving little or no impression from its statements — and the reading of the same volume with fixed and careful attention, every word observed, every sentiment weighed, and the whole mental energy directed to the subject in hand. We pass, in the streets of a crowded and busy city, many persons whom we do not stop to observe, and of whose appearance we could afterward give no account whatever. Presently, some one in the crowd attracts our notice. We observe his appearance, we watch his movements, we notice his peculiarities of dress, gait, manners, etc., and are able afterward to describe them with some degree of minuteness. In the former case we perceive, but do not attend. In the latter, we attend, in order to perceive.

Sometimes the sole Occupation. — Attention seems to be at times the sole occupation of the mind for the moment, as when we have heard some sound that attracts our notice, and are listening for its repetition. In this case the other faculties are for the time held in suspense, and we are, as we say, all attention. The posture naturally assumed in such a case is that indicated by the etymology of the word, and may have suggested its use to designate this faculty, viz., attention — ad-tendo — a *bending to*, a *stretching toward*, the object of interest.

Analysis of the mental Process in Attention. — If we closely analyze the process of our minds in the exercise of this power, we shall find, I think, that it consists chiefly in this — the arresting and detaining the thoughts, excluding thus the exercise of other forms of mental activity, in consequence of which the mind is left free to direct its whole energy to the one object in view. The process may be compared to the operation of the detent in machinery, which checks the wheels that are in rapid motion, and gives opportunity for any desired change; while it may be compared, as regards the result of its action, to the helm that directs the motion of the ship, now this way, now that, as the helmsman wills.

Objects of Attention. — The objects of attention are of course as various as the objects of thought. Like consciousness, it may confine itself to our own mental states; and, unlike consciousness, it may comprehend also the entire range of objective reality. In the former case it is more commonly designated by the term reflection, in the latter, observation.

Importance of Habits of Attention. — The importance of habits of attention, of the due exercise and development of this faculty of the mind, is too obvious to require special comment. The power of controlling one's own mental activity, of directing it at will into whatever channels the occasion may demand, of excluding for this purpose all other and irrelevant ideas, and concentrating the energies of the mind on the one object of thought before it, is a power of the highest value, an attainment worth any effort, and which, in the different degrees in which it is possessed, goes far to make the difference between one mind and another in the realm of thought and intellectual greatness. While the attention is divided and the mind distracted among a variety of objects, it can apprehend nothing clearly and definitely; the rays are not brought to a focus, and the mental eye, instead of a clear and well-defined image, perceives nothing but a shadowy and confused outline. The mind while in this state acts to little purpose. It is shorn of its strength.

The power of commanding the attention and concentrating the mental energy upon a given object, is, however, a power not easily acquired nor always possessed. The difficulty of the attainment is hardly less than its importance. It can be made only by earnest effort, resolute purpose, diligent culture and training. There must be strength of will to take command of the mental faculties, and make them subservient to its purpose. There must be determination to succeed, and a wise discipline and exercise of the mind with reference to the end in view. This faculty, like every other, requires education in order to its due development.

Whether certain Acts are performed without any Degree of Attention. — It is a question somewhat discussed among philosophers, whether those acts which from habit we have learned to perform with great facility, and, as we say, almost without thinking, are strictly voluntary; whether they do or do not involve an exercise of attention. Every one is aware of the facility acquired by practice in many manual and mechanical operations, as well as in those more properly intellectual. A musician sits at his instrument, scarcely conscious of what he is doing, his attention absorbed, it may be, with some engrossing topic of thought or conversation, while his fingers wander *ad libitum* among the keys and strike the notes of some familiar tune. Is there in such a case a special act of volition and attention preceding each movement of the fingers as they glide over the keys? And in more rapid playing, even when the attention is in general directed to the act performed, *i.e.*, the execution of the piece, is there still a special act of attention to the production of each note as they follow each other with almost inconceivable rapidity? Dr. Stahl, Dr. Reid, and others, especially many able physiologists, have answered this question in the negative, pronouncing the acts in question to be merely automatic and mechanical, and not properly involving any activity of mind. The mind, they would say, forms the general purpose to execute the given piece, but the particular movements and muscular contractions requisite to produce the individual notes, are, for the most part, involuntary, the result of habit, not of special at tention or volition.

The opposite View. — On the other hand, Mr. Stewart maintains that all such acts, however easily and rapidly performed, do involve mental activity, some degree of attention, some special volition to produce them, although we may not be able to recollect those volitions afterward. The different steps of the process are, by the association of ideas, so connected, that they present themselves successively to the mind without any effort to recall them, without any hesitation or reflection on our part, and with a rapidity proportioned to our experience. The attention and the volition are instantaneous, and therefore not subsequently recollected. Still, he would say, the fact that we do not recollect them is no proof that we did not exercise them. The musician can, at will, perform the piece so slowly, as to be able to observe and recall the special act of attention to each note, and of volition to produce it. The difference in the two cases lies in the rapidity of the movement, not in the nature of the operation.

Objection to this View. — The only objection to this view, of much weight, is the extreme rapidity of mental action, which this view supposes. An accomplished speaker will pronounce, it is said, from two to four hundred words, or from one to two thousand letters in a minute, and each letter requires a distinct contraction of the muscles, many of them, indeed, several contractions. Shall we suppose then so many thousand acts of attention and volition in a minute?

Reply to this Objection. — To this it may be replied that the very objection carries with it its own answer, since if it be true that the muscles of the body move with such wonderful rapidity, it is surely not incredible that the mind should be at least equally rapid in its movements with the body. To show that both mind and body often do act with great rapidity, Mr. Stewart cites the case of the equilibrist, who balances himself on the slack rope, and at the same time balances a number of rods or balls upon his chin, his position every instant changing, according to the accidental and ever-varying motions of the several objects whose equilibrium he is to preserve, which motions he must therefore constantly and closely watch. Now to do this, the closest attention, both of the eye and of the mind, to each of these instantaneous movements, is absolutely necessary, since the movements do not follow each other in any regular order, as do the notes of the musician, and cannot, therefore, by any association of ideas, be linked together, or laid up in the mind.

The Question undecided. — The question is a curious one, and with the arguments on either side, as now presented, I leave it to the reader's individual judgment and decision. Mr. Stewart is doubtless correct as to the rapidity of mental and muscular action. At the same time it seems to me *there are* actions, whatever may be true in the cases supposed, that are purely *automatic* and *mechanical.*

Whether we attend to more than one thing at once. — Analogous to the question already discussed, is the inquiry whether the mind ever attends or can attend to more than one thing at one and the same time; as when I read an author, my attention meanwhile being directed to some other object than the train of thought presented by the page before me, so that at the end of a paragraph or a chapter I find that I have no idea of what I have been reading, and yet I have followed with the eye, and perhaps pronounced aloud, every word and line of the entire passage. To do this must have required some attention. Have I then the power of attending to two things at once? So, when the musician carelessly strikes up a familiar air while engaged in animated conversation, and when the equilibrist balances both his own body upon the rope, and also a number of bodies upon different parts of his body, each movement of each requiring constant and instant attention, the same question arises.

Opinion of Mr. Stewart. — Mr. Stewart, in accordance

with the view already expressed of the rapidity of the mind's action, maintains that we do not under any circumstances attend at one and the same time to two objects of thought, but that the mind passes with such rapidity from one to another object in the cases supposed, that we are unconscious of the transition, and seem to ourselves to be attending to both objects at once.

Illustration of this View. — An illustration of this we find in the case of vision. Only one point of the surface of any external object is at any one instant in the direct line of vision, yet so rapidly does the eye pass from point to point, that we seem to perceive at a glance the whole surface.

How it is possible to compare different Objects. — It may be asked, How is it that we are able to compare one object with another, if we are unable to bring both before the mind at once? If, while I am thinking of A, I have no longer any thought whatever of B, how is it possible ever to bring together A and B before the mind so as to compare them?

The answer I conceive to be this, that the mind passes with such rapidity from the one to the other object, as to produce the same effect that would be produced were both objects actually before it at the same instant. The transition is not usually a matter of consciousness; yet if any one will observe closely the action of his own mind in the exercise of comparison, he will detect the passing of his thoughts back and forth from one object to the other many times before the conclusion is reached, and the comparison is complete.

CHAPTER III.

CONCEPTION.

Character of this Power. — This term has been employed in various senses by different writers. It does not denote properly a distinct faculty of the mind. I conceive of a thing when I make it a distinct object of thought, when I apprehend it, when I construe it to myself as a possible thing, and as being thus and thus. This form of mental activity enters more or less into all our mental operations; it is involved in perception, memory, imagination, abstraction, judgment, reasoning, etc. For this reason it is not to be ranked as one of, and correlate with, these several specific faculties. Like the power of thought, and hardly even more limited than that, it underlies all the special faculties, and is essential to them all. Such at least is the ordinary acceptation of the term; and when we employ it to denote some specific form of mental activity, we employ it in a sense aside from its usual and established meaning.

Objects of Conception. — I conceive of an absent object of sight, as, *e. g.*, the appearance of an absent friend, or of a foreign city, of the march of an army, or the eruption of a volcano. I conceive also of a mathematical truth, or a problem in astronomy. My conceptions are not limited to former perceptions or sensations, nor even to objects of sensible perception. They are not limited to material and sensible objects. They embrace the past and the future, the actual and the ideal, the sensible and the super-sensible.

Conceptions neither true nor false. — Our conceptions are neither true nor false, in themselves considered; they become so only when attended with some exercise of judgment or of belief. We conceive of a mountain of gold or of glass, and this simple conception has nothing to do with truth or error. When we conceive of it, however, as actually existing, and in this or that place, or when we simply judge that such a mountain is somewhere to be found, then such judgment or belief is either true or false; but it is no longer simple conception.

Not always Possibilities; nor possible Things always conceivable. — Our conceptions are not always possibilities. We can conceive of some things not within the limits of possibility. On the other hand, not every thing possible even is conceivable. Existence without beginning or end is possible, but it is not in the power of the human mind, strictly speaking, to conceive of such a thing. I know that Deity thus exists. I understand what is meant by such a proposition, and I believe it. But I cannot construe it to myself as a definite intellection, an apprehension, as I can conceive of the existence of a city or a continent, or of the truth of a mathematical proposition.

The same may be said of the ideas of the infinite and the absolute. They are not properly within the limits of thought, of apprehension, to the human mind. Thought in its very nature imposes a limitation on the object which is thought of — fathoms it — passes around it with its measuring line — apprehends it: only so far as this is done is the thing actually thought; only so far as it can be done is the thing really thinkable. But the infinite, the unconditioned, the absolute, in their very nature unlimited, cannot be shut up thus within the narrow lines of human thought. They are inconceivable. They are not, however, contradictory to thought. They may be true; they are true and real, though we cannot properly conceive them.

The Inconceivable becomes Impossible, when. — Not every thing then which is inconceivable is impossible, nor, on the other hand, is every thing which is impossible inconceivable. The inconceivable is impossible, at least it can be known to be so, only when it is either self-contradictory — as that a thing should be and not be at the same time — that a part is equal to the whole, etc.; or when it is contradictory of the laws of thought, as that two straight lines should enclose a space — that an event may occur without a cause — that space is not necessary to the existence of matter, or time to the succession of events. These things are unthinkable but they are more than that, contradictory of the established laws of thought; and they are impossible, because thus contradictory, and not merely because inconceivable. It is hardly true, as is sometimes affirmed, and as Dr. Wayland has stated, that our conceptions are the limits of possibility.

Mr. Stewart's use of the term Conception. — Mr. Stewart has employed the term Conception in a somewhat peculiar manner, and has assigned it a definite place among the faculties of the mind. He uses it to denote "that power of the mind which enables it to form a notion of an absent object of perception, or of a sensation which we have formerly felt." It is the office of this faculty "to present us with an exact transcript of what we have felt or perceived." In this respect it differs from imagination, which gives not an exact transcript, but one more or less altered or modified, combining our conceptions so as to form new results. It differs from memory in that it involves no idea of time, no recognition of the thing conceived, as a thing formerly perceived.

Objection to this use. — This use of the term is, on some accounts, objectionable. It is certainly not the ordinary sense of the word, but a departure from established usage. It is an arbitrary limitation of a word to denote a part only instead of the whole of that which it properly signifies. There is no reason, in the nature of the case, why the notion we form of an absent object of perception, or of a sensation, should be called a conception, rather than our notion of an abstract truth, a proposition in morals, or a mathematical problem. I am not aware that any special importance attaches to the former more than to the latter class of conceptions. Indeed, Sir W. Hamilton limits the term to the latter. But this again is not in accordance with established usage.

INTELLECTUAL FACULTIES.

PART FIRST.

THE PRESENTATIVE POWER.

THE

PRESENTATIVE POWER.

SENSE, OR PERCEPTION BY THE SENSES.

§ I. — General Observations.

This Faculty the Foundation of our Knowledge. — Of the cognitive powers of the mind, the first to be noticed, according to the analysis and distribution already given, is the Presentative Power — the power of cognizing external objects through the senses. This claims our first attention, inasmuch as it lies, chronologically at least, at the foundation of all our cognitive powers, and in truth, of our entire mental activity. We can, perhaps, conceive of a being so constituted as to be independent of sense, and yet possess mental activity; and we can even conceive such a mind as taking cognizance, in some mysterious way, of objects external to itself. But not such a being is man — not such the nature of the human mind. Its activity is first awak ened through sense; from sense it derives its knowledge of the external world, of whatever lies without and beyond the charmed circle of self; and whether *all* our knowledge is, strictly speaking, derived from sense, or not — a question so much disputed, and which we will not here stay to discuss — there can be no doubt that the activity of sense, and the knowledge thus acquired, is at least the beginning and foundation of all our mental acquisitions. We are constantly receiving impressions from without through the senses. In this way the mind is first awakened to activity.

and from this source we derive our knowledge of the external world.

General Character of this Faculty. — In its general character the faculty now under consideration, as the name indicates, is *presentative* and *intuitive.* It presents rather than represents objects, and what the mind thus perceives it perceives intuitively, rather than as the result of reflection. The knowledge which it gives is *immediate* knowledge, the knowledge of that which is now and here present, in time and space.

Involves a twofold Element. — Looking more closely at the character of this faculty, we find it to involve a twofold element, which we cannot better indicate than by the terms *subjective* and *objective.* There is, in the first place, the knowledge or consciousness of our own sentient organism as affected, and there is also the knowledge of something external to, and independent of the mind itself, or the me, as the producing cause of this affection of the organism. We know, by one and the same act, ourselves as affected, and the existence and presence of an external something affecting us. This presupposes, of course, the distinct independent existence of the *me* and the *not-me* — of ourselves as thinking and sentient beings, and of objects external to ourselves, and material,— a distinction which lies at the foundation of all sense-perception. All perception by the senses involves, and presupposes, the existence of a sentient being capable of perceiving, and of an object capable of being perceived. It supposes, also, such a relation between the two, that the former is affected by the presence of the latter. From this results perception in its twofold aspect, or the knowledge, on the part of the sentient mind, at once of itself as affected, and of the object as affecting it. According as one or the other of these elements is more directly the object of attention, so the subjective and the objective character predominate in the act of perception. If the former, then we think chiefly of the me as affected, and are scarcely conscious of the external object as the source or the producing cause; if the latter, the reverse is true.

§ II — Analysis of the Perceptive Process.

Simple Sensation. — The nature of the presentative power may be better understood by observing closely the different steps of the process. As we come into contact with the external world, the first thing of which we are conscious, the first step in the process of cognition, is doubtless simple sensation. Something touches me, my bodily organism is thereby affected, and I am conscious, at once, of a certain feeling or sensation. I do not know as yet what has produced the sensation, or whether any thing produced it. I do not as yet recognize it as the result of an affection of the bodily organism, or even as pertaining to that organism in distinction from the spiritual principle. I am conscious only of a certain feeling. This is simple *sensation* — a purely subjective process.

Recognition of it as such. — We do not, however, stop here. The mind is at once aroused by the occurrence of the phenomenon supposed, the attention is directed to it. I cognize it as sensation, as feeling. If it be not the first instance of the kind in my experience, I distinguish it from other sensations which I have felt.

Distribution of it to the Parts affected. — More than this; I am conscious not only of the given sensation, but of its being an affection of my bodily organism, and of this or that part of the organism; I distinguish the body as the seat of the sensation, and this or that part of the body as the part affected. The organism as thus affected becomes itself an object of thought as distinct from the thinking mind that animates and pervades it. It becomes to me an externality, having extension and parts out of and distinct from each other. As thus viewed, and brought now for the first time under the eye of consciousness, it becomes known to me as the *non-ego*, still connected, however, by sensation with the ego, the sentient principle and as thus viewed, I become aware that the sensation which I feel is an affection of that organism, and of a certain portion of it, as the hand, or the foot. This cognizance of the sensation as such, as pertaining to the organism, and to this or that part of the same, and the consequent cognizance of the organism as such, as distinct from the sentient mind, and as thus and thus affected, is no longer simple *sensation*, it is *perception.*

Cognition of something external to the Organism itself. — This is the most simple form of immediate perception. The process does not, however, necessarily stop here. I am conscious not only of this or that part of my organism as affected, but of something external to the organism itself, in contact with and affecting it. This organism with which I find myself connected, the seat of sensation, the object of perception, is capable of self-movement in obedience to my volitions. I am conscious of the effort to move my person, and conscious also of being resisted in those movements by something external in contact with my organism. This yet unknown something becomes now the object of attention and perception — this new phenomenon — resistance, something resisting. To perceive that I am resisted, is to perceive that something resists, and to perceive this is to perceive the object itself which offers such resistance. I may not know every thing pertaining to it, what sort of thing it may be, but I know this respecting it, that it exists, that it is external to my organism, that it resists my movements. Thus the outer world becomes directly an object of perception — passes under the immediate eye of consciousness.

In what Sense these several Steps distinct. — In the preceding analysis, in order more clearly to illustrate the nature of the process, we have regarded the act of perception as broken into several distinct parts, or steps of progress. This, however, is not strictly correct as regards the psychology of the matter. Logically, we may distinguish the simple sensation as mere feeling, from the reference of the same to this or that part of the bodily organism as affected, and each of these again, from the cognizance of the external object, which by contact or resistance produces the sensation. Chronologically, the act is one and indivisible. The sensation and the perception are synchronous. We cannot separate the act of sense-perception into the consciousness of a sensation, the consciousness of the bodily organism a. affected by that sensation, and the consciousness of an external something as the proximate cause of that affection. To experience a sensation, is to experience it as here or there in the sentient organism, and to perceive contact or resistance, is to perceive something in contact or resisting. There may, however, be sensation without cognizance of the external producing cause.

Restricted Sense of the term Perception. — According to the view now advanced, perception is *immediate;* not a matter of inference, not a roundabout reflective process. It is a cognizance direct and intuitive of the bodily organization as thus and thus affected, and of an external something in correlation with it, affecting and limiting that organism in its movements.

Usually, however, a wider range has been given to the term, and the faculty thereby denoted. It has been made to comprehend any mental process by which we refer a specific sensation to something external as its producing cause. It is thus employed by Reid and Stewart, and such has been in fact the prevalent use of the term. According to this, when we experience the sensation of fragrance, and refer that sensation to the presence of a rose, or the sensation of sound, and refer it to the stroke of a bell, or a passing carriage, we exercise the faculty of perception. Evidently, however, our knowledge in these cases is merely a matter of inference, of judgment, not of immediate direct perception, not in fact of perception at all. All that we properly perceive in such a case, all that we are directly conscious of, is the fragrance or the sound. That these are produced by the rose and the bell is not perceived, but only *conceived*, inferred — known, if at all, only by the aid of previous experience.

Sensation as distinguished from Perception. — According to the view now presented, *sensation*, as distinguished from *perception*, is the *simple feeling* which results from a certain affection of the organism. It is known to us merely *as* feeling. Perception takes cognizance of the feeling *as an affection of the organism*, and also of the organism as thus affected, and consequently as external to the me, extended, having parts, etc. It apprehends also objects external to the organism itself limiting and affecting its movements. Sensation is the indispensable condition of perception. If there were no sensation, there would be no perception. The one does not precede, however, and the other follow in order of time, but the one being given, the other is given along with it. The two do not, however, coexist in equal strength, but in the relation, as stated by Hamilton, of *inverse ratio;* that is, beyond a certain point, the stronger the sensation, the weaker the perception, and *vice versâ.*

Sensation as an Affection of the Mind. — It has been common to speak of sensation as lying wholly in the mind. Primarily, however, it is an affection of the nervous organism, and through that organism, as thus affected, an impression is made on the mind. If it were not for the mind present with the organism, and susceptible of impression from it, and thus cognizant of changes in it, the same changes might be produced in the organism as now, but we should be entirely unconscious of and insensible to them. In certain states of the system this actually happens, as in sound sleep, the magnetic state, the state produced by certain medicinal agents as ether, chloroform, opium, and the intoxicating drugs of the East. In those cases, the connection between the mind and the nervous organism seems to be in some manner interrupted or suspended, and consequently there is for the time no sensation. The nerves may be irritated, divided even, and still no pain is felt.

It is not true, however, that the sensation is wholly in the mind. It is in the living animated organism, as pervaded by the mind or spiritual principle, mysteriously present in every part of that organism, and cognizant of its changes; and neither the body alone, nor the mind alone, can be said to possess this faculty, but the two united in that complex mysterious unity which constitutes our present being.

§ III. — Analysis and Classification of the Qualities of Bodies.

Difference of Qualities. — The qualities of bodies as known to us through sensation and perception are many and various. On examination, a difference strikes us as existing among these qualities, which admits of being made the basis of classification. Some of them are qualities which strike us at once as essential to the very existence of matter, at least in our notion of it, so that we cannot in thought divest it of these qualities, and still retain our conception of matter. Others are not of this nature. Extension, divisibility, size, figure, situation, and some others, are of the former class. If matter exists at all, it must, according to our own conceptions, possess these qualities. We cannot think them away from it, and leave matter still existing. But we can conceive of matter as destitute of color, flavor, savor, heat, cold, weight, sound, hardness, etc. These are contingent and accidental properties not necessary to its existence.

How named and distinguished. — Philosophers have called the former class *primary*, the latter *secondary* qualities. The former are known *à priori*, the latter by experience. The former are known as qualities, in themselves, the latter only through the affections of our senses.

The primary qualities then have these characteristics:

1. They are essential to the very existence of matter, at least in our conception.

2. They are to be known *à priori.*

3. They are known as such, or in themselves.

The secondary, on the contrary, are:

1. Accidental, not essential to the notion of matter.
2. To be known only by experience.
3. To be learned only through the affection of the senses.

Further Division of secondary Qualities. — A further division, however, is capable of being made. The secondary qualities, as now defined, comprise, in reality, two classes. There are some, which, while known to us only through the senses, have still an existence as qualities of external objects, independent of our senses. As such they are objects of direct perception. Others, again, are known, not as qualities of bodies, but only as affections of sense, not as objective, but only as subjective, not as perceptions, but only as sensations. Thus I distinguish the smell, the taste, and the color of an orange. What I distinguish, however, is after all only certain sensations, certain affections of my own organism. What may be the peculiar properties or qualities in the object itself which are the exciting cause of these sensations in me, I know not. My perception does not extend to them at all. It is quite otherwise with the qualities of weight, hardness, compressibility, fluidity, elasticity, and others of that class. They are objects of perception, and not of sensation merely.

These Classes, how distinguished. — The class first named, are qualities of bodies as related to other bodies. The other class are qualities of bodies as related only to our nervous organization. The former all relate to bodies as occupying and moving in *space*, and come under the category of *resistance.* The latter relate to bodies only as capable of producing certain sensations in us. We may call the former *mechanical*, the latter *physiological.*

Connection of Sensation with the external Object. — From long habit of connecting the sensation with the external body which produces it, we find it difficult to per suade ourselves that taste and smell are mere affections of our senses, or that color is really and simply an affection of the optic nerve of the beholder, and that what is actually perceived in these instances is not properly a quality of the external object. A little reflection, however, will convince us that all which comes to our knowledge in these cases, all that we are properly cognizant of, is the affection of our own nervous organism, and that whatever may be the nature of the qualities in the object which are the producing cause of these sensations in us, they are to us occult and wholly unknown.

Power of producing these Sensations.—It is not to be denied, of course, that there is in external objects the power of producing these sensations in us, under given circumstances; but to what that power is owing, in what peculiarity of constitution or condition it consists, we know not. We have but one name, moreover, for the power of producing, and the effect produced. Thus the color, taste, smell, etc., of an object may denote either the sensation in us, or the unknown property of matter by virtue of which the sensation is awakened. It is only in the sense last mentioned, that the qualities under consideration may properly be called qualities of bodies.

Enumeration of the several Qualities as now classed.—According to the classification now made, the qualities of bodies may be thus enumerated.

I. *Primary.*—Extension, divisibility, size, density, figure absolute incompressibility, mobility, situation.

II. *Secondary.*—A. *Objective*, or *mechanical*—as heavy or light, hard or soft, firm or fluid, rough or smooth, compressible or incompressible, resilient or irresilient, and any other qualities of this general nature resulting from attraction, repulsion, etc.

B. *Subjective* or *physiological*—as color, sound, flavor, savor, temperature, tactual sensation, and certain other affections of the senses of this nature.

§ IV. — Organs of Sense. — Analysis of their Several Functions

Number of the Senses. — The different senses are usually reckoned as five in number. They may all be regarded, however, as modifications of one general sense, that of touch — or, in other words, the susceptibility of the nervous system to be excited by foreign substances brought into contact with it. This is the essential condition of sensation in any case, and the several senses, so called, are but so many variations in the mode of manifesting this excitability. There is a reason, nevertheless, for assigning five of these modifications and no more, and that is, that the anatomical structure indicates either a distinct organ, as the ear, the eye, etc., or at least a distinct branch of the nervous apparatus, as in the case of smell and taste, while the whole nervous expansion as spread out over the surface of the body contributes to the general sense of touch.

The Senses related to each other. — *Distinct Office of each.* — It is evident enough that these several senses sustain a certain relation to each other. They are so many and no more, not merely by accident; not merely because so many could find room in the bodily organization; not merely because it might be convenient to have so many. Let us look at the office performed by each, and we shall see that while each has its distinct function, not interchangeable with that of any other, it is a function more or less necessary to the animal economy. Remembering that the design and use of the several senses is to put us in possession of data, by means of which, directly or indirectly, we may gain correct knowledge of the external world, let us suppose the inquiry to be raised, What senses ought man to have for this purpose? What does he need, the material universe remaining what it is?

Function of the Sense of Touch. — Things exist about us in space, having certain properties and relations. We need a sense then, first and chiefly, that shall acquaint us with objects thus existing, taking cognizance of what lies immediately about us in space. This we have in the general sense of touch, making us acquainted with certain objective or mechanical qualities of external objects.

This Sense, how limited. — This, however, avails only for objects within a short distance, and capable of being brought into contact. It operates also synthetically and slowly, part after part of the object being given as we are brought into contact with different portions of it successively, until the process is so far complete that, from the ensemble of these different parts, our understanding can construct the whole.

Possibility of a Sense that shall meet these Limitations. — We can conceive of a sense that should differ in both these respects — that should take cognizance of distant objects, not capable perhaps of being brought into contact — and that should also operate analytically, or work from a given whole to the parts, and not from the parts to a whole, thus giving us possession at once of a complete object or series of objects. Such a sense, it is easy to see, would possess decided advantages, and in connection with the one already considered, would seem to bring within the sphere of our cognizance almost the complete range of external nature. This we have, and this exactly, in the sense of *vision.* It takes in objects at a distance, and takes in the whole at a glance.

This new Sense still limited. — This new sense, however, convenient and useful as it is, has evidently its limitations. It is available only through a given medium, the light. Strictly speaking, it is the light only that we see, and not the distant object; that is known indirectly by means of the light that, variously modified, travels from it to the eye. When this fails, as it does during several hours of the twenty-four, or when it is intercepted by objects coming between and shutting out the forms on which the eye seeks in vain to rest, then our knowledge from this source is cut off.

Still another Sense desirable.—Under these circumstances, might it not be well, were there given an additional sense, of the same general nature and design, but operating through a different medium, sure to be present wherever animal life exists, so that even in the darkness of the night, or the gloom of the dungeon, we might still have means of knowing something of the surrounding objects. And what f this medium, or avenue of sense, were of such a nature as to be capable of modification, and control, to some extent, on our part, and at our pleasure, so as to form a means of voluntary communication with our fellow-beings. Would not such an arrangement be of great service? Exactly these things are wanted; exactly these wants are met, and these objects accomplished, by a new sense answering to these conditions—the sense of *hearing*—the cognizance of sound. This we produce when we please by the spoken word, the vocal utterance, whether of speech, or musical note, or inarticulate cry, varied as we please, high, low, loud, soft—a complete alphabet of expression, conveying thus by signals, at once rapid and significant, the varying moods and phases of our inner life to other beings that had else been strangers, for the most part, to the thoughts and feelings which agitate our bosoms.

Senses for another Class of Qualities.—The senses, as thus far analyzed, have reference primarily to the number, magnitude, and distance of objects as occupying space—to quantities rather than qualities. Were it possible now to add to these a sense, or senses that should take cognizance of quality, as well as existence and quantity—that should detect, to some extent at least, the *chemical* properties of bodies as connected especially with the functions of respiration and nutrition—the list of senses would seem to be complete. This addition is made, this knowledge given, in the senses of *smell* and *taste.*

Possibility of additional Senses.—To those already named, other senses might doubtless have been added by the Creator, which would have revealed, it may be, properties of matter of which we have now no conception. It is not to be supposed that we know every thing respecting the nature and qualities of even the most familiar and common objects. Many things there may be, actual, real, in the world about us, of which we know nothing, because they come not within the range of any of our senses. But all that is essential to life, and happiness, and highest welfare s doubtless imparted by the present arrangement; and when closely studied, no one of these senses will be found superfluous, no one overlapping the province of another, but working each its specific end, and all in harmony.

The proper Office of Psychology in respect to the Senses.— It is the province of the anatomist and the physiologist to explain the mechanical structure of the several organs of sense, and their value as parts of the physical system. The psychologist has to do with them only as instruments of the mind, and it is for him to show their connection and proper office as such. This has been attempted in the preceding analysis.

The kind of Knowledge afforded by the Senses. — It is to be noticed, in addition, that with the exception of the tactual sense, and possibly of sight, these senses give us no direct, immediate knowledge of external things. They simply furnish data, signs, intimations, by the help of which the understanding forms its conclusions of the world with out. They are the *receiving* agents of the mind. This is, in fact, the chief office of sense, to receive through its various avenues the materials from which the understanding shall frame conceptions of things without; to convey, as it were, a series of telegraphic despatches along those curious and slender filaments that compose the nervous organization, by means of which the soul, keeping her hidden seat and chamber within, may receive communication from the distant provinces of her empire. These signs the understanding interprets; and in so far as this is the true nature of the process, it is not a process of immediate and proper perception. I hear, for example, a noise. All that I really perceive in this case is the sensation of sound. I refer it, however, to an external cause, to a carriage passing in the street. I specify, moreover, the kind of carriage, perhaps a coach, or a wagon with iron axles. I have observed, have learned by experience, that sounds of this nature are produced in this way, that is, by carriages passing, and by such carriages. Hence I judge that the sound which I now hear is produced in the same way. It is an *inference*, a conception merely. All that sense does is to receive and transmit the sign, which the understanding interprets by the aid of former experience. And the same is true of the other senses, with the exceptions named.

Not therefore of little Value. — We are not to infer, however, that these senses are on this account of no special value or importance to us. They do precisely what is needed. They put us in possession of just the data wanted in order to the necessary information concerning external things. It is only the theorist who undervalues the senses, and he only in his closet. No man, in the full possession of his reason, and his right mind, can go forth into this fair and goodly world, and not thank God for every one of those senses — sight, hearing, taste, touch, and smell. Their true and full value, however, we never learn till we come to be deprived of their use ; till with Milton we exclaim,

> " Seasons return ; but not to me returns
> Day, or the sweet approach of even or morn."

§ V. — Amount of Information Derived from the Respective Senses.

A further Question as to one Class of the Senses. — The relations and specific functions of the several senses have been already described. Some further questions arise, however, respecting the precise amount and kind of information afforded by that class of the senses which, as we have seen, relates to the spatial properties of bodies, in distinction from the chemical, viz.: hearing, sight, and touch.

What is given in Hearing.—And first, as to the sense of *hearing*. What is it precisely that we hear? When we listen to a sound, we speak of hearing the object that produces the sound; we say, I hear a bell, a bird, a gun, etc. Strictly speaking, we do not hear the object, but only the sound. It is not the bell or the bird that we hear, but the vibration of the air produced by bell and bird. This has been already illustrated by reference to a carriage passing in the street. It is only by experience, aided by other senses, that we learn to refer the sound to its producing cause.

Hearing not properly Perception.—Is hearing then a sensation merely, or is it a perception? If by perception we mean a direct knowledge of the external object—which is the proper sense of the word—hearing certainly is not perception. It gives us no such immediate knowledge. What we perceive in hearing is merely the sensation of sound. It may be doubted whether by this sense alone we should ever get the idea that what we hear is any thing external to ourselves.

Affords the means of Judging.—As it is, however, we judge, not only of the existence and nature, but of the distance and direction of the external object whence the sound proceeds. We learn to do this with great correctness, and with great facility. No sooner do we hear a sound, in most instances, than we form an opinion at once, from what direction it comes, and what produces it; nor are we often mistaken in our judgment. The faculty of judging by the ear as to the direction of the sound, and the nature of the object producing it, may be cultivated by care and practice to a remarkable degree of accuracy. Napoleon was seldom mistaken as to the direction and distance of a cannonade. It is said that the Indian of the north-western prairies by applying his ear to the ground, will detect the approach of a body of cavalry at a distance beyond the reach of vision, and distinguish their tread from that of a herd of buffaloes.

Number of Sounds. — The number of sounds which the ear can distinguish is almost without limit. There are, it is said, five hundred distinct tones which an ear of usual accuracy can recognize, and each of these tones admits of five hundred variations of loudness, giving, in all, two hundred and fifty thousand different sounds.

Power of Sound over the Mind. — The power of sound to affect the mind, and especially the feelings, is too well known to require specific statement. The note of an instrument, the tone of a human voice, the wild warbling of a bird, the tinkling of a bell, the variations of speech and of song, from the high and shrill to the low and heavy intonation, from the quick and impetuous to the slow and plaintive movement, these simple varieties of tone affect powerfully the heart, and find their way at once and irresistibly to the feelings. Hence the power of music over even the uncultivated mind; hence too in no small degree the power of the skilful orator over the feelings of his audience. It is not merely, nor so much, the thing said, in many cases, as the way of saying it, that touches and sways the assembled multitude. Tones and sounds have a natural meaning. They are the natural language of the heart. They express emotion, and hence awaken emotions in others.

The Question as to Sight. — Turning now from the sense of *hearing* to that of *sight*, the question arises, What is it precisely that we perceive by the eye? When we fix the eye upon any object, more or less remote, what is it, strictly speaking, that we see, extension and figure, or only color? Is it by vision that we learn primarily the distance of objects and their locality? These are points requiring investigation.

Does Sight give Extension and Figure. — As to the first of these questions, whether extension and figure are objects of direct visual perception. No doubt they are associated in our minds with the act of vision, so that the moment we see an object we obtain an idea of it as extended, and of such and such dimensions and figure. The question is, whether it is really through the sense of sight that we obtain this idea, or in some other way. Had we no other means of information, would sight alone give us this? When we first open our eyes on external objects, do we receive the idea of extension and figure, or only of color? The fact that as matters are, we cannot in our experience separate the notion of some surface extension from the sensation of color, is not decisive of these questions. We cannot, as Dr. Brown observes, separate the color from the convexity and magnitude of an oak before us, but this does not prove that convexity and magnitude are objects of immediate and original perception. If every surface in nature had been convex, suggests the same writer, we should probably have found the same difficulty in attempting to conceive of color as separate from convexity, that we now find in attempting to conceive of it as separate from length and breadth. As it is, however, our sensation of color has not always been associated with convexity, while it has been always associated with surface extension. Hence it is, he maintains, that we seem to perceive, by the eye, the length, and breadth, and objects along with their color.

Argument from the Affection of a Portion of the Retina. — The fact that in vision a certain portion of the retina in length and breadth is actually affected by the light falling on it, has been supposed by some to be conclusive of the fact that we perceive the length and breadth of the external object by the eye. This does not necessarily follow. As Dr. Brown contends, it is equally true that a certain part of the organ of smell is affected by odors, and a certain part of the auditory nerve is affected by sounds, yet we are not conscious of any perception of extension by either of these organs; we neither smell nor hear the length, and breadth, and magnitude of objects; nor is there any reason to suppose that the particular portion of the retina affected has any thing to do with the original sensation of sight.

Amount of the preceding Arguments. — These arguments, however, do not strike me as conclusive. They merely show the *possibility* that extension and figure *may be* acquired rather than original perceptions. They do not amount to positive evidence that they *are* so.

An Argument to the Contrary. — On the other hand, there is one consideration of a positive character, which to most minds will be likely to outweigh the merely negative arguments already adduced. Color is a property of light, and light comes to us reflected from objects occupying space; we perceive it only as we perceive it spread over and reflected from some surface. Extension, then, surface expansion of the reflecting object, is the indispensable condition of the visibility of light itself, and so of color, as reflected from the object. Now it is difficult to persuade ourselves that what we know to be an essential condition of the perception of color, and what we seem to perceive along with the color, and cannot, even in thought, wholly separate from it, is not, after all, really perceived by the eye.

Argument from recent Discoveries. — Indeed, recent discoveries in science seem to vindicate that not only surface extension, but trinal extension, or *solidity*, may be an object of direct perception by the eye. I refer to the researches of Wheatstone, in binocular vision, which go to show, that in consequence of the difference of the images formed upon the right and the left eye, as occupying different positions with reference to the object seen, we are enabled by the eye to cognize the solidity as well as the extension of objects. The difference of figure in the two images gives us this. That such is the case is shown by an instrument, the stereoscope, so constructed as to present separately the image as formed on each eye, which, when separately viewed, appear as mere plane surfaces, but when viewed together, the right image with the right eye, and the left one with the left eye, at the same time, present no longer the appearance of plane surfaces, but the two images combine to form one distinct figure, and that a solid, having length, breadth, thickness, and standing out with all the semblance of the real object.

It is hardly necessary to say that if extension is an object of perception by the eye, so also is figure, which is merely the *limitation* of extension in different directions.

Second Question — Does Sight give Distance? — Is it also by vision that we obtain the idea of the *distance* of objects and their externality? Does vision alone give the idea that what we see is numerically distinct from ourselves, and that it occupies this or that particular locality? So it would seem, judging from the impression left upon the mind in the act of vision. We seem to see the object as here or there, external, more or less distant in space. We distinguish it from ourselves.

The negative View. — This is denied by some. All that we see, they contend, is merely the light coming from the object, and from the variations and modifications which this exhibits we learn to judge by experience of the distance and locality of the object. It is a matter of judgment and not of perception. We have learned to associate the two things, the visual appearance and the distance.

Argument in the Negative. — In proof of this they adduce the fact that we are frequently mistaken in our estimate of the distance of objects. If there be more or fewer intervening objects than usual, if the atmosphere be more or less clear than usual, or any like circumstance affords a variation from our ordinary experience, we are misled as to the distance of the object. Hence we mistake the distance of ships at sea, or of objects on a prairie or a desert, the width of rivers, the height of steeples, towers, etc.

Further Argument in the Negative. — It is further contended that facts show that the impressions of sight alone, uncorrected by experience, do not convey the idea of distance at all, but that what we see seems to be in connection with the eye itself, until we learn the contrary by the aid of other senses. This, it is said, is the experience of persons who have been operated upon for cataract, particularly of a patient whose case is described by Cheselden, and who thought every thing which he saw, touched his eyes. It is said also to have been the same with Caspar Hauser, when first liberated from the long confinement of his dungeon, and permitted to look out upon the external world. The goodly landscape seemed to him to be a group of figures, drawn upon the window.

Force of this Argument. — This, however, is not inconsistent with the perception of externality by vision, since even what seems to be in contact with the eye, nay, what is known to be so, may still be known as external. Contact implies externality. It is very much to be doubted, moreover, whether the cases now referred to, coincide with the usual experience of those who are learning to see. The little child seems to recognize the externality and remoteness from his own person of the objects which attract his attention, as soon as he learns to observe surrounding objects at all, and, though he may not judge correctly of their relative distance from himself, never seems by his movements to suppose that they are in contact with his eye or with any part of his person. The young of animals, also, as soon as they are born, seem to perceive by the eye, the externality, the direction, and the distance of objects, and govern their movements accordingly. It is not, in these cases, a matter of experience, but of direct perception. These facts render it doubtful, to say the least, whether the common impression — that which in spite of all arguments to the contrary, is, and always will be made upon the mind in the act of vision, viz., that we see objects as external, as having locality, and as more or less remote from us — is not, after all, the correct impression.

Learning to judge of Distance not inconsistent with this

View. — Nor does it conflict with this view that we learn to judge of the true distance of objects, and are often deceived in regard to it. The *measurement* of distance, the more or less of it, is of course a matter of experience, a thing to be learned by practice. It does not follow, however, that we may not by the eye directly, and at first, perceive an object to be external, and removed from us, in other words distant, though we may not know at first *how* distant. The rays of light that come to us from this external object, may give us direct perception of the object as external, as extended, and as occupying apparently a given locality in space more or less remote, while at the same time it may be left to other senses and to experience to determine how great that distance is.

Questions as to Touch. — Passing now from the sense of sight to that of *touch*, we find similar questions discussed among philosophers respecting the precise information afforded by this sense. Does touch give us immediate perception of externality, extension, form, hardness, softness, etc., including the various mechanical properties of bodies? To this sense it has been common to ascribe these faculties of perception. They are so attributed by Reid, Upham, Wayland, and, I believe, by modern writers generally, with the exception of Brown and Hamilton.

Probability of another Source of Information. — It may be questioned, I think, whether, as regards some of these qualities at least, it is not rather the consciousness of resistance to muscular effort, than the sense of touch, properly speaking, that is the informing source. So, for example, as to hardness; the application of an external body lightly to the hand awakens the sense of touch, but conveys no idea of hardness. Let the same object be allowed to rest with gradually increasing weight upon the hand until it becomes painful, and we get the idea of weight, gravitation, but not of the hardness or impenetrability of the object. It is only when our muscular effort to move or penetrate the external body is met and resisted by the same, that we learn the impenetrability of the opposing body.

Other Perceptions attributable to the same Source. — So with regard to externality, extension, and form. When an external object, a cube, for example, or an ivory ball, is placed on the palm of the hand, sensation is awakened, but is that sensation necessarily accompanied with the perception of the external object as such? Does the mere tactual sensation, in the first instance, and of itself, inform us that there is something external to ourselves, that what we feel is not a part of our own organism? We are conscious of a change in the sensation of the part affected, but are we immediately conscious that this change is produced by something external? Let there be given, however, the consciousness of resistance to our muscular movements, as when the cube or ball, for instance, prevents the effort to close the hand, or when our locomotion is impeded by the presence of some obstacle, and will not the same resistance inform us of the extension of the resisting body, and so of its form and figure? We learn whereabout in space this resistance occurs, and where it ceases. The tactual sensation would indeed very soon come to our aid in this cognition, and serve as a guiding sense, even in the absence of the former. The question is, whether this alone would, in the first instance, give us such cognitions?

Our first Ideas of Extension, how derived. — We have had reference in this discussion only to the qualities of *external* bodies. There can be little question that our *first* ideas of extension are derived from our own sentient organism, the consciousness of sensations in different parts of the body, distinct from, and out of each other, thus affording the knowledge of an extended sentient organization. The idea of externality, or outness, and extension, thus acquired, the transition is easy from the perception of our own bodies as possessing these qualities, to the cognizance of the same qualities in external objects.

§ VI. — Credibility of our Sensations and Perceptions.

Denied by some. — There have always been those who were disposed to call in question the testimony of the senses. Such were the Eleatics and the Skeptics among the Greek philosophers, and there have not been wanting among the moderns minds of acuteness and ingenuity that have followed in the same path. While admitting the *phenomena* of sense, the *appearance* of things as being so and so, they have called in question the corresponding objective reality. Things appear to me to be thus and thus — such and such impressions are made on my senses — that I cannot deny; but how do I know that the reality corresponds to my impressions, or, in fact, that there is any reality? How know we our senses to be reliable? What evidence have we that they do not habitually deceive us?

Evidence demanded. — It were perhaps a sufficient answer to this question to reply, What *evidence* have we, or can we have, that they *do* deceive us? In the absence of all evidence to the contrary, is it not more reasonable to suppose that our perceptions correspond to realities, than that they are without foundation, uncaused, or caused by something not at all answering to the apparent object of perception; more reasonable to suppose that there is a real table or book answering to my perception of one, than that I have the perception while there is no such reality? It remains with those, then, who question and deny the validity of sense-perception, to show reasons for such denial. And this becomes the more imperative on them, inasmuch as they contradict the common belief and universal opinion of mankind—nay, what, in spite of all their arguments, is still, by their own confession, their own practical conviction and belief.

Evidence impossible. — But whence is this evidence to come? Where is it to be sought? How are we to prove that sense deceives us, except by arguments drawn from sense? And if sense is not reliable in the first instance, why re.y upon it in the second, to prove that it is not reliable? If the senses do habitually deceive us, manifestly it can never be shown that they do. And, even if this could be shown, it would be impossible to find any thing better to rely upon in their stead. We have these guides or none. We have these instruments of observation provided for the voyage of life. We may pronounce them worthless, and throw them into the sea, but we cannot replace them.

Inconsistent and contradictory Testimony of Sense.— But it may be replied that the testimony of sense is often inconsistent with itself, and contradictory of itself. What is sweet to one is sour and bitter to another. What seems a round tower in the distance becomes a square one as you approach; and the straight stick that you hold in your hand appears crooked when thrust into the water. There is in reality, however, no contradiction or inconsistency in the cases supposed. The change of circumstances accounts in every instance for the change of appearance. In the case of the stick, for example, the different density of the water accounts for the refraction of the rays of light that pass through it, and this accounts for the crooked appearance of the stick that is only partially submerged. So in the other cases; it is no contradiction that an object which appears round at a distance of ten miles, should appear square at the distance of so many rods — or that the taste of two persons should not agree as to the savor of a given object.

Deceptions of Sense. — It may be further objected that in certain states of the physical organism, sensations are experienced which seem to be of external origin, but are really produced by internal changes; and that in such cases we have the same perceptions, see the same objects, hear the same things, that we should if there were a corresponding external reality, while nevertheless there is no such reality, and it can be proved that there is none. If this may happen in some cases, why not in others, or in all?

Reply. — I reply, the simple fact, that in the case supposed the deception can be detected and proved, shows the difference between that and ordinary perception. If the senses were not habitually reliable, we could not detect the mistake in this particular instance. If all coin were counterfeit, how could we detect a counterfeit coin? We know, moreover, how to account for the mistake in the case before us. It occurs, by the supposition, only in a certain state of he organism, that is, only in a diseased, abnormal condition of the system. The exception proves the rule.

Distinction of direct and indirect Testimony. — A distinction is to be made, in the discussion of this subject, between the direct and indirect testimony of the senses, between that which is strictly and properly perception, and that which is only conception, judgment, inference. What I really perceive, for example, in the case of the distant tower, or the stick partially under water, is only a given appearance; I *infer* from that appearance that the tower is round and the stick crooked, and in that inference I am mistaken. My judgment is at fault here, and not my senses. They testified truly and correctly. They gave the real appearance, and this was all they could give, all they ever give. This has been well stated by Dr. Reid, and, long before him, the same ground was taken, in reply to the same objection, by Aristotle and also by Epicurus.

Direct Perception gives what. — In regard to direct and immediate perception, the case is different. Here the testimony is positive to the existence of the object. When something resists my voluntary movement, I am conscious of that resistance, conscious of something external and resisting. I cannot deny the fact of that consciousness. I may, however, deny the correctness, the truthfulness of what consciousness affirms. To do this, however, is to put an end to all reasoning on the subject, for, when we give up consciousness as no longer reliable, there is nothing left to fall back upon. If any one chooses to leap from this precipice, we can only say *finis.*

§ VII. — Historical Sketch.

I. Of Different Divisions of the Qualities of Bodies.

The Greek Philosophers. — The distinction of the qualities of bodies into two classes, differing in important respects, is by no means a modern one. It was recognized by some of the earlier Greek philosophers, who held that the sweet, bitter, hot, cold, etc., are rather affections of our own senses than proper qualities of matter, having independent existence. Subsequently the view was adopted by Protagoras, and by the Cyrenean and Epicurean schools. Plato held it, and especially and very fully, Aristotle, who calls the qualities to which we have referred, and which are usually denominated secondary, *affective* qualities, because they have the power of affecting the senses, while the qualities now usually termed primary, as extension, figure, motion, number, etc., he regards as not properly objects of sense. The former class he calls proper sensibles, the latter, common.

The Schoolmen. — The *schoolmen* made much of this distinction, and held, with Aristotle, that the qualities now called primary, require, for their cognition, other faculties than those of sense.

Doctrine of Galileo. — *Galileo* points out the true ground and philosophy of this distinction, and also gives the name *primary* to the class referred to, viz., *those qualities which are necessary to our conception of body*, as for example, figure, size, place, etc., while, on the contrary, colors, tastes, etc., are not inherent in bodies, but only in us, and we can conceive of body without them. The former are real qualities of bodies, while the latter are only conceptions which give us no real knowledge of any thing external, but only of the affections of our own minds.

The Moderns. — *Descartes* and *Locke* merely adopted these distinctions as they found them, without essential modification. So also did *Reid* and *Stewart*, although both included among the primary qualities some which are properly secondary, as roughness, smoothness, hardness, softness. Indeed Stewart restricted the primary qualities to those and such as those just named.

Hamilton. — No writer has so fully elaborated this matter as Sir William Hamilton, to whom we are indebted mainly for the historical facts now stated, and whose dissertations are and must ever remain an invaluable thesaurus on the philosophy of perception. So complete and elaborate is his classification of the qualities of matter, that I shall be pardoned for giving a synopsis of its principal points in this connection.

Hamilton's Scheme — General Divisions. — He divides the qualities of bodies into three classes, which he calls primary, secundo-primary, and secondary. The primary are thought as essential to the very notion of matter, and may be deduced *à priori*, the bare notion of matter being given; while the secundo-primary and the secondary, being accidental and contingent, must be deduced *à posteriori*, learned by experience. His deduction of the primary qualities is as follows:

Primary Qualities. — We can conceive of body only as, I. Occupying space; II. Contained in space. Space is a necessary form of thought, but we are not obliged to conceive of space as occupied, that is, to conceive of matter. When conceived it must be under the conditions now named.

I. The property of occupying space is *Simple Solidity*, which implies, *a.* Trinal extension, or length, breadth, and thickness; *b.* Impenetrability, or the property of not being reduced to non-extension. Trinal extension involves, 1. Number, or Divisibility; 2. Size, including Density; 3. Shape.

II. The attribute of being contained in space, affords the notion, 1. Of Mobility; 2. Of Position.

The essential and necessary constituents then of our notion of matter are, 1. Extension (comprising under it, 2 Divisibility; 3. Size; 4. Density; 5. Figure); 6. Ultimate Incompressibility; 7. Mobility; 8. Situation. These are the primary qualities, products, in a sort, of the understanding, developing themselves with rigid necessity out of the given notion of substance occupying space.

Secundo-Primary Qualities. — The secundo-primary are contingent modifications of the primary, all have relation to space, and motion in space, *all are contained under the category of resistance*, or *pressure*, all are learned or included as results of experience, all have both an objective and subjective phase, being at once qualities of matter, and also affections of our senses.

Considered as to the *sources* of resistance, there is, I. That of *Co-attraction*, under the forms of *a*, Gravity, *b*, Cohesion; II. That of Repulsion; III. Inertia; all which are capable of minute subdivision. Thus from cohesion follow the hard and soft, firm and fluid, tough and brittle, rigid and flexible, rough and smooth, etc., etc. From repulsion are derived compressible and incompressible, resilient and irresilient.

Secondary Qualities. — The secondary qualities are, as apprehended by us, not properly attributes of body at all, but only affections of our nervous organism. They belong to bodies only so far as these are furnished with the power of exciting our nervous organism to the specific action thus designated. To this class belong color, sound, flavor, savor, tactile sensation, feeling of heat, electricity, etc. Such also are titillation, sneezing, shuddering, and the various sensations, pleasurable or painful, resulting from the action of external stimuli.

These Classes further distinguished. — Of the qualities thus derived, the primary are known immediately in themselves, the secondary only mediately in their effects on us, the secundo-primary both immediately in themselves, and mediately in their effects on us. The primary are qualities of body in relation to body simply, and to our organism as such; the secundo-primary are qualities of body in relation to our organism, not as body in general, but as body of a particular sort, viz.: propelling, resisting, cohesive; the secondary are qualities of body in relation to our organism as excitable and sentient. The primary may be roundly characterized as mathematical, the secundo-primary as mechanical, the secondary as physiological.

Reasons for retaining the twofold Division.—Such, in brief outline, are the principal points of Hamilton's classification. While following in the main the distinctions here indicated, I have preferred to retain the old division into primary and secondary, as at once more simple, and sufficiently accurate, merely dividing the secondary into two classes, the mechanical (secundo-primary of Hamilton), and physiological. We are thus enabled, not merely to retain a division and nomenclature which have antiquity and authority in their favor, and are well-nigh universally received, but we avoid the almost barbarous terminology of Sir William's classification—while, at the same time, we indicate with sufficient precision the important distinction between the so-called secundo-primary and secondary qualities.

II. Of Different Theories of Perception.

Realists and Idealists.—There are two leading theories, quite distinct from each other, which have widely prevailed, and divided the thinking world, as to the philosophy of perception. The one maintains that in perception we have *direct cognizance* of a real external world. This is the view taken in the preceding pages, and now generally held by psychologists in this country, and to some extent in Europe. But for a long period, the prevalent, and in fact, until the time of Reid in Scotland, and Kant in Germany, the almost universally-received opinion was the reverse of this—that in perception, as in any and all other mental acts, the mind is conscious only of its own ideas, cognizant of itself and its own states only, incapable, in fact, of knowing any thing external to itself. Those who hold the former view are termed *Realists*, the latter *Idealists*.

Further division of the latter. — The latter, however, are of two classes. The *Absolute Idealists* hold that the notion we have of external things is purely subjective, having no external counterpart, no corresponding outward reality. In distinction from this the greater part maintain that while we are cognizant, directly and strictly, of nothing beyond our own minds, nevertheless there is an external reality corresponding to the idea in our minds, and which that idea represents. Hence they have been designated *Representative Idealists*, or, as Sir William Hamilton terms them, Cosmothetic Idealists.

Further Distinction. — Of these latter, again, some hold the idea which we have of an external world to be merely a state or modification of the mind itself; others regard it as a sort of intermediate connecting link between mind and matter. The former may be called egoistic, and the latter non-egoistic.

Summary of Classes. — We have then these three great classes — the *Natural Realists*, the *Absolute Idealists*, and the *Representative Idealists* comprising the Egoistic and Non-Egoistic divisions.

Distinguished Writers of the different Classes. — On the roll of absolute idealism are names of no small distinction: Berkley and Hume, in England, Fichte and Hegel, in Germany, are of the number ; while among the representative idealists one finds Descartes, Arnauld, Malebranche, Leibnitz, Locke, in fine, the greater number of philosophic writers from Descartes onward to the time of Reid. Subsequently even, we find a writer of no less repute than Dr. Brown assuming, as the basis of his philosophy of perception, the exploded theory of representative idealism, under the egoistic form. Of natural realists since the time of Reid, Sir W. Hamilton is the most distinguished.

Origin of Representative Idealism. — The doctrine of

representative perception doubtless originated in the difficulty of conceiving how a purely spiritual existence, the human mind, can, by any possibility, take cognizance of, or be affected by, a purely material substance, the external world. The soul seated in its presence-chamber, the brain, can cognize nothing beyond and without, for nothing can act except where it is present. It must be, then, said the philosophers, that in order to the mind's perceiving any thing of that which lies beyond and without its own immediate locality, there must come to the mind from that outer world certain little images bearing some resemblance to the things without, and *representing* to the soul that external world. These images — more refined than matter, less spiritual than mind itself, of an intermediate nature between the two — they termed ideas.

Tendency of Representative to Absolute Idealism. — It is easy to see how such a doctrine would lead almost inevitably to *absolute idealism.* If we do not in perception take cognizance directly of matter external, but only of certain images or ideas in our own minds, then how do we know that these images *correctly represent* the external reality, which we have never cognized, and never shall? How do we know, in fact, that there *is* any such external reality? What evidence have we, in a word, of the existence of any thing beyond and without our own minds? This was the actual result to which Berkley and Hume drove the then prevalent philosophy of Europe, as to a legitimate and inevitable result.

Relation of Dr. Reid to this Controversy. — To Dr. Reid belongs the credit of rescuing philosophy from this dangerous extreme, by showing the utter falsity of the ideal theory. He took the ground that the existence of any such representative images in the mind is wholly without proof, nay more, is inconceivable; that while we can conceive of an image of form or figure, we cannot conceive of an image of sound, or of taste or smell. The hypothesis is wholly without foundation. But even if it were conceivable and established by sufficient evidence, still it would explain nothing as to the manner in which the mind perceives external objects. It relieves no difficulty. If the representative image be itself material, how can the mind take cognizance of it? If not material, how can it represent matter, and how can the mind know that it does represent correctly the external object?

State of the Matter since Reid.—Since the time of Dr. Reid, this theory of representative perception, at least in this non-egoistic form, has been for the most part abandoned, and philosophers have been content to take the ground indicated by consciousness, and the common sense of mankind, that in perception we take direct cognizance of the external object.

Position of Hamilton.—It remained for Sir W. Hamilton to complete the work which Dr. Reid began, by showing that the representative theory, in its finer or egoistic form, as held by Dr. Brown and others, is equally untenable or unsound; that it makes little difference whether we regard the image or idea, which we take to represent the external object, as something distinct from the mind itself, or whether we view it as a mere modification or state of the mind, so long as we make any thing of the sort the direct object of perception instead of the real external thing. Idealism is the result in either case, and philosophical skepticism the goal. In place of any and all such views, Hamilton maintains, with great power and earnestness, the doctrine of natural realism—that in perception we are cognizant immediately and directly of the external object.

As no other writer has so fully elaborated this department of science, it may be of service to present in this connection the chief points of his theory.

Chief Points of Hamilton's Theory of Perception.—All perception is immediate cognition; we perceive only what we apprehend as now and here existent; and hence what we perceive is either in our own organism, viewed as material, extended, etc., or else is in immediate correlation to it. The organism is, in perception, viewed as not-me; in sensation, as of the me.

What is given in Perception proper. — What we apprehend in perception proper is: 1. The primary qualities of body as pertaining to our own organism; 2. The secundo-primary qualities of bodies in correlation to it. (See Hamilton's division of qualities of bodies, as above.)

Primary Qualities of external Objects, how known. — The primary qualities of things external to our organism we do not perceive immediately, but only infer, from the effects produced on us by them. Neither in perception nor sensation do we apprehend immediately, or in itself, the external cause of our affection or sensation. That is always unknown to consciousness, known only by inference or conjecture.

External Existence, how learned. — The existence of the world without is apprehended not in a perception of the primary qualities of things external, but of the secundo-primary — *i. e.*, in the consciousness that our movements are resisted by something external to our organism. This involves the consciousness of something external, resisting. The two things are conjunctly apprehended.

This presupposes what. — This experience presupposes the notion of space, and motion in space. These are inherent, instinctive native elements of thought, and it is idle to inquire how we come by them. Every perception of sensations *out of*, and distinct from, other sensations gives occasion for conceiving the idea of space. *Outness* involves it.

Points of Difference between this Theory and Reid's. — The system, as thus stated, differs in some respects materially from the doctrine of perception advanced by Dr. Reid, and generally adopted since his time by the English and Scotch philosophers. According to Hamilton, perception is not, as held by Reid and others, the *conception* of an object *suggested* by sensation, but the direct cognition of something. We do not merely *conceive* of the object as existing, and *believe* it to exist, we *know* it and *perceive* it to exist. Nor does sensation precede, and perception follow, as generally stated, but the two are, in time, conjunct, coëxistent. Nor do we perceive the secondary qualities of bodies, as such, but only *infer* them from our sensations. Neither do we perceive distant objects through a medium, as usually held, but what we perceive is either the organism itself, as affected thus and thus, or what is directly in contact with it, as affecting and resisting it. Extension and externality, again, are not first learned by *touch*, as Reid holds, and most subsequent writers, both English and American, but in other ways; the former, by the perception of the primary qualities of our own organism, as the seat of sensations distinct from other sensations elsewhere localized; the latter, by the resistance which we experience to our own locomotive force. Finally, sensation proper is not, as with Reid and others, an affection purely of the mind, but of mind and body as complex. Its subject is as much one as the other.

INTELLECTUAL FACULTIES.

PART SECOND.

THE REPRESENTATIVE POWER.

THE

REPRESENTATIVE POWER.

GENERAL OBSERVATIONS.

Nature of this Power — Its various Forms. — It is in the mind's power to conceive or represent to itself an object not at the time present to the senses. This may take place in several forms. There may be the simple reproduction in thought of the absent object of sense. There may be, along with the reproduction or recurrence of the object, the *recognition* of it as a former object of sensation or perception. There may be the reproduction of the object not as it is, or was, when formerly perceived, but with variations, the different elements arranged and combined not according to the actual and original, but according to the mind's own ideals, and at its will. This latter form of conception is what is usually termed imagination — while the general term memory, as ordinarily employed, is made to include the two former. While using the term in this general sense, we may properly distinguish, however, between mental reproduction, and mental recognition, the latter being strictly the office of memory.

All these are but so many forms of the representative power. We may designate them respectively as the *reproductive*, *recognitive*, and *creative* faculties. The mind's activity is essentially the same under each of these forms. The object is not *given* but *thought*, not presented to sense, but *represented* to the mind. The process is reflective rather than intuitive. It is a matter of *understanding* rather than of *sense* or of *reason.* It is a conception, not a perception or an intuition, and it is a simple conception of the object as it is or is conceived to be, in itself considered, and not in relation to other objects.

CHAPTER I.

MEMORY.

§ I. — Mental Reproduction.

I. Nature of the Process.

General Character. — As now defined, this is that form of mental activity in which the mind's former perceptions and sensations are reproduced in thought. The external objects are no longer present — the original sensations and perceptions have vanished — but by the mind's own power are reproduced to thought, giving, as it were, a representation or image of the original.

Example. — Suppose, for instance, that I have seen Strasburg minster, or the cathedral of Milan. Months, perhaps years pass away. By-and-by, in some other and remote part of the world, something reminds me of that splendid structure; I see again its imposing front, its lofty towers, its airy pinnacles and turrets. The solemn pile rises complete, as by magic, to the mind's eye, and, regardless of time or distance, the faculty of simple conception reproduces the object as it is.

Conceptions of Sound. — In like manner I form a conception, more or less distinct, of sounds once heard. The chanting of the evening service in the Church of the Madeleine at Paris, and the prolonged note of a shepherd's horn among the Alps, are instances of musical sound that frequently recur with startling distinctness to the mind,

The same is to some extent true of the sensations and perceptions derived from the other senses. With more or less vividness the objects of all such sensations and perceptions are capable of being reproduced in conception.

The Conceptions not of Necessity connected with the Recollection of Self as the Percipient. — In these cases there may or may not be a connection of the object, as it lies before our minds, with our own personal history as the former percipients of that object. The time, place, circumstance, of that perception may not be distinctly before us; even the fact that we have ourselves seen, heard, felt, what we now conceive, may not, at the moment, be an object of thought. These are the elements of memory or mental recognition, and are certainly very likely to stand associated in our minds with the conception of the object itself. But not always nor of necessity is it so. There may be simple conception of the object, mental reproduction, where there is, for the time being, no recognition of any thing further. The Strasburg minster, the chanting of the choir, the note of the mountain horn, the snowy peak of Jungfrau, may stand out by themselves before the mind, abstracted from all thought of the time, the place, the circumstances in which they were originally perceived, or even from all thought of the fact that we have at some former time actually perceived these very objects. They may present themselves as pure conceptions.

Conceptions vary in some Respects. — Our conceptions vary in respect to definiteness and clearness. The objects of some of the senses are more readily and also more distinctly conceived than those of others. The sense of sight is peculiar in this respect. A visible object is more easily and more distinctly conceived than a particular sound or taste. The sense of hearing is, perhaps, next to that of sight in this respect; while the sensations of taste and smell are so seldom the objects of distinct conception, that some have even denied the power of conceiving them. Dr. Wayland maintains this view. That we do form conceptions more or less distinct of the objects both of taste and smell, as, *e.g.*, of the taste of a melon, or the smell of an orange, hardly admits of question; while, at the same time, it is doubtless true that we have less occasion to reproduce in thought the objects now referred to than those of sight and hearing, that they are recalled with less facility, and also with less listinctness.

Stewart's Theory. — Dugald Stewart has ingeniously suggested that the reason why a sound or a taste is less readily conceived than an object of sight, may be that the former are single detached sensations, while visible objects are complex, presenting a series of connected points of observation, and our conception of them as a whole is the result of many single conceptions, a result to which the association of ideas largely contributes. We more readily conceive two things in connection than either of them separately. On the same principle a series of sounds in a strain of music is more readily conceived than a single detached note.

Importance of this Power. — The value of this power to the mind is inestimable. Without it, the passing moment, the impression or sensation of the instant, would be the sum total of our intellectual life, of our conscious being. The horizon of our mental vision would extend no further than our immediate present perceptions. The past would be a blank as dark and uncertain even as the future. Conception lights up the otherwise dreary waste of past existence, and eproducing the former scenes and objects, gives us mental possession of all that we have been, as well as of the present moment, and lays at our feet the objects of all former knowledge. The mind thus becomes in a measure independent of sense and the external world. What it has once seen, heard, felt, becomes its permanent acquisition, even when the original object of perception is for ever removed. I may have seen the grand and stately minster, or the snowy Alp but once in all my life; but ever after it dwells among my conceptions, and in after years, on other continents, and amid far other scenes, that vision of beauty and grandeur passes before me as an angelic vision; that succession of sweet sounds traverses again the silent chambers of the brain, with all the freshness of first reality. It is only a conception now, but who shall estimate the worth of that simple power of conception?

The Talent for Description as affected by this Power.— The following remarks of Mr. Stewart illustrate happily one of the many uses to which this power is subservient:

"A talent for lively description, at least in the case of sensible objects, depends chiefly on the degree in which the describer possesses the power of conception. We may remark, even in common conversation, a striking difference among individuals in this respect. One man, in attempting to convey a notion of any object he has seen, seems to place it before him, and to paint from actual perception; another, although not deficient in a ready elocution, finds himself, in such a situation, confused and embarrassed among a number of particulars imperfectly apprehended, which crowd into his mind without any just order and connection. Nor is it merely to the accuracy of our descriptions that this power is subservient; it contributes, more than any thing else, to render them striking and expressive to others, by guiding us to a selection of such circumstances as are most prominent and characteristic; insomuch that I think it may reasonably be doubted if a person would not write a happier description of an object from the conception than from the perception of it. It has often been remarked, that the perfection of description does not consist in a minute specification of circumstances, but in a judicious selection of them; and that the best rule for making the selection is to attend to the particulars that make the deepest impression on our own minds. When the object is actually before us, it is extremely difficult to compare the impressions which different circumstances produce; and the very thought of writing

a description, would prevent the impressions which would otherwise take place. When we afterward conceive the object, the representation of it we form to ourselves, however lively, is merely an outline, and is made up of those circumstances which really struck us most at the moment, while others of less importance are obliterated."

Conceptions often Complex.—It is to be further remarked especting the power now under consideration, that the notion, or conception which we form of an object, by means of this faculty, is frequently complex. The particular perceptions and sensations formerly experienced, and now represented, are combined, forming thus a notion of the object as a whole. The figure, magnitude, color, and various other properties, of any object, as, *e. g.*, a table, are objects each of distinct and separate cognition, and as such are mentally reproduced, distinctly, and separately; but when thus reproduced, are combined to form the complete conception of the table, as it lies in my mind. The notion or conception of the object as a whole being thus once formed, any single perception as, *e.g.*, of color, figure, etc., is afterward sufficient to recall and represent the whole.

Often passes for Perception.—It was remarked, in treating of perception, that very much which passes under that name is in reality only conception. I hear, for example, a carriage passing in the street. All that I really perceive is the sound; but that single perception recalls at once the various perceptions that have formerly been associated with it, and so there is at once reproduced in my mind the *conception* of the passing carriage. Our conviction of the existence and reality of the object thus conceived, is hardly inferior to that produced by actual and complete perception.

Correctness of our Conceptions.—In general it may be remarked, that our conceptions are more or less adequate and correct representations of the objects to which they relate, according as they combine the reports of more or

fewer different senses, respecting more or fewer different qualities, and as these reports are more or less clear and distinct.

II. Laws of Mental Reproduction.

Conceptions not uncaused.—It is evident that our conceptions arise not uncaused and at hap-hazard, but according to some law. There is a method about the phenomena of mental reproduction. There is a reason why any particular scene or event of former experience, any perception or sensation, is brought again to mind, when it is, and as it is, rather than some other in its place. A careful observation and study of the laws which regulate in general the succession of thought, will furnish the explanation and true philosophy of mental reproduction.

Principle of Suggestion.—Every thought which passes through the mind is directly or indirectly connected with, and suggested by something which preceded; and that something may be either a sensation, a perception, a conception, or an emotion. The precedence may be either immediate or remote. Some connection there always is between any given thought or feeling at any moment before the mind, and some preceding thought or feeling, which gives rise to, occasions, suggests, the latter. These suggestions follow certain general rules or laws, which are usually called the *laws of association*. These laws, so called, are only the different circumstances under which the suggestions take place, and are termed laws only to indicate the regularity and uniformity with which, under given circumstances given thoughts and feelings are awakened in the mind.

This the Basis of mental Reproduction.—It is to this general principle of suggestion or association that we are indebted for all mental reproduction. It is only as one idea or feeling is suggested by some other which has gone before, and with which it is in some way, and for some reason, associated in our minds, that any former thought or sensa

tion is recalled, that any object which we have perceived, or any scene through which we have passed, is mentally reproduced. It is thus that the sight of an object brings to mind occurrences connected with it in our history, that the name recalls the thing, that the words of a language bring to mind the ideas which they denote, or the characters on the musical staff, the tones which they represent.

Not a distinct Faculty. — It has been customary to speak of association of ideas as a distinct faculty of the mind. It is not properly so ranked. It is a law of the mind rather than a faculty of it — a rule or method of its action in certain cases; and the particular power of mind to which this rule applies is that form of simple conception which we term mental reproduction.

The Term Suggestion preferred by Brown. — In place of the term association, Dr. Brown would prefer the term suggestion as more correct. To speak of the association of ideas implies that they have previously coëxisted in the mind, and that the one now recalls the other in consequence of that previous coëxistence. That this is often the case is doubtless true, but it is also true that in many cases one idea suggests another with which it has not previously been associated in our minds. It is not necessary to the suggestion that there should be any prior association. An object seen *for the first time* suggests many relative conceptions. The sight of a giant suggests the idea of a friend of diminutive stature, not because the two ideas have previously been associated, or the two objects have coëxisted, either in perception or conception, but because it is a law of the mind that one conception shall suggest another, either as similar, or as opposite, or in some other way related to it. This may be as truly a law of the mind, independent of association, as that light falling on the retina shall produce vision. It may seem mysterious that this should be so. Is it not equally mysterious that ideas which have formerly coëxisted should recall each other? The real mystery is

the recurrence in any mode, and from any source, of the idea, without the recurrence of the external producing cause. For these reasons, Dr. Brown prefers the term *suggestion* to *association*.

The Term Conception preferable to either. — As regards the activity of *the mind itself*, in the process of mental reproduction, the term conception seems to me to express more nearly the exact state of the case than either association or suggestion. An idea is *suggested to* the mind by some external object; the mind *conceives* the idea thus suggested. The flute which I perceive lying on the table in the room of my friend suggests at once to my mind the idea of that friend. The action of the mind in this case is simply an act of conception. All that the flute does — all that we mean when we say the flute suggests the idea of the friend — is simply to place the mind in such a state that the conception follows. Whether we speak then of the laws of *association*, laws of *suggestion*, or laws of mental *conception*, is immaterial, provided we bear in mind the real nature of the process as now defined.

Question stated. — But what are the laws of association, or suggestion, so-called — in other words, of mental conception? Under what circumstances is a given conception awakened in the mind by some preceding conception or perception? This is an important subject of inquiry, and one which has not escaped the attention of philosophers.

Primary Laws. — It has been usual to enumerate as primary laws of suggestion, the following: *resemblance, contrast, contiguity in time or place;* to which has sometimes been added *cause and effect.* There can be little doubt that these are important laws of suggestion; that a given object of thought is likely to suggest to the mind that which is like itself, that which is unlike, that which is connected with itself in time and place, that of which it is the cause or the effect. Whether these principles are exhaustive, and whether they may not be reduced to some one general principle comprehensive of them all, may admit of question.

Law of Similars. — To begin with *resemblance.* It seems to be a law of our nature, that like shall remind us of like. The mountain, the forest, the river, that I see in my morning walk to-day, remind me of similar objects that were familiar to my childhood. Nor is it necessary that the resemblance should be complete. A single point of similarity is sufficient to awaken the conception of objects the most remote, and, in other respects, dissimilar. I pass in the street a person with blue eyes, or dark hair, or having some peculiarity of expression in the countenance, and am at once reminded of a very different person whom I knew years ago, or whom I met perhaps in another land; yet the two may be as unlike, except in the one point which attracts my attention, as any two persons in the world. An article of dress peculiar to the Elizabethan age, or to the court of Louis XIV. reminds us of the lordly dames and courtiers, or gallant warriors of those periods. A single feature in the landscape, perhaps a single tree, or projecting crag, on the mountain side, brings before us the picture of a scene widely different in most respects, but presenting only this one point of resemblance to the scene before us.

Not confined to Objects of Sight. — Nor is it the objects of sight alone that are suggestive of similar objects. The other senses follow the same law. Sounds suggest similar sounds; tastes, similar tastes; and along with the sounds, tastes, etc., thus recalled, are awakened conceptions of many things having no resemblance to the suggesting object, but associated in our previous perceptions with the object suggested. A certain succession of musical sounds, for example, recalls to the Swiss his native valley, and the mountains that shut it in, and brings back to his mind the scenes of his childhood, and the peculiar customs of his father-land, where he heard in former years that simple melody. With what a train of associations is a single name often fraught what power of magic lies often in a single word!

Illustrations of other Laws. — Of the other principles of

suggestion or association which have been named, it is not necessary to speak minutely. Their operation is obvious and indisputable. Illustrations will occur to every one. The palace of the king reminds us by contrast of the hovel of the peasant. The splendor of wealth and luxury suggests the wretchedness of poverty and want. The giant reminds us of the dwarf, and the dwarf of the giant. On the principle of contiguity in time and place, the sight of an object reminds us of events that have occurred in connection with it; the name Napoleon suggests Waterloo, and Wellington, and the marshals of the empire; St. Peter's and the Vatican suggest Raphael and his Transfiguration; a book, casually lying on my table, reminds me of the volume that formerly stood by its side on the shelf, and so carries me back to other scenes, and other days.

In like manner, if it be not indeed the operation of the same principle, cause suggests the effect, and effect its cause. The wound reminds me of the instrument, and the instrument awakens the unpleasant conception of the wound which it once inflicted.

Why one Conception rather than another. — Inasmuch as any one conception may awaken in the mind a great variety of other conceptions — since a picture, for example, may recall the person whose likeness it is, or the artist who painted it, or the friend who possesses it, or the time and place in which it was sketched, or the room in which it formerly hung, or any circumstance or event connected with it — the question arises, why, in any given instance, is *one* of these conceptions awakened in the mind rather than any *other* in its stead? It is evident that the action of the associating principle is not uniform, sometimes one conception being awakened, sometimes another.

Secondary Laws. — In answer to this, Dr. Brown has shown that the action of these general and primary laws of suggestion, now named, is modified by a variety of circumstances, which may be called *secondary* laws of suggestion, and which will account for the variety in question. These modifying circumstances are: 1. Continuance of attention. 2. Vividness of feeling. 3. Frequency of repetition. 4. Lapse of time. 5. Exclusiveness of association. 6. Original constitutional differences. 7. State of mind at the time. 8. State of body. 9. Professional habits. Any one of these circumstances may so modify the action of the primary laws of suggestion, that one conception shall be awakened in the mind rather than another, by that which has preceded.

Correctness of this View. — There can be little doubt as to the correctness of this view. The attention, for example, which a given object or event excites at the time of its occurrence, and the strength and liveliness of feeling which it awakened in us, have very much to do, as every one knows, with our subsequent remembrance of that object or event. So also has the frequency with which the train of thought has been repeated — a fact illustrated in the process of committing to memory.

The more frequently two things come together before the mind, the more likely will it be, when one is again presented, to think of the other. In the process of learning a thing by rote, we repeat the lines over and over, until they become so associated, and linked together, that the suggestion of one recalls the whole. Frequently, however, we find it difficult to pass from one sentence to another, or from one stanza or paragraph to another, while we find no difficulty in completing the sentence or paragraph once commenced. The reason is, we have repeated each sentence or stanza by itself in the process of learning, and have not connected one with another. The last words of one sentence, and the first words of another, have not been repeatedly conjoined in the mind — have not frequently *coëxisted.*

Sometimes, however, a more than usual vividness of conception will make up for the want of this frequent coexistence. When, for any reason, as excited feeling, or extraordinary interest in what we perceive, we grasp with peculiar clearness and force the idea presented, this vividness of mental conception will, of itself, insure the remembrance of the object contemplated. A man, on trial for his life, will be likely to recollect the faces and tones of each of the different witnesses on the stand, and the different judges and advocates, even if he never sees them afterward.

We all know, also, that the lapse of time weakens the impression of any object or event upon the mind, and so lessens the probability of its recurrence to the thoughts. We more readily recall places and objects seen in a recent tour, than those seen a year ago. The exclusiveness of the connection is also an important circumstance. An air of music, which I have heard played or sung only on one occasion, and by one musician only, is much more likely, when heard again, to bring to mind the former player, than if it had also been associated with other occasions and other performers. Much depends, moreover, on native differences of temperament, on the habitual joyousness, or habitual gloom, which may pervade the spirits, on the lights and shadows which passing events may cast, in quick succession, on the mind, as good or bad news, the arrival of a friend, the failure of an enterprise, a slight derangement of any of the bodily functions, or even the state of the atmosphere. All these circumstances have much to do with the question, whether one conception or another shall be awakened in the mind by any object presented to its thoughts.

These Laws distinguished as Objective and Subjective.— It will be observed that the primary laws of suggestion, so called, are such as arise from the relations which our thoughts sustain to each other, while the secondary are such as arise from the relations which they sustain to ourselves, the thinking subjects. Hence the former have been called *objective*, the latter, *subjective* laws.

Possibility of reducing the primary Laws to one comprehensive Principle.—I have already suggested that possibly the primary laws admit of being reduced to some one general and comprehensive principle. This is a point deserving attention. Were we required to name some one principle which should comprehend these several specific laws of association, it would be that of the prior existence in the mind of the suggesting and the suggested idea. The two conceptions have, for some reason, and at some time, stood together before the mind, and hence the one recalls the other. *It seems to be a general law of thought, that whatever has been perceived or conceived in connection with some other object of perception or thought, is afterward suggestive of that other.* The relation may be that of part to whole, of resemblance, of contiguity, or contrast, or cause; it may be a natural or an artificial relation; whatever it is that serves as the connecting link between one thought and another, as they come before the mind at first, that will also serve as the ground of subsequent connection, when either of these thoughts shall present itself again to the mind. The one will suggest the other.

Application of this Principle to the several Laws of Suggestion. — Why is it, for example, that things contiguous in time and place suggest each other? In consequence of that contiguity they were viewed by the mind in connection with each other; as, *e. g.*, the handle, and the door to which it belongs, the book, and its neighbor on the shelf. It is because Napoleon and his marshals, Wellington and Waterloo, have been presented together to the thoughts, that one now recalls the other. For the same reason the light hair and blue eyes of the person passing in the street recall the friend of former years; that peculiarity of hair and of eyes has been, in my mind, previously connected with the conception of my friend. So also a part suggests the whole with which it has been ordinarily connected, as, for example, the crystal and the watch.

Further Application of the same Principle. — On the same principle cause and effect are naturally suggestive. We have been accustomed to observe the elision of a spark in connection with the forcible collision of flint and steel; and whenever we have observed the application of fire to gunpowder, certain consequences have uniformly attracted our attention; hence the one of these things awakens immediately in our minds the conception of the other, with which it has previously coëxisted. For the same reason the instrument suggests the idea of the wound, and the wound of the instrument. The sight of a rose, and the sensation of fragrance, have usually coëxisted; hence either recalls the other.

The connection in this case is natural. Let us suppose a case in which it shall be arbitrary, or artificial. Suppose I happen to hold a rose in my hand, at the same moment a certain unusual noise is heard in the street, or at the moment when an eclipse of the sun becomes visible; on seeing the rose the next day I am instantly reminded of the noise, or of the eclipse, that was connected with it in my previous perception.

Application to the Law of Opposites. — On the same principle opposites also suggest each other. They sustain a certain relation to each other in our thoughts, and are in a sense necessary to each other in thought, as, *e.g.*, white and black, crooked and straight, tall and short; which are *relative* ideas, neither of which is complete by itself without the other; the one the complement of the other; each, so to speak, the extreme term of a comparison. As such they stand together before the mind, in its ordinary perceptions, and hence the one almost of necessity recalls the other.

The same Principle suggested by Dr. Brown. — The possibility of reducing the laws of association to one common principle, as now attempted, namely that of prior coëxistence in the mind, has not altogether escaped the notice of philosophers. Dr. Brown, in more than one passage, advances the idea, that on a sufficiently minute analysis "all suggestion may be found to depend on prior coëxistence, or, at least, on such immediate proximity, as is itself, very probably, a modification of coëxistence." In order to this nice reduction, however, he adds, we must take into account "the influence of emotions, and other feelings that are very different from ideas; as when an analogous object suggests an analogous object by the influence of an emotion or sentiment, which each separately may have produced before, and which is therefore common to both." As illustrative of this, he refers, among others, to cases of remote resemblance; as when, "for example, the whiteness of untrodden snow brings to our mind the innocence of an unpolluted heart; or a fine morning of spring, the cheerful freshness of youth." In such cases, he says, "though there may never have been in the mind any proximity of the very images compared, there may have been a proximity of each to an emotion of some sort, which, as common to both, might render each capable, indirectly, of suggesting the other. The same principle he applies to suggestion by contrast, as when the sight of a person with a remarkably long nose brings to mind some one whom we have seen with a nose as remarkable for brevity; the common feeling in the two cases being that of surprise or wonder at the peculiarity of this feature of the countenance.

Theory of Mahan. — Mahan, in his Intellectual Philosophy, carries out the suggestion of Dr. Brown, and makes the emotion awakened in common by two or more objects, the sole law, or ground of association. One object recalls another only by means of the feeling or state of mind common to both.

This View questionable. — That this is the philosophy of the suggesting principle in those cases in which two objects have not previously coëxisted in the mind — that is, in cases of suggestion, and not of *association* properly — I am disposed to admit, but that it is the philosophy of *association*, strictly speaking, that it is the reason why objects which have been viewed together by the mind should afterward recall each other, is to be questioned. It seems to be an established law of mental action that objects once viewed in connection by the mind, afterward retain that connection. This is a grand and simple law of thought. I doubt whether any explanation can make it more simple, whether any thing is gained by calling in the influence of emotion to account for it. The emotion may, or may not, be the cause why objects, once coëxistent in the mind, recall each other. It is enough that the simple law of previous coëxistence, as now stated, covers the whole ground, and accounts for all the phenomena of mental association.

The same Rule given by Aristotle. — Long before the days of Brown and his successors, this same law had suggested itself to one of the closest thinkers, and most acute observers of mental phenomena, whom the world has ever seen, as a principle comprehensive of all the specific laws of association. *Aristotle* — as quoted by Hamilton — expresses the rule in the following terms: *Thoughts, which have at any time, recent or remote, stood to each other in the relation of coëxistence, or immediate consecution, do, when severally reproduced, tend to reproduce each other.* Under this general law he includes the specific ones of similars, contraries, and coädjacents, as comprehending all the possible relations of things to each other.

Further Question. — View of Rosenkranz. —It may still be questioned whether the specific laws of association, as usually given, viz., resemblance, contrast, contiguity, and cause, are a complete and exhaustive list. Are there not relations of things to each other, and so relations of thought, which do not fall under any of the categories now named? A distinguished psychologist of the Hegelian school, Rosenkranz, denies even that there are any laws of association. Law is found, he says, where the manifoldness still evinces unity, to which the manifold and accidental are subject But association is not subject to any such unity. It is a free process. There are indeed certain limitations or categories of thought, but these so-called laws of association are not to be confounded with those categories; they are not exhaustive of them. Why not also introduce the law by which we pass from quality to quantity, being to appearance, the universal to the particular, the end to the means, etc., etc.? In short, all metaphysical and logical categories lay claim to be included in the list of such laws. No one can calculate the possible connections of one conception with another. Each is, for us, the middle point of a universe from which we can go forth on all sides. What diverse trains of thought, for example, may the Strasburg minster awaken in my mind: the material of which it is built, the architect, the middle ages, the gothic style, etc., etc. There is, in a word, no law of association.

Objections to this View. — Such, in substance, is the view maintained by this able writer. We cannot altogether coincide with it. That the specific laws of Aristotle, Hume, and Brown, are not exhaustive, may very likely be true; that there is no law, no unity to which this manifoldness of conception is subject, is yet to be shown. Take the very case supposed. The gothic minster of Strasburg reminds me of the gothic style of architecture. What is that but an instance under the law of similarity? It reminds me of the middle ages. What is that but the operation of the law of contiguity in time? It brings to mind the architect. What is that but the relation of cause to effect? Or, if I think of the material of which the building is composed, the marble of this minster reminding me of the class, marble, does not that again fall under the relation of a part to the whole, which is comprehended under the general law of coadjacence, or contiguity in space? So quality and quantity, matter and form, being and appearance, as parts of a comprehensive whole, recall each other. The instances given, then, so far from proving that there is no law of association actually fall under the specific laws enumerated.

The Law of Contiguity includes what. — It is contended that this gives a wider extension to the law of contiguity in time and space than properly belongs to it. I reply, not wider than is intended by those who make use of this expression. Aristotle, the earliest writer who attempts any classification of the laws of suggestion, distinctly includes under the law of *coadjacence* whatever stand as parts of the same whole, as, *e. g.*, parts of the same building, traits of the same character, species of the same genus, the sign and the thing signified, different wholes of the same part, correlate terms, as the abstract and concrete, etc., etc.

Reference to the subjective Laws. — If it still is asked why does the minster of Strasburg, or any given object, suggest one of these several conceptions, and not some other in its place? the reason for this must doubtless be sought in the state of the mind at the time; in other words, in those subjective or secondary laws of suggestion, of which we have already spoken, as given by Brown and others. Aristotle has more concisely answered the question in the important rule which he adds as supplementary of his general law; viz., that, of two thoughts, one tends to suggest the other, in proportion, 1. To its comparative importance; 2. Its comparative interest. For the first reason, the foot is more likely to suggest the head than the head the foot. For the second reason, the dog is more likely to suggest the master than the master the dog.

§ II. — Mental Recognition, as Distinguished from Mental Reproduction.

I. General Character of this Process.

The Faculty as thus far considered. — Thus far we have considered the faculty of mental representation only under one of its forms, viz., as *reproductive.* By the operation of this power, the intuitions of sense are replaced before the mind, in the absence of the original objects; images, so to speak, of the former objects of perception are brought out from the dark back-ground of the past, and thrown in relief upon the mental canvas. Picture after picture thus comes up, and passes away. The mind has the power of thus reproducing for itself, according to laws of suggestion already considered, the objects of its former perception. This it is constantly doing. No small part of our thinking is the simple reproduction of what has been already, in some form, before the mind.

An additional Element. — The intuitions of sense, thus replaced in the absence of the external objects, present themselves to the mind as mere conceptions, involving no reference to ourselves as the perceiving subject, nor to the time, place, and circumstances of the original perception. But suppose now this latter element to be superadded to the former; that along with the conception or recalling of the object, there is also the conception of ourselves as perceiving, and of the circumstances under which it was perceived; in a word, the recalling of the *subjective* along with the *objective* element of the original perception, and we have now that form of mental representation which we term *recognitive*, or mental recognition.

The two Forms compared and distinguished. — The two taken together, the reproduction, and the recognition, constitute what is ordinarily called memory, which involves, when closely considered, not only the reproduction, in thought, of the former object of perception, but also the consciousness of having ourselves perceived the same. The conception is given as before, but it is no longer mere conception in the abstract, standing by itself; it is connected now by links of time, place, and circumstance, with our own personal history. It is this *subjective* element that constitutes the essential characteristic of memory proper, or mental recognition, as distinguished from mere conception, or mental reproduction.

Specification of Time and Place. — It is not necessary that the *specific time* and *place* when and where we previously perceived the object, or received the impression, should be recalled along with the object or impression; this may or may not be. More frequently, perhaps, these do recur to the mind, and the object itself is recalled or suggested by means of these specific momenta; but this is not essential to the act of memory. It is enough that we recognize the representation or conception, now before the mind, as, in general, an object of former cognition, a previous possession of the mind, and not a new acquisition.

Not of necessity voluntary.—Nor is it necessary to the fact of memory, that this recurrence and recognition of former perceptions and sensations, as objects of thought, should be the result of special volition on our part. It may be quite involuntary. It may take place unbidden and unsought, the result of casual suggestion.

Distinction of Terms.—Memory is usually distinguished from *remembrance*, and also from *recollection*. Memory is, more properly, the power or faculty, remembrance the exercise of that power in respect to particular objects and events. When this exercise is voluntary—when we set ourselves to recall what has nearly or quite escaped us, to *re-collect*, as it were, the scattered materials of our former consciousness—we designate this voluntary process by the term *recollection*. We recollect only what is at the moment out of mind, and what we *wish* to recall.

Possibility of recalling.—But here the question arises how it is possible, by a voluntary effort, to recall what is once gone from the mind. Does not the very fact of a volition imply that we have already in mind the thing willed and wished for? How else could we will to recall it? This is a philosophical puzzle with which any one, who chooses, may amuse himself. I have forgotten, for instance, the name of a person: I seek to recall it; to recall what? you may ask. That name. *What* name? Now I do not know what name; if I did, I should have no occasion to recall it. And yet, in another sense, I do know what it is that I have forgotten. I know that it is a name, and I know whose name it is; the name, viz., of this particular person. And this is all I need to know in order to have a distinct, definite object of volition before my mind.

The Mode of Operation. — The process through which the mind passes in such a case, is, to dwell upon some circumstances not forgotten, that are intimately connected with the missing idea, and through these, as so many connecting links, to pass over, if possible, to the thing sought. I cannot, for example, recall the name, but I remember the names of other persons of the same family, class, or profession, or I remember that it begins with the letter B, and then think over all the names I know that begin with that letter; and, in this way, seek to recall, by association, the name that has escaped.

Memory not an immediate Knowledge. — It has been held by some that memory gives us an *immediate* knowledge of the past. This is the view of Dr. Reid. If, by immediate knowledge, we mean knowledge of a thing as existing, and as it is in itself — nothing intervening between it as a present reality, and our direct cognizance of it — then not in this sense is memory an immediate knowledge; for a past event is no longer existent, and cannot be known as such, or as it is in itself; it no longer *is*, but only *was*. Hence an immediate knowledge of it, is, as Sir William Hamilton affirms, a contradiction. Still, we may know the past *as it was*, not less really and positively than we know the present as it is. I as really know that I sat at this table yesterday as I know that I sit here now. I am conscious of being here now. I was conscious of being here then. That consciousness is not to be impeached in either case. If the senses deceived me yesterday, they may deceive me to-day. If consciousness testified falsely then, it may now. But if I was indeed here yesterday, and if I knew then that I was here, and that knowledge was certain and positive, then I know *now* that I was here yesterday, for memory recognizes what would otherwise be the mere conception of to-day, as identical with the positive knowledge of yesterday. Memory may possibly be mistaken as to the so-called positive knowledge of yesterday; and so sense may be mistaken as to the so-called positive knowledge of the present moment.

Belief attending Memory. — The remarks of Dr. Reid on this point are worthy of note. "Memory is always accompanied with the belief of that which we remember, as perception is accompanied with the belief of that which we perceive, and consciousness with the belief of that whereof we are conscious. Perhaps in infancy, or in disorder of mind, things remembered may be confounded with those which are merely imagined; but in mature years, and in a sound state of mind, every man feels that he must believe what he distinctly remembers, though he can give no other reason for his belief, but that he remembers the thing distinctly; whereas, when he merely imagines a thing ever so distinctly he has no belief of it upon that account.

This belief, which we have from distinct memory, we account real knowledge, no less certain than if it was grounded on demonstration; no man, in his wits, calls it in question, or will hear any argument against it. The testimony of witnesses in causes of life and death depends upon it, and all the knowledge of mankind of past events is built on this foundation. There are cases in which a man's memory is less distinct and determinate, and where he is ready to allow that it may have failed him; but this does not in the least weaken its credit, when it is perfectly distinct."

Importance of this Faculty. — The importance of memory as a power of the mind, is shown by the simple fact, that, but for it, there could be no consciousness of *continued existence*, none of *personal identity*, for memory is our only voucher for the fact that we existed at all at any previous moment. Without this faculty, each separate instant of life would be a new existence, isolated, disconnected with aught before or after; nay, there would, in that case, scarcely be any consciousness of even the present existence, for we are conscious only as we are *cognizant of change*, says Hamilton, and there is involved in it the idea of the *latest past* along with the present. Memory, then, is essential to all intelligent mental action, whether intellectual, sensational, or voluntary. The ancients seem to have been aware of this, when they gave it the name μνημη (from μνημος, μναομαι), appellations of the *mind itself*, as being, in fact, the chief characteristic faculty of the mind.

II. What is implied in an Act of Memory.

Several Conditions. — Every act of memory involves these several conditions: 1. Present existence. 2. Past existence. 3. Mental activity at some moment of that past existence. 4. The recurrence to the mind of something thus thought, perceived, or felt. 5. Its recognition as a past or former thought or impression, and that our own. These last, the recurrence and the recognition, are strictly the essential elements of memory, yet the others are implied in it. In order to my remembering, for example, an occurrence of yesterday, I must exist at the present time, else I cannot remember at the present time; I must have existed yesterday, else there can be no memory of yesterday; my mind must have been active then, else there will be nothing to remember; the thoughts, perceptions, sensations, then occupying the mind, must now recur, else it is the same as if they had never been; they must recur, not as new thoughts and impressions, but as old ones, else I no longer remember, but only conceive or perceive.

III. Qualities of Memory.

Distinctions of Stewart and Wayland. — It has been customary to designate certain qualities as essential to a good memory. Susceptibility, retentiveness, and readiness, are thus distinguished by Mr. Stewart; the first denoting the facility with which the mind acquires; the second, the permanence with which it retains; and the third, the quickness with which it recalls and applies its original acquisitions. And these qualities are rarely united, he adds, in the same person. The memory which is susceptible and ready, is not commonly very retentive. Dr. Wayland makes the same distinction. Some men, he says, retain their knowledge more perfectly than they recall it. Others have their knowledge always at command. Some men acquire with great rapidity, but soon forget what they have learned. Others acquire with difficulty, but retain tenaciously.

Objections to this View. — Although supported by such authority, it admits of question whether this distinction is strictly valid. Facility of acquisition, the readiness with which the mind perceives truth, is hardly to be reckoned as an attribute of memory. It is a quality of mind, a quality possessed in diverse degrees by different persons, doubtless, but not a quality of mind in its distinctive capacity and office of *remembering.* It is no part, psychologically considered, of the function of *mental reproduction.* It is essential, indeed, to the act of memory that there should be something to remember, but the acquisition of the thing remembered, and the remembering, are two distinct and different mental acts; nor is it of any consequence to the mind, in remembering, whether the original acquisition was made with more or less facility. Indeed, so far as that bears upon the case at all, facility of acquisition, as even these writers admit, is likely to be rather a hindrance than a help to subsequent remembrance, since what is most readily acquired is not most readily recalled.

The Mind retentive in what Sense. — Nor is it altogether proper to speak of retentiveness as a *quality* of memory — a quality which may pertain to it in a greater or less degree in different cases. The truth is, *all* memory is retentive, or, more properly, retentiveness *is itself* memory. It is a quality of mind; a power or faculty possessed in different degrees by different persons; and the power which the mind possesses of retaining thus, wholly, or in part, what passes before it, is the faculty of memory. But in what sense does the mind retain anything which has once occupied its thoughts? Not, of course, in the sense in which a hook retains the hat and coat that are hung upon it, ready to be taken down when wanted. We are not to conceive of the mind as a convenient receptacle, in which may be stowed away all manner of old thoughts, sensations, impressions, as old clothes are put by in a press, or guns in an armory. Not in any such sense is the mind retentive. What we mean, when we say the mind is retentive, is simply this, that it is in its power to repossess itself of what has once passed before it, to regain a thought or impression it has once had. And this is done by the operation of those laws of suggestion already considered. That, and that only is *retained* by the mind, which under the appropriate circumstances is by the principle of suggestion *recalled* to the mind. We are not to distinguish, then, the power to retain and the power to recall, as two separate things; nor, for the same reason, can we conceive of a memory that is other than retentive, or that is retentive but not ready. So far as these expressions denote any real distinction, it amounts simply to this, that some minds are more retentive than others; in other words, more susceptible of the influence of the suggesting principle in recalling ideas that have once been before them. Such a difference undoubtedly exists. Some remember much more readily and extensively than others. This may be owing, partly, to some difference of mental constitution and endowment; but more frequently to differences of mental habit and culture. It is not necessary to refer again to the laws of mental reproduction which have been already discussed. It is sufficient to say, that *the more clearly any fact or truth is originally apprehended, and the more deeply it interests the mind*, the more readily will it subsequently recur, and the longer will it be retained.

IV. Memory in Relation to Intellectual Strength

The common Opinion.—The question has arisen, how far the power of memory may be regarded as a test of intellectual ability. The opinion has been somewhat prevalent, that a more than usual development of this faculty is likely to be attended with a corresponding deficiency in some other mental power, and especially that it is incompatible with a sound judgment. To this opinion I cannot subscribe. Doubtless it is true that many persons, deficient in the power of accurate discrimination, have possessed wonderful power of memory. The mind, in such cases, undisciplined, uncultivated, with little inventive and self-moving power, lies passive and open to the influence of every-chance suggestion from without, as the lyre is put in vibration by the stray winds that sweep across its strings. Facts and incidents of no value, without number, and without order, are thrown into relief upon the confused background of the past, as sea-weed, sand, and shells are heaped by the unmeaning waves upon the shore.

But if a weak mind may possess a good memory, it is equally true, that a strong and well disciplined mind is seldom deficient in it. Men of most active and commanding intellect have been men also of tenacious and accurate memory. Napoleon was a remarkable instance of this. So also was the philosopher Leibnitz. While, then, we cannot regard the memory as a test of intellectual capacity, neither can it be considered incompatible with, or unfavorable to, mental strength. On the contrary, we can hardly look for any considerable degree of mental vigor and power where this faculty is essentially deficient.

Memory as affected by the Art of Printing.—It is remarked by Miss Edgeworth, and the remark is noticed with approval by Dugald Stewart, that the invention of printing, by placing books within the reach of all classes of people, has lowered the value of those extraordinary powers of memory which some of the learned were accustomed to display in former times. A man who had read, and who could repeat, a few manuscripts, was then not merely a remarkable, but a very useful man. It is quite otherwise now. There is no occasion now for any such exercise of memory. Hence instances of extraordinary memory are of unfrequent occurrence.

Failure of Memory accompanies failure of mental Power. — A decline of mental vigor, whether produced by disease or age, is usually attended with loss of memory to some extent. The first symptoms of this failure are usually forgetfulness of proper names and dates, and sometimes of words in general. A stroke of palsy frequently produces this result, and in such cases the name sometimes suggests the object, while the object no longer recalls the name. This is probably owing to the fact that the sign, being of less consequence than the thing signified, and making less impression on the mind, is more readily forgotten; hence the name, if suggested, recalls the thing, while, at the same time, the thing may not recall the name. In general, we pass more readily from the sign to the thing signified, than the reverse, and for the reason now given. Mr. Stewart remarks, that this loss of proper names incident to old men, is chiefly observable in men of science, or those much occupied with important affairs — a fact resulting, he thinks, partly from their habits of general thought, and partly from their want of constant practice in that trivial conversation which is every moment recalling particulars to the mind.

The Memory of the Aged. — In the principles which have been advanced, we find an explanation, I think, of some facts respecting memory, which every one has noticed, but of which the philosophy may not be at first sight apparent. Why is it that aged people forget? that, as we grow old, while perhaps other powers of the mind are still vigorous, the memory begins to lose its tenacity? Not, I suspect, from any special change which the brain undergoes, for why should such changes affect *this* faculty more than any other? I should seek the explanation in a failure of one or other of the conditions already mentioned as essential to a good memory; either in the want of a sufficiently frequent coëxistence of associated ideas, or else in the want of a sufficiently vivid conception of them when presented; or, more likely, in both. And so the facts would indicate. Age involves usually the gradual failure and decay of the powers of perception; the ear fails to report what is said, the eye what is passing in space; and as memory is dependent on prior perception, of course a diminished activity of the one brings about a diminished activity of the other. In proportion as this ensues, the mind's interest in passing events is likely to fail, for what is no longer clearly apprehended no longer awakens the same interest and attention as formerly. This directly affects the vividness of conception, and indirectly also reacts upon the frequency of coëxistence, for what we do not clearly apprehend, nor feel much interest in, will not be likely often to recur to mind, nor shall we dwell upon it when presented. There is thus brought about, by the mutual action and reaction of the causes now specified, a failure more or less complete of the essential conditions of a retentive memory.

The old man dwells accordingly much in the *past.* His life is behind him, and not in advance. He is unobservant of passing events, because he neither clearly apprehends them, now that his connection with the outer world is in a measure interrupted by the decay of sense, nor does he much care about them, for the same reason. His attention and interest, withdrawn in a manner from these, revert to the past. Those things he remembers, the sports and companions of his youth, and the stirring events of his best and most active years, for those things *have* been frequently associated in his mind, linked with each other, and with all the past of his life, and they *have* deeply interested him. Hence they are remembered while yesterday is forgotten.

Varieties of Memory. — Why is it, you ask, that memory seems to select for itself now one and now another field of operation, one man remembering dates, another events or facts in history, another words or pages of a book, while in each case the memory of other things, of every thing that lies beyond or without the favorite range of topics, is defective? Manifestly for much the same reason already given. The mind has its favorite subjects of investigation and thought; to these it frequently recurs, and dwells on them with interest; there is, consequently, frequency of coexistence, and vividness of conception — the very conditions of retentiveness — while, at the same time, the mind being preöccupied with the given subjects, and the attention and interest withdrawn from other things, the memory of other things is proportionably deficient. We remember, in other words, just those things best, in which we are most interested, and with which we have most to do.

This explains why we forget names so readily. We have more *to do with*, and are more interested in, *persons*, than their names; the latter we have occasion to think of much less often than the former. The *sign* occurs less frequently than the *thing signified.*

V. Cultivation of Memory.

The principles already advanced furnish a clue to the proper and successful cultivation of the memory. Like all other powers, this may be cultivated, and to a wonderful degree; and, like all other powers, it gains strength by *use*, by exercise. The first and chief direction, then, if you would cultivate and strengthen this faculty of the mind, is, *exercise* it; train it to do its work — to do it quickly, easily, accurately, and well — as you train yourself to handle the keys of an instrument, or to add up a column of figures with promptness and accuracy.

To be more specific. — As regards any particular thing which you wish to remember: 1. Grasp it fully, clearly, defin itely in the mind; be sure you have it exactly — *it*, and not something like it or something about it. 2. Connect it with other things that are known; suffer it to link itself with other ideas and impressions already in the mind, that you may have something to recall it by. 3. Frequently revert to it, until you are sure that it has become a permanent possession, and one which you can at any time recall by any one of numerous connecting links. In this way you secure the two conditions already specified as essential, viz., frequency of coëxistence, and vividness of conception.

Systems of artificial Memory. — A thing is recalled by the suggestion of any *coëxisting* thought or feeling. Observing this, ingenious men have availed themselves of the principle of association to construct various mechanical or artificial systems of memory, usually termed *mnemonics.* The principle of the construction is this: should you see an elm or an oak-tree, or hear a particular tune whistled, at the same time that you were going through a demonstration in Euclid, you would be likely to think of the tree or the tune whenever next you had occasion to repeat that demonstration. The sight of the diagram would recall the associated object. They *stand together* in your mind afterward. This we have already found to be the groundwork and chief element of all association of ideas and feelings, viz., *prior coexistence* in the mind. Suppose, now, you wish to fix in the mind the list of English kings. Make out a corresponding list of simple figures, or images of objects, giving each its invariable place in relation to the series: No. 1. a pump: No. 2. a goose, etc., till you reach a sufficient number, say a hundred. These are committed to memory, fixed indelibly in the mind. You then associate with those figures your English kings; Charles I. stands by the pump; Charles II. pursues the goose; James hugs the bear, and so on. These things thus once firmly linked together, remain afterward associated, and the figure serves at once to recall the associate monarch, and to fix his place in the series. The same series of figures, of course, will serve for any number of different series of events, personages, etc., which are to be remembered.

Utility questioned. — It may be seriously questioned, I think, whether such systems are of real value; whether they do not really weaken the memory and throw it into disuse, by departing from the ordinary laws and methods of suggestion, and substituting a purely artificial, arbitrary and mechanical process; whether, morevoer, they really accomplish what they propose; whether, since the signs or figures have no natural relation to each other, and none to the things signified, but only the arbitrary relation imposed by the system, it is not really as difficult to fix the connection of the two things in your mind, *e.g.*, to remember that Charles the Second is represented by a dog or by a goose, as it would be simply, and in the natural way, to remember the things themselves without any *such* association.

Extent to which the Memory may be cultivated. — The extent to which the cultivation of the memory may be carried by due training and care, is a topic worthy of some attention. Men of reflection and thought, and generally men of studious habits, literary men and authors, do not, for the most part, rely so much upon the memory as men of a more practical cast and of business pursuits; for this reason, viz., the want of due exercise, this faculty of their minds is not in the most favorable circumstances for development. Some striking exceptions, however, we shall have occasion presently to mention.

It has been already remarked, that prior to the art of printing, the cultivation of the memory was an object of far greater importance, to those who were destined for public life, than it is in modern times, and consequently instances of remarkable memory are much more frequently to be met with among the ancients than among the men of our times. The same remark will apply to men of different pursuits in any age: the more one has occasion to employ the memory, the more striking will be its development.

Instances of extraordinary Memory. — Cyrus, it is said, knew the name of every officer, Pliny has it of every soldier, that served under him. Themistocles could call by name each one of the twenty thousand citizens of Athens. Hortensius could sit all day at an auction, and at evening give an account from memory of every thing sold, the purchaser, and the price. Muretus saw at Padua a young Corsican, says Mr. Stewart, who could repeat, without hesitation, thirty-six thousand names in the order in which he heard them, and then reverse the order and proceed backward to the first.

Dr. Wallis of Oxford, on one occasion, at night, in bed, proposed to himself a number of fifty-three places, and found its square root to twenty-seven places, and, without writing down numbers at all, dictated the result from memory twenty days afterward. It was not unusual with him to perform arithmetical operations in the dark, as the extraction of roots, *e.g.*, *to* forty *decimal* places. The distinguished Euler, blind from early life, had always in his memory a table of the first six powers of all numbers, from one to one hundred. On one occasion two of his pupils, calculating a converging series, on reaching the seventeenth term, found their results differing by one unit at the fiftieth figure, and in order to decide which was correct, Euler went over the whole in his head, and his decision was found afterward to be correct. Pascal forgot nothing of what he had read, or heard, or seen. Menage, at seventy-seven, commemorates, in Latin verses, the favor of the gods, in restoring to him, after partial eclipse, the full powers of memory which had adorned his earlier life.

The instances now given are mentioned by Mr. Stewart; but perhaps the most remarkable instance of great memory, in modern times, is the case of the celebrated *Magliabechi*, librarian of the Duke of Tuscany. He would inform any one who consulted him, not only who had directly treated of any particular subject, but who had indirectly touched upon it in treating of other subjects, to the number of perhaps one hundred different authors, giving the name of the author, the name of the book, the words, often the page, where they were to be found, and with the greatest exactness.

To test his memory, a gentleman of Florence lent him at one time a manuscript he had prepared for the press, and, some time afterward, went to him with a sorrowful face, and pretended to have lost his manuscript by accident. The poor author seemed inconsolable, and begged Magliabechi to recollect what he could, and write it down. He assured the unfortunate man that he would, and setting about it, wrote out the entire manuscript without missing a word. He had a *local* memory also, knew where every book stood. One day the Grand Duke sent for him to inquire if he could procure a book which was very scarce. "No, sir," answered Magliabechi; "it is impossible: there is but *one* in the world; that is in the Grand Seignior's library at Constantinople, and is the *seventh book, on the seventh shelf, on the right hand as you go in.*"

VI. Effects of Disease on the Memory.

Forgetfulness of certain Objects. — Of the effect of certain forms of disease, and also of age, in weakening the power of remembering names, I have already spoken. There are other effects, occasionally produced by disease upon this faculty of the mind, which are not so readily explained. In some cases, a certain class of objects, or the knowledge of certain persons, or of a particular language or some part of a language, as substantives, *e. g.*, seems to be lost to the mind; in other cases, a certain portion of life is obliterated from the recollection. In cases of severe injury to the head, persons have forgotten some particular language; others have been unable to recall afterward the names of the most common objects, while the memory was at no loss for adjectives. A surgeon mentioned by Dr. Abercrombie, so far recovered from a fall as to give special directions respecting his own treatment, yet, for several days, lost all idea of having either a wife or children. The case of Mr. Tennent, who on recovering from apparent death, lost all knowledge of his past life, and was obliged to commence again the study of the alphabet, until after considerable time his knowledge suddenly returned to him, is too well known to require minute description.

Former Objects recalled. — In other instances, precisely the reverse occurs. Disease brings back to mind what has been long forgotten. Thus, persons in extreme sickness, or at the point of death, not unfrequently converse in languages which they have known only in youth. The case cited by Coleridge, and so frequently quoted, of the German servant girl, who in sickness was heard repeating passages of Greek, Latin, and Hebrew, which she had formerly heard her master repeat, as he walked in his study, but of whose meaning she had no idea, is in point in this connection. So also is the case of the Italian mentioned by Dr. Rush, who died in New York, and who, in the beginning of his sickness, spoke English, in the middle of it, French, but on the day of his death, nothing but Italian. A Lutheran clergyman of Philadelphia told Dr. Rush that it was not uncommon for the Germans and Swedes of his congregation, when near death, to speak and pray in their native languages, which some of them had probably not spoken for fifty years. These facts are sufficiently numerous to constitute a class by themselves; they seem to fall under some law of the physical system not yet clearly understood, and are, therefore, in the present state of our knowledge, incapable of explanation.

Inference often drawn from these Facts. — Certain writers have inferred, from the recurrence of things long forgotten, as in the cases now cited, that all knowledge is indestructible, and that all which is necessary to the entire reproduction of the past life is the quickened activity of the mental powers, an effect which is produced in the delirium of disease. From this they have derived an argument for future retribution.

Coleridge has made such use of it, and has been followed by Upham, and in part, at least, though with more caution, by Wayland.

The true Inference. — It may be doubted, perhaps, whether the absolute indestructibility of all human knowledge is a legitimate inference from these facts. The most that can with certainty be concluded from them, is, not that all our past thoughts and consciousness *must* or *will* return, but that much of it *may* — perhaps all of it; and this is all we need to know in order to perceive the *possibility* of a future retribution. It is enough to know, that in the constitution of the mind *means exist* for recalling, in some way to us mysterious, and under certain conditions not by us fully understood, the objects of our former consciousness, in all the freshness and vividness of their past cognizance, long after they seem to have passed finally from the memory.

Importance of a well-spent Life. — This simple fact, together with the well-known tendency of the mind in advancing age to revert to the scenes and incidents of early life, certainly presents in the clearest light the importance of a well-spent life, of a mind stored with such recollections as shall cast a cheerful radiance over the past, and brighten the uncertain future in those hours of gloom and despondency when the shadows lengthen upon the path of earthly pilgrimage, and life is drawing to a close. If the thoughts and impressions of the passing moment are liable, by some casual association, by some mysterious law of our being, under conditions which may at any moment be fulfilled, to recur at any time to subsequent consciousness, with all the minuteness and power of present reality, it becomes us, as we regard our own highest interests, to guard well the avenues of thought and feeling against the first approach of that which we shall not be pleased to meet again, when it will not be in our power to escape its *presence*, or avoid its recognition.

VII. Influence of Memory on the Happiness of Life.

The Pleasures of the Past thus retained. — Of the importance of this faculty as related to other intellectual powers, I have already spoken. I refer now to its value as connected with human happiness, as the source of some of the purest pleasures of life. The present, however joyous, is fleeting and evanescent. Memory seizes the passing moment, fixes it upon the canvas, and hangs the picture on the soul's inner chambers for her to look upon when she will. Thus, in an important sense, the former years are past, but not gone. We live them over again in memory.

Instance of Niebuhr. — It is related of Carsten Niebuhr, the Oriental traveller, that "when old and blind, and so feeble that he had barely strength to be borne from his bed to his chair, the dim remembrance of his early adventures thronged before his memory with such vividness that they presented themselves as pictures upon his sightless eye-balls. As he lay upon his bed, pictures of the gorgeous Orient flashed upon his darkness as distinctly as though he had just closed his eyes to shut them out for an instant. The cloudless blue of the eastern heavens bending by day over the broad deserts, and studded by night with southern constellations, shone as vividly before him, after the lapse of half a century, as they did upon the first Chaldean shepherds whom they won to the worship of the host of heaven; and he discoursed with strange and thrilling eloquence upon those scenes which thus, in the hours of stillness and darkness, were reflected upon his inmost soul."

The same Thing occurs often in old Age. — Something of this kind not unfrequently occurs in advanced life. Picture to yourself an old man of many winters. The world in which his young life began has grown old with him and around him, and its brightest colors have faded from his vision. The life and stir, the whirl and tumult of the busy world, the world of to-day and yesterday, move him not. He heeds but slightly the events of the passing hour. He lives in a past world. The scenes of his childhood, the sports and companions of his youth, the hills and streams, the bright eyes and laughing faces on which his young eyes rested, in which his young heart delighted — these visit him again in his solitude, as he sits in his chair by the quiet fireside. He lives over again the past. He wanders again by the old hills, and over the old meadows. He feels again the vigor of youth. He leads again his bride to the altar. He brings home toys for his children, and enters again into their sports. And so the extremes of life meet. Age completes the circuit, and brings us back to the starting-point. We close where we began, Life is a magic ring.

The recollection of past Sorrow not always painful. — But life is not all joyous. Mingled with the brighter hues of every life are also much sadness and sorrow, and these, too, are to be remembered. It might be supposed that, while memory, by recalling the pleasing incidents of the past, might contribute much to our happiness, she would add, in perhaps an equal degree, to our sorrow, by recalling much that is painful to the thoughts. Such, however, I am convinced, is not the fact. The benevolence of the Creator has ordered it otherwise. To no one, perhaps, is memory the source of greater pleasure, strange as it may seem, than to the mourner. The very circumstances that tend to renew our grief, and keep alive our sorrow, in case of some severe calamity or bereavement, are still cherished with a melancholy satisfaction of which we would not be deprived. There is a luxury in our very grief, and in the remembrance of that for which we grieve. We would not forget what we have lost. Every recollection and association connected with it are sacred. Time assuages our grief, but impairs not the strength and sacredness of those associations, nor diminishes the pleasure with which we recall the forms we shall see no more, and the scenes that are gone forever. Every memento of the departed one is sacred; the books, the flowers, the favorite walks, the tree in whose shadow he was wont to recline, all have a significance and a value which the stricken heart only can interpret, and which memory only can afford.

We recollect the Past as it was. — It is to be noticed, also, that, in such cases, the picture which memory furnishes is a transcript of the past as it was; the image is stereotyped and unchangeable. Other things change, we change; that changes not. It has a fixed value. A mother, for instance, loses a child of three years. It ever remains to her a child of three years. She remembers it as it was. She grows old; twenty summers and winters pass; yet as often as she visits the little mound, now scarce to be distinguished from the level surface, there comes to her recollection that little child as he was, when she hung, for the last time, over that pale, sweet face that she should see no more. She still thinks of him, dreams of him, as a child, for it is as such only that she remembers him.

Blessed boon, that gives us just the past; when all things change, fortunes vary, friends depart, the world grows unkind, and we grow old, the former things remain treasured in our memory, and we can stand as mourners at the grave of what we once were.

VIII. Historical Sketch. — Different Theories of Memory.

Ancient Theory. — The idea formerly, and almost universally entertained respecting the *modus operandi* of the faculty we call memory, was, that in perception and the various operations of the senses, certain impressions are made on the sensorium — certain forms and types of things without, certain *images* of them — which remain when the external object is no longer present, and become imprinted thus on the mind. Such, certainly, was the doctrine of the earliest Greek commentators on Aristotle. Such, I must think, is substantially the doctrine of Aristotle himself.

Theory of Aristotle. — His idea is, that memory, as well as imagination, primarily and directly, relates only to sensible objects, and gives us only *images* of these objects, and even when it gives us strictly intellectual objects, gives us these only by images. One cannot *think*, he says, without images. Its source and origin, then, he concludes, is the sensibility, and so it pertains to *animals*, as well as men; only to those, however, which have the perception of time, since memory is a modification of sensation or intellectual conception, under the condition of *time past.* Such being, in his view, the nature and source of memory, he goes on to ask how it is that only a modification (or state) of the mind being present, and the object itself absent, one recalls that absent object?

"Manifestly," he replies, "we must believe that the impression which is produced, in consequence of the sensation, in the soul, and in that part of the body which perceives the sensation, is analogous to a species of painting, and that the perception of that impression constitutes precisely what we call memory. The movement which then takes place in the mind *imprints there a sort of type of the sensation* analogous to the *seal which one imprints on wax with a ring.* Hence it is that those who by the violence of the impression, or by the ardor of age are in a great excitement (movement) have not the memory of things, as if the movement and seal had been applied to running water. In the case of others, however, who are in a sort cold, as the plaster of old edifices, the very *hardness* of the part which receives the impression prevents the image from leaving the least trace. Hence it is that young children and old men have so little memory. It is the same with those who are too lively, and those who are too slow. Neither remember well. The one class are too *humid*, the other too hard. The image dwells not in the soul of the one, makes no impression whatever on that of the other.

"How is it now," he goes on to ask, "that this stamp, impression, image, or painting, in us, a mere mode of the mind, can recall the absent object?" His answer is, that the impression or image is a *copy* of that object, while, at the same time, it is, in itself considered, only a modification of our mind, just as a painting is a mere picture, and yet a *copy* from nature. (Parva Naturalia: Memory, ch. 1.)

Defence of Aristotle. — Sir W. Hamilton defends Aristotle against the strictures of Dr. Reid, upon this subject, by the supposition that he used these expressions not in a literal, but in a figurative or analogical sense. The figure, however, if it be one, is very clearly and boldly sustained, and constitutes, in fact, the whole explanation given of the process of memory — the entire theory. Take away these expressions, and you take away the whole substance of his argument, the whole solution of the problem. Sensation, or intellectual conception, produces an *impression* on the soul, and *imprints there a type* of itself, not unlike a painting or the stamp of a seal on wax, and the *perception* of this is *memory*. Such is in brief his theory.

Theory of Hobbes. — Not far remote from this was the theory of Hobbes, who regarded memory as a decaying or vanishing sense; that of Hume, who represents it as merely a somewhat weaker impression than that which we designate as perception; and that of the celebrated Malebranche, who accounted for memory by making it to depend entirely on the changes which take place in the fibres of the brain. "For even as the branches of a tree which have continued some time bent in a certain form, still preserve an aptitude to be bent anew after the same manner, so the fibres of the brain having once received certain impressions by the course of the animal spirits, and by the action of objects, retain a long time some facility to receive these same dispositions. Now the memory consists only in this faculty, since we think on the same things when the brain receives the same impressions."

He goes on to explain how, as the brain undergoes a change in different periods of life, the mind is affected accordingly. "The fibres of the brain in children are soft, flexible, and delicate; a riper age dries, hardens, and strengthens them; but in old age they become wholly inflexible." * * * "For as we see the fibres which compose the flesh harden by time, and that the flesh of a young partridge is, without dispute, more tender than that of an old one, so the fibres of the brain of a child or youth will be much more soft and delicate than those of persons more advanced in years."

Strictures upon this Theory.—Without disputing what is here stated as to the difference in the fibres of the brain at different periods of life, it remains to be proved that all this has any thing to do with the differences of memory in different persons, or with the phenomena of memory in general.

These theories, it will be observed, all assume that in perception and sensation some physical effect is produced on the system, which remains after the orginal sensation or perception has ceased to act, and that memory is the *result* of that remaining effect, the perception, or conscious cognizance of it by the mind. The process is a purely physiological one. Without insisting on the expressions made use of to represent this process, all which convey the idea strongly of a mechanical effect—type imprinted on the soul, impression made on it as of a seal on wax, image, picture, copy, etc.; allowing these to be mere metaphors; allowing, moreover, that the essential fact all along assumed, is a fact, viz., that in sensation, perception, etc., some physical effect *is* produced on the sensorium; there are still two essential propositions to be established before we can admit any of these theories: 1. That this physical effect *remains* any time after the cause ceases to operate; 2. That if so, it is in any way concerned in the production of memory; and even if these points could be made out, it would still be an open question, in WHAT way, possible or conceivable, this effect or impression on the sensorium gives rise to the phenomenon of memory; for this is, after all, the chief thing to be explained.

CHAPTER II.

IMAGINATION.

§ I. — General Character of this Faculty.

The Point at which we have arrived. — We have thus far treated of those forms of mental representation which are concerned in the reproduction of what has once been perceived or felt, and in the recognition of it as such. It remains still to investigate that form of the representative power, which has for its office something quite distinct from either of these, and which we may term the *creative* faculty.

Office of this Faculty. — By the operation of this power, the former perceptions and sensations are replaced in thought, and combined as in mental reproduction, but not, as in mental reproduction, according to the *original* and *actual*, so that the past is simply repeated, but rather according to the mind's own *ideal*, and at its own will and fancy; so that while the groundwork of the representation is something which has been, at some time, an object of perception, the picture itself, as it stands before the mind in its completeness, is not the copy of any thing actually perceived, but a creation of the mind's own. This power the mind has, and it is a power distinct from either of those already mentioned, and not less wonderful than either. The details of the original perception are omitted; time, place, circumstance fall out, or are varied to suit the fancy; the scene is laid when and where we like; the incidents follow each other no longer in their actual order; the original, in a word, is no longer faithfully transcribed, but the picture is conformed to the taste and pleasure of the artist. The conception becomes IDEAL. This is imagination in its true and proper sphere — the creative power of the mind.

§ II. — Relation of this to other Faculties.

The true province of imagination may be more definitely distinguished by comparing it with other powers of the mind.

Imagination as related to Memory. — How, then, does imagination differ from *memory?* In this, first and chiefly, that memory gives us the actual, imagination, the ideal; in this also, that memory deals only with the past, while imagination, not confined to such limits, sweeps on bolder wing, and without bound, alike through the future and the past. In one respect they agree. Both give the *absent* — that which is not now and here present to sense. Both are representative rather than presentative. Both also are forms of conception.

To Perception. — In what respect does it differ from *perception?* In perception the object is given, presented; in imagination it is thought, conceived; in the former case it is given as *actual*, in the latter, conceived not as actual but as ideal.

To Judgment. — Imagination differs from *judgment*, in that the latter deals, not like the former, with things in themselves considered, but rather with the relations of things — is, in other words, a form not of *simple*, but of *relative* conception; and also in that it deals with these relations as *actual*, not as ideal. It has always specific reference to truth, and is concerned in the formation of opinion and belief, as resting on the evidence of truth, and the perception of the actual relations of things.

To Reasoning. — In like manner it differs from *reasoning*, which also has to do with truths, facts — has for its object to ascertain and state those facts or principles; its sole and simple inquiry being, what is *true?* Imagination concerns itself with no such inquiry, admits of no such limitation. Its thought is not what *did* actually occur, but what in given circumstances *might* occur. Its question is not what really *was*, or *is*, or *will be*, but what *may* be; what may be *conceived* as possible or probable under such or such contingencies.

Reasoning, moreover, reaches only such truths as are involved in its premises, and may fairly be deduced as conclusions from those premises. It furnishes no new material, but merely evolves and unfolds what lies wrapped up in the admitted premises. Imagination lies under no such restriction. There is no necessary connection between the wrath of Achilles, and the consequences that are made to result from it in the unfolding of the epic.

To Taste. — Imagination and *taste* are by no means identical. The former may exist in a high degree where the latter is essentially defective. In such a case the conceptions of the imagination are, it may be, too bold, passing the limits of probability, or, it may be, offensive to delicacy, wanting in refinement and beauty, or in some way deficient in the qualities that please a cultivated mind. This is not unfrequently the case with the productions of the poet, the painter, the orator. There is no lack of imagination in their works, while, at the same time, they strike us as deficient in taste. Taste is the regulating principle, whose office is to guide and direct the imagination, sustaining to it much the same relation that conscience does to free moral action. It is a lawgiver and a judge.

To Knowledge. — Still more widely does imagination differ from simple knowledge. There may be great learning and no imagination, and the reverse is equally true. We know that which is — the actual; we imagine that which is not — the ideal. Learning enlarges and quickens the mind, extends the field of its vision, augments its resources, expands its sphere of thought and action; in this way its powers are strengthened, its conceptions multiplied and vivified. There is furnished, consequently, both more and better material for the creative faculty to work upon. Further than this, the imagination is little indebted to learning.

Illustration of these Differences. — To illustrate the differences already indicated: I stand at my window and look out on the landscape. My eye rests on the form and dark outline of a mountain, pictured against the sky. Perception, this. I go back to my desk, I shut my eyes. That form and figure, pencilled darkly against the blue sky, are still in my mind. I seem to see them still. That heavy mass, that undulating outline, that bold rugged summit — the whole stands before me as distinctly as when my eye rested upon it. Conception, this, replacing the absent object. I not only in my thoughts seem to see the mountain thus reproduced, but I *know* it when seen; I recognize it as the mountain which a moment before I saw from my window. Memory, this, connecting the conception with something in my past experience. The picture fades perhaps from my view, and I begin to estimate the probable distance of the mountain, or its relative height, as compared with other mountains. Judgment, this, or the conception of relations. I proceed to calculate the number of square miles of surface on a mountain of that height and extent. Reasoning, this. And now I sweep away, in thought, the actual mountain, and replace it with one vastly more imposing and grand. Eternal snows rest upon its summits; glaciers hold their slow and stately march down its sides; the avalanche thunders from its precipices. *Imagination* now has the field to herself.

§ III. — Active and Passive Imagination.

View of Dr. Wayland. — "If we regard the several act of this faculty," says Dr. Wayland, "we may, I think, observe a difference between them. We have the power to originate images or pictures for ourselves, and we have the power to form them as they are presented in language. The former may be called active, and the latter passive imagination. The active, I believe, always includes the passive power, but the passive does not always include the active. Thus we frequently observe persons who delight in poetry and romance, who are utterly incapable of creating a scene or composing a stanza. They can form the pictures dictated by language, but are destitute of the power of original combination."

Correctness of this View questioned. — That many who enjoy the creations of the poet and the splendid fictions of the dramatist and novelist, are themselves incapable of producing like creations, is doubtless true. The same is true in other departments of the creative art. Many persons enjoy a fine painting or statue, good music, or a noble architectural design, who cannot themselves produce these works of art. This does not prove them deficient, however, in imagination, for the inability may be owing to other causes, as want of training; nor, on the other hand, does the simple enjoyment of ideal creations involve a different kind of imagination from that exercised in creating. Imagination is, as it seems to me, always active, never passive. Where it exists, and whenever it is called into exercise, it acts, and its action is, in some sense, creative. It conceives the ideal, that which, as conceived, does not exist, or at least is not known to the senses as existing. It matters not in what way these ideal conceptions are suggested, whether by the signs of language written or spoken, or by those characters which the painter, the sculptor, or the architect presents, each in his own way, and with his own material, or by one's own previous conceptions. *Every* ideal conception is suggested by *something* antecedent to itself. All active imagination is, in other words, passive, in the sense here intended, and all passive imagination, so called, is in reality active, so far as it is, properly speaking, imagination at all. The difference between the faculty that produces and that which merely enjoys, is a difference of *degree* rather than of kind. The one is an imagination peculiarly active; the other slightly so; or, more properly, the one mind has *much*, the other *little* imagination.

Philosophic Imagination.—The term *philosophic* imagination, in distinction from *poetic*, is employed by the same distinguished writer to denote the faculty, possessed by some minds of a high order, of discovering new truths in science; of so classifying and arranging known facts as to bring to light the laws which govern them, or, by a happy conjecture, assigning to phenomena hitherto unexplained, a theory which will account for them. Whether the faculty now intended is properly imagination, admits of question. Its field is that of conjecture, supposition, theory, invention. It involves the exercise of judgment and reason. It seeks after truth. It is a process of discovering what is. Imagination deals with the ideal only — inquires not for the true.

§ IV. — Imagination a Simple Faculty.

Common Theory. — The view which has been very generally entertained of the faculty now under consideration, both in this country, and by the Scotch philosophers, resolves it partially or wholly into other powers of the mind, as abstraction, association, judgment, taste. In this view, it is no longer a simple faculty, if indeed it can with propriety be called a faculty at all, inasmuch as the effects ascribed to it can be accounted for by the agency of the other powers now named.

A different View.—It seems to me that imagination, while doubtless it presupposes and involves the exercise of the suggestive and associative principle, of the analytic or divisive principle by which compounds are broken up into their distinct elements, and also, to some extent, of judgment, or the principle which perceives relations, is, nevertheless, itself a power distinct from each of these, and from all of them in combination. Memory *presupposes* perception, or something to be reproduced and remembered. It is not, therefore, to be regarded as a complex faculty, comprising the perceptive power as one of its factors. The power to combine, in like manner, *presupposes* the previous separation of elements capable of being reunited, but is not to be resolved into that power which produces such separation. It *involves* some exercise of judgment along with its own proper and distinctive activity, but is not to be confounded with, or resolved into the power of perceiving relations.

The faculty of ideal conception is really a power of the mind, and it is a simple power, a thing of itself, although it may involve and presuppose the activity of other faculties along with its own. Abstraction, association, judgment, taste — none of them singly, nor all of them combined, are what we mean by it.

Theory of Brown. — Dr. Brown resolves the faculty now in question into simple suggestion, accompanied, in the case of *voluntary* imagination, with desire, and with judgment. There is nothing in the process different from what occurs in any case of the suggestion of one thought by another, he would say. We think of a mountain, we think of gold, and some analogy, or common property of the two, serves to suggest the complex conception, mountain of gold. Even where the process is not purely spontaneous, but accompanied with desire on our part, it is still essentially the same process. We think of something, and this suggests other related conceptions, some of which we approve as fit for our purpose, others we reject as unfit. Here is simple suggestion accompanied with desire and judgment; and these are all the factors that enter into the process. " We may term this state, or series of states, imagination or fancy, and the term may be convenient for its brevity. But in using it we must not forget that the term, however brief and simple, is still the name of a state that is complex, or of a succession of states, that the phenomena comprehended under it being the same in nature, are not rendered, by the use of a mere word, different from those to which we have already given peculiar names expressive of them as they exist separately; and that it is to the classes of these elementary phenomena, therefore, that we must refer the whole process of imagination in our philosophic analysis."

Strictures on this Theory. — This view, it will be perceived, in reality sweeps the faculty of imagination entirely from the field. To this I cannot yield my assent. Is not this state, or affection of the mind, as Dr. Brown calls it, quite a distinct thing from other mental states and affections? Has it not a character *sui generis?* Is not th operation, the thing done, a *different* thing from what is done in other cases, and by other faculties; and has not the mind the *power* of doing this new and different thing; and is not that power of doing a given thing what we mean in any case by a *faculty* of the mind? Is there not an element in this process under consideration which is *not* involved in other mental processes, viz.: the *ideal* element; the conception, not of the actual and the real, as in the case of the other faculties, but of the purely ideal? And if the mind has the faculty of forming a class of conceptions so entirely distinct from the others, why not give that faculty a name, and its own proper name, and allow it a place, its own proper place, among the mental powers?

§ V. — Imagination not merely the Power of Combination.

The prevalent View. — This question is closely connected with that just discussed. The usual definitions make the faculty under consideration a mere process of combining and arranging ideas previously in the mind, so as to form new compounds. You have certain conceptions. These you combine one with another, as a child puts together blocks that lie before him, to suit himself, now this uppermost, now that, and the result is a work of imagination. It is the mere arrangement of previous conceptions, and not itself a power of producing or conceiving any thing. And even this arrangement of former conceptions is itself a *spontaneous* casual process, according to Dr. Brown, not properly a *power* of the mind.

Makes Imagination little else than Invention. — According to this view, imagination is hardly to be distinguished from mere *invention* in the mechanic arts, which is the result of some new combination of previously existing materials. The construction of a steam-pump with a new kind of valve, is as really a work of imagination, as Paradise Lost. The man who contrives a carding-machine, and the man who conceives the Transfiguration, the Apollo Belvidere, or th Iliad, are exercising both the same faculty — merely combining in new forms the previous possessions of the mind.

This View inadequate. — This is a very meagre and inadequate view, as it seems to me, of the faculty of imagination. It fixes the attention upon, and elevates into the importance of a definition, a circumstance in itself unimportant, while it overlooks the essential characteristic of the faculty to be defined. The *creative activity* of the mind is lost sight of in attending to the *materials* on which it works.

The Distinctive Element of Imagination overlooked. — Imagination I take to be the power of conceiving the ideal. The elements which enter into and compose that ideal conception, are, indeed, elements previously existing, not themselves the mind's creations; but the conception itself is the mind's own creation, and this creative activity, this power of conceiving the purely ideal, is the very essence of that which we are seeking to define. True, the separate conceptions which enter into the composition of Paradise Lost — trees, flowers, rivers, mountains, angels, deities — were already in the poet's mind before he began to meditate the sublime epic. They were but the material on which he wrought. Has he then created nothing, conceived nothing? Have we truly and adequately described that immortal poem when we say that it is a mere combination of trees, rivers, hills, and angels, in certain proportions and relations not previously attempted?

Illustration drawn from the Arts. — The artist makes use

of colors previously existing when he would produce a painting, and of marble already in the block, when he would chisel a statue or a temple. In reality he only combines. Yet it would be but a poor definition of any one of these sublime arts to say that painting, sculpture, architecture, is merely the putting together of previous materials to form new wholes. We object to such a definition, not because it affirms what is not true, but because it does not affirm the chief and most important truth; not because of what it states, but because of what it omits to state. These are creative arts. They give us indeed not new substances, but new forms, new products, new ideas. So is imagination a creative faculty. The individual elements may not be new, but the grand product and result is new, a creation of the mind's own. And this is of more consequence than the fact that the elementary conceptions were already in the mind. The one is the essential characteristic, the other a comparatively unimportant circumstance; the one describes the thing itself, the other the mere *modus operandi* of the thing.

Illustration drawn from the Creation of the material World. — What is *creation* in its higher and more proper sense, as applied to the formation, by divine power, of the world in which we dwell? There was a moment, in the eternity of the past, when the omnipotent builder divided the light from the darkness, and the evening and the morning were the first day. The elements may have existed before — heat, air, earth, water, the various material and diffused substance of the world about to be — but latent, confused, chaotic those elements, not called forth and appointed each to its own proper sphere. Light slumbers amid the chaotic elements unseen. He speaks the word, and it comes forth from its hiding-place, and stands revealed in its own beauty and splendor. Has God made nothing, in so doing? Has he conceived nothing, *created* nothing? And when the work goes on, and is at length complete, and the fair new world hangs poised and trembling on its axis, perfect in every part, and rejoicing the heart of the builder, is there no new power displayed in all this, no creation here? And do we well and adequately express the sublime mystery when we say that the deity has merely arranged and combined materials previously existing, to form a new whole?

Art essentially creative. — So when the poet, the painter, the skillful architect, the mighty orator, call forth from the slumbering elements new forms of beauty and power, are not they, too, in their humble way, creators? True, they have in so doing combined conceptions previously existing in the mind. The writer combines in new forms the existing letters of the alphabet, the painter combines existing colors, the architect puts together previously-existing stones. But is this all he does? Is it the chief thing? Is this the soul and spirit of his divine art? No; there is a new power, a new element, not thus expressed—the power of conceiving, and calling into existence, in the realm of thought, that which has no actual existence in the world of sober reality. He who has this power is a *maker* — ποιητής. It is a power conferred, in some degree, on all, in its highest degree, on few. The poet, painter, orator, the gifted creative man, whoever he is, belongs to this class.

§ VI. — Imagination limited to Sensible Objects.

Law of the Imagination. — It is a law of the imagination, that whatever it represents, it realizes, clothes in sensible forms, conceives as visible, audible, tangible, or in some way within the sphere and cognizance of sense. Whatever it has to do with, whatever object it seizes and presents, it brings within this sphere, invests with sensible drapery. Now, strictly speaking, there are no objects, save those of sense, which admit of this process, which can be, even in conception, thus invested with sensible forms, pictured to the eye, or represented to the other senses as objects of their cognizance. If I conceive of objects strictly immaterial as thus presented, I make them, by the very conception, to depart from their proper nature and to become sensible. Imagination has nothing to do, then, strictly speaking, with abstract truths and conceptions, with spiritual and immaterial existences, with ideas and feelings as such, for none of these can be represented under sensible forms, or brought within the sphere and cognizance of the senses. Sensible objects are the groundwork, therefore, of its operation — the materials of its art.

But not to visible Objects. — It is not limited, however, to *visible* objects merely — is not a mere picture-forming, image-making power. It more frequently, indeed, fashions its creations after the conceptions which sight affords than those of the other senses; but it deals also with conceptions of sound, as in music, and the play of storm and tempest, and with other objects of sense, as the taste, the touch, pressure, etc. Thus the *gelidi fontes* of Virgil is an appeal to the sense of delicious coolness not less than to that of sparkling beauty. A careful analysis of every act of the imagination will show, I think, a *sensible basis* as the groundwork of the fabric — something seen, or heard, or felt — something said or done — some sensible reality — something which, however ideal and transcendental in itself and in reality, yet admits of expression in and through the senses; otherwise it were a mere conception or *abstraction* — a mere idea — not an imagination.

§ VII. — Imagination limited to New Results.

The simple reproduction of the *past*, whether an object of perception, or sensation, or conception merely, the simple reproduction or bringing back of that to the mind, we have assigned as the office of another faculty. Imagination, we have said, departs from the reality, and gives you not what you have had before, but something new, other, different. It is not the simple image-making power, then, for mental reproduction gives you an image or picture of any former object of perception, *as* you have seen it — a portrait of the past, true and faithful to the original.

Some writers would differ from the view now expressed. Some of the Germans assign to imagination the double office of producing the new and reproducing the old; the latter they call imaginative reproduction. In what respect this latter differs from the faculty of mental reproduction in general, it is difficult to perceive. When I remember a word spoken, or a song, I have the conception of a *sound*, or a series of sounds. When I remember an object in nature, as a mountain, a house, etc., I have the conception of a material object, having some definite form, and figure, outline, proportion, magnitude, etc. The conception of the absent object presents itself in such a case, of course, as an image or picture of the object to the mental eye. It is as really the work of conception reproductive, however, to replace, in this case, the absent object as once perceived, as it is to bring back to mind any thing else that has once been before it; *e. g.*, a spoken word or a date in history. We may, if we please, term this faculty, as employed on objects of sight, conception *imaginative*, and distinguish it from the same faculty as employed in reproducing other objects; but it were certainly better to appropriate the term imagination to the single and far higher province of creation — the office of conceiving the ideal under the form of the sensible.

§ VIII. — Imagination a Voluntary Power, or Process.

Is it an act which the mind puts forth when it will, and withholds when it will? Or is it a mere passive susceptibility of the mind to be impressed in this particular way? As the harp lies passive to the wind, which comes and goes we know not how or whither, so does the mind lie open to such thoughts and fancies as flit over it, and call forth its hidden harmonies as they pass by? Those who, with Dr. Brown, resolve imagination into mere suggestion, of course take the latter view.

Often spontaneous. — Undoubtedly, the greater part of our ideal conceptions are spontaneous — the thoughts that rise at the instant, unpremeditated, uncalled, the suggestions of the passing moment or event. This is true of our daily reveries, and all the little romances we construct, when we give the reins to fancy, and a "varied scene of thought" — to use the beautiful expression of Cudworth — passes before us, peopled with forms unreal and illusive. There is no special volition to call up these conceptions, or *such* as these. They take their rise and hue from the complexion of the mind at the time, and the character of the preceding conceptions, in the ever moving, ever varying series and procession of thought. They are like the shifting figures on the curtain in a darkened room, shadows coming and going, as the forms of those without move hither and thither. So far, all is spontaneous. Nay, more: It is, doubtless, impossible, by direct volition, to call up any conception, ideal or otherwise; since this, as Dr. Brown has well argued, would be "either to will without knowing what we will, which is absurd," or else to have already the conception which we wished to have, which is not less absurd.

If no intentional Activity, then Imagination not a Faculty. — Is there then no intentional creation of new and ideal conceptions, of images, similes, metaphors, and other like material of a lively and awakened fancy, but merely a *casual* suggestion of such and such thoughts, quite beyond any control and volition or even purpose of ours? If so, then, after all, is it proper to speak of a faculty of imagination, since we have not, in this case, the *power* of *doing* the thing under consideration? We merely sit still in the darkened room, and watch the figures as they come and go, with some desire that the thing may go on, some appreciation of it, some critical judgment of the different forms and movements.

The Mind not wholly passive in the Process. — I reply, this is not altogether so. The mind is not altogether *passive* in this thing; there is an *activity* involved in the process, and that of the mind's own. There is a power, either original or acquired, of conceiving such thoughts as are now under consideration, a readiness for them, a proneness to them, a bias, propensity, inclination, more powerful in some than in others, by virtue of which this process occurs. We may call this a faculty, though, more strictly, perhaps, a *susceptibility*, but it is, in truth, one of the endowments of the mind, part of its furniture, one form of its activity.

A more direct voluntary Element. — But there is, further than this, and more directly, a voluntary element in the process. It is in our power to yield, or not, to this propensity, this inclination to the ideal; to put forth the mental activity in this direction, or to withhold it; to say whether or not the imagination shall have its free, full play, and with liberated wing soar aloft through her native skies; whether our speech shall be simple argument, unadorned stout logic, or logic not less stout, clothed with the pleasing, rustling drapery which a lively imagination is able to throw, like a splendid robe, over the naked form of truth.

There is, then, really a mental activity, and an activity in some degree under control of the will, in the process we are considering.

Same Difficulty lies elsewhere. — The same difficulty which meets us here, meets us elsewhere, and lies equally against other mental powers. We cannot, by direct volition, remember a past event, for this implies, as in the case of the volition to imagine a given scene, either that the thing is already in view, or else that we will we know not what. Yet, as every one knows, there is a way of recalling past events; a faculty or power of doing this thing; a faculty which we exercise when we please.

The same may be said of the power of thought in general. We cannot, by direct volition, *think* of any given thing, for to will to th nk of it is already to have thought of it, yet there is mental activity involved in every process of thought, a mental power exercised, a faculty of some sort exercised. Nor is it a power altogether beyond our own control. We can direct our thoughts, can govern them, can turn them, as we do a water course, that *will* flow somewhere, but whose channel we may lead this way or that.

§ IX. — Use and Abuse of Imagination.

Influence upon the Mind. — As to the benefits arising from the due use and exercise of this faculty, not much, perhaps, is requisite to be said. It gives vividness to our conceptions, it raises the tone of our entire mental activity, it adds force to our reasoning, casts the light of fancy over the sombre plodding steps of judgment, gilds the recollections of the past, and the anticipations of the future, with a coloring not their own. It lights up the whole horizon of thought, as the sunrise flashes along the mountain tops, and lights up the world. It would be but a dreary world without that light.

Influence on the Orator. — By its aid the orator presents his clear, strong argument in its own simple strength and beauty, or commands those skilful touches, that, by a magic spell, thrill all hearts in unison. There floats before his mind, ever as he proceeds, the *beau ideal* of what his argument should be; toward this he aspires, and those aspirations make him what he is. No man is eloquent who has not the imagination requisite to form and keep vividly before him such an ideal.

On the Artist. — By its aid the artist breathes into the inanimate marble the breath of life, and it becomes a living soul. By its aid, deaf old Beethoven, at his stringless instrument, calls up the richest harmony of sound, and blind old Milton, in his darkness and desolateness, takes his magician's wand, and lo! there rises before him the vision of that Paradise where man, in his primeval innocence, walked with God.

On other Minds. — Nor is it the poet, the orator, the artist, alone, that derive benefit from the exercise of this faculty, or have occasion to make use of it. It is of inestimable value to us all. It opens for us new worlds, enlarges the sphere of our mental vision, releases us from the bonds and bounds of the actual, and gives us, as a bird let loose, the wide firmament of thought for our domain. It gilds the bald, sullen actualities, and stern realities of life, as the morning reddens the chill, snowy summits of the Alps, till they glow in resplendent beauty.

On the Spectator and Observer. — It is of service, not to him who writes alone, but to him who reads; not to him who speaks alone, but to him who hears; not to the artist alone, but to the *observer* of art; for neither poet, nor orator, nor artist, can convey the full meaning, the *soul*, the inspiration of his work, to one who has not the imagination to appreciate and feel the beauty, and the power, that lie hidden there. There is just as much meaning in their works, to us, as there is soul in us to receive that meaning. The man of no imagination sees no meaning, no beauty, no power, in the Paradise Lost, the symphonies of Beethoven and Mozart, the Transfiguration of Raphael, the Aurora of Guido, or the master-pieces of Canova and Thorwalsden.

Errors of Imagination. — Undoubtedly there are errors, mistakes, prejudices, illusions of the imagination; mistakes in judgment, in reasoning, in the affairs of practical life, the source of which is to be found in some undue influence, some wrong use, of the imagination. We mistake its conceptions for realities. We dwell upon its pleasing visions till we forget the sober face of truth. We fancy pleasures, benefits results which will never be realized, or we look upon the dark and dreary side of things till all nature wears the sombre hue of our disordered fancy.

Not, therefore, to set aside its due Culture. — All this we

7*

are liable to do. All these abuses of the imagination are possible, likely enough to occur. Against them we must guard. But to cry out against the culture and due exercise of the imagination, because of these abuses to which it is liable, is not the part of wisdom or highest benevolence. To hinder its fair and full development, and to preclude its use, is to cut ourselves off, and shut ourselves out, from the source of some of the highest, purest, noblest, pleasures of this our mortal life.

No Faculty perhaps of more Value.—It is not too much to say, that there is, perhaps, no faculty of the mind which, under due cultivation, and within proper bounds, is of more real service to man, or is more worthy of his regard, than this. Especially, is it of value in forming and holding before the mind an ideal of excellence in whatever we pursue, a standard of attainment, practicable and desirable, but loftier far than any thing we have yet reached. To present such an ideal, is the work of the imagination, which looks not upon the actual, but the possible, and conceives that which is more perfect than the human eye hath seen, or the human hand wrought. No man ever yet attained excellence, in any art or profession, who had not floating before his mind, by day and by night, such an ideal and vision of what he might and ought to be and to do. It hovers before him, and hangs over him, like the bow of promise and of hope, advancing with his progress, ever rising as he rises, and moving onward as he moves; he will never reach it, but without it he would never be what he is.

§ X.—Culture of the Imagination.

Strengthened by Use.—In what way, it is sometimes asked, may the faculty under consideration be improved and strengthened? To this it may be replied, in general, that the ideal faculty, like every other, is developed and strengthened by exercise, weakened and impaired by neglect. There is no surer way to secure its growth than to call its present powers, whatever they may be, into frequent exercise. The mental faculties, like the thews and muscles of the physical frame, develop by use. Imagination follows the same general law.

Study of the Works of others. — I do not mean by this exclusively the direct exercise of the imagination in ideal creations of our own, although its frequent employment in this way, is of course necessary to its full development. But the imagination is also exercised by the study of the ideal creations of others, especially of those highly gifted minds which have adorned and enriched their age with productions of rarest value, which bear the stamp and seal of immortality. With these, in whatever department of letters or art, in poetry, oratory, music, painting, sculpture, architecture — whatever is grand, and lofty, and full of inspiration, whatever is beautiful and pleasing, whatever is of choicest worth and excellence in its own proper sphere; with these let him become familiar who seeks to cultivate in himself the faculty of the ideal. Every work of the imagination appeals to the imagination of the observer, and thus develops the faculty which it calls into exercise. No one can be familiar with the creations of Shakspeare and Milton, of Mozart and Beethoven, of Raphael and Michael Angelo, and not catch something of their inspiration.

Study of Nature. — Even more indispensable is the study of nature; and it has this advantage, that it is open to those who may not have access to the sublime works of the highest masters of art. Nature, in all her moods and phases — in her wonderful variety of elements — the grand and the lowly, the sublime and the beautiful, the terrible and the pleasing — nature in her mildest and most fearful displays of power, and also in her softest and sweetest attractions, is open to every man's observation, and he must be a close observer and a diligent student of her who would cultivate in himself the ideal element. The most gifted sons of genius, the minds most richly endowed with the power of ideal creation, have been remarkable for their love and careful study of nature.

Mistake on this Point. — I must notice in this connection, however, a mistake into which some have fallen in regard to this matter. The simple description of a scene in nature, just as it is, is not properly a work of the imagination. It is simply perception or memory that is thus exercised, along with judgment and artistic power of expression. Imagination gives not the actual, but the ideal. She never satisfies herself with an exact copy. The mere portrait painter, however skillful, is not in the highest sense an artist. The painter, mentioned by Wayland, who copied the wing of the butterfly for the wing of the Sylph, was not, in so doing, exercising his imagination, but only his power of imitation. So, too, when Walter Scott gives us, in the cave of Denzel, a precise description of some spot which he has seen, even to the very plants and flowers that grow among the rocks, that scene, however pleasing and life-like, is not properly a creation of his own imagination; it is a description of the actual, and not a conception of the ideal. Much that is included under the general title of works of the imagination is not properly the production of that faculty.

Coleridge has made essentially the same remark, that in what is called a work of imagination, much is simple narration, much the filling up of the outline, and not to be attributed to that faculty.

The Student of Nature not a mere Copyist. — The true study of nature, is not to observe simply that we may copy what she presents, but rather to gather materials on which our own conceptive power may work, and which it may fashion after its own designs into new combinations and results of beauty. Nature, too, is full of hints and suggestions which a discerning mind, and an eye practised to the beautiful, will not fail to catch and improve. It is only when we do this, when we begin, in fact, to depart from, and go beyond the actual, that we exercise the imagination.

Difference illustrated by an Example. — The difference between simple description, and the creations of the conceptive faculty, may be shown by reference to a single example:

> "The twilight hours, like birds, flew by,
> As lightly and as free;
> Ten thousand stars were in the sky,
> Ten thousand in the sea;
> For every wave, with dimpled cheek,
> That leaped upon the air,
> Had caught a star in its embrace,
> And held it trembling there."

The quiet stillness of the evening, the reflection of the stars in the sea, are the two simple ideas which enter into this beautiful stanza. They would have been faithfully and fully expressed, so far as regards all the perfections of exact description, by the simple propositions which follow: "The evening hours passed swiftly and silently; many stars appeared in the sky, and each was reflected in the sea."

The poet is not content with this description. The swiftness and silentness of those passing hours remind him of the flight of birds along the sky. The resemblance strikes him as beautiful. He embodies it in his description. It is an ideal conception. He goes further. He sees in the water, not the reflection merely of the stars, but the stars themselves, as many in the sea as in the sky. Here is a departure from the truth, from the actual, an advance into the region of the ideal. Imagination, thus set free, takes still further liberties: attributes to the inanimate wave the *dimpled cheek* of beauty, ascribes its restlessness not to the laws of gravitation, but to the force of a strictly human passion, under the influence of which it leaps into the air toward the object of its affection, seizes it, and holds it, trembling, in its embrace.

§ XI. — Historical Sketch.

Various Definitions and Theories of Imagination by Different Writers.

Definition of Dr. Reid. — *Reid* makes it nearly synonymous with simple apprehension. "I take imagination, in its most proper sense, to signify a lively conception of *objects of sight*," the conception of things as they appear to the eye. *Addison* employs the term with the same limitation, that is, as confined to objects of sight.

Of Stewart. — *Stewart* regards this as incorrect, holds that imagination is not confined to *visible* or even *sensible* objects. He regards it as a complex, not a simple power, including simple apprehension, abstraction, judgment, or taste, and association of ideas; its province being to select, from different objects, a variety of qualities and circumstances, and combine and arrange them so as to form a new creation of its own.

Of Brown. — *Brown* differs not essentially from the view of Stewart. He also makes imagination a complex operation, involving conception, abstraction, judgment, association. He distinguishes between the *spontaneous* and the *voluntary* operation of the imaginative power; in the former case, there is no voluntary effort of selection, combination, etc., but images arise independently of any desire or choice of ours, by the laws of suggestion; and this he holds to be the most frequent operation of the faculty. In the case of voluntary imagination, which is attended with desire, this desire is the prominent thing, and serves to keep the conception of the subject before the mind, in consequence of which, a variety of associated conceptions follow, by the laws of suggestion, in regular train. Of these suggested conceptions and images, some, we approve, others, we do not; the former, by virtue of our approval, become more lively and permanent, while the latter pass away. Thus, without any direct effort or power of the will to combine and separate these various conceptions, they shape themselves according to our approval and desire, in obedience to the ordinary laws of suggestion.

Of Smith. — *Sydney Smith* regards imagination in much the same light — a faculty in which association plays the principal part, assisted by judgment, taste, etc., amounting, in fact, to much the same thing that we call invention; the process by which a poet constructs a drama, or a machinist a steam-engine, being essentially the same.

Of Wayland and Upham. — *Wayland*, in common with most of the authors already cited, makes imagination a complex faculty, involving abstraction, and association; "the power by which, from simple conceptions already existing in the mind, we form complex wholes or images." Some form of abstraction necessarily precedes the exercise of this power. The different elements of a conception must be first mentally severed before we can reunite them in a new conception. "It is this power of reuniting the several elements of a conception at will, that is, properly, imagination. Imagination may then be designated the power of combination." *Upham* takes the same view. The same view, essentially, is also given by *Amandè Jacques*, a French writer of distinction.

View of Tissot. — *Tissot*, as also many of the German philosophers, gives imagination the double province of recalling sensible intuitions, objects of sight, such as we have known them, and also of conceiving objects altogether differently disposed from our original perceptions of them, varied from the reality. The former they call imagination *reproductive*; the latter, *creative*. That form of the imagination which is purely spontaneous, in distinction from the voluntary, they term *fancy*.

Of Coleridge and Mahan. — *Coleridge*, followed by *Ma-*

han, regards imagination as the power which recombines the several elements of thought into conceptions, which conform not to *mere existences*, but to *certain fundamental ideas in the mind itself*, ideas of the beautiful, sublime, etc.

These Definitions agree in what.—These definitions, it will be perceived, with scarcely an exception make imagination to be a complex faculty, and regard it as merely *the power of combining*, in new forms, the various elements of thought already in the mind. The correctness of each of these ideas has been already discussed.

INTELLECTUAL FACULTIES.

PART THIRD.

THE REFLECTIVE POWER.

THE REFLECTIVE POWER.

GENERAL OBSERVATIONS.

Office of this Power. — We have thus far treated of that power of the mind by which it takes cognizance of objects as directly presented to sense, and also of that by which it represents to itself former objects of cognition in their absence. But a large portion of our knowledge and of our mental activity does not fall under either of these divisions. There is a class of mental operations which differ from the former, in that they do not give us directly sensations or perceptions of things, do not present objects themselves; and from the latter, in that they do not represent to the thought absent objects of perception; which differ from both, in that they deal not with the things themselves, but with the properties and relations of things — not with the concrete, but with the abstract and general. This class of operations, to distinguish it from the preceding classes, we have named, in our analysis, the *reflective* power of the nind. It comprises a large part of our mental activity.

Specific Character. — The form of mental activity which is characteristic of this faculty, is the perception of relations, that which Dr. Brown calls *relative suggestion*, but which we should prefer to term *relative conception.* The mind is so constituted that when distinct objects of thought are presented, it conceives at once the notion of certain relations existing between those objects. One is larger, one smaller, one is here, the other there, one is a part in relation to a whole, some are like, others unlike each other. The several relations that may exist and fall under the notice of this power of the mind are too many to be easily enumerated. The more important are, position, resemblance, proportion, degree, comprehension. All these may, perhaps, by a sufficiently minute analysis, be resolved into one — that of comprehension, or the relation of a whole to its parts.

Comprehensive of several Processes. — The faculty now under consideration will, on careful investigation, be found to underlie and comprehend several mental processes usually ranked as distinct operations and faculties of the mind, but which are at most only so many forms of the general power of relative conception. Such are the mental operations usually known as *judgment*, *abstraction*, *generalization*, and *reasoning*. Of these, and their relation to the general faculty comprehensive of all, we shall have occasion to speak further as we proceed.

Two Modes of Operation. — As the relations of object to object may all be comprised under the general category of comprehension, or the whole and its parts, there are manifestly two modes or processes in which the reflective faculty may put forth its activity. It may combine the several parts or elements to form a complex whole, or it may divide the complex whole into its several parts and elements. In the one case, it works from the parts, as already resolved, to the whole; in the other, from the whole, as already combined, to the parts. The one is the compositive or synthetic, the other, the analytic or divisive process. Each will claim our attention.

CHAPTER I.

THE SYNTHETIC PROCESS — GENERALIZATION.

§ I. — Nature of the Synthetic Process.

Our Conceptions often Complex. — If we examine attentively the various notions or conceptions of the mind, we find that a large part of them are in a sense complex — comprising, in a word, a certain aggregate of properties, which, taken together, constitute our conception of the object. Thus, my notion of table, or chair, or desk, is made up of several conceptions, of form, size, material, color, hardness, weight, use, etc., etc., all which, taken together, constitute my notion of the object thus designated.

Originally given as discrete. — These several elements that enter into the composition of our conceptions of objects, it is further to be noticed, are, in the first instance, given us in perception, not as a complex whole, but as discrete elements. Thus, sight gives us form and color; touch gives us extension, hardness, smoothness, etc.; muscular resistance gives us weight, and so, by the various senses, we gather the several properties which make up our cognizance of the object, and which, taken together, constitute our conception of it.

Conceptions of Classes. — But a large part of our conceptions, if we carefully observe the operations of our own minds, are not particular, but general, not of individual objects, but of classes of objects. Of this, any one may satisfy himself on a little reflection. How are these conceptions formed?

Such Conceptions, how formed. — The process of forming a general conception, I take to be this: The several elements that compose our conception of an individual object, being originally presented, as we have already said, one by one, in the discrete, and not in the concrete, it is of course in our power to conceive of any one of these elements by itself. No new power or faculty is needed for this. By the usual laws of suggestion any one of these elements may be presented to the mind, distinct from those with which, in perception, it is associated, and as such it may be the object of attention and thought. I may thus conceive of the color, the form, the size, or the fragrance of a flower.

Extension of the Process to other Objects. — It is of the form, color, etc., of some particular flower, as yet, however, and not of form and color in general, that I conceive. Suppose, now, that other flowers are presented to my notice, possessing the same form and color, for example, red. Presently I observe other objects, besides flowers, that are of the same color — horses, cows, tables, books, cloths. As the field of observation enlarges, still other objects are added to the list, until that which I first conceived of as the peculiar property of a single flower, the rose, and of a single specimen, no longer is appropriated in my thoughts to any individual object or class of objects, but becomes a general conception. It is an abstraction and also a generalization; an abstraction because it no longer denotes or connotes any individual object, but stands before the mind as simple, pure quality, red, or redness; a generalization inasmuch as it is a quality pertaining equally to a great variety of objects.

The Process carried still further. — Having thus obtained the general conception of red, and, in like manner, of blue, violet, yellow, indigo, orange, etc., etc., I may carry the process still further, and form a conception more general than either, and which shall include all these. These are all varieties denoting the certain peculiarity of appearance which external objects present to the eye. Fixing my thought upon this, their common characteristic, I no longer conceive of red, or blue, or violet, as such, but of color in general.

In like manner, I observe the properties of different triangles — right-angled, obtuse-angled, acute-angled, equilateral, isosceles. I leave out of view whatever is peculiar to each of these varieties, retaining only what is common to them all — the property of three-sidedness; and my conception is now a general one — triangle.

It is in this manner that we form the conceptions expressed by such terms as animal, man, virtue, form, beauty, and the like. A large proportion of the words in ordinary use, are of this sort. They are the names or expressions of abstract, general, conceptions: abstract, in that they do not relate to any individual object; general, in that they comprehend, and are equally applicable to a great variety of objects.

Process of Classification. — The process of *classification* is essentially the same with that by which we form general abstract conceptions. Observing different objects, I find that they resemble each other in certain respects, while in others they differ. Objects A, B, and C, differ, for instance, in form, and size, and weight, and fragrance, but agree in some other respect, as in color. On the ground of this resemblance, I class them together in my conceptions. In so doing, I leave out of view all other peculiarities, the points in which they differ, and take into account only the one circumstance in which they agree. In the very act of forming a class, I have formed a general conception, which lies at the basis of that classification.

Tendency of the Mind. — The tendency of the mind to group individual objects together on the ground of perceived resemblances, is very strong, and must be regarded as one of the universal and instinctive propensities of our nature, one of the laws of mental action. As we have already remarked, respecting general abstract terms, a large portion of the language of ordinary life is the language of classification. The words which constitute by far the greater part of the names of things, are common nouns, that is, names of classes. The names of individual objects are comparatively few. Adjectives, specifying the qualities of objects, denote groups or classes possessing that common quality. Adverbs qualifying verbs or adjectives, designate varieties or classes of action and of quality. Indeed, the very existence of language as a medium of communication, and means of expression, involves and depends upon this tendency of the mind to class together, and then to designate by a common noun, objects diverse in reality, but agreeing in some prominent points of resemblance. In no other way would language be possible to man, since, to designate each individual object by a name peculiar to itself, would be an undertaking altogether impracticable.

Rudeness of the earlier Attempts. — The first efforts of the mind at the process of classification are, doubtless, rude and imperfect. The infancy of the individual, and the infancy of nations and races, are, in this respect, alike ; objects are grouped roughly and in the mass, specific differences are overlooked, and individuals differing widely and essentially are thrown into the same class, on the ground of some observed and striking resemblance. As observation becomes more minute, and the mind advances in culture and power of discrimination, these ruder generalizations are either abandoned or subdivided into genera and species, and the process assumes a scientific form. What was at first mere classification, becomes now, in the strictest sense, *generalization.*

Scientific Classification. — Classification, however scientific, is still essentially the process already described. We observe a number of individuals, for example, of our own species. Certain resemblances and differences strike us. Some have straight hair, and copper complexion, others, woolly hair, and black complexion, others, again, differ from the preceding in both these respects. Neglecting minor and specific differences, we fix our attention on the grand points of resemblance, and thus form a general conception, which embraces whatever characteristics belong, in common, to the several individuals which thus resemble each other. To this general conception we appropriate the name Indian, Negro, Caucasian, etc., which henceforth represent to us so many classes or varieties of the human race. Bringing these classes again into comparison with each other, we observe certain points of resemblance between them, and form a conception still more general, that of man.

Further Illustration of the same Process. — In this way the genera and species of science are formed. On grounds of observed resemblance, we class together, for example, certain animals. They differ from each other in color, size, and many other respects, but agree in certain characteristics which we find invariable, as, for example, the form of the skeleton, number of vertebræ, number and form of teeth, arrangement of organs of digestion. We give a name to the class thus formed — carnivora, rodentia, etc. The class thus formed and named, we term the genus, while the minor differences mark the subordinate varieties or species included under the genus. In the same way, comparing other animals, we form other genera. Bringing the several genera also into comparison, we find them likewise agreeing in certain broad resemblances. These points of agreement, in turn, constitute the elements of a conception and classification still wider and more comprehensive than the former. Under this new conception I unite the previous genera, and term them all mammalia. And so on to the highest and widest generalizations of science.

Having formed our classification we refer any new specimen to some one of the classes already formed, and the more complete our original survey, the more correct is this process of individual arrangement. It is remarked by Mr. Stewart, that the islanders of the Pacific, who had never seen any species of quadruped, except the hog and the goat, naturally inferred, when they saw a cow, that she must belong to one or the other of these classes. The limitations of human knowledge may lead the wisest philosopher into essentially the same error.

It is in the way now described that we form genera, and species, and the various classes into which, for purposes of science, we divide the multitude of objects which are presented in nature, and which, but for this faculty, would appear to us but a confused and chaotic assemblage without number, order, or arrangement. The individuals exist in nature — not the classes, and orders, and species: these are the creations of the human mind, conceptions of the brain, results of that process of thought now described as the reflective faculty in its synthetic form.

Importance of this Process. — It is evident at a glance that this process lies at the foundation of all science. Had we no power of generalization — had we no power of separating, in our thoughts, the quality from the substance to which it pertains, of going beyond the concrete to the abstract, beyond the particular to the general — could we deal only with individual existences, neither comparison nor classification would be possible; each particular individual object would be a study to us by itself, nor would any amount of diligence ever carry us beyond the very alphabet of knowledge.

Existence of general Conceptions questioned. — Important as this faculty may seem when thus regarded, it has been questioned by some whether, after all, we have, in fact, or can have, any general abstract ideas; whether triangle, man, animal, etc., suggest in reality any thing more to the mind than simply some particular man, or triangle, or animal, which we take to represent the whole class to which the individual belongs.

There can be no question, however, that we do distinguish in our minds the thought of some particular man, as Mr. A, or some particular sort of man, as black man, white man, from the thought suggested by the term man; and the thought of an isosceles or right-angled triangle, from the thought suggested by the unqualified term triangle. They do not mean the same thing; they have not the same value to our minds. Now there are a great multitude of such general terms in every language, they have a definite meaning and value, and we know *what* they mean. It must be then that we have general abstract ideas, or general conceptions.

Argument of the Nominalist. — But the nominalist replies. The term man, or triangle, awakens in your mind, in reality and directly, only the idea of some particular individual or triangle, and this stands as a sort of *type* or *representation* of other like individuals of whom you do not definitely think as such and so many. I reply, this cannot be shown; but even if it were so, the very language of the objection implies the power of having general conceptions. If the individual man or triangle thought of stands as a type or representation, as it is said, of a great number of similar men and triangles, then is there not already in my mind, prior to this act of representation, the *idea of a class of objects*, arranged according to the law of resemblance, in other words, a *general abstract idea* or *conception?* If I had not already formed such an idea, the particular object presented to my thoughts could not stand as type or representation of any such thing, or of any thing beyond itself, for the simple reason that there would be nothing of the sort to represent.

Further Reply. — Besides, there is a large class of general terms to which this reasoning of the nominalist would not at all apply — such terms as virtue, vice, knowledge, wisdom, truth, time, space — which manifestly do not awaken in the mind the thought of any particular virtue or vice, any particular truth, any definite time, any definite space, but a general notion under which all particular instances may be included. To this the nominalist will perhaps reply, that in such cases we are really thinking, after all, of mere *names* or *signs*, as when we use the algebraic formula $x-y$, a mere term of convenience, having indeed some value, we do not know precisely what, *itself* the terminus and object of our thought for the time being. In such cases the mind stops, he would say, with the term itself, and does not go beyond it to conjure up a general conception for it. So it is with the terms virtue, vice; so with the general terms, class, species, genus, man, animal, triangle; they are mere collective terms, *signs*, formulas of convenience, to which you attach no more meaning than to the expression $x-y$. If you would find their meaning and attach any definite idea to them, you must resolve them into the *particular* objects, the particular vices, virtues, etc., which go to make up the class.

I reply to all this, you are still classifying, still forming a general conception, the expression of which is your so called formula, $x-y$, alias virtue, man, and the like.

§ II. — Province and Relation of several Terms employed to denote, in Part, or as a Whole, this Power of the Mind.

We are now prepared to consider the proper province and relation of several terms frequently employed, with considerable latitude and diversity of meaning, to denote, in part, or as a whole, the process now described. Such are the terms *abstraction*, *generalization*, *classification*, and *judgment.*

I. Abstraction.

Term often used in a Wide Sense. — This term is frequently employed to denote the entire synthetic process as now described — the power of forming abstract general conceptions, and of classifying objects according to those conceptions. It is thus employed by Stewart, Wayland, Mahan, and others. There is, perhaps, no objection to this use of the word, except that it is manifestly a departure from the strict and proper sense of the term.

More limited Sense. — There is another and more common use of the term abstraction, which gives it a more limited sense. As thus employed, it denotes that act of the mind by which we fix our attention on some one of the several parts, properties, or qualities of an object, to the exclusion of all the other parts or properties which go to make up the complex whole. In consequence of this exclusive direction of the thoughts to that one element, the other elements or properties are lost sight of, drop out of the account, and there remains in our present conception only that one item which we have singled out from the rest. This is denominated, in common language, *abstraction.* Such is the common idea and definition of that term. It is Mr. Upham's definition.

This not really Abstraction. — Whether this, again, is the true idea of abstraction, is, to say the least, questionable. When I think of the cover of a book, the handle of a door, the spring of a watch, in distinction from the other parts which make up a complex whole, I am hardly exercising the power of abstract thought; certainly no new, distinct faculty is requisite for this, but simply attention to one among several items or objects of perception. Hardly ever can it be called analysis, with Wayland. It is the simple direction of the thought to some one out of several objects presented. A red rose is before me. I may think of its color exclusively, in distinction from its form and fragrance; that is, of the redness of this particular rose, this given surface before me. The object of my thought is purely a sensible object. I have not abstracted it from the sensible individual object to which it belongs. It is in no sense an abstract idea, a pure conception. There has been nothing done which is not done in any case where one thing, rather than another of a group or assemblage of objects, is made the object of attention.

The true Nature of Abstraction. — But suppose now that instead of thinking of the redness of this rose in particular, I think of the color red in general, without reference to the rose or any other substance; or, to carry the process further, of color in general, without specifying in my thought any particular color, evidently I am dealing now with abstractions. I have in my thought *drawn away* (abstraho) the color from the substance to which it belongs, from all substance, and it stands forth by itself a pure conception, an abstraction, having, as such, no existence save in my mind, but there it does exist a definite object of contemplation. The form of mental activity now described, I should call *abstraction*. It is not necessary, perhaps, to assign it a place as a distinct faculty of the mind. It is, in reality, a part, and an important part, of the synthetic process already described. But it is not the whole of that process, and the term abstraction should not, therefore, in strict propriety, at least as now defined, be applied as a general term to designate that class of mental operations. The synthetic process involves something more than mere abstraction; viz.:

II. Classification as Distinguished from Generalization.

Classification. — When the general idea or conception has been formed in the mind, we proceed to bring together and arrange, on the basis of that general conception, whatever individual objects seem to us to fall under that general rule. This we call classification. Thus, forming first the abstract, or general conception red, we bring together in our thought a variety of objects to which this conception is applicable, as red horses, red flowers, red books, red tables, etc., etc., thus forming classes of objects on the ground of this common property. The difference between *classification* and *generalization*, in so far as they are not synonymous, I take to be simply this, that in the former we group and arrange objects according to no general law, but mere appearance or resemblance, often, therefore, on fanciful or arbitrary grounds; while in the latter case, we proceed according to some general and scientific principle or law of classification, making only those distinctions the basis of our arrangement which are founded in nature, and are at once invariable and essential.

III. Judgment as Related to Classification.

Judgment. — We have already spoken of that specific process by which, having formed a given conception, or a given rule, we bring the individual objects of perception and thought under that rule, or reject them from it, according as they agree or disagree with the conception we have formed. The process itself we have called classification. The mental activity thus employed is technically termed *judgment* — the power of subsuming, under a given notion or conception, the particular objects which properly belong there. Thus, the botanist, as he meets with new plants, and the ornithologist, as he discovers new varieties of birds, refers them at once to the family, the genus, the species to which they belong. His mind runs over the generic types of the several classes and orders into which all plants and birds are divided, he perceives that his new specimen answers to the characteristic features of one of these families, or classes, and not to those of the others, and he accordingly assigns it a place under one, and excludes it from the rest. So doing, he exercises judgment. All classification involves and depends upon this power; closely viewed, the action of the mind, in the exercise of this power, amounts simply to this, the perception of agreement or disagreement between two objects of thought. In the case supposed, the genus or species, as described by those who have treated of the particular science, is one of the objects contemplated; the new specimen of plant or bird, as carefully observed and studied, is the other. These two objects of thought are compared; the one is perceived to agree or not to agree with the other; and on the ground of this agreement or disagreement, the classification is made. This perception of agreement in such a case is an act of judgment, so called.

Not a distinct Faculty. — The form of mental activity now described, is hardly to be ranked as a distinct faculty of the mind, although it has been not unfrequently so treated by writers on mental science. It enters more or less fully into all mental operations; like consciousness and attention, it is, to some extent, involved in the exercise of all the faculties, and cannot, therefore, be ranked, with propriety, as coördinate with them. It is not confined to the investigations of science, but is an activity constantly exercised by all men. We have in our minds a multitude of general conceptions, the result of previous observation and thought. Every moment some new object presents itself. With the quickness of thought, we find its place among the conceptions already in the mind: it agrees with this, it is incompatible with that, it belongs with the one, it is excluded from the other. This is the form of most of our thinking; indeed, no small part of our mental activity consists in this perception of argreements and disagreements, and in the referring of some particular object of experience, some individual conception, to the class or general conception under which it properly belongs. The expression of such a judgment is a proposition. We think in propositions, which are only judgments mentally expressed. We discourse in propositions, which are judgments orally expressed. We cannot frame a proposition which does not affirm, or deny, or call in question, something of something.

Judgment in relation to Knowledge. — Are judgment and knowledge identical? Is all knowledge only some form of judgment? So Kant, Tissot, and other writers of that school, would affirm. "Judgment is the principal operation of the mind, since it is concerned in all knowledge properly so called." "All our knowledges are judgments. To know, is to distinguish, and to distinguish, is at once to affirm, and to deny." Such was also Dr. Reid's doctrine, in opposition to Locke, who distinguished between knowledge and judgment. Reid, on the contrary, regards knowledge as only one class of judgments, namely, those about which we are most positive and certain. According to this view, judgment seems to cover the whole field of mental activity. Sir William Hamilton thus regards it. We cannot even experience a sensation, he maintains, without the mental affirmation or judgment that we are thus and thus affected.

Common Speech distinguishes them. — It must be admitted, however, that in common use there is a distinction between knowing and judging, the one implying the comparative certainty of the thing known, the other implying some room and ground for doubt, the existence of opinion and belief, rather than of positive knowledge. The word itself, both in its primitive signification, and its derivation, indicating, as it does, the decision by legal tribunal of doubtful cases, favors this usage. That an exercise of judgment is, strictly speaking, involved in all knowledge, is, nevertheless true, since, to know that a thing is thus and thus, and not otherwise, is to distinguish it from other things, and that is to judge.

§ III. — Historical Sketch.

The Realist and Nominalist Controversy.

The Question at Issue. — No question has been more earnestly and even more bitterly discussed, in the whole history of philosophical inquiry, than the point at issue between the Realist and Nominalist, as to what is the precise object of thought when we form an abstract general conception. When I use the term *man*, for example, is it a mere *name*, and nothing more, or is there a *real existence* corresponding to that name, or is it neither a mere name on the one hand, nor, on the other, a real existence, but a conception of my own mind, which is the object of thought?

These three answers can be made, these three doctrines held, and essentially only these three. Each has been actually maintained with great ability and acuteness. The names by which the three doctrines are respectively designated are, Realism, Nominalism, and Conceptualism.

Early History of Realism. — Of these doctrines, the former, Realism, was the first to develop itself. To say nothing of the ancients, we find traces of it in modern philosophy, as early as the ninth century. Indeed, it would seem to have been the prevalent doctrine, though not clearly and sharply defined; a belief, as Tissot has well expressed it, "spontaneous, blind, and without self-consciousness." John Scotus Erigena, and St. Anselm, Archbishop of Canterbury, both philosophers of note, together with many others of less distinction, in the ninth, tenth, and eleventh centuries, were prominent Realists. The Platonic view may, in fact, be said to have prevailed down to that period. The early fathers of the Christian Church were strongly tinged with Platonism, and the Realistic theory accordingly very naturally engrafted itself upon the philosophy of the middle ages. The logical and the ontological, existence as mere thought of the mind, and existence as reality, were not distinguished by the leading minds of those centuries. The reality of the thought as thought, and the reality of an actual existence, corresponding to that thought, were confounded the one with the other. As the rose of which I conceive has existence apart from my conception, so man, plant, tree, animal, are realities, and not mere conceptions of the mind.

Rise of Nominalism. — It was not till nearly the close of the eleventh century, that the announcement of the opposite doctrine was distinctly made, in opposition to the prevalent views. This was done by Roscelinus, who maintained that universal and general ideas have no objective reality; that the only reality is that of the individuals comprised under these genera; that there are no such existences as man, animal, beauty, virtue, etc.; that generality is only a pure form given by the mind to the matter of its ideas, a pure abstraction, a mere name.

In this we have the opposite extreme of Realism. If the Realist went too far in affirming the objective reality of his conception, the Nominalist erred on the other in overlooking its subjective reality as a mode or state of the mind, and reducing it to a mere name.

Dispute becomes theological. — The dispute now, unfortunately, but almost inevitably, became theological. The Realist accused the Nominalist of virtually denying the doctrine of the Trinity, inasmuch as, according to him, the idea of Trinity is only an abstraction, and there is no Being corresponding to that idea. To this, Roscelinus replied, with at least equal force and truth, that on the same ground the Realist denied the doctrine of divine unity, by holding a doctrine utterly incompatible with it. Roscelinus, however, was defeated, if not in argument, at least by numbers and authority, and was condemned by council at the close of the eleventh century.

Rise of Conceptualism. — It was about this time, that Abelard, pupil of Roscelinus, proposed a modified view of the matter, avoiding the extreme position both of the Realist and the Nominalist party, and allowing the *subjective*, but not the *objective* reality, of general ideas. This is substantially the doctrine of Conceptualism. The general abstract idea of man, rose, mountain, etc., has indeed no existence or reality as an external object, nor is there among external objects any thing corresponding to this idea; but it has, nevertheless, a reality and existence as a thought, a conception of my mind.

Prevalence of Realism during the twelfth and thirteenth Centuries. — The doctrine, as thus modified, gained some prevalence, but was condemned by successive councils and by the Pope. Sustained by such authority, as well as by the names of men greatly distinguished for learning and philosophy, Realism prevailed over its antagonists during the latter part of the twelfth and the whole of the thirteenth century. The fourteenth witnessed again the rise and spread of the Conceptualist theory, under the leadership of Occam. The dispute was bitter, leading to strife and even blood.

Later History of the Discussion.—In the seventeenth century we find Hobbes, Hume, and Berkley advocating the doctrine of the Nominalists, while Price maintains the side of Realism. Locke and Reid were Conceptualists, Stewart a Nominalist.

CHAPTER II.

THE ANALYTIC PROCESS—REASONING.

Relation to the Synthetic Process.—We have thus far considered that form or process of the reflective faculty, by which we combine the elements of individual complex conceptions, to form general conceptions and classes, on the basis of perceived agreements and differences. This we have termed the synthetic process. The divisive or analytic process remains to be considered. This, as the name denotes, is, so far as regards the method of procedure, the opposite of the former. We no longer put together, but take apart, no longer combine the many to form one, but from the general complex whole, as already formed and announced, we evolve the particular which lies included in it. This process comprehends what is generally called analysis, and also reasoning.

In discussing this most important mental process, we shall have occasion to treat more particularly of its *nature*, its *forms*, and its *modes*.

§ I. — The Nature of the Process.

Conceptions often Complex. — It was remarked, in speaking of our conceptions, that many of them are complex. My notion of a table, for example, is that of an object possessing certain qualities, as form, size, weight, color, hardness, each of which qualities is known to me by a distinct act of perception, if not by a distinct sense, and each of which is capable, accordingly, of being distinctly, and by itself, an object of thought or conception. The understanding combines these several conceptions, and thus forms the complex notion of a table. The notion thus formed, is neither more nor less than the aggregate, or combination of the several elementary conceptions already indicated. When I am called on to define my complex conception, I can only specify these several elementary notions which go to make up my idea of the table. I can say it is an object round, or square, of such or such magnitude, that it is of such or such material, of this or that color, and designed for such and such uses.

Virtual Analysis of complex Conceptions. — Now when I affirm that the table is round, I state one of the several qualities of the object so called, one of the several parts of the complex notion. It is a partial analysis of that complex conception. I separate from the whole, one of its component parts, and then affirm that it sustains the relation of a part to the comprehensive whole. The separation is a virtual analysis. The affirmation is an act of judgment expressed in the form of a proposition. Every proposition is, in fact, a species of synthesis, and implies the previous analysis of the conception, or comprehensive whole, whose component parts are thus brought together. Thus, when I say snow is white, man is mortal, the earth is round, I simply affirm of the object designated, one of the qualities which go to make up my conception of that object. Every such statement or proposition involves an analysis of the complex conception which forms the subject of the proposition, while the thing predicated or affirmed is, that the quality designated — the result of such analysis — is one of the parts constituting that complex whole.

Reasoning, what. — Reasoning is simply a series of such propositions following in consecutive order, in which this analysis is carried out more or less minutely. Thus, when I affirm that man is mortal, I resolve my complex notion of man into its component parts, among which I find the attribute of mortality, and this attribute I then proceed to affirm of the subject, man. I simply evolve, and distinctly announce, what was involved in the term man. But this term expresses not merely a complex, but a general notion. Resolving it as such into its individual elements, I find it to comprehend among the rest, a certain person, Socrates, *e. g.*, and the result of this analysis I state in the proposition, Socrates is a man. But on the principle that what is true of a class must be true of the individuals composing it, it follows that the mortality already predicated of the class, man, is an attribute of the individual, Socrates. When I affirm, then, that Socrates is mortal, I announce, in reality, only what was virtually implied in the first proposition — man is mortal. I have analyzed the complex general conception, man, have found involved in it the particular conception, mortal, and the individual conception, Socrates, and by a subsequent synthesis have brought together these results in the proposition, Socrates is mortal, a proposition which sustains to the affirmation, man is mortal, the simple relation of a part to the whole.

Reasoning and Analysis, how related. — This analytic process, as applied to propositions, for the purpose of evolving from a complex general statement, whatever is involved or virtually contained in it, is called reasoning; as applied not to propositions, but to simple conceptions merely, it is known as simple analysis. The psychological process is, in either case, one and the same.

Illustration by Dr. Brown. — Dr. Brown has well illustrated the nature of the reasoning process in its relation to the general proposition with which we set out, by reference to the germ enclosed in the bulb of the plant. "The truths at which we arrive, by repeated intellectual analysis, may be said to resemble the premature plant which is to be found enclosed in that which is itself enclosed in the bulb, or seed which we dissect. We must carry on our dissection more and more minutely to arrive at each new germ; but we do arrive at one after the other, and when our dissection is obliged to stop, we have reason to suppose that still finer instruments, and still finer eyes, might prosecute the discovery almost to infinity. It is the same in the discovery of the truths of reasoning. The stage at which one inquirer stops is not the limit of analysis in reference to the object, but the limit of the analytic power of the individual. Inquirer after inquirer discovers truths which were involved in truths formerly admitted by us, without our being able to perceive what was comprehended in our admission. * * * There may be races of beings, at least we can conceive of races of beings, whose senses would enable them to perceive the ultimate embryo plant enclosed in its innumerable series of preceding germs; and there may, perhaps, be created powers of some higher order, as we know that there is one Eternal Power, able to feel, in a single comprehensive thought, all those truths, of which the generations of mankind are able, by successive analyses, to discover only a few, that are, perhaps, to the great truths which they contain, only as the flower, which is blossoming before us, is to that infinity of future blossoms enveloped in it, with which, in ever renovated beauty, it is to adorn the summers of other ages."

Inquiry suggested. — But here the inquiry may arise, How happens it that, if the reasonings which conduct to the profoundest and most important truths, are but successive and continued analyses of our previous conceptions, we should have admitted those preceding truths and conceptions without a suspicion of the results involved in them? The reason is probably to be found, as Dr. Brown suggests, in the fact that in the process of generalizing we form classes and orders before distinguishing the minuter varieties; we are struck with some obvious points of agreement which lead us to give a common place and a common term to the objects of such resemblance, and this very circumstance of agreement which we perceive, may involve other circumstances which we do not at the time perceive, but which are disclosed on minute and subsequent attention. "It is as if we knew the situations and bearings of all the great cities in Europe, and could lay down, with most accurate precision, their longitude and latitude. To know thus much, is to know that a certain space must intervene between them, but it is not to know what that space contains. The process of reasoning, in the discoveries which it gives, is like that topographic inquiry which fills up the intervals of our map, placing here a forest, there a long extent of plains, and beyond them a still longer range of mountains, till we see, at last, innumerable objects connected with each other in that space which before presented to us only a few points of mutual bearing."

The Position further argued from the Nature of the Syllogism. — That all deductive reasoning, at least, is essentially what has now been described, an analytic process, is evident from the fact that the syllogism to which all such argument may be reduced, is based upon the admitted principle that whatever is true of the class, is true of all the individuals comprehended under it. Something is affirmed of a given class; an individual or individuals are then affirmed to belong to that class; and on the strength of the principle just stated, it is thereupon affirmed that what was predicated of the class is also true of the individual. Nothing can be plainer than that in this process we are working from the given whole to the comprehended parts, from the complex conception stated at the outset, to the truths that lie hidden and involved in it. In other words, it is a process of analysis which we thus perform, and as all reasoning, when scientifically stated, is brought under this form, it follows that all reasoning is essentially analytic in its nature.

Inductive Reasoning no Exception.—It may be supposed that the inductive method of reasoning is an exception to this rule, inasmuch as we proceed, in that case, not from the general to the particular, but the reverse. Whatever may be true of deduction, is not induction essentially a synthetic process? So it might, at first, appear. I have observed, for example, that several animals of a particular species, sheep, for instance, chew the cud. Having observed this in several instances, I presently conclude that the same is true of the whole class to which these several individuals belong, in other words, that all sheep are ruminant. Extending my observation further, I find other species of animals likewise chewing the cud. I observe, moreover, that every animal, possessing this characteristic, is distinguished by the circumstance of having horns and cloven hoofs; I find, so far as my observation goes, the two things always associated, and hence am led, on observing the one, immediately to infer the other. The proposition that was at the outset particular, now becomes general, viz., all animals that have horns and cloven hoofs are ruminant. Is the conclusion at which I thus arrive, involved in the premiss with which I start? Is the fact that all horned and cloven-footed animals are ruminant, implied and contained in the fact that *some* horned and cloven-footed animals, that is, so many as I have observed, are so?

Even here the Evidence of the Conclusion lies in the Premiss. — A little reflection will convince us that these questions are to be answered in the affirmative. If the conclusion be itself correct and true, then it is a truth involved in the previous proposition; for whatever evidence I have of the truth of my conclusion, that all animals of this sort are ruminant, is manifestly derived from, and therefore contained in, the fact that such as I have observed are so. I have no other evidence in the case supposed. If this evidence is insufficient, then the conclusion is not established. If it be sufficient, then the conclusion which it establishes, is derived from and involved in it.

The argument fully and scientifically stated, runs thus:

A, B, C, animals observed, are ruminant. But A, B, C, represent the class Z to which they belong.

Therefore, class Z is ruminant.

Admitting now the correctness of my observation in respect to A, B, C, that they are ruminant, the argument turns entirely upon the second proposition that A, B, C, represent the class Z, so that what is true of them in this respect, is true of the whole class. If A, B, C, *do* represent the class Z, then to say that A, B, C, are ruminant, is to say that Z is so. The one is contained in the other. If they do *not*, then the conclusion is itself groundless, and there is no occasion to inquire in what it is contained, or whether it is contained in any thing. It is no longer a valid argument, and therefore cannot be brought in evidence that some reasoning is not analytic.

What sort of Propositions constitute Reasoning. — It is hardly necessary to state that not any and every series of propositions constitute reasoning. The propositions must be consecutive, following in a certain order, and not only so, but must be in such a manner connected with and related to each other, that the truth of the final proposition shall be manifest from the propositions which precede. To affirm that snow is white, that gold is more valuable than silver, and that virtue is the only sure road to happiness, is to state a series of propositions, each one of which is true, but which have no such relation to each other as to constitute an argument. The truth of the last proposition does not follow from the truth of the preceding ones.

§ II. — Relation of Judgment and Reasoning

Judgment Synthetic, Reasoning Analytic. — The relation of judgment and reasoning to each other becomes evident from what has been said of the nature of the reasoning process. Judgment is essentially synthetic. Reasoning, essentially analytic. The former combines, affirms one thing to be true of another; the latter divides, declares one truth to be contained in another. All reasoning involves judgment, but all judgment is not reasoning. The several propositions that constitute a chain of reasoning, are so many distinct judgments. Reasoning is the evolution or derivation of one of these judgments, viz., the conclusion, from another, viz., the premiss. It is the process by which we arrive at some of our judgments.

Mr. Stewart's View. — Reasoning is frequently defined as a combination of judgments, in order to reach a result not otherwise obvious. Mr. Stewart compares our several judgments to the separate blocks of stone which the builder has prepared, and which lie upon the ground, upon any one of which a person may elevate himself a slight distance from the ground; while these same judgments, combined in a process of reasoning, he likens to those same blocks converted now, by the builder's art, into a grand staircase leading to the summit of some lofty tower. It is a simple combination of separate judgments, nor is there any thing in the last step of the series differing at all in its nature, says Mr. Stewart, from the first step. Each step is precisely like every other, and the process of reaching the top is simply a repetition of the act by which the first step is reached.

This View called in Question. — It is evident that this position is not in accordance with the general view which we have maintained of the nature of the reasoning process. According to this view, reasoning is not so much a combination as an analysis of judgments; nor is the last of the several propositions in a chain of argument of the same nature precisely as the first. It is, like the first, a judgment, but unlike the first, it is a particular sort of judgment, viz., an inference or conclusion, a judgment involved in and derived from the former.

In the series of propositions, A is B, B is C, therefore A is C, the act of mind by which I perceive that A is B, or that B is C, is not of the same nature with that by which I perceive the consequent truth that A is C; no mere repetition of the former act would amount to the latter. There is a new sort of judgment in the latter case, a deduction from the former. In order to reach it, I must not merely perceive that A is B, and that B is C, but must also perceive the connection of the two propositions, and what is involved in them. It is only by bringing together in the mind these two propositions, that I perceive the new truth, not otherwise obvious, that A is C, and the state or act of mind involved in this latter step seems to me a different one from that by which I reach the former judgments.

§ III. — Different Kinds of Reasoning.

Two Kinds of Truth. — The most natural division is that according to the subject-matter, or the materials of the work. The truths which constitute the material of our reasoning process are of two kinds, *necessary*, and *contingent*. That two straight lines cannot enclose a space, that the whole is greater than any one of its parts, are examples of the former. That the earth is an oblate spheroid, moves in an elliptical orbit, and is attended by one satellite, are examples of the latter.

The Difference lies in what. — The difference is not that one is any *less certain* than the other, but of the one you cannot conceive the opposite, of the other you can. That three times three are nine, is no more true and certain, than that Cæsar invaded Britain, or that the sun will rise to-morrow a few minutes earlier or later than to-day. But the one admits of the contrary supposition without absurdity, the other does not; the one is contingent, the other necessary. Now these two classes of truths, differing as they do, in this important particular, admit of, and require, very different methods of reasoning. The one class is susceptible of *demonstration*, the other admits only that species of reasoning called *probable* or *moral*. It must be remembered, however, that when we thus speak we do not mean that this latter class of truths is deficient in proof; the word probable is not, as thus used, opposed to *certainty*, but only to *demonstration*. That there is such a city as Rome, or London, is just as *certain* as that the several angles of a triangle are equal to two right-angles; but the evidence which substantiates the one is of a very different nature from that of the other. The one can be demonstrated, the other cannot. The one is an eternal and necessary truth, subject to no contingence, no possibility of the opposite. The other is of the nature of an event taking place in time, and dependent on the will of man, and might, without any absurdity, be supposed not to be as it is.

I. Demonstrative Reasoning.

Field of Demonstrative Reasoning. — Its field, as we have seen, is necessary truth. It is limited, therefore, in its range, takes in only things abstract, conceptions rather than realities, the relations of things rather than things themselves, as existences. It is confined principally, if not entirely, to mathematical truths.

No degrees of Evidence. — There are no *degrees* of evidence or certainty in truths of this nature. Every step follows irresistibly from the preceding. Every conclusion is inevitable. One demonstration is as good as another, so far as regards the certainty of the conclusion, and one is as good as a thousand. It is quite otherwise in probable reasoning.

Two Modes of Procedure. — In demonstration, we may

proceed directly, or indirectly; as, *e. g.*, in case of two triangles to be proved equal. I may, by super-position, prove this directly; or I may suppose them unequal, and proceed to show the absurdity of such a supposition; or I may make a number of suppositions, one or the other of which *must* be true, and then show that all but the one which I wish to establish are false.

Force of Mathematical reasoning. — The question arises whence the peculiar force of mathematical, in distinction from other reasoning? — a fact observed by every one, but not easily explained: how happens this, and on what does it depend, this irresistible cogency which compels our assent? Is it owing to the pains taken to define the terms employed, and the strict adherence to those definitions? I think not; for other sciences approximate to mathematics in this, but not to the cogency of its reasoning. The explanation given by Stewart is certainly plausible. He ascribes the peculiar force of demonstrative reasoning to the fact, that the first principles from which it sets out, *i. e.*, its definitions, are *purely hypothetical*, involving no basis or admixture of facts, and that by simply reasoning strictly upon these assumed hypotheses the conclusions follow irresistibly. The same thing would happen in any other science, could we (as we cannot) construct our definitions to suit ourselves, instead of proceeding upon *facts* as our data. The same view is ably maintained by other writers.

If this be so, the superior certainty of mathematical, over all other modes of reasoning, if it does not quite vanish, becomes of much less consequence than is generally supposed. Its truths are necessary in no other sense than that certain definitions being assumed, certain *suppositions* made, then the certain other things follow, which is no more than may be said of any science.

Confirmation of this View. — It may be argued, as a confirmation of this view, that whenever mathematical reasoning comes to be applied to sciences involving facts either as the data, or as objects of investigation, where it is no longer possible to proceed entirely upon hypothesis, as, *e. g.*, when you apply it to mechanics, physics, astronomy, practical geometry, etc., then it ceases to be demonstrative, and becomes merely probable reasoning.

Mathematical reasoning supposed by some to be identical. — It has been much discussed whether all mathematical reasoning is merely identical, asserting, in fact, nothing more than that $a=a$; that a given thing is equivalent to itself, capable of being resolved at last into merely this. This view has been maintained by Leibnitz, himself one of the greatest mathematicians, and by many others. It was for a long time the prevalent doctrine on the Continent. Condillac applies the same to all reasoning, and Hobbes seems to have had a similar view, *i. e.*, that all reasoning is only so much addition or subtraction. Against this view Stewart contends that even if the propositions themselves might be represented by the formula $a=a$, it does not follow that the various steps of reasoning leading to the conclusion amount merely to that. A paper written in cipher may be said to be identical with the same paper as interpreted; but the evidence on which the act of deciphering proceeds, amounts to something more than the perception of identity. And further, he denies that the propositions are identical, *e. g.*, even the simple proposition $2 \times 2=4$. 2×2 express one set of quantities, and 4 expresses another, and the proposition that asserts their equivalence is not identical; it is not saying that the same quantity is equal to itself, but that two different quantities are equivalent.

II. Probable Reasoning.

Not opposed to Certainty. — It must be borne in mind, as already stated, that the probability now intended is not opposed to certainty. That Cæsar invaded Britain is *certain*, but the reasoning which goes to establish it, is only probable reasoning, because the thing to be proved is an event in history, contingent therefore, and not capable of demonstration.

Sources of Evidence. — Evidence of this kind of truths is derived from three sources: 1. Testimony; 2. Experience; 3. Analogy.

1. *Evidence of Testimony.*

In itself probable. — This is, à priori, *probable.* We are so constituted as to be inclined to believe testimony, and it is only when the incredibility of the witness has been ascertained by sufficient evidence, that we refuse our assent. The child believes whatever is told him. The man, long conversant with human affairs, becomes wary, cautious, suspicious, incredulous. It is remarked by Reid that the evidence of testimony does not depend altogether on the character of the witness. If there be no *motive* for deception, especially if there be weighty reasons why he should speak truth, or if the narrative be in itself probable and consistent, and tallies with circumstances, it is in such cases to be received even from those not of unimpeachable integrity.

Limits of Belief. — What are the limits of belief in testimony? Suppose the character of witnesses to be good, the narrative self-consistent, the testimony concurrent of various witnesses, explicit, positive, full, no motive for deception; are we to believe in that case whatever may be testified? One thing is certain, we do in fact believe in such cases; we are so constituted. Such is the law of our nature. Nor can it be shown irrational to yield such assent. It has been shown by an eminent mathematician that it is always possible to assign a number of independent witnesses, so great that the falsity of their concurrent testimony shall be mathematically more improbable, and so more incredible, than the truth of their statement, *be it what it may.*

Case supposed. — Suppose a considerable number of men of undoubted veracity, should, without concert, and agreeing in the main as to particulars, all testify, one by one, that they witnessed, on a given day and hour, some very strange occurrence, as, *e.g.*, a ball of fire, or a form of angelic brightness, hovering in the air, over this building, or any like unwonted and inexplicable phenomenon. Are we to withhold or yield our assent? I reply, if the number of witnesses is large, and the testimony concurrent, and without concert, and no motive exists for deception, and they are men of known integrity, especially if they are sane and sober men, not easily imposed upon, I see not how we can reasonably withhold assent. Their testimony is to be taken as true testimony, *i.e.*, they did really witness the phenomenon described. The proof becomes stronger or weaker in proportion as the circumstances now mentioned coëxist to a greater or less extent, *i.e.*, in proportion as there are more or fewer of these concurring and corroborating circumstances. If there was but a single witness, or if a number of the witnesses were not of the best character, or if there were some possible motive for deception, or if they were not altogether agreed as to important features of the case, so far the testimony would of course be weakened. But we may always suppose a case so strong that the falsity of the witnesses would be a greater miracle than the truth of the story. This is the case with the testimony of the witnesses to our Saviour's miracles.

Distinction to be made.—An important distinction is here to be noticed between the falsity, and the incorrectness, of the witness, between his intention to deceive, and his being himself deceived. He may have seen precisely what he describes; he may be mistaken in thinking it to have been an angel, or a spirit, or a ball of fire. Just as in the case of certain illusions of sense—an oar in the water—the eye correctly reports what it sees, but the judgment is in error, in thinking the oar to be crooked. So the witness may be true, and the testimony true in the case of a supposed miracle or other strange phenomenon; the *appearance* may have been just as stated, but the question may still be raised, were the witnesses correct, in their inference, or judgment, as to what was the cause of the said appearance, as to *what it was* that they saw or heard?

This must be decided by the rules that govern the proceedings of sensible men in common affairs of life.

2. *Reasoning from Experience.*

Induction as distinguished from Deduction. — This is called *induction*, the peculiar characteristic of which, in distinction from deductive reasoning, is that it begins with individual cases, and from them infers a general conclusion, whereas, the deductive method starts with a general proposition, and infers a particular one. From the proposition all men are mortal, the syllogism infers that Socrates is mortal. From the fact that Socrates, Plato, Aristotle, Pliny, Cæsar, Cicero, and any number of other individuals, are mortal, induction leads you to conclude that all men are so. The premises here are facts occurring within the range of observation and experience, and the reasoning proceeds on the principle of the general uniformity of nature and her laws. Induction, then, is, in other words, the process of inferring that what we know to be true in certain observed cases, is also true, and will be found to be true, in other like cases which have not fallen under our observation.

Basis of this Mode of reasoning. — The groundwork of induction, as I have already said, is the axiom or universal proposition of the uniformity of nature. Take this away, and all reasoning from induction or experience fails at once. This is a truth which the human mind is, by its nature and constitution, always disposed to proceed upon. It may not be embodied in the shape of a definite proposition, but it is tacitly assumed and acted upon by all men. How came we by this general truth. Is it *intuitive?* So say the disciples of certain schools, so says Cousin, and so say the Scotch metaphysicians, and the German. Others, however, contend that it is itself an induction, as truly as any other, a truth learned from experience and observation, and by no means the first, but rather among the latest of our inductions. Without stopping to discuss this question, it is sufficient for our purpose to notice the fact, that this simple truth is universally admitted, and constitutes the basis of all reasoning from experience.

Incorrect Mode of Statement. — The proposition is sometimes incorrectly stated, as, *e. g.*, that the future will resemble the past. This is not an adequate expression of the great truth to which we refer. It is not that the future merely will resemble the past merely, but that the unknown will resemble the known. The idea of time is not properly connected with the subject. That which is unknown may lie in the future, it may lie in the present or the past.

Limits of this Belief. — An important question here arises. What are the limits, if limits there are, to this belief of the uniformity of nature, and to the reasoning based on that belief? Are we warranted, in all cases, in inferring that the unknown will be, in similar circumstances, like the known — that what we have found to be true in five, ten, or fifty cases, and without exception, will be universally true? We do reason thus very generally. Such is the tendency of the mind, its nature. Is it correct procedure? Is it certain that our experience, though it be uniform and unvaried, is the universal experience? If not, if limits there are to this method of reasoning, what are they?

Erroneous Induction. — The inhabitants of Siam have never seen water in any other than a liquid or gaseous form. They conclude that water is never solid. The inhabitants of central Africa may be supposed never to have seen or heard of a white man. They infer that all men are black. Are these correct inductions? No; for they lead to false conclusions. They are built on insufficient foundations. There was not a sufficiently wide observation of facts to justify so wide a conclusion. Evidently, we cannot infer from our own non-observation of exceptions, that exceptions do not exist. We must first know that if there were exceptions we should have known them. In both the cases now supposed, this was overlooked. The African has only seen men who were natives of Africa. There may be, in other countries, races that he has not seen, and has had no opportunity to see. The world may be full of exceptions to this general rule, and yet he not know it. Correct induction in his case would be this: I have seen many men, natives of central Africa, and they have all been black men, without exception. I conclude, therefore, that *all* the natives of central Africa are black. In a word, it is only *under like circumstances* that we can infer the uniformity of nature, and so reason inductively from the known to the unknown.

Superstitious Belief of the Ancients. — The tendency of men to believe in the universal permanence of nature, and, on that ground, to generalize from insufficient data, is illustrated in the superstitious and widely prevalent idea among the ancients, and some of the moderns also, of grand cycles of events extending both to the natural and the *moral* world. According to this idea, the changes of the atmosphere, and all other natural phenomena, as observed at any time, would, after a period, return again in the same order of succession as before; storms, and seasons, and times, being subject to some regular law. It was supposed, in fact, "that all the events" — to use the language of one of these theorists — "within the immeasurable circuit of the universe, are the successive evolutions of an extended series, which, at the return of some vast period, repeats its eternal round during the endless flux of time." This is a sufficiently grand induction, startling in its sweep and range of thought, but requiring for its data a somewhat wider observation of facts than can fall to the lot of short-lived and short-sighted man, during the few years of his narrow sojourn, and pilgrimage, in a world like this.

3. *Reasoning from Analogy.*

Meaning of the term Analogy. — This word, analogy, is used with great variety of meaning, and with much vagueness, therefore. It properly denotes any sort of resemblance, whether of relation or otherwise; and the argument from analogy is an argument from resemblance, an argument of an inductive nature, but not amounting to complete induction. A resembles B in certain respects; therefore it probably resembles it, also, in a certain other respect: such is the argument from *analogy*. A resembles B in such and such properties, but these are always found connected with a certain other property; therefore A resembles B also in regard to that property: such is the argument from *induction*. Every resemblance which can be pointed out between A and B creates a further and increased probability that the resemblance holds also in respect to the property which is the object of inquiry. If the two resembled each other in all their properties, there would be no longer any doubt as to this one, but a positive certainty, and the more resemblances in other respects so much the nearer we come to certainty respecting the one that happens to be in question.

Illustration of this Principle. — It was observed by Newton, that the diamond possessed a very high refractive power compared with its density. The same thing he knew to be true of combustible substances. Hence, he conjectured that the diamond was combustible. He conjectured the same thing, and for the same reason, of water, *i. e.*, that it contains a combustible ingredient. In both instances, he guessed right — reasoning from analogy.

Further Illustration of Reasoning from Analogy. — Reasoning from analogy, I might infer that the moon is inhabited, thus: The earth is inhabited — land, sea, and air, are all occupied with life. But the moon resembles the earth in figure, relation to the sun, movement, opacity, etc.; moreover, it has volcanoes as the earth has; therefore, it is *probably* like the earth in this other respect, that of being inhabited. To make this out by induction, I must show that the moon not only resembles the earth in these several respects, but that these circumstances are in other cases observed to be connected with the one in question; thus, in other cases, bodies that are opaque, spherical, and moving in elliptical orbits, are known to be inhabited. The same thing is probably true then in all cases, and inasmuch as the moon has these marks, it is therefore inhabited.

Counter Probability. — On the other hand, the points of dissimilarity create a counter probability, as, *e. g.*, the moon has no atmosphere, no clouds, and therefore no water; but air and water are, on our planet, essential to life; the presumption is, then, looking at these circumstances merely, that the moon is uninhabited. Nay, more: if life exists, then it must be under very different conditions from those under which it exists here. Evidently, then, the greater the resemblance in other respects between the two planets, the less probability that they differ in this respect (*i. e.*, the mode of sustaining life), so that the resemblances already proved, become, themselves, presumptions *against* the supposition that the moon is inhabited.

Amount of Probability. — The analogy and diversity, when they come thus into competition and the arguments from the one conflict with those of the other, must be weighed against each other. The extent of the resemblance, compared with the extent of the difference, gives the amount of probability on one side or the other, so *far as these elements are known.* If any region lies unexplored, we can infer nothing with certainty or probability as to that. Suppose, then, that so far as we have had the means of observing, the resemblances are to the differences as four to one; we conclude with a probability of four to one, that any given property of the one will be found to belong to the other. The chances are four out of five.

Value of Analogical Reasoning. — The chief value of

analogy, as regards science, however, is as a guide to con jecture and to experiment; and even a faint degree of anàlogical evidence may be of great service in this way, by directing further inquiries into that channel, and so conducting to eventual probability, or even certainty.

It is well remarked by Stewart, that the tendency of our nature is so to reason from analogy, that we naturally confide in it, as we do in the evidence of testimony.

Liable to mislead. — It must be confessed, however, that it is a species of reasoning likely to mislead in many cases. Its chief value lies not in proving a position, but in rebutting objections; it is good, not for assault, but defence. As thus used it is a powerful weapon in the hands of a skilful master. Such it was in Butler's hands.

§ IV. — Use of Hypotheses and Theories in Reasoning.

Theory, what. — The terms hypothesis and theory are often used interchangeably and loosely. Confusion is the result. It is difficult to define them accurately.

Theory (from the Greek, θεωρια; Latin, theoria; French, théorie; Italian, teoria; from θεωρεω, to perceive, see, contemplate) denotes properly any philosophical explanation of phenomena, any connected arrangement and statement of facts according to their bearing on some real or imaginary law. The facts, the phenomena, once known, proved, rest on independent evidence. Theory takes survey of them as such, with special reference to the law which governs and connects them, whether that law be also known or merely conjectured.

Hypothesis, what. — *Hypothesis* (ὑπο-τιθημι) denotes a gratuitous supposition or conjecture, in *the absence* of all positive knowledge as to what the law is that governs and connects the observed phenomena, or as to the cause which will account for them.

Theory may or may not be Hypothesis. — Hypothesis is, in

its nature, conjectural, and therefore uncertain; has its degrees of probability — no certainty. The moment the thing supposed is proved true, or verified, if it ever is, it ceases to be hypothesis. Theory, however, is not necessarily a matter of uncertainty. After the law or the cause is ascertained, fully known, and no longer a hypothesis at all, there may be still a theory about it; a survey of the facts and phenomena, as they stand affected by that law, or as accounted for by that cause. The motion of the planets in elliptical orbits, was originally matter of conjecture, of hypothesis. It is still matter of theory.

Probability of Hypothesis. — The probability of a hypothesis is in proportion to the number of facts or phenomena, in the given case, which it will satisfactorily explain, in other words, account for. Of several hypotheses, that is the most probable which will account for the greatest number of the given phenomena — those which, if the hypothesis be true, ought to fall under it as their law. If it accounts for all the phenomena in the case, it is generally regarded as having established its claim to certainty. So Whewell maintains. This, however, is not exactly the case. The hypothesis can be verified only by showing that the facts or phenomena in the case cannot possibly be accounted for on any *other* supposition, or result from any *other* cause; not simply that they can be accounted for, or can result from this. This is well stated by Mill in his System of Philosophy. The hypothesis of the undulating movement of a subtle and all-pervading ether will account for many of the known phenomena of light; but it has never been shown, and in the nature of the case never can be, probably, that no *other* hypothesis possible or supposable will also account for them.

Use of Hypotheses. — As to the *use* of hypotheses in science, Reid's remarks are altogether too sweeping, and quite incorrect. It is not true that hypotheses lead to no valuable result in philosophy. Almost all discoveries were at first hypotheses, suppositions, lucky guesses, if you please to call them so. The Copernican theory that the earth revolves on its axis was a mere hypothesis at the outset. Kepler's theory of the elliptical orbits of the planets was such; he made and abandoned nineteen false ones before he hit the right. This discovery led to another — that planets describe equal areas in equal times. Newton never framed hypotheses, if we may believe him. But his own grand discovery of the law of gravity as the central force of the system, depends for one of its steps of evidence on his previous discovery that the force of attraction varies as the inverse square of the distance, and this was suggested by him at first as a mere hypothesis; he was able to verify it only by calling in the aid of Kepler's discovery of equal areas in equal times, which latter, as already stated, was itself the result of hypothesis. Had it not been for one hypothesis of Newton, verified by the results of another hypothesis of Kepler, Newton could never have made his own discovery.

A hypothesis, it must be remembered, is any supposition, with or without evidence, made in order to deduce from it conclusions agreeable to known facts. If we succeed in doing this, we verify our hypothesis (unless, indeed, it can be shown that some other hypothesis will equally well suit these facts), and our hypothesis, when verified, ceases to be longer a hypothesis, takes its place as known truth, and in turn serves to explain those facts which would, on the supposition of its truth, follow from it as a cause. It is simply a short-hand process of arriving at conclusions in science. Suppose the problem to be the one already named — to prove that the central force of the solar system is one and the same with *gravity*. Now it may not be easy, or even possible in some cases, to establish the first step or premiss in such a chain of reasoning. The inductions leading to it may not be forthcoming. Hypothesis steps in and supplies the deficiency, by substituting in place of the induction a supposition. Assuming that distant bodies attract each other with a power inversely as the square of the distance, it proceeds on that supposition, and arrives at the desired conclusion.

In what Cases admissible. — Now this method is always allowable, and strictly scientific, whenever it is possible to verify our hypothesis, *i. e.*, in every case in which it is possible to show that no law but the one assumed can lead to these same results; that no *other* hypothesis can accord with the facts.

In the case supposed, it would not be possible to prove that the same movements might not follow from some other law than the one supposed. It is not certain, therefore, that the moving force of the solar system is identical with gravitation, *merely because* the latter would, if extended so far, produce the same results. In many other cases it *is* practicable; indeed, *in all cases where the inquiry is not tc ascertain the cause, but, the cause being already known, to ascertain the law of its action.*

Even in cases where the inquiry is not of this nature, hypothesis is of use in the suggestion of future investigations, and, as such, is frequently indispensable.

View of Mr. Mill. — Nearly every thing which is now theory, was once hypothesis, says Mill. "The process of tracing regularity in any complicated, and, at first sight, confused set of appearances, is necessarily tentative: we begin by making any supposition, even a false one, to see what consequences will follow from it; and by observing how these differ from the real phenomena we learn what corrections to make in our assumption. The simplest supposition which accords with any of the most obvious facts, is the best to begin with, because its consequences are the most easily traced. This rude hypothesis is then rudely corrected, and the operation repeated, until the deductive results are at last made to tally with the phenomena. Let any one watch the manner in which he himself unravels any complicated mass of evidence; let him observe how, for instance, he elicits the true history of any occurrence from the involved statements of one or of many witnesses. He will find that he does not take all the items of evidence into his mind at once, and attempt to weave them together; the human faculties are not equal to such an undertaking; he extemporizes, from a few of the particulars, a first rude theory of the mode in which the facts took place, and then looks at the other statements, one by one, to try whether they can be reconciled with the provisional theory, or what corrections or additions it requires to make it square with them. In this way, which, as M. Comte remarks, has some resemblance to the methods of approximation of mathematicians, we arrive by means of hypothesis at conclusions not hypothetical."

§ V. — Different Forms of Reasoning.

It remains to treat briefly of the *different forms* of reasoning, as founded in the laws of thought.

How far these Forms fall within the Province of Psychology. — As there are different kinds or modes of reasoning, according to the difference of the subject-matter or material about which our reasoning is employed, so there are certain general forms into which all reasoning may be cast, and which, according to the laws of thought, it naturally assumes. To treat specifically of these forms, their nature, use, and value, is the business of *logic;* but, in so far as they depend upon the laws of thought, and are merely modes of mental activity as exercised in reasoning, they are to be considered, in connection with other phenomena of the mind, by the psychologist. Briefly to describe these forms, and then to consider their value, is all that I now propose. I begin with the proposition, as the starting-point in every process of reasoning.

I. Analysis of the Proposition.

What constitutes a Proposition. — All reasoning deals

with propositions, which are judgments expressed. Every proposition involves two distinct conceptions, and expresses the relation between them; affirms the agreement or disagreement of the one with the other. As when I say, Snow is white, the conception of snow is before my mind, and also of whiteness; I perceive that the latter element enters into my notion of snow, and constitutes one of the qualities of the substance so called; I affirm the relation of the two, accordingly, and this gives the proposition enunciated. Every proposition then consists of these several parts, a word or words expressing some conception, a word or words expressing some other conception, a word or words expressing the relation of the two. The words which designate these two conceptions are called the *terms* of the proposition, and, according to the above analysis, there are, in every proposition, always two terms. That term or conception of which something is affirmed, is called the *subject*, that which is affirmed of the same, the *predicate*, and the word which expresses the relation of the two, the *copula*. In the above proposition, snow is the subject, white, the predicate, and is, the copula.

Quality and Quantity.—Propositions are distinguished as to *quality* and *quantity*. The former has reference to the affirmative or negative character of the proposition, the latter to its comprehensiveness. Every proposition is either affirmative or negative, which is called its quality. As to quantity, every proposition is either *universal*, affirming something of the whole of the subject—as, All men are mortal; or else *particular*, affirming something of only a part of the subject—as, Some tyrants are miserable.

Four kinds of categorical Propositions.—We have, then, four kinds of categorical propositions, viz., universal affirmative, universal negative, particular affirmative, particular negative. That is, with the same subject and predicate, it is always possible to state four distinct propositions; as, every A is B, no A is B, some A is B, some A is not B.

For the sake of convenience, logicians designate these different kinds of propositions severally by the letters A, E, I, O. Propositions that thus differ in quantity and quality are said to be opposed to each other. Of these, the two universals, A and E, are called contraries; the two particulars, I and O, sub-contraries; the universal affirmative, and the particular affirmative, A and I, also the universal negative and the particular negative, E and O, are respectively subalterns; while the universal affirmative and the particular negative, A and O, as also the universal negative and particular affirmative, E and I, are contradictories.

Rules of Opposition. — The following rules will be found universally applicable to propositions as opposed to each other. If the universal is true, so is the particular. If the particular is false, so is the universal. Contraries are never both true, but may be both false. Sub-contraries are never both false, but may be both true. Contradictories are never both true, or both false, but always one is true, the other false. The truth of these maxims will be evident on applying them to any proposition and its opposites, as for example, to the affirmation, Every man is mortal.

Categorical and hypothetical Propositions. — Propositions may be further distinguished as categorical or hypothetical; the one asserting or denying directly, as, *e. g.*, The earth is round; the other conditionally, — as, If the earth is round, it is not oblong.

Pure, and Modal. — The proposition, moreover, may be either pure or modal, the former asserting or denying without qualification, — as, Man is liable to err; the latter qualifying the statement, — as, Man is extremely or unquestionably liable to err.

II. Analysis of the Syllogism.

Proposition the Link, Syllogism the Chain. — All reasoning admits of being reduced to the form of a syllogism. Having discussed the proposition which forms the material or groundwork of every connected chain of argument, we are prepared now to examine the syllogism, or chain itself, into which the several propositions, as so many links, are wrought.

Syllogism defined. — A syllogism is an argument so expressed that the conclusiveness of it is manifest from the mere form of expression. When, for example, I affirm that all A is B, that all B is C, and that, consequently, all A is C, it is impossible that any one who is able to reason at all, and who comprehends the force of these several propositions taken singly, should fail to perceive that the conclusion follows inevitably from the premises. That which is affirmed, may or may not be *true*, but it is *conclusive*. If the premises are true, so is the conclusion; but whether they are true or not, the argument, as such, is conclusive; nay, even if they are false, the conclusion may possibly be true. For example, Every tyrant is a good man; Washington was a tyrant; therefore, Washington was a good man. Both the premises are false, but the argument, as regards the form, is valid, and the conclusion is not only correctly drawn, but is, moreover, a true proposition. In a word, the syllogism concerns itself not at all with the truth or falsity of the thing stated, but only with the form of stating, and that form must be such, that the premises being conceded, the conclusion shall be obvious and inevitable. All valid reasoning admits of such statement.

Composition of a Syllogism. — Every syllogism contains three propositions, of which two state the grounds or reasons, and are called the premises, the other states the inference from those positions, and is called the conclusion. These three propositions contain three, and only three, distinct terms, of which one is common to both premises, and is called the *middle* term; the others are the extremes, one of which is the subject of the conclusion, and is called the *minor* term; the other the predicate of the conclusion, and is called the *major* term, from the fact that it denotes the class to which the subject or minor term belongs. In the syllogism, — Every man is mortal; Socrates is a man; therefore, Socrates is mortal, — the three terms are, man, mortal, and Socrates: of these, Socrates, or the subject of the conclusion, is the minor; mortal, or the predicate of the conclusion, is the major; and man, with which both the others are compared, is the middle term.

Major and minor Premiss. — The premiss which contains the *major* term, and compares it with the middle, is called the *major premiss;* that which, in like manner, compares the *minor* term with the middle, is called the *minor premiss.* In the syllogism already given, 'Every man is mortal' is the major premiss; 'Socrates is a man' is the minor premiss.

The Order variable. — The order of the terms in the respective propositions, and even the order of the propositions themselves, is not invariable, but depends on circumstances. In the above proposition, it is immaterial whether I say, Every man is mortal, or, Mortal is every man; it is immaterial whether I state first the major or the minor premiss; nay, it is allowable even to state the conclusion first, and then the grounds and reasons for the same.

III. Laws of Syllogism.

The following rules or maxims will be found applicable to all cases, and may be regarded as laws of the syllogism.

Middle Term unequivocal. — *The middle term must not be equivocal.* This rule is violated in the following syllogism. Nothing is heavier than lead; feathers are heavier than nothing; therefore, feathers are heavier than lead. The middle term, nothing, is here used in different senses in the two premises.

Middle Term to be distributed. — Essentially the same thing occurs when the middle term is not, at least once, in the premises, used in its most complete and comprehensive sense, or, as the logicians express it, *distributed.* As, for example, when I say, White is a color, the term color is not here distributed, for it properly includes many things besides white. If now I introduce into another proposition the same term in a similar manner, as Black is a color, I evidently include under the term, as now used, some part of the class of things denoted by the general word color, which was not included under the same term as first used. The color which is affirmed to agree with black, is not the same color which is affirmed to agree with white. The term, in fact, denotes one thing in the one proposition, and another in the other. A syllogism thus constructed, is invalid. Hence the rule, that the *middle term must be distributed*, or taken in its completeness, to include the whole class which it properly denotes, *at least once in the premises*. This is done either by making it the *subject of an affirmative*, or the *predicate of a negative proposition;* as, All men are mortal, or, No vice is useful. Here the term man in the one case, and the term useful in the other, are each distributed or taken in their completeness. There is no individual to whom the term man can properly be applied, who is not included in the expression, all men, nor is there any useful thing which is not here denied of vice.

What distributed in the Conclusion. — On the same principle, *no term must be distributed in the conclusion which was not distributed in one of the premises.* This rule is violated in the following syllogism, All birds are bipeds; no man is a bird; therefore, no man is a biped. Here the term biped, in the major premiss, is not taken in its completeness, since many creatures besides birds are bipeds. Birds are only one sort of bipeds. In the conclusion, however, the term biped, being the predicate of a negative proposition, is distributed, the whole class of bipeds is spoken of, and man is excluded from the whole class. The syllogism is, of course, invalid.

Law of negative Premiss. — It is further a law of the syllogism, that *from negative premises nothing can be inferred.* Also, that *if one premiss is negative, the conclusion will be negative.*.

Law of particular Premiss. — *From two particular premises nothing follows, but if one premiss is particular, the conclusion will be so.*

These rules are too obvious, and too easily verified, to require illustration.

IV. Different Kinds of Syllogism.

Syllogisms differ. — We have mentioned as yet only those properties of the syllogism which universally belong to it. There are differences, however, which require to be noticed, and which constitute a distinction of some importance, presenting, in fact, two distinct kinds of syllogism.

Two Modes of procedure. — There are manifestly two entirely distinct modes of procedure in reasoning. We may infer from the whole to the parts, or from the parts to the whole. The former is called deductive, the latter inductive reasoning. The one is precisely the reverse of the other in method of procedure. Each is a perfectly valid method of reasoning, and each is, in itself, a distinct and valid kind of syllogism. Each requires the other. The deductive is wholly dependent on the inductive for its major premiss, which is only the conclusion of a previous induction, while, on the other hand, the induction is valuable chiefly as preparing the way for subsequent deduction. Each has equal claims with the other to be regarded as a distinct and independent form of syllogism. They have not, however, been so treated by logicians, but, on the contrary, the inductive method has been regarded, almost universally, as a mere appendage of the deductive, an imperfect form of one or another of the several figures of the syllogism deductive. Of this we shall have occasion to speak more fully in the historical sketch.

The two Modes compared. — The precise relation of the two modes will best appear by the comparison of the following syllogisms. The inductive syllogism runs thus: x, y, z, are A; x, y, z, constitute B; therefore, B is A.

The deductive runs thus: B is A; x, y, z, constitute B; therefore, x, y, z, are A.

The latter, it will be seen at a glance, is the precise counterpart of the other, beginning where the former ends, and exactly reversing the several steps in their order.

The Law of each. — The general law or rule which governs the former, is, What belongs (or does not belong) to all the constituent parts, belongs (or does not belong) to the constituted whole. The law of the latter is, What belongs (or not) to the containing whole, belongs (or not) to all the contained parts.

Application of the inductive Method. — Applying the inductive method to a particular case, we reason thus: Magnets x, y, z, etc., including so many as I have observed, attract iron. But it is fair to presume that what I have observed as true of x, y, z, is equally true of e, f, g, and all other magnets; in other words, x, y, z, do represent, and may fairly be taken as constituting the whole class of magnets; consequently, I conclude that all magnets attract iron. Thus stated, the truth which was at first observed and affirmed only of particular instances, becomes a general proposition, and may, in turn, become the premiss of a process of deduction. Thus, from the general proposition, obtained as now explained by the inductive mode, that all horned animals ruminate, I may proceed, by the deductive mode, to infer that this is true of deer or goats, or any particular species or individual whose habits I have not as yet observed.

V. Different Forms of Syllogism.

The Form of Statement not invariable. — As there are different kinds of syllogism, so also there are different *forms* in which any kind of syllogism may be stated. These forms are not essential, pertaining to the nature of the syllogism itself, but accidental, pertaining merely to the order of announcing the several propositions. It has already been remarked, in speaking of the general structure of the syllogism, that the order of propositions is not essential. Either premiss may precede, either follow. Nay, we may state *first the conclusion*, and *then the reasons, or grounds.* This latter method, as Hamilton has shown in his *New Analytic of Logical forms*, is perfectly valid, though usually neglected by writers on logic. It is not only valid, but the more natural of the two methods. When asked if Socrates is mortal, it is more natural to say, He is mortal, for he is a man, and all men are mortal, than to say, All men are mortal, he is a man, and therefore, he is mortal. In fact, most of our reasoning takes the first of these forms. The two are designated by Hamilton, respectively, as the *analytic* and *synthetic* syllogism.

Order of Premises may vary. — As to the order of the premises, which shall precede the other, this, too, is quite unessential and accidental. The earlier method, practised by Greek, Arabian, Jewish and Latin schools, was to state first the minor premiss, precisely the reverse of our modern custom.

Order of Terms not essential. — The order of the *terms*, in the several propositions, is also accidental rather than essential. There are several possible and allowable arrangements of these terms with reference to the order of precedence and succession, giving rise to what are called *figures* of the syllogism. These arrangements and figures have usually been reckoned as four; three only are admitted by Hamilton, the fourth being abolished. The first figure occurs when the middle term is the subject of one premiss and the predicate of the other. The second figure gives the middle term the place of predicate in both premises. The third makes it the subject of both.

A further Variation. — There is still another form of statement, in which the terms compared are not, as above, severally subject and predicate, but, in the same proposition, are both subject, or both predicate, as when we say, A and B are equal; B and C are equal; therefore, A and C are equal. This is a valid synthetic syllogism, though not recognized by logicians previously to the *New Analytic* of Hamilton. It is termed by him the unfigured syllogism.

Hypothetical reasoning not syllogistic. — It has been customary to treat of *hypothetical* reasoning, in its two forms of conditional and disjunctive, as forms or kinds of syllogism. As when we say, if A is B, C is D; but A is B, therefore C is D; or, disjunctively, either A is B, or C is D; but A is not B, therefore C is D. These, however, are not properly syllogisms. The inference is not mediate, through comparison with a common or middle term, but *immediate*, whereas the syllogism is, in all its forms, a process of mediate inference.

Summary of Distinctions. — To sum up the distinctions now pointed out. All inference is either immediate, as in the case of hypothetical reasoning, whether conjunctive or disjunctive, or else mediate, as in the syllogism. The latter may be inductive or deductive; and, as to form, analytic or synthetic, figured or unfigured.

VI. Laws of Thought on which the Syllogism depends.

Statement. — There are certain universal laws of thought on which all reasoning, and, of course, all syllogisms, depend. These laws, according to Hamilton, are the principles of *identity*, of *contradiction*, and of *excluded middle*; from which primary laws results a fourth, that of *reason and consequent.*

Law of Identity, what. — The principle of *identity* compels us to recognize the equivalence of a whole and its several parts taken together, as applied to any conception and its distinctive characters. As, for example, the sameness or equivalence of the notion *man* with the aggregate of qualities or characters that constitute that notion.

Law of Contradiction, what. — The law of contradiction is the principle that what is contradictory is unthinkable;

as, for example, that A has, and yet has not, a given quality, B.

Law of excluded Middle. — The principle of *excluded middle* is this, that of two contradictory notions, we must think one or the other to be true; as, that A either has or has not the quality B.

Law of Reason and Consequent. — From these primary principles results the law of *reason and consequent.* All logical inference is based on that law of our nature, that one notion shall always depend on another. This inference is of two kinds, from the whole to the parts, or from the parts to the whole, respectively called deductive and inductive, as already explained.

Certain Points not included in the preceding Synopsis. — I have presented, as was proposed, in brief outline, a synopsis of the forms of reasoning. For a full treatment of these forms, and the laws which govern them, the treatises on logic must be consulted.

Some things usually considered essential to logical forms, as the *modality* of propositions and syllogisms, and the *conversion* of the other figures of the syllogism into the first, I have not included in the above outline, for the reason that the former does not properly fall within the province of logic, which has to do only with the *form* and not with the *matter* of a proposition or an argument, while, as to the latter, it is only an accidental, and not an essential circumstance, what may be the figure of a syllogism, and it is, therefore, of no importance to reduce the second and third figures to the first.

VII. Use and Value of the Syllogism.

Having considered the various forms which the syllogism may assume, as also the laws or canons which govern it, we proceed to inquire, finally, as to it *use* and *value* in reasoning.

All mediate reasoning syllogistic. — It must be conceded, I think, that all *mediate* reasoning, all inference, which is not immediate and direct, but which, in order to reach its conclusion, compares one thing with another, is essentially syllogistic. The greater part of our reasoning processes are of this sort. When fully and explicitly stated, such reasoning resolves itself into some form of syllogism. It is not, as sometimes stated, *a* mode of reasoning, but *the* mode which all reasoning, except such as is direct and immediate, tends to assume. Not always, indeed, is this reasoning fully drawn out and explicitly stated, but all valid reasoning admits of being thus stated; nay, it is not, as to form at least, complete until it is so expressed.

Not always syllogistically expressed. — In ordinary conversation, and even in public address, we omit many intermediate steps in the trains and processes of our arguments, for the reason that their statement is not essential to our being understood, the hearer's mind supplying, for itself, the connecting links as we proceed; just as in speaking or writing, we make many abbreviations, drop out some letters and syllables here and there, in our hasty utterance, and yet all such short-hand processes imply and are based upon the full form; and it would be as correct and as reasonable to say that the fully written or fully spoken word is merely *a* mode of speaking and writing, which, when the grammarian and rhetorician come into contact with common people, they lay aside for the ordinary forms of speech, as to say that syllogism is merely *a* mode of reasoning, which the logician lays aside when he comes out of his study, and reasons with other men.

Chief Value of the Syllogism. — The chief use of the syllogism, I apprehend, however, to be, not in presenting a train of argument for the purpose of convincing and persuading others; for the laws of thought do not require us in such a case to state every thing that is even essential to the argument, but only so much as shall clearly indicate our meaning, and enable the hearer or reader to follow us; but rather in testing the soundness or detecting the unsoundness of an argument, whether our own, or that of an opponent. For this purpose, an acquaintance with the forms and laws of syllogism may be of great service to the writer and to the orator.

Objection to the Syllogism. — But it is objected to the syllogism that it is of no value in the discovery and establishment of truth, inasmuch as, by the very laws of the syllogism, there can be nothing more in the conclusion than was assumed in the premises. There is, and can be, in this way, no progress from the known to the unknown. The very construction of the syllogism, it is said, involves a *petitio principii.* When I say, All men are mortal; Socrates is a man; therefore, Socrates is mortal; the major premiss, it is said, affirms the very thing to be proved; that Socrates is mortal is virtually affirmed in the proposition that *all* men are so. Either, then, the syllogism proves nothing which was not known before, or else the general proposition, with which it sets out, is unwarranted, as asserting more than we know to be true, and, in that case, the conclusion is equally unreliable; in either case nothing is gained by the process; the syllogism is worthless.

Lies equally against all reasoning. — This objection, if valid against the syllogism, is valid against and overthrows not the syllogism merely, but all reasoning of whatever kind, and in whatever form. It is an objection which really applies, not to the form which an argument may happen to assume, but to the essential nature of reasoning itself. As was shown in discussing the nature of the reasoning process, all reasoning is, in its nature, essentially analytic. It is the evolution of a truth that lies involved in some already admitted truth. It simply develops, draws out, what was therein contained. Its starting-point must always be some admitted position, its conclusions must always be some inevitable necessary consequence of that admission. The mortality of Socrates is, indeed, involved and contained in the general proposition which affirms the mortality of all men, and so, also, is every inferred truth contained in that from which it is inferred.

Conclusion not affirmed in the Premiss. — But while *contained*, it is not *affirmed*, in the premiss. To say that all men are mortal, is not to say that Socrates is so, but only to say what implies that. The conclusion which draws out and affirms what was involved, but not affirmed, in the premiss, is an advance in the order of thought, a step of progress, and not merely an idle repetition, and the syllogism, as a whole, moves the mind onward from the starting-point to a position not otherwise explicitly and positively reached. It is a movement onward, and not merely a rotation of the wheel about its own axis.

The Form accidental. — In so far as the objection of *petitio principii* relates, not to the *nature* of reasoning, but only to its *form*, this is entirely a matter of accident, and does not pertain to the syllogism as such. As was shown in treating of the different forms of syllogism, the order of the propositions is not essential. We may, if we like, state the conclusion first, and then the reasons, as, All A is C, for all A is B, and all B is C; or we may state the same thing in a different form, as, A and B are equal; B and C are equal; therefore, A and C are equal. Both are syllogisms, the former *analytic*, the latter *unfigured*, but to neither does the objection of *petitio principii* apply so far as regards the mere form of statement. Nor does it apply to that form of syllogism in which the major premiss is a singular proposition, as, *e. g.*, Cæsar was fortunate; Cæsar was a tyrant; therefore, a tyrant may be fortunate. Here the subject of the conclusion is not formally contained in that of the major premiss, as Socrates is contained in the expression, all men, a part of the whole.

Objection inapplicable to the inductive Syllogism. — Nor does the objection apply again to the *inductive* syllogism, in which the conclusion is more comprehensive than the premiss. The objection applies, in fact, only to the deductive syllogism, and to that only in its synthetic form, and to that only as figured, and as presenting, in its major premiss, other than a singular proposition.

Major Premiss, whence derived. — But whence, it may still be asked, comes the general proposition which every deductive syllogism contains, whether analytic or synthetic, the proposition *e. g.*, that all men are mortal? Whether this be stated before or after the conclusion is a mere matter of form; but what is our authority for stating such a proposition at all? How do we know that which is here affirmed?

I reply, it is a truth reached by previous induction. Every deduction implies previous induction. I observe the mortality of individuals, *x*, *y*, *z*. I find no exceptions. My observation extends to a great number of cases, insomuch that I am authorized to take those cases as fairly representing the whole class to which they belong. I conclude, therefore, that what I have observed of the many is true of the whole. So comes the general proposition, All men are mortal.

Authority for this Belief. — But what reason have I to believe that what is true of the many is true of the whole; and how do I know this? I reply, I do not know it by observation, nor by demonstration; my belief of it rests upon, and resolves itself into, that general law or constitution of the mind according to which I am led to expect, under like circumstances, like results, in other words, that nature acts uniformly. This is my warrant, and my only warrant, for the inference, that what I have observed in many cases is true in others that I have not observed.

A Difficulty suggested. — But in what manner, now, shall this mere belief of mine, for it is nothing more, come to take its place as a general proposition, as positive categorical affirmation in the syllogism whose major premiss reads, All men are mortal?

A law of the mind may be a sufficient explanation of my belief; but the science of syllogisms cannot take cognizance of laws of the mind, as such, and has nothing to do with beliefs, but is concerned only with the *forms* in which an argument shall be presented. Those forms must be conclusive. How shall I convert, then, my conjecture, my plausible belief, in the present case, into that general positive affirmation which alone will answer the demands of the syllogism?

The Process explained. — The process is this: The precise result of my observation stands thus — *x*, *y*, *z*, are mortal. But I know that *x*, *y*, *z*, are so numerous as fairly to represent the class to which they belong. On the strength of this position, the inductive syllogism takes its stand, and overlooking the fact that there are some cases which have not fallen under my observation, *positively affirms* what I only *believe* and *presume* to be true, and the argument then reads, *x*, *y*, *z*, are mortal. But *x*, *y*, *z*, are all men, therefore, all men are mortal.

The general proposition thus reached by induction becomes, in turn, the major premiss of the deductive syllogism, which concludes, from the mortality of all men, that of Socrates in particular.

Position of Mill. — An able and ingenious writer, Mr. Mill, in his treatise on logic, takes the ground that we have no need to embody the result of our observations in the form of a general proposition, from which again to descend to the particular conclusion, but that, dispensing with the general proposition altogether, and with the syllogism of every kind and form, we may, and virtually do, reason directly from one particular instance to another, as, *e. g.*, *x*, *y*, *z*, are mortal; therefore, *f*, *g*, *h*, are so. "If from our experience of John, Thomas, etc., who were once living, but are now dead, we are entitled to conclude that all human beings are mortal, we might surely, without any logical inconsequence, have concluded at once, from those instances, that the Duke of Wellington is mortal. The mortality of

John, Thomas, and company, is, after all, the whole evidence we have of the mortality of the Duke of Wellington. Not one iota is added to the proof by interpolating a general proposition." Our earliest inferences, he contends, are precisely of this sort. The child burning his fingers, reasons thus: "That fire burnt me, therefore this will." He does not generalize, "All fire burns; this is fire; therefore, this will burn." The only use of a general proposition, Mill contends, is simply to furnish collateral security for the cor rectness of our inference.

Remarks upon this View. — This view sweeps away at once, and forever, all mediate reasoning, and shuts us up to the narrow limits of such inference alone as proceeds from a given instance directly to a conclusion therefrom. No doubt we do sometimes reason thus. But it is a reasoning, the conclusiveness of which is not, and cannot be made, apparent by any form of statement. If called in question, we can only say, I think so, or, I believe so. The mortality of John does not prove the mortality of Thomas. It may not even render it probable; it is only when I have observed such and so many cases as to leave no reasonable doubt that the property in question is *a law of the class as such*, and *not a mere accident of the individual*, that I am really warranted in the belief that any individual, not as yet observed, will come under the same law, because belonging to the same class. To reason in this way is to generalize; whatever process stops short of this, stops so far short of any and all conclusive evidence of the truth of what it affirms.

VIII. Historical Sketch of the Science of Logic.

Indian Logic earlier than that of Aristotle. — It is of the Greek logic, that of Aristotle, that we usually speak when we have occasion to refer to this science. It is usually attributed to Aristotle, indeed, as his peculiar glory, that he should at once have originated, and brought to perfection, a science which, for more than two thousand years, has received few alterations, found few minds capable of suggesting improvements. Recent labors of Orientalists have, however, brought to light the fact that in India, long before the palmy days of Grecian philosophy, logic was pursued with vigor as a study and science. The Nyâya of Gotama holds, in the Indian systems of philosophy, much the same place that the Organon of Aristotle holds with us. The two, however, are quite independent of each other. Aristotle was no disciple of Gotama.

Aristotle's Logic not perfect. — Nor, on the other hand, was the logic of Aristotle by any means perfect, as it is often represented. Its imperfections are many, and have been, for the most part, faithfully copied by his disciples.

Aristotle the first Greek Logician. — Previous to Aristotle there had been nothing worthy the name of science in this department of philosophy. The Sophists had made some attempts at logic, but of no great value. Plato had not devoted much attention to it. Aristotle himself says, in the close of his Organon, that he had worked without models or predecessors to guide him.

Subsequent Writers. — The work of Aristotle is in six parts, the first four treating of logic pure, the remaining two of its application. The school of Aristotle carried the cultivation and study of logic to a high degree. Theophrastus and Eudemus labored assiduously as commentators on their master, but made no change in the essential principles of the system. The Stoics, however, gave logic more attention and honor, more time and care, than did any other of the rival schools of philosophy. They sought to enlarge its boundaries and make it an instrument for the discovery of truth. It held the first place in their system, ethics and physics ranking after it.

St. Hilaire is wrong in saying that with Epicurus logic was of little consideration, that sensation was the source and criterion of thought with that school. The Epicurean logic was a peculiar system, differing from the Aristotelian, and very little known in the subsequent centuries.

In Alexandria the logic of Aristotle was in great honor, and had numerous commentators in the first centuries of the Christian era.

Introduced into Rome.—For a time the original works of Aristotle were lost. They lay buried in an obscure retreat whither they had been carried for safe preservation, and no one knew what they were. Sylla, capturing the city, brought them to Rome, where they were discovered to be the works of the great master, and Cicero gives them, with some labor and learning, to the public. But the Roman mind never mastered the logic of Aristotle. In all Roman philosophy, says St. Hilaire, there is scarcely a logician worthy of the name.

For several centuries, if not in Rome, yet in Alexandria and Athens, in Greece and in Egypt, the logic of Aristotle continued to be assiduously cultivated.

Logic in the Middle Ages. — It was in the middle ages, however, that logic received its chief cultivation and its highest honors. Aristotle was for some six centuries almost the only teacher of the human mind, and the Organon was the foundation of his knowledge. Nor during the irruption of the northern hordes, and the revolutions of society, and empire, and human manners, which followed, did the philosophy and logic of Aristotle pass out of sight or out of mind. It seemed impossible for any revolution of empire or of time to shake its foundations or break its sceptre over the human mind. In the seventh century, Isidore of Seville, and Bede the Venerable, gave it their labors and renown. In the eighth, Alcuin introduced it into the court of Charlemagne. In the twelfth, Abelard, and the controversy between the Realists and Nominalists, gave this science still more importance.

Logic in the Arabian Schools. — Meanwhile, the Mohammedans had been in advance of the Christians in the study of this science. The Arabs had inherited the learning of antiquity, and had carried the cultivation of the peripatetic philosophy to a high degree of perfection more than a century before it had received the homage of the West. From Arabia it passed, with the march of conquest, into Spain, and some of the ablest commentators Europe has produced, on the works of Aristotle, have been the Moors of Spain.

Continuance of Aristotle's Dominion.—The Crusades tended only to enlarge the sphere of this influence. Such men as Albert the Great, and Thomas Aquinas, became, in the thirteenth century, expounders of Aristotle. Not till the sixteenth century did this long dominion over the human mind show symptoms of decadence.

The Reformers.—Luther, among the Protestant reformers, sought to banish logic from the schools; but it was retained, and in the Protestant universities was still professed.

Attacks upon Aristotle.—It now became the fashion, however, in certain quarters, especially among the mystics in the Catholic communion, to decry Aristotle, and each original genius took this way to show his independence. Ramus is noted among these. Bacon followed in this track, and did little more than repeat the invectives of his predecessors. He attempted to set aside the syllogism, and put in its place induction.

Induction, however, in some form, is as old as the syllogism. From Plato and Aristotle downward, a thousand philosophers had availed themselves of this method of reasoning, and had also stated and defended it.

The Moderns.—From Bacon and Descartes till our day logic has been in process of decadence. Locke condemns it Reid and the Scotch school ridicule its pretensions. Kant and Hegel, on the other hand, give it a due place in their systems—the latter especially; while in France, it has admirers in St. Hilaire, Cousin, and others of like genius; and in Edinburgh, the great Hamilton devoted to it the powers of his unrivalled intellect.

Logic of Hamilton. — As no writer, since the days of Aristotle, has done more to complete and perfect the science of reasoning, than Sir William Hamilton, it seems due that even so brief a sketch of the history of logic as the present, should indicate, at least, the more important changes which his system introduces. Whatever may be thought of some of his views and proposed reforms in this ancient science and sanctuary of past learning, it is not too much to say, that no writer on logic can henceforth present a claim to be considered, who has not, at least, thoroughly mastered and carefully weighed these views and proposed changes, even if he do not adopt them. They are, moreover, for the most part, changes so obviously demanded in order to the completeness of the science, and so thorough-going withal, that they are destined, it would seem, to be sooner or later adopted, and if adopted, to work a radical change in the whole structure of this ancient and time-honored science.

I shall attempt nothing more, in this connection, than, in the briefest manner, to enumerate some of the more important of these improvements.

Assigns Induction its true Place. — Hamilton is the first, so far as I know, to elevate to its true place the inductive method of reasoning, making it coördinate with the deductive, and assigning its true character and value as a form of syllogism.

Recognizes the analytic Syllogism. — He is the first to bring to notice the claims of the *analytic* syllogism to a distinctive place and recognition in logic; a form of reasoning, which, however natural and necessary, and in use almost universal, had been strangely overlooked by logicians from Aristotle down.

Rejects Modality. — He strenuously and consistently rejects the modality of the proposition and the syllogism, on the ground that logic is not concerned with the character of the matter, whether it be true or false, necessary or contingent, but only with the form of statement, and consequently, all distinctions founded on the truth or falsity, the necessity or contingence of the matter, are utterly irrelevant to the science — a principle admitted by others, but not previously carried out to its true results.

Doctrine of Figure. — He shows that the figure of the syllogism is a matter accidental, rather than essential, that it may be even entirely *unfigured;* abolishes the fourth figure as superfluous; and sets aside, as quite useless and unnecessary, the old laborious processes of reducing and connecting the several figures to the first.

Rejects hypothetical Syllogism. — He throws out of the syllogism entirely, the so-called *hypothetical* forms, both conjunctive and disjunctive, as reducible to *immediate* inference, and not, therefore, to be included under syllogistic reasoning, which is always mediate.

The single Canon. — He reduces the several laws and canons of the figured syllogism to a single comprehensive canon.

Quantification of the Predicate. — But the most important discovery made by Hamilton in this science, is the quantification of the predicate. The predicate is always a given quantity in relation to the subject, and that quantity should be stated. This, logicians have always overlooked, quantifying only the subject, as, All men, Some men, etc., but never the predicate. Fully quantified, the proposition reads, All man is *some* animal, no animal, etc., *i. e.*, some sort or species of animal. This doubles the number of possible propositions, giving eight in place of four, and gives a corresponding increase in the number of words. These eight propositions are shown to be, not only possible, but admissible and valid. They are thus enumerated and named:

	AFFIRMATIVE.	NEGATIVE.
I. *Toto-total:*	All A is all B.	Any A is not any B.
II. *Toto-partial:*	All A is some B.	Any A is not some B.
III. *Parti-total:*	Some A is all B.	Some A is not any B.
IV. *Parti-partial:*	Some A is some B.	Some A is not some B.

Reference. — For a more full and exact account of Hamilton's system, the reader is referred to the article on logic in the volume of *Discussions on Philosophy and Literature*, by Sir W. Hamilton; also, to "*An Essay on the New Analytic of Logical Forms*," by Thomas Spencer Baynes, L. L. B. On the history of logic in general, see *Dictionnaire des Sciences Philosophiques* — Article *Logique*, by Barthèleme St. Hilaire, Professor of Philosophy to the College of France, member of the Institute, etc., etc.; also, Blakey's *History of Logic*. The *Memoir* of St. Hilaire, on the logic of Aristotle, is one of the best works of modern times on the subject of which it treats.

INTELLECTUAL FACULTIES.

PART FOURTH.

THE INTUITIVE POWER.

INTUITIVE POWER.

CHAPTER I.

EXISTENCE AND NATURE OF THE INTUITIVE FACULTY.

Office of this Power. — In our analysis of the powers of the mind, one was described as having for its office the conception of truths that lie apart from the region and domain of sense — first principles and primary ideas, fundamental to, and presupposed in, the operations of the understanding, yet not directly furnished by sense. They are awakened in the mind on occasion of sensible experience, but it is not sensible experience which produces them. On the contrary, they spring up in the mind as by intuition, whenever the fitting occasion is presented. We must attribute their origin to a special power of the mind by virtue of which, under appropriate circumstances, it conceives the truths and ideas to which we refer. This power we have termed the *originative* or *intuitive* faculty.

Specific Character. — In its specific character and function it is quite distinct from any of the faculties as yet considered It does not, like the presentative power, bring before us, in direct cognizance, sensible objects; nor does it, like the representative faculty, replace those objects to thought, in their absence. It neither presents, nor represents, any object whatever. It forms no picture of any thing to the mind's eye. It is a power of simple conception; and yet it differs in an important sense from the other conceptive powers, and that is, that it is not *reflective* but intuitive in its action. Its data are conceptions, but conceptions necessary and intuitive, seen at a glance, not the results of the reflective and discursive process. These data are ideas of reason, rather than notions of the understanding, or processes of reflection. There is no sensible object corresponding to these ideas. We do not see, or hear, or feel, or by any means cognize, any thing of the sort; nor can we form a picture, or represent to ourselves any such thing as, *e.g.*, time, or space, or substance, or cause, and the like. They are conceptions of the mind, and yet we conceive of them as *realities*. We cannot think them the mere creations and figments of the brain. And in this respect, again, they differ from the notions of the understanding — those classes and genera which we know to be the mere creations of the mind.

Existence of such a Faculty. — If any are disposed to doubt the existence of the faculty under consideration, as a distinct power of the mind, we have only to ask, whence come these ideas? They are given, not by perception, evidently, nor by memory, nor by imagination, for they fall not within the sphere of any of these faculties, that is the sphere of sense. They relate not to the sensible, but to the super-sensible.

Nor are they the result of abstraction, as might at first appear. Particular instances being given, certain times, certain spaces, certain substances, certain instances of right and wrong conduct — it is the province of the faculty now named, to form, from these concrete ideas, the abstract notions of time, space, etc. But whence comes, in the first instance, the concrete idea? Whence comes the notion of *a* time, *a* space, *a* substance, *a* cause, *a* right or wrong act? Abstraction cannot give these. Manifestly, however, we have a faculty of forming such conceptions, of perceiving such truths and realities; and as manifestly, it is a faculty distinct from any hitherto considered. There are such realities as time, space, substance, cause, right and wrong, etc.

The mind takes cognizance of them as such, knows them, and knows them to be realities; has, therefore, the faculty of knowing such truths. We may call it, if we please, the faculty of original and intuitive conception.

Generally admitted. — The existence of ideas not directly furnished by sense or experience, and not given by the faculties whose office it is to deal with objects of sense, is a doctrine now generally admitted by the most eminent philosophers. Nor is it a doctrine peculiar to any one school. Under different names it is the doctrine substantially of Reid, Stewart, Brown, Price, among English metaphysicians; Kant and his disciples in Germany; Cousin, Jouffroy and others in France. It is denied by Hobbes, Condillac, Gassendi, and others of that class who trace all our ideas to sense as their ultimate source and parentage.

Opinion of Locke. — The position of Locke respecting this matter, has been the subject of much controversy. By a certain class of writers he has been regarded as denying the existence of any and all ideas not derived from sense, and has been classed with the school of Hobbes, Condillac, etc. His philosophy has been regarded by many as of doubtful and dangerous tendency, as leading to the denial of all truth and knowledge not within the narrow domain of sense, and so conducting to materialism and skepticism. This can by no means be fairly charged upon him, nor upon his philosophy. He held no such views, nor are they implied or contained in his doctrine. Locke, indeed, takes the ground that all our ideas may be traced ultimately to one of two sources, sensation or reflection; the one taking cognizance of external objects, the other of our own mental operations: and that, whatever other knowledge we have, not given directly by these faculties, is produced by adding, repeating, and variously combining, in our own minds, the simple ideas derived from these sources. In this process, however, of adding, combining, etc., he really includes what we prefer to designate as a separate faculty of the mind, and by another name. He distinctly recognizes the existence of the ideas which we attribute to this faculty — ideas of space, power, etc. — and gives a clear, and for the most part correct account of their origin. The mind, he says, observes what passes without — the changes there occurring; it reflects also on what passes within — the changes of its own ideas and purposes; it concludes that like changes will be produced in the same things, under the same circumstances, in future; it considers the possibility of effecting such changes, and so comes by the idea of *power*. In this Locke really includes essentially what we mean by suggestion or original conception. Experience, it is universally admitted, furnishes the occasion, suggests the idea, must precede as the indispensable condition of the mind's having that idea, and is, at least in this sense, the source of it, that it suggests the idea to the mind. All this, Locke fully admits, while, at the same time, he fails to draw the dividing line clearly between the ideas of sense and those in question.

Objections to the term Suggestion. — The name original suggestion has been commonly applied, of late, especially in this country, to designate the faculty now under consideration. It is so used by Professor Upham, and by Dr. Wayland. It is liable, however, to serious objections. The term suggestion does not seem to me to express the peculiar characteristic, the distinctive element and office of this faculty. It is not peculiar to the ideas now in question, that they are *suggested* to the mind; many other ideas, all ideas, in fact, are suggested by something. This class of our thoughts, therefore, is no more entitled to that name than any other class. Nor is it peculiar to this class that they are *original* suggestions. The mind has many other equally original ideas that are likewise suggestions from things without, or from its own operations — mere fancies many of them, imaginations. We need to distinguish, in this case, the merely fanciful, the ideal, from the real. The terms intuitive and intuition, while they imply the reality of the thing perceived, indicate, also, the immediateness of the process.

More serious Objection. — But there is a still further and more serious objection to the term suggestion as thus employed. The word does not, and cannot, with propriety, be made to denote what is now intended. It has a transitive significance, and cannot be made to denote a purely subjective process. Objects external suggest certain ideas to my mind. I suggest ideas to other minds. The faculty of suggestion lies, properly, not with the mind that receives the suggestion, but with the mind or object that gives it. But when we say the mind has the faculty of original suggestion, we do not mean that it has the power of suggesting original ideas to other minds; we refer to that power of the mind by which, in virtue of its constitution, certain ideas, not strictly derived from sense, are awakened in it when the occasion presents itself. We intend not a power of suggesting, but rather of receiving suggestions, a power of *conceiving* ideas, a power of original and intuitive conceptions. To say that the mind suggests to itself ideas of space, time, etc., is a singular use of terms. I understand what is meant by suggesting ideas to others, and what it is to receive suggestions from others, and to have ideas suggested by events, occurrences and objects without, and how one thought may, by some law of association, suggest another. But how the mind suggests ideas to *itself*, is not so clear. A man, in a fit of abstraction, talks to himself, but whether he suggests ideas to himself in that way, so that he finds his own conversation instructive and profitable, may admit of question. The truth is, the idea is suggested, not *by* the mind, but *to* the mind—suggested from without. The mind has the power of conceiving certain ideas, which are awakened or excited in it by the occasion which presents itself. To call this faculty a faculty of suggestion, is simply a misnomer.

The true Doctrine. — All we can truly say, is, that the idea is awakened or called up in the mind when the occasion presents, is suggested *to* it, not by it, suggested by the occasion, and not by the mind itself. The mind has the idea within, has, moreover, the faculty of *conceiving* the idea, is so constituted, that, under certain circumstances, in view of what it observes without, or is conscious of within, the given idea is naturally and universally awakened in it; but the *source* of the suggestion lies not within the mind itself, and is not to be confounded with the mind's faculty of conception.

Use of the term by Reid and others.—Dr. Reid has been referred to as authority for the use of the word suggestion to denote the faculty in question. Dr. Reid makes use of the word, but not in the sense now intended, not to denote a specific faculty of the mind, coördinate with perception, memory, imagination, etc., not, in fact, as a faculty at all. He refers to the well known fact, that ideas are suggested to the mind by objects and events without, and by the sensations thus awakened; as, *e. g.*, a certain sound suggests the passing of a coach in the street. So, also, one idea or sensation will suggest another. He uses the term to denote the suggestion of one thing *to* the mind *by* another thing, and not to denote a power in the mind of suggesting things to itself. This is the correct use, and was not original with Reid. Berkley had used the term in the same way before him. Locke had used the word *excited*, in the same sense. The idea expressed by these terms, and the use of the same or similar terms by which to express it, may be traced back as far, at least, as to the Christian Fathers. St. Augustine so uses it. Reid expressly applies the term to the perception of external objects, as, *e. g.*, certain sensations suggest the notion of extension and space. This is correct use.

The Facts in the Case.—The truth is, things exist thus and thus, and we are constituted with reference to them as thus existing. Sense and experience inform us of these existences and realities. Some of them are objects of direct perception by the senses, as matter and its qualities. Some of them are not directly objects of perception, but are suggested to the mind by the operations of sense, and are intuitively perceived by the mind, and recognized as truths and realities when thus suggested, as time, space, substance, cause, the right, the wrong, the beautiful, etc.

The mind has the faculty of receiving and recognizing such truths and realities as thus suggested; and this faculty we call the power of *original and intuitive conception.*

These Ideas of internal Origin, in what Sense. — It has been customary of late, especially in our country, to speak of the class of ideas now referred to as of *internal origin*, in distinction from other ideas, derived more directly from sense, and which are consequently designated as of external origin. As it is desirable to be exact in our use of terms, it may be well to inquire in what sense any of our ideas are of external, and in what sense of internal origin, and wherein the ideas, now under consideration, differ from any others in respect to their source.

Ideas of external Origin. — A large class of our ideas evidently relate to objects of sense, objects external and material, of which we take cognizance through the senses. Such ideas may be said to be of external origin, inasmuch as they relate to things without, and are dependent on the external object as the indispensable condition of their development. Were it not for the external object producing the sensation of color or of hardness, I should not have the idea of redness or of hardness; were it not for the external object resisting my movements, I should not get the idea of externality. The idea is, in these cases, dependent on, and limited by, the sensation or the perception. They correspond as shadow and substance. The idea of resistance, and the perception of it, the idea of sound or color, and the sensation of it, are coëxtensive, synchronous, and, as to contents, identical.

These, in a Sense, internal. — In another sense, however,

even these ideas are of internal origin, that is, they are the mind's own ideas; they spring up in the mind, and not out of it; they are, as ideas, strictly internal states, affections, acts of the mind itself. Take away intelligence, reason, the light divine, from the soul of man, and the external objects may exist as before, and produce the same effect on the organs of sense, but the ideas no longer follow. The physical organs of the idiot are affected in the same way by external objects as those of any other person, but he gets not the same ideas. These, it is the office of the mind to produce and fashion for itself out of the occasion and material furnished by sense. And this is as true of ideas relating to external objects as to any other.

Sensation an internal Affection. — It may even be said of this class of ideas, that their *suggestion* is of internal origin. The immediate occasion of the mind's having the idea of extension, weight, hardness, color, etc., is not the existence of the object itself, possessing such and such qualities, but the impression produced by the object and its qualities on the sense; in other words, the sensation awakened in us. This it is which awakens and calls forth in the mind the idea of the external object. Were there, for any reason, no sensation, then the objects might exist as now, but we should have no idea of them. But sensation is an internal affection, revealed by consciousness, and the ideas awakened by it and dependent on it, are immediately of internal origin, though mediately dependent on some preceding external condition and occasion.

Ideas of internal Origin. — If we examine, now, the ideas of internal origin, so called, furnished by the faculty of original and intuitive conception, we find that, while they do not directly relate to objects of sense external and material, they nevertheless depend, in like manner, on some preceding operation of sense as the occasion of their development. Observation of what goes on without, or consciousness of what goes on within furnishes the occasion, as all admit, on which these ideas are awakened in the mind. The idea of time, *e. g.*, is connected with the succession of events, external or internal — things without and thought and feeling within following each other — which succession is matter of observation or of consciousness. The idea of space is connected with the observation or sensation of body as extended. The idea of beauty and deformity is awakened by the perception of external objects as possessing certain qualities which we thus designate. The idea of right and wrong in like manner connects with something observed in human conduct. So of all ideas of this class. They are not disconnected with, nor independent of, the appropriate objects of observation and consciousness. These objects must exist, these occasions must be furnished, as the *indispensable condition* of the existence of the idea in the mind. Dispense with the succession of events or the observation of it, and you dispense with the idea of time in the human mind.

Conclusion. — So far as regards the origin of the ideas in question, it is not easy to draw a dividing line, then, between the two classes, marking the one as *external*, the other as *internal.* Both are of external origin, and equally so, in this sense — that they both depend, and equally depend, on some previous exercise of sense as the occasion and condition of their development. Both are of internal origin, in another sense — that they are both awakened in the mind — are both the product of its own activity.

Difference lies in what. — The difference is not so much that of externality or internality of origin, as it is a difference of character. The one relates to objects of sense, which can be seen, heard, felt; the other to matters not less real, not less obvious, but of which sense does not take direct cognizance. In either case they spring from the constitution and laws of the mind. Such is my constitution that external and material objects, affecting my senses, furnish me ideas relating to such objects. And such is my constitution that certain relations and qualities of things not directly cognizable by sense, and certain realities and facts of an æsthetic and moral nature, likewise impress my mind, and thus awaken in me the idea of such relations and realities. The objects, the relations, the realities, exist, they are perceived by the mind, and thus the first idea of them is obtained. Color exists, and the eye is so constituted as to be able to perceive it, and thus the idea of color is awakened in the mind. So right and wrong exist, and the mind is so constituted as to be able to perceive and recognize their existence, and thus the idea of right is awakened in the mind. The faculty we call perception in the one case, original conception in the other.

CHAPTER II.

TRUTHS AND CONCEPTIONS FURNISHED BY THIS FACULTY.

§ I. — Primary Truths.

Primary Truths and Primary Ideas as distinguished.— The faculty in question may be regarded as the source of primary beliefs, truths, cognitions, intuitively *perceived*, and also of primary and original conceptions, notions, ideas, also intuitively *conceived.*

The difference between a conception or idea, and a belief or truth, is obvious. The notion of existence, and the knowledge or belief that I, myself, exist, are clearly distinguishable. The idea of cause, and the conviction that every event has a cause, are distinct mental states. The one is a primitive and intuitive conception, the other a primitive and intuitive truth. Every primary truth involves a primitive and original conception.

Existence of first Truths. — All science and all reasoning depend ultimately on certain first truths or principles, not learned by experience, but prior to it, the evidence and certainty of which lie back of all reasoning and all experience. Take away these elementary truths, and neither science nor reasoning are longer possible, for want of a beginning and foundation. Every proposition which carries evidence with it, either contains that evidence in itself, or derives it from some other proposition on which it depends. And the same is true of this other proposition, and so on forever, until we come, at last, to some proposition which depends on no other, but is self-evident, a first truth or principle. Whence come these first principles? Not of course from experience, for they are involved in and essential to all experience. They are native or *à priori* convictions of the mind, instinctive and intuitive judgments.

Existence of first Truths admitted.—The existence of first truths or principles, as the basis of all acquired knowledge, has been very generally admitted by philosophers. They have designated these elementary principles, however, by widely different appellations. By some, they have been termed *instinctive* beliefs, cognitions, judgments, etc., an appellation mentioned by Hamilton as employed by a very great number of writers from Cicero downward, including, among the rest, Scaliger, Bacon, Descartes, Pascal, Leibnitz, Hume, Reid, Stewart, Jacobi. Others, again, have termed them *à priori* or *transcendental* principles, cognitions, judgments, etc., as being prior to experience, and transcending the knowledge derived from sense. So Kant and his school termed them. By the Scotch writers they have been termed, also, principles of *common sense*, in place of which expression Stewart prefers the title, *fundamental laws of human belief.*

Criteria of primary Truths.—It becomes an important inquiry, in what manner we may recognize and distinguish first truths from all others. Besides common consent, or universality of belief on the part of those who have arrived at years of discretion, *Buffier* relies, also, upon the following, as criteria of first principles; that they are such truths as can neither be defended nor attacked by any propositions, either more manifest or more certain than themselves; and that their practical influence extends even to those who would deny them. Reid gives, among other criteria, the following: consent of ages and nations; the absurdity of the opposite; early appearance in the mind, prior to education and reasoning; practical necessity to the conduct and concerns of life. *Hamilton* gives the following as tests or criteria of first truths: 1. *Incomprehensibilty.* — We comprehend that the thing is, but not *how* or *why* it is. 2. *Simplicity.* — If the cognition or belief can be resolved into several cognitions or beliefs, it is complex, and so, no longer original. 3. *Necessity, and consequent universality.* — If necessary, it is universal, and if absolutely universal, then it must be necessary. 4. *Comparative evidence and certainty.*

Summary of Criteria. — The following may be regarded as a summary of the more important criteria by which to distinguish primary truths from all others.

a. As first truths, or primary data of intellegence, they are, of course, not derived from observation or experience, but are prior and necessary to such experience.

b. They are *simple* truths, not resolvable into some prior and comprehending truth from which they may be deduced.

c. As simple truths, they *do not admit of proof*, there being nothing more certain which can be brought in evidence of them.

d. While they do not admit of proof, *the denial of them involves us in absurdity.*

e. Accordingly, as simple, and as self-evident, they are universally admitted.

Enumeration of some of the Truths usually regarded as primary. — Different writers have included some more, some fewer, of these first principles in their list; while no one has professed, so far as I am aware, to give a complete enumeration of them. Such an enumeration, if it were possible, would be of great service in philosophy. The following have been generally included among primary truths by those who have attempted any specification, viz.; our personal existence, our personal identity, the existence of efficient causes, the existence of the material world, the uniformity of nature; to which would be added, by others, the reliability of memory, and of our natural faculties generally, and personal freedom or power over our own actions and volitions.

Correctness of this Enumeration. — That the truths now specified are in some sense primary, that they are generally admitted and acted upon, among men, without process of reasoning, and that, when stated, they command the universal and instant assent of even the untaught and unreflecting mind, there can be little doubt. Whether, in all cases, however, they come strictly under the rules and criteria now given; whether, for example, our own existence and identity are primary data of consciousness; or whether, on the contrary, they are not *inferred* from the existence of those thoughts and feelings of which we are directly conscious, as, for example, in the famous argument of Descartes, *Cogito, ergo sum*, may admit of question.

§ II. — Intuitive Conceptions.

Of the results or operations of the faculty under consideration, we have considered, as yet, only that class which may be designated as primary *truths*, in distinction from primitive or intuitive *conceptions*. To this latter class let us now direct our attention.

Proposed consideration of some of the more important. — Without undertaking to give a complete list of our original or intuitive conceptions, there are certain of the more important, which seem to require specific consideration. Such are the ideas of space, time, identity, cause, the beautiful, the right — ideas difficult to define and explain, but, on that account, requiring the more careful investigation. Let us, then, take up these conceptions one by one, and inquire more particularly into their nature.

I. Space.

Subjective View. — What is space? Is it a mere idea, a mere conception of the mind, or has it reality? This is a question which has much perplexed philosophers. Kant and his school regard both time and space as merely subjective, mere conceptions or forms which the mind imposes upon outward things, having no reality, save as conceptions, or laws of thought.

Opposite View. — On the other hand, if we make space a reality, and not a mere conception, what is it, and where is it? Not matter, and yet real, a something which exists, distinct from matter, and yet not mind. Pressed with these difficulties, some distinguished and acute writers have resolved time and space into qualities of the one infinite and absolute Being, the divine mind. Such was the view of Clarke and Newton, a view favored also by a recent French writer of some note — C. H. Bernard, Professor of Philosophy in the Lycée Bonaparte.

A middle Ground. — These must be regarded as, on either hand, extreme views. But is there a middle ground possible or conceivable? Let us see. What, then, is the simple idea of space? What mean we by that word?

Idea of Space. — When we contemplate any material object, any existence of which the senses can take cognizance, we are cognizant of it as *extended, i. e., occupying space*, nor can we possibly conceive of it as otherwise. The idea of space, then, is involved in the very idea of extended substance, or material existence, given along with it, impossible to be separated from it. We may regard it, therefore, as *the condition or postulate of being, considered as material existence*, *posseesing extension*, etc. The idea of it is essential to the idea of matter, the reality of it to the reality of matter; for if there were no space, there could be no extension in space, and, without extension, no matter.

Not a mere Conception. — Is space, then, a mere conception of the mind, merely subjective? Unquestionably not. It is not, indeed, a *substance* or *entity*, it has nc *being*. It is not matter, for it is, itself, the *condition* of matter; it is not spirit, for then it were intelligent. It is not an *existence*, then, strictly speaking, not a thing created, nor is it in the power of deity either to create or to annihilate it, for creation and annihilation relate only to *existence*. And yet space is a *reality*, and not a *mere conception* of the mind. For, if so, then were there no longer any mind to conceive it, there would be no longer any space; if no mind to think, then no thought. Were the whole race of intelligent beings, then, to be blotted out of existence, and all things else to remain as now, space would be gone, while, yet, matter would exist, extension — worlds moving on as before. Extension in what, motion in what? Not in space, for that is no longer extant; defunct, rather, with the last mind whose expiring torch went out in the gloom of night. Unless we make *matter*, then, to be also a mere conception of the mind, space is not so. If the one is real, the other is. If one is a mere conception, so is the other; and to this result the school of Kant actually come. Matter, itself, is a subjective phenomenon, a mode of mind, or, rather, if it be any thing more, we have no means of knowing it to be so.

If, on the contrary, as we hold, matter *exists*, and is an object of immediate perception by the senses, then there is such a thing as space also, the *condition* of its existence, a *reality*, though not an *entity*, the idea of it given along with that of matter, the reality of it implied in the reality of matter. Matter *presupposes* it, depends on it as its *sine quâ non.*

It depends on nothing. Were there no matter, there would be none the less space, but only space unoccupied. In that case, the idea of space might never occur to any mind, but the reality would exist just as now. Were all matter and all mind to be blotted out of being, space would still be what it is now.

The Idea, how awakened — How come we by our Idea of Space? — Sense gives us our first knowledge of matter, as extended, etc., and so furnishes the *occasion* on which the idea of space is first awakened in the mind. In this sense, and no other, does it originate in sensation or experience. It is a simple idea, *logically* prior to experience, because the very notion of matter *presupposes* space; yet, *chronologically*, as regards the matter of development in the mind, subsequent to experience and cognizance of matter.

II. TIME.

Idea and Definition. — What we have said of space will enable us better to understand what is the nature of that analogous and kindred conception of the mind, in itself so simple, yet so difficult of definition and explanation — *Time.* The remarks already made, respecting space, will almost equally apply to this subject also.

Space, we defined as the *condition of being, regarded as extended, material.* Time is the *condition of being, regarded as in action, movement, change.*

Sense informs us not only of magnitudes, extensions, material objects, and existences, as around us in nature, but of movements and changes continually taking place among these various existences; as *extension* is essential to those material forms, so *succession* is essential to these movements and changes; they cannot take place, nor be conceived to take place, without it; and as space is involved in, and given along with, the very idea of *extension*, so time is involved in, and given along with, the very idea of *succession.* Time, then, is the condition of action, movement, change, event, as space is of extended and material existence. It is that which is required in order that something should *take place* or occur, just as space is that which is required in order that something should exist as material and having form. As space gives us the question *where*, time gives us the question *when.* It is the place of events, as space is of forms.

Brown's View. — Dr. Brown defines time to be the mere relation of one event to another, as prior and subsequent. It follows, from this view, that if there were no *events*, then no *time*, since the latter is a mere relation subsisting among the former. Is this so? No doubt we derive our *idea* of time from the succession of events; but is time merely an idea, merely a conception, merely a relation, or has it reality out of and aside from our mind's conceiving it, and independent of the series of events that take place in it?

Not a mere Conception. — Like space, it is a law of thought, a conception, and like space it is not a *mere* law of thought, not a mere conception of the mind, not altogether subjective. Nor is it a mere relation of one event to another in succession. It is, on the contrary, *necessary to*, and prior to, all succession and all events. It does not depend on the occurrence of events, but the occurrence of events depends on *it.* As space would still exist were matter annihilated, so time would continue were events to cease. But were time blotted out there could be no succession, no occurrence or event. Time is essential, not to the mere thought or *conception* of events, but to the *possibility* of the thing itself. It is not, then, a mere idea, or conception of the mind, nor a mere relation. It has, in a sense, objectivity and reality, since it is the ground and condition of all continuous active existence, as space is of all extended formal existence, the *sine quâ non*, without which not merely our idea and conception of such existence would vanish, but the thing itself. There could be no such thing as active continuous existence, either of mind or matter, since mind and spirit, as continuous and persistent in any of its moods and phases, much more as passing from one to another of those moods, implies succession. Time is to mind what space is to matter. *Matter* protends in *space*, *mind* in *time*. Time is even less purely subjective than space, for should we say that both matter and space are mere subjective phenomena, mere conceptions, yet even to those very conceptions, to those subjective phenomena, as states of mind, time is essential.

Whence our Idea of Time. — It is with the idea of time as with that of space. *Logically*, time is the condition, à priori, of all experience, because of all continuous existence and all consciousness; but *chronologically* it is à posteriori, *i.e.*, it is, to us, a matter of sensible experience. Sense is the occasion on which the idea of time is first awakened in our minds. We first exist, continue to exist, are conscious of that existence, conscious of succession, thoughts, feelings, sensations, and so we get the idea of time.

Time is necessary to *succession;* yet had there been no succession known to us, we should have had no *idea* of time. We are to distinguish, of course, between our *idea* of time and the thing itself. Locke is incorrect in making the idea of succession prior to that of duration, *in itself considered*, and not merely as regards our knowledge. In this respect, Cousin has ably and justly criticised the philosophy of Locke.

Time a relative Idea. — Looking at time merely as an idea or conception of our own minds, it is simply the perception of *relation;* the relation of passing events to each other, the relation of our various modes and states of being, our thoughts, feelings, etc., to each other, as successive, or to external objects and events, as also successive; the whereabouts, in a word, of one's self, one's present consciousness, in relation to what passes, or has passed, within or without, the relation of the present me to the former me, as regards both the succession of internal or external events.

Hence the mind has only to withdraw itself completely from the consciousness of its former states and of events passing without, and it *loses* altogether its idea of time.

Thus in Sleep. — This we find to be the case in sleep. The thinking goes on; the idea of present self is kept up, but not of self in relation to the objects that are really about us, or to the actual part of its own existence. Whatever relation seems to exist, is imaginary and untrue. We no longer know where we are, nor exactly who we are. The avenues of communication with the external world are shut up, the eye, the ear, etc., are inactive, the spirit withdraws from the outward into itself, as far as this is possible, while the connection of body and mind still continues; its relations to former things and to present things are forgotten and unknown. What is the consequence? We lose all idea of *time;* the moment of falling asleep and of our beginning to awake, if the sleep have been sound, is apparently one and the same moment. The first effect of returning consciousness is to resume the broken thread of time, to find your place again in the series of things, whether it is morning or night, what morning or what night it is; to find yourself, in fact. You had *forgotten yourself*, to use a familiar phrase exactly descriptive of the present case. What of yourself had you forgotten? Simply your *relation* to the order and succession of things without, and of thoughts and feelings within — your place in the series. In sleep, your existence, so far as it is an object of consciousness at all, is simply that of each passing moment by itself.

Thus in absorbing Pursuits. — You have only, in your waking moments, to lose sight as completely of that relation and succession of the present self to the past self, of the me to the not me, and you lose as completely all idea of time. Does this ever occur? Partially, whenever the attention is absorbed in any intensely interesting pursuit or study. Time passes insensibly then. We are abstracted from the series, our attention is withdrawn from surrounding objects and events, and even from our own thoughts, *as such.* We lose sight of the me, and, of course, of the relation of the me, to passing events, and therefore lose the sense of time. When the spell is at last broken we must go to seek ourselves again, as we would seek a child, that, in its play, had wandered from our side.

Also in Disease. — Something of the same sort occurs in severe and protracted sickness. The mind loses its reckoning, so to speak, as a ship in a storm loses latitude and longitude, and wanders from its course, unable longer to take its daily observations.

Idea of Time in Children. — You have doubtless noticed that children have little idea of time. It is much the same to them, one day with another, one week with another; it is morning, or afternoon, or night indifferently. The distinction and recognition of time, and of one time as different from another, is slowly acquired, and with difficulty. They have not that self-consciousness, that apprehension of the present and of the past, as related to each other in the series of events, which is involved in the idea of time. They are more like one in sleep, like one dreaming, like one in reverie, wholly absorbed with the present moment, the present consciousness.

Time longer to a Child than an Adult. — What has been said explains, also, the well-known fact, that time seems longer to a child than to an adult person. It is, as we have seen, the relation of the present self, as affected by changes internal and external, to the past self as thus affected, that gives us the idea and the standard of time. Of course, the shorter the line that represents the past, the longer, in comparison, that present duration which is measured by it. Now the child has fewer past thoughts and events with which to compare the present ones; hence, they hold a greater comparative magnitude to him than to us, who have a greater range of past existence and past consciousness with which to connect the passing moments. Hence, the longer we live, the more quickly pass our years, the shorter appears any given period of duration.

Applied to eternal Duration. — You have but to apply this thought to Him whose going forth is from of old, who *inhabiteth eternity*, and you have a new meaning in the beautiful thought of the Hebrew poet, that with Him a thousand years are but as a day. To that eternal mind, the remoteness of the period when the first star lighted up the vault of night at his bidding, may be recent as an event of yesterday.

III. Identity.

Difficult of Explanation. — Perhaps no subject, in the whole range of intellectual philosophy, has been the occasion of more perplexity and embarrassment than this. It is, in itself, a difficult subject to comprehend and explain. We know what we mean by identity, but to tell what that meaning is, to state the thing lucidly, and explain it philosophically, is another matter. It becomes necessary to examine the subject, therefore, with some care, in order to avoid confusion of ideas, and positively erroneous opinions. The subject is one of some importance in its theological, as well as its strictly philosophical bearings.

Not Similarity. — Identity is *not similarity*, not mere resemblance — *similar* things are not the *same* thing. We may suppose two globes or spheres precisely alike in every respect — of the same size, color, form, of the same material, of the same chemical composition and substance, presenting to the eye and the touch, and every other sense, the very same appearance and qualities, so that, if viewed successively, we should not recognize the difference; yet they are not identical; they are, by the very supposition, *two* distinct globes, two entities, two substances, and to say that they are identical, is to say that two things are only one. *Similarity* is not identity; so far from it, as Archbishop Whately has well remarked, it is not even implied of necessity in identity. A person may so far change as to be quite unlike his former self in appearance, size, etc., and yet be the same person. Not only are the two ideas quite distinct, but the one may be, and in fact is, in most cases, the virtual *negation* of the other. Resemblance, in most cases, implies difference of objects, the opposite of identity. To say that A and B resemble each other, is to say that, as known to us, they are *not* one and the same, not identical. It is only when one and the same object falls under cognizance at diverse times, so that we compare the object, as now known, with the same object as previously known, that resemblance and identity can possibly be predicated of the same thing.

Identity is only another term for *sameness* (*idem*); any one who knows what that means, knows what identity means, and that it does not mean mere similarity or resemblance.

Not sameness of chemical Composition. — Nor does sameness of chemical composition constitute identity. This is merely similarity. Two bodies may be composed of the same chemical elements, in the same proportion, and possessing the same general form and structure, yet they are not the same body. A given piece of wood or iron may be divided into a number of parts, each closely resembling the others, of the same appearance, size, figure, color, weight, and of the same chemical components; yet no one of these is identical with any other. When we say, in such a case, that the different pieces are of the same material, we use the word *same* with some latitude, to denote, not that they are composed of strictly the same particles, that the substance of the one is the very identical substance of the other, but only that they consist of the same *sort* or *kind* of substance, that they are, *e. g.*, both wood, or both iron. But this does not constitute identity.

There is no limit to the number of identical bodies which it is possible to conceive on this theory of identity. The same power that constructs one body of given chemical elements, and of given form and structure, may make two such, or ten, and if the first two are identical, the ten are, and they may exist at one and the same time, beside each other, identical with each other, yet ten, every one of which is itself, and yet every one is each of the others!

A relative Term. — Identity is a relative term, like most others that are expressive of quality. The term straight implies the idea of that which is not straight; beauty, the idea of deformity; greatness, its opposite; and so of others. Identity stands related to *diversity* as its opposite. To have the idea of identity, is to have that of diversity also. To affirm the former, is to deny the latter, and to deny is to have the idea of that which is denied. I do not say there can be no *identity* without diversity, but only that there can be no *idea* of the one without the idea, also, of the other, any more than there can be the idea of a tall man without the idea of short men.

Opposite of Diversity. — To affirm identity, then, is simply to deny *diversity*, to predicate unity, sameness, oneness. Other objects there are, like this, it may be, similar in every respect, capable of being confounded with it, and mistaken for it, but they are *other* and not *it*. This we affirm when we affirm identity, *non-diversity*, *non-otherness*. Whatever it be that marks off and distinguishes a thing from all other like or unlike objects — whatever constitutes its *individuality*, its *essence* — *in that consists its identity.*

Different applications of the Term. — Evidently, then, the word has somewhat different senses as applied to different classes of objects, whose individuality or essence varies. There are three distinct classes of objects to which the term is applicable. 1. Spiritual existence. 2. Organic and animate material existence. 3. Inorganic matter.

As applied to the first Class. — As regards the first class, *spiritual existences*, their identity consists in simple oneness and continuity of existence. It is enough that the soul or spirit exist, and continue to exist. So long as this is the case, identity is predicable of it. Should that existence cease, the identity ceases, since the object no longer exists of which identity can be affirmed. Should another spirit be created in its place, and even, *if the thing be supposable*, should it be endowed, not only with the same qualities, but the same *consciousness*, so as to be conscious of all that of which the former was conscious, still it would not be identical with the former. It is, by the very supposition, *another* spirit, and not the same. To be identical with it, it must be the very same essence, being, or existence, and not some other in its place.

It is only of spiritual immaterial existence that identity, in its strict and complete sense, is properly predicable, since it is only this class of existences that retains, unimpaired, its simple oneness, sameness, continuity of essence.

Personal Identity. — When we speak of *personal* identity, we mean that of the spirit, the soul, the ego, in distinction from the corporeal material part. The *evidence* of personal identity is *consciousness*. We know that the thinking conscious existence of to-day, which we call *self*, *me*, is one and the same with the thinking conscious self or me of yesterday, and not some other personal existence of like attributes and condition.

Locke's Idea. — Mr. Locke strangely mistook the *evidence* of personal identity for identity *itself*, and affirmed that our identity *consists* in our consciousness. If this were so, then, whenever our consciousness were interrupted, as in sound sleep, or in fainting, or delirium, our identity would be gone. This error has been pointed out, and fully explained, by Dr. Reid, and Bishop Butler, the former of whom makes this supposition: that the same individual is, at different periods of life, a boy at school, a private in the army, and a military commander; while a boy, he is whipped for robbing an orchard; when a soldier, he takes a standard from the enemy, and at that time recollects, perfectly, the whipping when a boy; when commander, he remembers taking the standard but not the whipping. It follows, according to Mr. Locke, that the soldier is identical with the boy, and the general with the soldier, because conscious of the same things, but the general is not identical with the boy, because not conscious of the same things, that is, *a* is *b*, and *b* is *c*, yet *a* is not *c*. The truth is, *identity*, and the *evidence* of it, are two things. Were there no consciousness of any thing past, there would still be identity so long as unity and continuity of existence remained.

2. *Identity as applied to the second Class.* — As regards *organic material* existence, whether animal or vegetable, the identity consists in that which constitutes the essence or being of the thing, which constitutes it an animal or vegetable existence. It is not mere body, not mere particles of matter, of such number and nature, or even of such arrangement and structure, but along with this, there is a higher principle involved — that of life. The continuity of this mysterious principle of life, under the same general structure and organization of material parts, making throughout one complex unity, one entity, one being, though with many changes, it may be, of separate parts and particles composing the organization; this constitutes the identity of the object.

The identity is no longer complete, no longer absolute, because there is no longer, as in the case of spiritual existence, absolute sameness of essence. Of the complex being under consideration, animal or vegetable, the life-principle is, indeed, one and the same throughout all periods of its existence, but the material organization retains not the same absolute essence, only the same general structure, and form, and adaptation of parts, while the parts and particles themselves are continually changing. It is only in a modified and partial sense, then, not in strict philosophical use of language, that we can predicate identity of any material organic existence. We mean by it, simply, *continuity of life* under the same general structure and organization; for so far as it has unity at all, this is it. This enables us to distinguish such an object from any and all other like objects of the same kind or sort.

3. *Identity as applied to the third Class.* — As regards mere inorganic matter, its identity consists, again, in its absolute oneness and sameness. There must be no change of particles, for the essence of the thing now considered lies not in any peculiarity of form, or structure, or life-principle, all which are wanting, but simply in the number and nature of the particles that make up the mass or substance of the thing, and if these change in the least, it is no longer the same essence. There is, properly, then, no such thing as identity in the cases now under consideration, since the particles of any material substance are liable to constant changes. It is only in a secondary and popular sense that we speak of the identity of merely inorganic material substance; strictly speaking, it has no identity, and continues not the same for any two moments.

We say, however, of two pieces of paper, that they are of the *same* color, meaning that they are both white or both red; of two coins, that they are of the same fineness, the same size, and weight, etc., meaning, thereby, only that the two things are of the same *sort* of color, the same degree of fineness, etc., and not that the color of the one or the fineness and size of the one is absolutely the essential and identical color, size, fineness of the other. It is by a similar use of terms, not in their strict and proper, but in a loose and secondary sense, that we speak of the identity or sameness of any material substance in itself considered. Strictly, it has no identity unless its substance is absolutely unchanged, which is not true of most, if, indeed, of any material existence, for any successive periods of time.

Popular Use. — There is a popular use of this term which requires further notice. We speak of the identity of a mountain, a river, a tree, or any like object in nature. It is the same mountain, we say, that we looked upon in childhood, the same tree under which we sat when a boy, the same river in which we bathed or fished in youth. Now there is a sense in which this is true and correct. There has been change of substance unquestionably, and therefore there is not *absolute* identity; but there is, after all, *numerical* sameness, and this is what we mean when we speak of the sameness or identity of the object. It constitutes a sufficient ground for such use of terms. You recognize the book, the mountain, the river, as one you have seen before. The tree that you pass in your morning walk you recognize as the very tree under which you sat ten years ago. Leaves have changed, bark and fibres have changed; branches are larger and more numerous; boughs, perhaps, have fallen by time and by tempest; it has changed as you have changed, it has grown old like yourself, with changing seasons; its verdure and foliage, like your hopes and plans, lie scattered around it, and yet it is *to you* the same tree. How so? It is the same numerical unity. Of a thousand or ten thousand *similar* trees, similar in species, in growth, and form, and adaptation of parts, in size, color, general appearance, etc., it is this individual one, and not some other of the same sort or species growing elsewhere, that you refer to. It is the same numerical unity and not some other one of the series. Still there must be continuity of existence in order to identity even in this popular sense of the term. Were the parts entirely changed and new ones substituted, as in the puzzle of the knife with several successive handles and blades, or the ship whose original timbers, planks, cordage, and entire substance, had, in course of time, by continued repairs, been removed and replaced by new; in such a case, we do not ordinarily speak or think of the object as being any longer the same.

This not absolute Identity. — In the cases now under consideration, in which, in popular language, objects are termed "same" and "identical," which are not strictly so, there is *comparative* rather than *absolute* unity and identity.

There is reference always in such cases to other objects of the same kind, sort, and description, a series of which the object of present cognition is one, and to which series it holds the same relation now that it held formerly. As when, of several books on a table, you touch *one*, and after the interval of some moments or hours touch the same again; you say, The book I last touched is the same I touched before, the *identical* one; you do not mean that its *substance* is absolutely unchanged, that it has the same precise number of particles in its composition as before — this is not in your mind at all — but only that the unity thus designated is the same unity previously designated, that, and not some other one of the series of similar objects. It is a *comparative* idea, a comparative identity, in which numerical unity is the element chiefly regarded.

Possible Plurality implied. — In all cases where the idea of identity arises in the mind, there is implied a *possible* plurality of objects of the same general character; the idea of such diversity or plurality is before the mind, and the foundation of that idea is the difference of cognition. The same object is viewed by the same person at *different times* or by *different persons* at the same time, and in that case, though the object itself should be absolutely one and the same, yet there have been distinct, separate cognitions of it, and this plurality or difference of cognition is a sufficient foundation for the idea of a possible diversity of object. The book *as known* to-day and the book *as known* yesterday, are two distinct objects of thought. The cognition now, and the cognition then, are two separate acts of the mind; and the question arises, Are the *objects* distinct, as well as the cognitions? This is the question of identity. You have an immediate, irresistible conviction that the object of these several cognitions is one and the same. You affirm its identity, absolute or comparative, as the case may be.

The Conception of Identity amounts to what. — In every

case of affirmed identity, then, there is implied a possible plurality of objects; a difference of cognition of a given object, whether one person cognizant at different times, or different persons at the same time; a question whether the possible plurality, as regards the object of these different cognitions, is an *actual* plurality; a conviction and decision that it is not, that the object is one and the same; and this sameness and unity are *absolute* or *comparative*, according as we use the language in its strict, primitive, philosophical meaning, or in its loose and popular sense. In the one case, it is sameness of absolute essence, in the other, sameness of nominal relation to others of a series or class.

IV. Cause.

Meaning of the Term. — The idea of cause is one with which every mind is familiar. It is not easy, however, to explain precisely what we mean by it, nor to fix its limits, nor to unfold its origin.

We mean by this term, I think, as ordinarily employed, that on which some consequence depends, that but for which some event or phenomenon would not occur. In order to affirm that one thing is the cause of another, I must know, not merely that they are connected, but that the existence of the one depends on that of the other. This is more than mere antecedence, however invariable. The approach of a storm may be invariably indicated by the changes of the barometer. These changes precede the storm, but are not the cause of it.

Origin of the Idea. — *Whence do we derive* the idea of cause? — a question of some importance, and much discussed.

Evidently not from sense. I observe, for example, the melting of snow before the fire, or wax before the flame of a taper. What is it that I see in this case? Merely the phenomenon, nothing more. All that sense conveys, all that the eye reports, is simply the melting of the one substance in the presence and vicinity of the other. I *see* no cause, no form transmitted from the one to the other, no action of the one on the other, but simply the vicinity of the two, and the change taking place in one. I *infer* that the change takes place in consequence of the vicinity. I believe it; and if the experiment is often repeated with the same results, I cannot doubt that it is so. The idea of causality is, indeed, *suggested* by what I have seen, but is not given by sense. I have not seen the cause; that lies hidden, occult, its nature wholly unknown, and its very existence known, not by what I have actually seen, but by that law of the mind which leads me to believe that every event must have a cause, and to look for that cause in whatever circumstance is known to be invariably connected with the given change or event.

Constitution of the Mind. — That such is the constitution of the mind, such the law of its action, admits of no reasonable doubt. No sooner is an event or phenomenon observed, than we conclude, at once, that it is an effect, and begin to inquire the cause. We cannot, by any effort of conception, persuade ourselves that there is absolutely no cause.

Not derived from Sense. — But is not this principle of causality derived from experience? We have already said that sense does not give it. I do not see with the eye the cause of the melting of the wax, much less does what I see contain the general principle, that *every* event must have a cause. Sense does not give me this.

Whether from Consciousness. — Still, may it not be a matter of experience in another way, given by *consciousness*, though not by *sense*. For example, I am conscious of certain volitions. These volitions are accompanied with certain muscular movements, and these, again, are followed by certain sensible effects upon surrounding objects. These changes produced on objects without are directly connected thus with my own mental states and changes, with the volitions of which I am directly conscious. Given, the volition on my part, with the corresponding muscular effort, and the external change is produced. I never observe it taking place without such preceding volition. I learn to regard my will as the *cause*, and the external change as the *effect*. I observe that it is in the power of others to produce changes in like manner. Thus I obtain the general idea of cause. It is given by consciousness and experience.

Notion of Causality not thus derived.—It is to this source that a very able and ingenious French philosopher would attribute our first idea of cause. I refer to Maine de Biran. I should agree with M. de Biran, that consciousness of our own voluntary efforts, and of the effects thus produced, may give us our first notion of cause. But it does not give us the law of causality. It extends to a given instance only, explains that, explains nothing further than that, cannot go beyond. I am conscious that in this given instance I have set in operation a train of antecedents and sequences which results in the given effect. I am not conscious that *every* event has, in like manner, a cause. My experience warrants no such assumption. No induction of facts and cases can possibly amount to this. Induction can multiply and generalize, but cannot stamp on that which is merely empirical and contingent, the character of universality and necessity. The law of causality, in a word, is to be distinguished from any given instance, or number of instances, of actually observed causation. The latter fall within the range of consciousness and experience, the former is given, if at all, as a law of the mind, a primary truth, an idea of reason.

Remarks of Professor Bowen.—As Professor Bowen has well observed, "The maxim, '*Every event must have a cause*,' is not, like the so-called laws of nature, a mere induction founded on experience, and holding good only until an instance is discovered to the contrary; it is a necessary and immutable truth. It is not derived from observation of natural phenomena, but is super-imposed upon such observation by a necessity of the human intellect. It is not made known through the senses; and its falsity, under any circumstances, is not possible, is not even conceivable. The *cause* to which it points us, is not to be found in nature. The mere physicist, after vainly searching, ever since the world began, for a single instance of it, has, at length, abandoned the attempt as hopeless, and now confines himself to the mere *description* of natural phenomena. The *true cause* of these phenomena must be sought for in the realm, not of *matter*, but of *mind*."

What constitutes Cause. — In this last remark, the author quoted touches upon a question of no little moment. What constitutes a cause? We cannot here enter into the discussion of this question. It is sufficient to remark, that in the ordinary use of the word, as denoting that, but for which a given result will not be, many things beside mind are included as causes. A hammer, or some like instrument, is essential to the driving of a nail. The hammer may be called the cause of the nail being driven; the blow struck by means of the hammer may also be so designated. More properly, the arm which gave the blow, and, more correctly still, the mind which willed the movement of the arm, and not the consequent blow of the hammer, may be said to be the cause. If we seek for *ultimate* and *efficient* causes, we must, doubtless, come back to the realm of mind. It is mind that is, in every case, the first mover, the originator of any effect, and it may, therefore, be called the true and prime cause, the cause of causes.

History of the Doctrine. — *Aristotle's View.* — The history of the doctrine of causality presents a number of widely different theories, a brief outline of which is all that we can here give. The most ancient division and classification of causes is that of Aristotle, which is based on the following analysis: Every work brought to completion implies four things: an agent by whom it is done, an element or material of which it is wrought, a plan or idea according to which it is fashioned, and an end for which it is produced.

Thus, to the production of a statue there must be a statuary, a block of marble, a plan in the mind of the artist, and a motive for the execution of the work. The first of these is termed the *efficient* cause, the second the *material* cause, the third the *formal*, and the fourth the *final* cause. This classification was universally adopted by the scholastic philosophers, and, to some extent, is still prevalent. We still speak of *efficient* and of *final* causes.

Locke's Derivation of Cause. — With regard to the origin of the idea of cause, there has been the greatest diversity of opinion. Locke derives it from sense; so do the philosophers of the sensationalist school. We perceive bodies modifying each other, and hence the notion of causality.

Theory of Hume and of Brown. — Hume denies the existence of what we call cause, or power of one object over another. He resolves it into succession or sequence of objects in regular order, and consequent association of them in our thoughts. Essentially the same is the theory of Brown, who resolves cause and effect into simple antecedence and sequence, beyond which we know nothing, and can affirm nothing.

Theory of Leibnitz. — The theory of Leibnitz verges upon the opposite extreme, and assigns the element of power or causal efficiency to every form of existence; every substance is a force, a cause, in itself.

Of Kant. — Kant and his school make cause a merely subjective notion, a law of the understanding, which it impresses upon outward things, a condition of our thought. We observe external phenomena, and, according to this law of our intelligence, are under the necessity of arranging them as cause and effect; but we do not know that, independent of our conception, there exists in reality any thing corresponding to this idea. The tendency of this theory, as well as that of Hume and Brown, to a thorough-going skepticism, is obvious at a glance. The theory of Maine de Biran has been already noticed.

V. The Idea of the Beautiful, and of Right.

These Ideas Intuitive. — Among the primary ideas awakened in the mind by the faculty of original or intuitive conception, ideas of reason, as some writers would prefer to call them, must be included the notion of the *beautiful*, and also that of *right* — ideas more important in themselves, and in their bearing on human happiness, than almost any others which the mind entertains. That these ideas are to be traced, ultimately, to the originative or intuitive faculty, there can be little doubt. They are simple and primary ideas. They have the characteristics of universality and necessity. They are awakened intuitively and instantaneously in the mind, when the appropriate occasion is presented by sense. There are certain objects in nature and art, which, so soon as perceived, strike us as beautiful. There are certain traits of character and courses of conduct, which, so soon as observed, strike us as morally right and wrong. The ideas of the beautiful and the right are thus awakened in the mind on the perception of the corresponding objects.

Things to be considered respecting them. — Viewed as notions of the intuitive faculty, or original conceptions, it would be in place to consider more particularly the *circumstances* under which each of these ideas originates, and the *characteristics* of each ; also what *constitutes*, in either case, the object, what constitutes the beautiful and the right.

These Topics reserved for separate Discussion. — These matters deserve a wider and fuller discussion, however, than would here be in place. The ideas under consideration are to be viewed, not merely as conceptions of the reason or intuition, but as constituting the material of two distinct and important departments of mental activity, two distinct classes of judgments, viz., the *æsthetic* and the *moral.* The conceptions of the beautiful and the right, furnished by the originative or intuitive power of the mind, constitute the material and basis on which the reflective power works, and, as thus employed, the mental activity assumes the form, and is known under the familiar names of *taste* and *conscience*, or, as we may term them, the æsthetic and moral faculties. As such, we reserve them for distinct consideration in the following pages, bearing in mind, as we proceed, that these faculties, so called, are not properly new powers of the mind, but merely forms of the reflective faculty, as exercised upon this particular class of ideas.

CHAPTER III.

THE CONCEPTION AND COGNIZANCE OF THE BEAUTIFUL.

§ I. — Conception of the Beautiful.

The Science which treats of this. — The investigation of this topic brings us upon the domain of a science as yet comparatively new, and which, in fact, has scarcely yet assumed its place among the philosophic sciences — *Æsthetics*, the science of the beautiful.

Difficulty of defining. — What, then, is the beautiful? — A question that meets us at the threshold, and that has received, from different sources, answers almost as many and diverse as the writers that have undertaken its discussion. It is easy to specify instances of the beautiful without number, and of endless variety; but that is not defining it. On the contrary, it is only increasing the difficulty; for, where so many things are beautiful, and so diverse from each other, how are we to decide what is that one property which they all have in common, viz., beauty? The difficulty is to fix upon any one quality or attribute that shall pertain alike to all the objects that seem to us beautiful. A figure of speech, a statue, a star, an air from an opera, all strike us as beautiful, all awaken in us the emotion which beauty alone can excite. But what have they in common? It were easy to fix upon something in the case of the statue, or of the star, which should account, perhaps, for the pleasure those objects afford us; but the same thing might not apply to the figure of speech, or to the musical air. It would seem almost hopeless to attempt the solution of the problem in this method. And yet there *must be*, it would seem, some principle or attribute in which these various objects that we call beautiful agree, which is the secret and substance of their beauty, and the cause of that uniform effect which they all produce upon us. Philosophers have accordingly proposed various solutions of the problem, some fixing upon one thing, some upon another; and it may be instructive to glance at some of these definitions.

Some make it a Sensation. — Of those who have undertaken to define what beauty is, there are some who make it a mere *feeling* or sensation of the mind, and not an objective reality of any sort. It is not this, that, or the other quality of the external object, but simply a subjective emotion. It lies within us, and not without. Thus, Sir George Mackenzie describes it as "a certain degree of a certain species of pleasurable effect impressed on the mind." So also Grohman, Professor of Philosophy at Hamburg, in his treatise on æsthetic as science, defines the beautiful to be "the infinite consciousness of the reason as *feeling*." As the true is the activity of reason at work as *intellect* or knowledge, and as the good is its province when it appears as *will*, so the beautiful is its activity in the domain of *sensibility*. Brown, Upham, and others, among English and American writers, frequently speak of the emotion of beauty, as if beauty itself were an emotion.

Others an Association. — Closely agreeing with this class of writers, and hardly to be distinguished from it, is that which makes beauty consist in certain *associations of idea and feeling* with the object contemplated. This is the favorite doctrine with the Scotch metaphysicians. Thus Lord Jeffrey, who has written with great clearness and force on this subject, regards beauty as dependent entirely on association, "the reflection of our own inward sensations." It is not, according to this view, a quality of the object external, but only a feeling in our own minds. Its seat is within and not without.

Theory that Beauty consists in Expression. — Of the same general class, also, are those who, with Alison, Reid, and Cousin, regard beauty as the *sign* or *expression* of some quality fitted to awaken pleasing emotions in us. Nothing is beautiful, say these writers, which is not thus expressive of some mental or moral quality or attribute. It is not an original and independent quality of any peculiar forms or colors, says Alison, for then we should have a definite rule for the creation of beauty. It lies ultimately in the mind, not in matter, and matter becomes beautiful only as it becomes, by analogy or association, suggestive of mental qualities. The same is substantially the ancient Platonic view. Kant, also, followed in the main by Schiller and Fichte, takes the subjective view, and makes beauty a mere play of the imagination.

All these Theories make it subjective. — Whether we regard beauty, then, as a mere emotion, or as an association of thought and feeling with the external object, or as the sign and expression of mental qualities, in either case we make it ultimately subjective, and deny its external objective reality.

Different Forms of the objective Theory. — Of those who take the opposite view, some seek for the hidden principle of beauty in *novelty;* others, as Galen and Marmontel, in *utility;* others, as Shaftesbury, Hutcheson, Hogarth, in the principle of *unity in variety;* others, in that of *order and proportion*, as Aristotle, Augustine, Crousez.

All these writers, while they admit the existence of beauty in the external object, make it to consist in some quality or conformation of matter, as such.

The spiritual Theory. — There is still another theory of the beautiful, which, while admitting its external objective reality, seeks to divest it of that material nature in which the writers last named present it, and searches for its essence among principles ethereal and spiritual. According to this view beauty is the *spiritual life in its immediate sensible manifestation;* the hidden, invisible principle — spirit in distinction from matter, animating, manifesting itself in, looking out through, the material form. It is not matter as such, it is not spirit as such, much less a mere mental quality or mental feeling; it is the expression of the invisible and spiritual under sensible material forms. This view was first fully developed by Schelling and Hegel, and is adopted, in the main, by Jouffroy in his Cours d'Esthetique, by Dr. August Ruhlert, of the university of Breslau, in his able system of æsthetics, and by many other philosophical writers of distinction in Europe.

Questions for Consideration. — The following questions grow out of these various and conflicting definitions, as presenting the real points at issue, and, as such, requiring investigation.

I. Is beauty something objective, or merely subjective and emotional?

II. If the former, then what is it in the object that constitutes its beauty?

I. *Question stated.* — Is beauty merely subjective, an emotion of our own minds, or is it a quality of objects? When we speak, *e. g.*, of the beauty of a landscape, or of a painting, do we mean merely a certain excitement of our sensitive nature, a certain feeling awakened by the object, or do we mean some quality or property belonging to that object? If the latter, then are we *correct* in attributing any such quality to the object?

Emotion admitted. — Unquestionably, certain pleasing emotions are awakened in the mind in view of certain objects which we term beautiful; unquestionably those objects are the cause or occasion of such emotions; they have, under favorable circumstances, the power of producing them; unquestionably they have this power by virtue, moreover, of some quality or property pertaining to them. All this will be admitted by those who deny the objective reality of beauty. The question is not, whether there is in the object any quality which is the occasion or cause of our emotion, but whether the term beauty is properly the name of that cause, or of the emotion it produces.

Beauty not an Emotion.—The question would seem a very plain one if submitted to common sense. It would seem strange that any one should deliberately and intelligently take the position that beauty and sublimity are merely emotions of our minds, and not qualities of objects: when we hear men speaking in this way, we are half inclined to suspect that we misunderstand them, or that they misunderstand themselves. I look upon a gorgeous sunset, and call it beautiful. What is it that is beautiful? That sky, that cloud, that coloring, those tints that fade into each other and change even as I behold them, those lines of fire that lie in brilliant relief upon the darker background, as if some radiant angel had thrown aside his robe of light as he flew, or had left his smile upon the cloud as he passed through the golden gates of Hesperus, these, these, are beautiful; *there* lies the beauty, and surely not in me, the beholder. An emotion is in my mind, but that emotion is not beauty; it is simple *admiration*, *i. e.*, wonder and delight. There is no such emotion as beauty, common as is the ambiguous expression "emotion of beauty." There are emotions of fear, hope, joy, sorrow, and the like, and these emotions I experience; I know what they mean; but I am not conscious of having ever experienced an emotion of *beauty*, though I have often been filled with wonder and delight at the sight of the beautiful in nature or art. When I experience an emotion of fear, of hope, of joy, or of sorrow, what is it that is joyful or sorrowful, hopeful or fearful? My mind, of course, that is, I, myself. The object that occasions the emotion on my part, is in no other sense fearful or joyful than as it is the occasion of my being so. If, in like manner, beauty is an emotion, and I experience that emotion, it is, of course, my mind that is beautiful, and not the object contemplated. It is I, myself, that am beautiful, not the sunset, the painting, the landscape, or any thing of that sort, whatever. These things are merely the occasion of *my* being beautiful. Could any doctrine be more consoling to those who are conscious of any serious deficiency on the score of personal attractions! Can any thing be more absurd?

The common View correct.—I beg leave to take the common-sense view of this question, which I cannot but think is, in the present instance, the most correct, and still to think and speak of the beauty of *objects*, and not of our own minds. Such is certainly the ordinary acceptation and use of the term, nor can any reason be shown why, in strictest philosophy, we should depart from it. There is no need of applying the term to denote the emotion awakened in the mind, for that emotion is not, in itself, either a new or a nameless one, but simply that mingled feeling of wonder and delight which we call admiration, and which passes, it may be, into love. To make beauty itself an emotion, is to be guilty of a double absurdity. It is to leave the quality of the object which gives rise to the emotion altogether without a name, and bestow that name where it is not needed, on that which has already a name of its own.

Beauty still objective, though reflected from the Mind.—If to this it be replied, that the beauty which we admire and which *seems* to be a property of the external object, is, nevertheless, of internal origin, being merely a transfer to the object, and association with it, of certain thoughts and feelings of our own minds, a reflection of our own consciousness gilding and lighting up the objects around us, which objects are then viewed by us as having a light and beauty of their own, I answer, that even on this supposition, the external object, as thus illumined, has the power of awakening the pleasing emotion within us, and that power is its beauty, a property or quality of the object still, although borrowed originally from the mind; just as the moon, though it give but a reflected light, still shines, and with a beauty of its own. So long as those thoughts and feelings lay hidden in the mind, untransferred, unassociated with the external object, they were not *beauty*. Not until the object is invested with them, and they have become a property of that object, do they assume, to the mental eye, the quality of beauty. So, then, beauty is even still an objective reality, something that lies without us, and not within us.

The Power of expressing an objective Quality, likewise.—In like manner, if it be contended that beauty is only the sign and expression of mental qualities, I reply, that power of signifying or expressing is certainly a property of the object, and that property is its beauty, and is certainly a thing objective, and not a mere emotion.

All Beauty not Reflection, nor Expression.—I am far from conceding, however, that all beauty is either the reflection or expression of what passes within the mind. There are objects which no play of the fancy, no transfer or association of the mental states, can ever render beautiful; while, on the other hand, there are others which require no such association, but of themselves shine forth upon us with their own clear and lustrous beauty. Suppose a child of lively sensibility, and with that true love of the beautiful, wherever discerned, which is one of the finest traits of the child's nature, to look for the first time upon the broad expanse of the ocean; it lies spread out before him a new and sudden revelation of beauty; its extent of surface, unbroken by the petty lines and boundaries that divide and mark off the lands upon the shore; its wonderful deep blue, a color he has seen hitherto only in the firmament above him, and not there as here—that deep blue relieved by the white sails, that, like birds of snowy wing, flit across its peaceful bosom, or lie motionless in the morning light on its calm expanse; its peculiar convexity of surface, as it stretches far out to the horizon, and lifts up its broad shoulders against the sky;—these things he beholds for the first time, they are associated with nothing in his past experience; he has never seen, never dreamed of such a vision; it is not the reflection of his own thoughts or fancies; but it is, nevertheless, to him a scene of rare and wondrous beauty, the recollection and first impression of which shall haunt him while he lives. If, in after life, he came to philosophize upon the matter, it would be difficult to convince him that what he thus admired was but the play of his own imagination, the transfer of his own mental state, the association of his own thought and feeling with the object before him; in a word, that the beauty which so charmed him lay not at all in the object contemplated, but only in his own mind.

A further Question.—That the beauty which we perceive is a quality of objects, and not merely a subjective emotion, that there is in the object something which, call it what we will, is the producing cause of the emotion in us, and that this objective cause, whatever it be, is, in the proper use of terms, to be recognized as beauty, this we have now sufficiently discussed. Admitting, however, these positions, the question may still arise, whether that which we call beauty in objects has, after all, an absolute existence, independent of the mind that is impressed by it? The beauty that I admire in yonder landscape, or in the wild flower that looms at my feet, is, indeed, the beauty of the landscape or the flower, and not of my mind; it pertains to, and dwells in, the object, and not in me; but dwells it there independently of me, the observer, and when I do not behold it? If there were no intelligent, observing mind, to behold and feel that beauty, would the object still be beautiful, even as now? This admits of question. Is the beauty a fixed, absolute quality, inherent in the object as such, and *per se*, or is it something springing out of the relation between the mind of the observer and the object observed.

No Evidence of its Existence except its Effect. — That it is relative, and not absolute, may be argued from the fact that we have no evidence of any such quality or cause, save as in operation, save as producing effects in us; and as we could never have inferred the existence of the cause, had it not been for the effect produced, so we have no reason to suppose its existence when and where it does not manifest itself in operation, that is to say, when and where it is not observed. As the spark from the smitten steel is not strictly to be regarded as itself a property of the steel, nor yet of the flint, but as a relative phenomenon arising from the collision of the two, so beauty, it may be said, dwells not absolutely in the object *per se*, nor yet in the intelligent subject, but is a phenomenon resulting from the relation of the two.

Further Argument from diversity of Effects. — The same may be argued from the diversity of the effects produced. If beauty is a fixed, absolute quality of objects, it may be said, then the effects ought to be uniformly the same; whereas there is, in fact, no such uniformity, no standard of beauty, none of taste, but what seems to one man exceedingly fine, excites only the aversion and disgust of another, and even the same person is at different times differently affected by the same object. Hence it may be inferred that the beauty is merely a relation between the mind and the object contemplated, varying as the mind varies.

Reply to the first Argument. — To these arguments I reply, in the first place, that it is not necessary that a cause should be in actual operation, under our immediate eye, in order that we should conclude its independent and constant existence. If, whenever the occasion returns, the effects are observed, we conclude that the cause exists *per se*, and not merely in relation to us. Otherwise we could never believe the absolute existence of any thing, but should, with

Berkley and Hume, call in question the existence of matter itself, save as phenomenal and relative to our senses. The same argument that makes the beauty of a rose relative merely to the observer, makes the rose itself merely a relative existence. How do I know that it exists? I see it, feel it, smell it; it lies upon my table; it affects my senses. I turn away now. I leave the room. How do I know *now* that the rose exists? It no longer affects my senses; the cause no longer operates; the effect is no longer produced. I have just as much reason to say it no longer exists, as to say it is no longer beautiful.

Reply to the second Argument. — To the argument from the diversity of effect, I reply, that admitting the fact to be as stated, viz., that the same object is differently regarded by different minds, the diversity may arise from either of two sources. The want of uniformity may lie in the cause, or it may lie in the minds affected by it. The exciting cause may vary, and the effects produced by it will then be diverse; or the minds on which it operates may differ, and in that case, also, the effects will be diverse. We are not to conclude, then, from diversity of effect that the cause is not uniform. A beautiful object, it is true, affects different observers differently, but the reason of the diversity may be in *them* and not in the object.

What then is the fact? Are the minds of all observers equally susceptible of impression from the beautiful? By no means. They differ in education, habit of thought, culture, taste, native sensibility, and many other things. Hardly two minds can be found that are not diverse in these respects. Ought we then to expect absolute uniformity of effect?

Not to be conceded that there is no Agreement. — It is by no means to be conceded, however, that there is no such thing as a standard of beauty or of taste, no general agreement among men as to what is or is not beautiful, no general agreement as to the emotions produced. There is such agreement in both respects. Within certain limits it is uniform and complete. Certain aspects of nature, and certain works of art, are, in all ages, and by all men, regarded as beautiful. The Apollo Belvidere, and the Venus of the Capitol, are to us what they were to the ancients; the perfection of the beautiful. The great work of Raphael, scarcely finished at his death, the last touches still fresh from his hand — that work which, as it hung above his bier, drew tears from all eyes, and filled with admiration all hearts — is still the wonder and admiration of men. And so it will be in centuries to come. And so of the emotions produced by the contemplation of the beautiful. Making due allowance for habits of association, mental culture, and differences of native sensibility, we shall find men affected much in the same way by the beautiful in nature or art. The men of the same class and condition as to these matters — the peasant of one age or country, and the peasant of another, the philosopher of one time, and of another, the wealthy, uneducated citizen, and the fashionable fool, of one period and nation, and of another — experience much the same effects in view of one and the same object. The same general laws, too, preside over and regulate the different arts which have relation to the beautiful, in all ages of the world.

Consequences of the Theory that Beauty is merely relative. — If beauty be not absolute but relative only, it follows, 1. That, if there were no observers of nature or art, neither would be longer beautiful. 2. If, for any reason any thing is for the time unseen, as, *e. g.*, a pearl in the sea, a precious stone in the mine, or a rich jewel in the casket, it has no beauty so long as it is there and thus. 3. As minds vary in susceptibility of impression, the same thing is beautiful to one person and not to another; at one time and not at another; nay, at one and the same moment it is both beautiful and not beautiful, according as the minds of the observers vary I cannot say with truth, that the Mosaics of St. Peter's, or the great diamond of the East, are, at this moment, really beautiful, because I do not know who, or whether any one, may, at this moment, be looking at them.

Intimate Relation between the Mind and the Object.—While I maintain, however, the existence of beauty as an absolute and independent quality of objects, and not merely as relative to the mind that perceives and enjoys it, I would, by no means, overlook the very intimate relation which subsists, in the present case, between the perceiving mind and the object perceived. Beauty makes its appeal primarily to the senses. It pleases and charms us, because we are endowed with senses and a nature fitted to receive pleasure from such objects. In the *adaptation* of our physical and mental constitution to the order and constitution of material things as they exist without, lies the secret of that power which the beautiful exerts over us.

Might have been otherwise constituted. — We might have been so constituted, doubtless, that the most beautiful objects should have been disgusting, rather than pleasing: the violet should have seemed an ugly thing, and the sweetest strains of music harsh and discordant. There are disordered senses, and disordered minds, to which, even now, those things, which we call beautiful, may so appear. For that adaptation of our sensitive nature to external objects, and of these objects to our sensitive nature, by virtue of which, the percipient mind recognizes and feels the beauty of the object perceived, and takes delight in it, we are indebted wholly to the wisdom and benevolence of the great Creator.

The Doctrine maintained. — Still, *given*, the present constitution and mutual adaptation of mind and matter, and we affirm the independent existence of the beautiful as an object *per se*, and not merely as an affection of the percipient mind. The perception and enjoyment of the beauty are subjective, relative, dependent; the beauty itself not so.

The second Question. — If beauty be, then, as we find reason to believe, not wholly a subjective affair, but a quality or property of external objects, the question now arises,

II. What is it in the object, that constitutes its beauty?

Theory of Novelty. — And first, is it the *novelty* of the thing? Is the novel the beautiful? Doubtless, novelty pleases us. It has this in common with the beautiful. Yet some things that are novel, are by no means beautiful. A mill for grinding corn is a great curiosity to one who has never seen such a machine before, but it might not strike him as particularly beautiful.

Every thing, when first beheld, is novel; but every thing is not beautiful. Let us look more closely at the element of novelty. That is novel which is new to *us* merely, which appears to us for the first time. It may be new to the intellect, a new idea, or to the sensibility, a new feeling, or to the will, a new act. As a new idea it satisfies our curiosity, as a new feeling it developes our nature, as a new volition it enlarges the sphere of our activity. In these respects, and for these reasons, novelty pleases, but in all this we discover no resemblance to the beautiful.

Novelty heightens Beauty. — It is not to be denied that novelty, in many cases, heightens the beauty of an object. By familiarity, we become, in a measure, insensible to the charms of that which, as first beheld, filled us with delight. The sensibility receives no further excitement from that to which it has become accustomed. To enjoy mountain scenery most highly, one must not always dwell among the mountains. To enjoy Niagara most highly, one must not live in the sight of it all his days. But beauty, and the *enjoyment* of the beautiful, are surely different things, and while novelty is accessory to the full effect of the beautiful on our minds, and even indispensable to it, it is not, itself, the element of beauty, not the ground and substance of it.

Not always pleasing. — Jouffroy even denies that novelty is always pleasing. Some things, he contends, *displease* us, simply because they are new. We become accustomed to them, and our dislike ceases. Thus it is, to some extent, with difference of color in the races.

Theory of the Useful. — Is, then, the *useful* the beautiful? This theory next claims our attention. The foundation of the emotions awakened in us by the beautiful in nature or art, is the perception of utility. We perceive in the object a fitness to conduce, in some way, to our welfare, to serve, in some way, our purposes, and for this reason, we are pleased. The utility is the beauty.

The most useful not the most beautiful. — That the beauty of an object may, in our perception, be heightened by the discovery of its fitness to produce some desirable end, or rather, that this may add somewhat to the pleasure we feel in view of the object, is quite possible; that this is the main element and grand secret, either of that emotion on our part, or of the beauty which gives rise to it, is not possible. It is sufficient to say, that, if this were so, the most useful things ought, of course, to be the most beautiful. Is this the case? A stream of water conducted along a ship canal is more useful than the same stream tumbling over the rapids, or plunging over a perpendicular precipice. Is it also more beautiful? A swine's snout, to use a homely but forcible illustration of Burke, is admirably fitted to serve the purpose for which it was intended; useful exceedingly for rooting and grubbing, but not, on the whole, very beautiful.

Dissimilarity of the two. — Indeed, few things can be more unlike, in their effect upon the mind, in the nature of the emotions they excite, than the useful and the beautiful. This has been well shown by Jouffroy in his analysis of the beautiful. Kant has also clearly pointed out the same thing. Both please us, but not in the same way, not for the same reason. We love the one for its advantage to us, the other *for its own sake.* The one is a purely selfish, the other a purely disinterested love, a noble, elevated emotion. The two are heaven-wide asunder. The glorious sunset is of no earthly use to us, otherwise than mere beauty and pleasure are in themselves of use. The gorgeous spectacle becomes at once degraded in our own estimation by the very question of its possible utility. We love it not for the benefit it confers, the use we can make of it, but for its own sake, its own sweet beauty, because it is what it is. There it lies, pencilled on the clouds, evanescent, momentarily changing. There it is, afar off. You cannot reach it, cannot command its stay, have no wish to appropriate it to yourself, no desire to turn it to your own account, or reap any benefit from it, other than the mere enjoyment; still you admire it, still it is beautiful to you. Of what use to the beholder is the ruddy glow and flash of sunrise on the Alpine summits as seen from the Rhigi or Mount Blanc? Of what use, in fact, is beauty in any case, other than as it may be the means of refining the taste, and elevating the mind? That it has this advantage we are free to admit; and it is certainly one of the noblest uses to which any thing can be made subservient; but surely this cannot be what is meant when we are told that beauty *consists* in utility, for this would be simply affirming that the cause consists in the effect produced. Beauty refines and elevates the mind, is a means of æsthetic and moral culture; as such it is of use, and in that use lies the secret and the subtle essence of beauty itself. In other words, a given cause produces a given effect, and that effect *constitutes* the cause!

The utility of Beauty an incidental Circumstance. — The truth is, that while the beautiful does elevate and ennoble the mind, and thus furnish the means of the highest æsthetic and moral culture, this advantage is wholly incidental to the existence of beauty, not even a necessary or invariable effect, much less the constituting element. This is not the reason why we admire the beautiful. It does not enter into our thoughts at the moment. As on the summit of Rhigi, I watch the play of the first rosy light on the snowy peaks that lift themselves in stately grandeur along the opposite horizon, I am not thinking, at that moment, of the effect produced on my own mind, by the spectacle before me; I am wholly absorbed in the magnificence of the scene itself. It is beautiful, not because it is useful, not because it elevates my mind, and cultivates my taste, and contributes, in various ways, to my development, but it produces these effects because it is beautiful. The very thought of the useful is almost enough, in such cases, to extinguish the sentiment of the beautiful.

Beauty cannot be appropriated. — That only is useful which can be *appropriated*, and turned to account. But the beautiful, in its very nature, cannot be appropriated or possessed. You may appropriate the picture, the statue, the mountain, the waterfall, but not their beauty. These do not belong to you, and never can. They are the property of every beholder. Hence, as Jouffroy has well observed, the possession of a beautiful object never fully satisfies. The beauty is ideal, and cannot be possessed. It is an ethereal spirit that floats away as a silver cloud, ever near, yet ever beyond your grasp. It is a bow, spanning the blue arch, many-colored, wonderful; yonder, just yonder, is its base, where the rosy light seems to hover over the wood, and touch gently the earth; but you cannot, by any flight or speed of travel, come up with it. It is here, there, everywhere, except where you are. It is given you to behold, not to possess it.

Theory of Unity in Variety. — Evidently we must seek elsewhere than in utility the dwelling-place of beauty. The secret of her tabernacle is not there. Let us see, then, if *unity in variety* may not be, as some affirm, the principle of the beautiful. The intellect demands a general unity, as, *e.g.*, in a piece of music, a painting, or a play, and is not satisfied unless it can perceive such unity. The parts must be not only connected but related, and that relation must be obvious. At the same time the sensibility demands variety, as *e.g.*, of tone and time in the music, of color and shade in the painting, of expression in both. The same note of a musical instrument continuously produced, or the same color unvaried in the painting, would be intolerable. The due combination of these two principles, unity and variety, say these writers, constitutes what we call beauty in an object. The waving line of Hogarth may be taken as an illustration of this principle.

Objection to this View. — Without entering fully into the discussion of this theory, it may be sufficient to say, that while the principle now named does enter, in some degree, into our conception of the beautiful, it can hardly be admitted as the ground and cause, or even as the chief element, of beauty. Not every thing is beautiful which presents both unity and variety. Some things, on the other hand, are beautiful which lack this combination. Some colors are beautiful, taken by themselves, and the same is true of certain forms, which, nevertheless, lack the element of variety. In the construction of certain mathematical figures, which please the eye by their symmetry and exactness, we may detect, perhaps, the operation of this principle. On the other hand, it will not account for the pleasure we feel when the eye rests upon a particular color that is agreeable. A bright red pebble, or a bit of stained glass, appears to a child very beautiful. It is the color that is the object of his admiration. We have simple unity but no variety there. On the other hand, in a beautiful sunset we have the greatest variety, but not unity, other than simply a numerical unity.

We cannot, on the whole, accept this theory as a complete and satisfactory resolution of the problem of the beautiful, although it is supported by the eminent authority of Cousin, who, while he regards all beauty as ultimately pertaining to the spiritual nature, still finds in the principle, now under consideration, its chief characteristic so far as it assumes external form.

Order and Proportion. — Shall we then, with Aristotle, Augustine, André, and others, ancient and modern, seek the hidden principle of beauty in the elements of *order and proportion?* What are order and proportion? Order is the arrangement of the several parts of a composite body. Proportion is the relation of the several parts to each other in space and time. Not every possible arrangement is order, but only that which appears conducive to the end designed, and not every possible arrangement of parts is proportion, but only that which furthers the end to be accomplished. To place the human eye in the back part of the head, the limbs remaining as they now are, would be *disorder*, for motion must in that case, as now, be forward, while the eye, looking backward, could no longer survey the path we tread. The limbs of the Arabian steed, designed for swiftness of locomotion, bear a proportion to the other parts of the body, somewhat different from that which the limbs of the swine, designed chiefly for support, and for movements slower, and over shorter distances, bear to his general frame. The proportion of each, however, is perfect as it is. Exchange each for each, and they are quite out of proportion.

Only another Form of the Useful.—Since order and proportion, then, have always reference to the end proposed to be accomplished, we have, in fact, in these elements, only another form of the useful, which, as we have already seen, is not the principle of beauty.

Not always Beautiful.—Accordingly, we find that order and proportion do not, in themselves, and when unassociated with other elements, invariably strike us as beautiful. The leg of the swine is as fine a specimen of order and proportion as that of the Arab courser, but is not so much admired for its beauty. It must be admitted, however, that these elements in combination, do with others, enter more or less fully into the formation of the beautiful, are intimately associated with its external forms. The absence or violation of these principles would mar the beauty of the object.

The spiritual Theory.—The only theory of beauty remaining to be noticed is the spiritual theory, which makes beauty consist, not in matter as such, nor in any mere arrangement of matter in itself considered, but in the manifestation or expression, under these sensible material forms, of the higher, the *hidden spiritual nature*, or element, appealing thus to our own spiritual nature, which is thereby awakened to sympathy. In the sensible world about us we find two elements diverse and distinct each from the other, the idea and the form, spirit and matter, the invisible and the visible. In objects that are beautiful we find these two elements united in such a way, that the one expresses or manifests the other, the form expresses the idea, the body expresses the spirit, the visible manifests the invisible, and our own spiritual nature recognizing its like, holds communion and sympathy with it as thus expressed. That which constitutes the beautiful, then, is this manifestation, under sensible forms, and so to our senses, of the higher and spiritual principle which is the life and soul of things.

Relation of the Beautiful to the True and the Good. — It differs from the true in that the true is not, like the beautiful, expressed under sensible forms, but is isolated, pure, abstract, not addressed to the senses, but to reason. It differs from the good, in that the good always proposes an end to be accomplished, and involves the idea of obligation, while the beautiful, on the contrary, proposes no end to be accomplished, acknowledges no obligation or necessity, but is purely free and spontaneous. Yet, though differing in these aspects, the good, the true, and the beautiful, are at basis essentially the same, even as old Plato taught, differing rather in their mode of expression, and the relations which they sustain to us, than in essence.

Relation of the Beautiful to the Sublime. — The relation of the beautiful to the *sublime*, according to this theory, is simply this: In the beautiful, the invisible and the visible, the finite and the infinite, are harmoniously blended. In the sublime, the spiritual element predominates, the harmony is disturbed, the sensible is overborne by the infinite, and our spirits are agitated by the presence, in an unwonted degree, of the higher element of our own being. Hence, while the one pleases, the other awes and subdues us.

Application of this Theory. — Such, in brief outline, is the theory. Let us see now whether it is applicable to the different forms of beauty, and whether it furnishes a satisfactory explanation and account of them.

Surveying the different forms of being, we find among them different degrees of beauty. Does, then, every thing which is beautiful express or manifest, through the medium, and, as it were, under the veil, of the material form, the presence of the invisible spiritual element? and the more beautiful it is, does it so much the more plainly and directly manifest this element?

The Theory applied to inorganic Forms. — And first, to begin with the lowest, how is it with the inanimate, inorganic, merely chemical forms of matter? Here we have certain lines, certain figures, certain colors, that we call beautiful. What do they express of the higher or spiritual element of being? In themselves, and directly, they express nothing, perhaps. Yet are they not, after all, suggestive, symbolical of an idea and spirit dwelling, not in them, but in him who made them, of the Creator's idea and spirit, inarticulate expressions, mere natural signs, of a higher principle than dwells in these poor forms? Do they not suggest and express to us ideas of grace, elegance, delicacy, and the like? Do we not find ourselves attracted by, and, in a sort, in sympathy with these forms, as thus significant and expressive? Is it not thus that lines, and figures, and mathematical forms, the regular and sharply cut angles of the crystal, the light that flashes on its polished surface, or lies hid in beautiful color within it, the order, proportion, and movement, by fixed laws, of the various forms of matter, appear beautiful to us? For what are order, proportion, regularity, harmony, and movement, by fixed laws, and what are elegance, and grace of outline and figure, but so many signs and expressions of a higher intelligence?

Theory applied to vegetable Forms. — Passing onward and upward in the scale of being, taking into view, now, the organic forms of vegetable life, do we not find a more definite articulate expression of the spiritual and invisible under the material form? The flower that blooms in our path, the sturdy tree that throws out its branches against the sky, or droops pensively, as if weighed down by some hidden sorrow, address us more directly, speak more intimately to our spirits, than the mere crystal can do, however elegant its form, or definite its outline. They express sentiments, not ideas merely. They respond to the sensibilities, they appeal to the inner life of the soul. They are strong or weak, timid or bold, joyous or melancholy. It requires no vigorous exercise of fancy to attribute to them the sensibilities which they awaken in us. When in lively communion and sympathy with nature, we can hardly resist the conviction that the emotions which she calls into play in our own bosoms are, somehow, her own emotions also; that under these forms so expressive, so full of meaning to us, there lurks an intelligence, a soul.

To the animal Kingdom. — In the animal kingdom, this invisible spiritual principle, the energy that lies hidden under all forms of animate and organized substance, becomes yet more strongly and obviously developed. The approach is nearer, and the appeal is more direct, to our own spiritual nature. We perceive signs, not to be mistaken, of intelligence and of feeling; passion betrays itself, love, hate, fear, the very principles of our own spiritual being, the very image of our own higher nature. Beauty and deformity are now more strongly marked than in the lower degrees of the scale of being.

To Man. — In man we reach the highest stage of animal existence with which we are conversant, the highest degree of life, intelligence, soul — the being in whom the spiritual shines forth most clearly through the material veil — and, shall we not say also, the being most beautiful of all? The highest style of beauty to be found in nature pertains to the human form, as animated and lighted up by the intelligence within. It is the expression of the soul that constitutes this superior beauty. It is that which looks out at the eye, which sits in calm majesty on the brow, lurks in the lip, smiles on the cheek, is set forth in the chiselled lines and features of the countenance, in the general contour of figure and form, and the particular shading and expression of the several parts, in the movement, and gesture, and tone; it is this looking out of the invisible spirit that dwells within, through the portals of the visible, this manifestation of the higher nature, that we admire and love; this constitutes to us the beauty of our species. Hence it is that certain features, not in themselves, perhaps, particularly attractive, wanting, it may be, in certain regularity of outline, or in certain delicacy and softness, are still invested with a peculiar charm and radiance of beauty from their peculiar expressiveness and animation. The light of genius, or the superior glow of sympathy, and a noble heart, play upon those plain, and, it may be, homely features, and light them up with a brilliant and regal beauty. Those, as every artist knows, are precisely the features most difficult to portray. The expression changes with the instant. The beauty flashes, and is gone, or gives place to a still higher beauty, as the light that plays in fitful corruscations along the northern sky, coming and going, but never still.

Man not the highest Type of Beauty.—Is then the human form the highest expression of the principle of beauty? It can hardly be; for in man, as in all things on the earth, is mingled along with the beauty much that is deformed, with the excellence much imperfection. We can conceive forms superior to his, faces radiant with a beauty that sin has never darkened, nor passion nor sorrow dimmed. We can conceive forms of beauty more perfect, purer, brighter, loftier than any thing that human eye hath seen or human ear heard. We conceive them, however, as existing only under some sensible form, as manifest in some way to sense, and the beauty with which we invest them is the beauty of the spiritual expressing itself in the outward and visible. It is the province of imagination to fashion these conceptions, and of art to attempt their realization. This, the poet, the painter, the sculptor, the architect, the orator, each in his way, is ever striving to do, to present under sensible forms, the ideal of a more perfect loveliness and excellence than the actual world affords.

This ideal can never be adequately and fully represented. The perfection of beauty dwells alone with God.

Consideration in favor of the Theory now explained. — It is in favor of the theory now under consideration, that it seems thus more nearly to meet and account for the various phenomena of beauty, than any other of those which have passed under our review, and that it accounts for them, withal, on a principle so simple and obvious. The crystal, the violet, the graceful spreading elm, the drooping willow, the statue, the painting, the musical composition, the grand cathedral, whatever in nature, whatever in art is beautiful, all mean something, all express something, and in this lies their beauty; and we are moved by them, because we, who have a soul, and in whom the spiritual nature predominates, can understand and sympathize with that which these forms of nature and art, in their semi-articulate way, seem all striving to express.

The Ideas thus expressed pertain not to Nature but to the divine Mind. — It is not necessary that, with the ancient Greeks, we should conceive of nature, as having herself an intelligent soul, of these forms as themselves conscious of their own meaning and beauty. It is enough that we recognize them as conveying a sentiment and meaning not their own, but his who made them, and made them representative and expressive of his own beautiful thought.

Words are not the only modes of expression. The soul speaks more earnestly and eloquently often in signs than in words. And when God speaks to men, he does it not always in the barren forms of human speech, but in the flower that he places by my path, in the tree, the mountain, the rolling ocean, the azure firmament. These are his *words;* and they are beautiful, and, when he will, they are terrible. Happy he who, in all these manifestations, recognizes the voice of God.

§ II. — Cognizance of the Beautiful.

Beauty an Object of Cognition. — We have treated, in the preceding section, of the idea of the beautiful, in itself considered. We proceed to investigate the action of the mind as cognizant of the beautiful in its actual manifestations, whether in nature or art. Beauty, as we have found reason to believe, is not a conception merely, existing only in the mind, but a quality of certain objects. As such it has objective value and existence, and the mind is cognizant of it as such, perceives it, observes it, compares it and the object to which it pertains with other like and unlike objects, judges and decides respecting it. This quality of objects makes its appeal, as do all objects of perception, first to the senses, and through them to the mind. There is thus awakened in the mind, or suggested to it, the original and intuitive conception of the beautiful; there is also, and beside this, the cognizance by the mind of the beautiful as an actual and present reality manifest in the object before it As it perceives other objects of a like nature, it classes them with the preceding, compares them severally, judges of their respective merits, their respective degrees and kinds of beauty. This discriminating power of the mind, as exercised upon the various objects of beauty and sublimity, whether in nature or art, we may designate by the general name of *taste*.

Nature of this Power. — There has been much difference of opinion as to the precise nature of this power, whether it is a distinct faculty of the mind, or the simple exercise of some faculty already known and described, whether it is of the nature of intellect, or of emotion, or the combination of both. Hence the various definitions of taste which have been given by different writers, some regarding it as strictly an intellectual faculty, others as an emotion, while the greater number regard it as including the action both of the intellect in perceiving, and of the sensibility in feeling, whatever is beautiful and sublime.

What has been already said, sufficiently indicates with which of these general views our own most nearly accords. We use the term taste to denote the mind's power of cognizing the beautiful, a power of knowing, of discriminating, rather than of feeling, an exercise of judgment and the reflective power, directed to one particular class of objects, rather than any distinct faculty of the mind. Feeling is doubtless awakened on the perception of the beautiful; it may even precede the judgment by which we decide that the object before us is truly beautiful; but the feeling is not *itself* the perception, or the judgment; is not itself *taste*, whatever may be its relation to taste.

Proposed Investigation. — As this is a matter of some importance to a correct psychology, and also of much difference of opinion, it seems necessary, for purposes of science, to investigate somewhat carefully the nature of this form of mental activity. It is not a matter to be settled by authority, by arbitrary definition, or dogmatic assertion. We must look at the views and opinions of others, and at the reasons for those opinions.

Definitions. — As preliminary to such investigation, I shall present some of the definitions of taste, given by the more prominent writers, representing each of the leading views already indicated.

Blair defines it "a power of receiving pleasure from the

beauties of nature and art." Montesquieu, a French author of distinction, defines it "something which attaches us to certain objects by the power of an internal sense or feeling." Gerard, author of an Essay on Taste, makes it consist in the improvement of the internal senses, viz., sense of novelty, sublimity, beauty, imitation, harmony, etc. Accordant with this are the lines of Akenside:

"What, then, is taste but those internal powers,
Active and strong, and feelingly alive
To each fine impulse?"

Nature of these Definitions. — The definitions now given, it will be perceived, make taste a matter of *sensibility*, of mere *feeling*, a sensation or sense, a passive faculty of being pleased with the beauties of nature and art.

Another Class of Definitions. — Differing from this, others have carefully distinguished between the rational and emotional elements, the power of *discriminating* and the power of *feeling*, and have made taste to consist properly in the former. Of this class is Brown. M'Dermot also takes the same view. This author, in his critical dissertation on the nature and principles of taste, defines it as the *power of discriminating* those qualities of sensible and intellectual being, which, from the invisible harmony that exists between them and our nature, excite in us pleasant emotions. The emotion, however, though it may be the parent of taste, he would not regard as a constituent element of it.

Definitions combining both Elements. — The greater number, however, of those who have written on this subject, have combined in their definitions of taste both these elements, the power of perceiving and the power of feeling. So Burke: "That faculty, or those faculties of the mind which *are affected with*, or which *form a judgment of*, the works of imagination and the elegant arts." Alison: "That faculty of the mind by which we *perceive* and *enjoy* whatever is beautiful or sublime in the works of nature and art."

Reid also makes it consist in "the power of discerning and relishing" these objects. Voltaire makes the feeling quite as essential as the perception. Benard, Professor of Philosophy in the College Royal at Rouen, in the excellent article on taste, in the Dictionnaire des Sciences Philosophiques, defines taste as "that faculty of the mind which makes us to discern and feel the beauties of nature, and whatever is excellent in works of art." It is a compound faculty, according to this author, inhabiting at once both worlds, that of sense and that of reason. Beauty reveals itself to us only under sensible forms, the faculty which contemplates the beautiful, therefore, seizes it only in its sensible manifestation. The pure idea, on the other hand, in its abstract nature, addresses not the taste but the understanding; it appears to us, not as the beautiful, but as the true. Taste, then, has to do with sense. Still, says Benard, "the essential element which constitutes it, pertains to the reason; it is, in truth, only one of the forms of this sovereign power, which takes different names according to the objects which it deals with; *reason*, properly speaking, when it employs itself in the sphere of speculative truth; *conscience*, when it reveals to us truths moral or practical; *taste*, when it appreciates the beauty and suitableness of objects in the real world, or of works of art."

These three Classes comprehensive. — Other authorities and definitions, almost without number, might be added, but they fall essentially under the three classes now specified. Which of these views, then, is the correct and true one? is the question now before us. Is taste a matter of feeling, or is it an intellectual discernment, or is it both? Evidently we cannot depend on authority for the decision of this question, since authorities differ. We must examine for ourselves.

Etymology of the Term. — To some extent the word itself may guide us. Borrowed, as are most if not all words expressing mental states and acts, from the sphere of sense, there was doubtless some reason why this word in particular was selected to denote the power of the mind now under consideration. Some close analogy, doubtless, was supposed to exist between the physical state denoted by this word in its primary sense, and the mental faculty to which we refer, so that, in seeking for a term by which to designate that intellectual faculty, none would more readily present itself, as appropriate and suggestive of the mental state intended, than the one in question. This analogy, whatever it be, while it cannot be taken as decisive of the question before us, is still an element not to be overlooked by the psychologist. What, then, is the analogy? How comes this word — *taste* — to be used, rather than any other, to denote the idea and power now under consideration?

Taste as a Sense. — In the domain of sense, certain objects brought in contact with the appropriate physical organ, affect us as sweet, sour, bitter, etc. This is purely an affection of the sensibility, mere feeling. We say the thing *tastes* so and so. The power of distinguishing such qualities we call the power or sense of taste. Primarily, mere sensation, mere feeling, we transfer the word to denote the power of judging by means of that sensation. There is, in the first instance, an affection of the organ by the object brought in contact with it, of which affection we are cognizant; then follows an intellectual perception or judgment that the object thus affecting us, possesses such and such qualities, is sweet, sour, bitter, salt, etc., The sensation affords the ground of the judgment. The latter is based upon the former. The sensation, the simple feeling, affords the means of discriminating, judging, distinguishing, and to this latter power or process the word taste, in the physical sense, is more frequently appropriated. We say of such or such a man, his taste is acute, or his taste is impaired, or dull, etc., meaning his power of perceiving and distinguishing the various properties of objects which affect the sense of taste.

Analogy of this to the mental Process called Taste. — It is easy to perceive, now, the analogy between the physical power and process thus described, and the psychological faculty under consideration, to which the name primarily denoting the former has been transferred. Objects in nature and art present themselves to the observation, and awaken pleasure as beautiful, or excite disgust as the opposite. A mere matter of sensibility, of feeling, this. Presently, however, we begin to notice, not the mere feeling of pleasure or aversion, but the character of the object that awakens it; we discriminate, we attribute to the object such and such qualities, take cognizance of it as possessing those qualities. This discriminating power, this judgment of the mind that the object possesses such properties, we call taste. As, in the sphere of sense, the feeling awakened affords the means of judging and distinguishing, as to the qualities of the object, so here. The beautiful awakens sensation — a vivid feeling of pleasure, delight, admiration; deformity awakens the reverse; and this feeling enables us to judge of the object, as regards the property in question, viz., beauty or deformity, whether, and how far, as compared with other objects of the mind, it possesses this quality. In either case — the physical and the psychological — the process begins with sensation or feeling, but passes on at once into the domain of intellect, the sphere of understanding or judgment; and while, in either case, the word taste may, without impropriety, be used to denote the feeling or susceptibility of impression which lies at the foundation of the intellectual process, it is more strictly appropriate to the faculty of discriminating the objects, and the qualities of objects, which awaken in us the given emotions.

So far as the word itself can guide us, then, it would seem to be in the direction now indicated.

Appeal to Consciousness. — Analogy, however, may mislead us. We must not base a doctrine or decide a question in psychology upon the meaning of a single term. Upon observation and consciousness of what actually passes in our own minds, in view of the beautiful, we must, after all, rely. Let us place ourselves, then, in the presence of the beautiful in nature or art, and observe the various mental phenomena that present themselves to our consciousness.

I stand before a statue of Thorwalsden or Canova. The spell and inspiration of high art are upon me. What passes now in my mind?

The first Element. — First of all, I am conscious of almost instant emotion in view of the object, an emotion of pleasure and delight. No sooner do my eyes rest upon the chiselled form that stands in faultless and wondrous beauty before me, than this emotion awakens. It springs into play, as a fountain springs out of the earth by its own spontaneous energy, or, as the light plays on the mountain tops, and flushes their snowy summits, when the sun rises on the Alps. It is by no volition of mine that this takes place.

A second Element. — Along with the emotion, there is another thing of which, also, I am conscious. Scarcely have my eyes taken in the form and proportions on which they rest with delight, scarcely has the first thrill of emotion, thus awakened, made itself known to the consciousness, when I find myself exclaiming, "How beautiful!" The soul says it; perhaps the lips utter it. If not an oral, it is, at least, a mental affirmation. The mind perceives, at a glance, the presence of beauty, recognizes its divinity, and pays homage at its shrine; not now the blind homage of feeling, merely, but the clear-sighted perception of the intellect, the sure decision of the understanding affirming, with authority, 'That which thou perceivest and admirest is beautiful.' This is an act of judgment, based, however, on the previous awakening of the sensibility. I know, because I feel.

A third Element. — In addition to these, there may, or may not be, another phase of mental action. I may begin, presently, to observe, with a more careful eye, the work before me, and form a critical estimate of it, scan its outline, its several parts, its effect as a whole, ascertain its merits, and its defects as a work of art, study its design, its idea, and how well it expresses that idea, and fulfills that design. I seek to know what it is in the piece that pleases me, and why it pleases me. This may, or may not, take place. Whether it shall occur, or not, will depend on the state of the mind at the moment, the circumstances in which it is placed, its previous training and culture, its habits of thought. This, too, is an exercise of judgment, comparing, distinguishing, deciding; a purely intellectual process. It is not so much a new element, as a distinct phase of that last named. It is the mind deciding and affirming now, not merely that the object is beautiful, but *in what* and *why* it is so.

Uniformity of Results. — I change now the experiment. I repeat it. I place myself before other works, before works of other artists — works of the painter, the architect, the musician, the poet, the orator. Whatever is beautiful, in art or nature, I observe. I perceive, in all cases, the same results, the occurrence of essentially the same mental phenomena. I conclude that these effects are produced, not fortuitously, but according to the constitution of my nature; that they are not specific instances, but general laws of mental action; in other words, that the mind possesses a susceptibility of being impressed in this manner by such objects, and also a faculty of judging and discriminating as above described. To these two elements, essentially, then, do the mental phenomena occasioned by the presence of the beautiful, reduce themselves.

The Question. — Which, then, of these elements is it that answers to the idea of taste, as used to denote a power of the mind? Is it the susceptibility of emotion in view of the beautiful, the power of feeling; or is it the faculty of judging and discriminating; or is it both combined? Our definitions, as we have seen, include both; the word, itself, may denote either; both are comprised in our analysis of the mental phenomena in view of the beautiful.

Not the first. — Is it the first? I think not. Taste is not mere emotion, nor mere susceptibility of emotion. A child or a savage may be deficient in taste, yet they may be as deeply moved in view of the beautiful, in nature or art, as the man of cultivated mind; nay, their emotion may exceed his. They may regard, with great delight and admiration, what he will view with entire indifference. So far from indicating a high degree of taste, the very susceptibility of emotion, in such cases, may be the sure indication of a want of taste. They are pleased with that which a cultivated and correct taste would condemn. The power of being moved is simply sensibility, and sensibility is not taste, however closely they may be related.

Taste the intellectual Element. — Is taste, then, the power of mental discrimination which enables me to say that such and such things are, or are not, beautiful, and which, in some cases, perhaps, enables me to decide why, or wherein they are so? Does it, in a word, denote the *intellectual* rather than the *emotional* element of the process? I am inclined to think this the more correct view. Susceptibility of emotion is, doubtless, concerned in the matter. It has to do with taste. It may be even the ground and foundation of its exercise, nay, of its existence. But it is not, itself, taste, and should not be included, therefore, in the definition.

Reason for distinguishing the two. — As we distinguish, in philosophical investigation, between an emotion and the intellectual perception that precedes and gives rise to it, or between the perception and the sensation on which it is founded, so I would distinguish *taste*, or the intellectual perception of the beautiful, from the *sensation* or *feeling* awakened in view of the object. The fact that both elements exist, and enter into the series of mental phenomena in view of the beautiful, is no reason why they should both be designated by the same term, or included in the same definition, but, rather, it is a reason why they should be carefully distinguished.

The precise nature of this faculty may be more distinctly perceived, if we consider, more particularly, its relation to the *judgment*, and also to the *sensibility*.

Taste, as related to Judgment. — According to the view now taken, taste is only a modification, or rather a particular direction of that general power of the mind which we call *judgment;* it is judgment exercised about the beautiful. It is the office of the judgment to form opinions and beliefs, to inform us of relations, to decide that things are thus and thus, that this is this, and that is that. As employed in different departments of thought, it appears under different forms, and is known under diverse names. As employed about the actual and sensible, we call it understanding; in the sphere of abstract truth it works under the cognomen of reason; in the sphere of practical truth, the thing that is good and right to be done by me, it is known as conscience; in the sphere of the ideal and the beautiful it is taste. In all these departments of mental activity it is exercised, employs itself upon all these subjects, giving us opinion, belief, knowledge, as to them all. The judgment as thus exercised in relation to the beautiful, that is to say, the mind observing, comparing, discriminating, deciding, forming the opinion, or reaching it may be the positive knowledge that this thing is, or is not, beautiful — for this is simply what we mean by judgment in any particular instance — judgment, as thus exercised, is known by the name of *taste.* More strictly speaking, it is not so much the *exercise* of the judgment in this particular way in given instances, as the *foundation* or *ground* of that exercise, the *discriminating faculty* or *power* of the mind by virtue of which it thus operates.

Judgment does not furnish the Ideas. — Does, then, the judgment, it may be asked, give us originally the ideas of the true, the beautiful, and the good? This we do not affirm. Judgment is not the source of ideas, certainly not of those now mentioned. It does not originate them. Their origin and awakening in the human mind is, we should say, on this wise. The beautiful, the true, the good, exist as simple, absolute, eternal principles. They are in the divine mind. They are in the divine works. In a sense they are independent of Deity. He does not create them. He cannot reverse them or change their nature. He works according to them. They are not created by, but only *manifested in*, what God does. We are created with a nature so formed and endowed as to be capable of recognizing these principles and being impressed by them. The consequence is, that no sooner do we open the eye of reason and intelligence upon that which lies around and passes before us, in the world, than the idea of the true, the beautiful, the morally good, is awakened in the mind. We instinctively perceive and feel their presence in the objects presented to our notice. They are the product of our rational intelligence, brought into contact, through sense, with the world in which we dwell. The idea of beauty or of the right, thus once awakened in the mind, when afterward examples, or, it may be, violations, of these principles occur, the judgment is exercised in deciding that the cases presented do or do not properly fall under the class thus designated; and the judgment thus exercised in respect to the beautiful, we call *taste*, in respect to the right, *conscience*.

Taste as now defined.—As now defined, taste is, as to its principle, *the discriminating power of the mind with respect to the beautiful or sublime in nature or art;* that certain state, quality, or condition of the mental powers and the mental culture, the result partly of native difference and endowment, partly of education and habit, by virtue of which we are able to judge more or less correctly as to the beauty, or deformity, the merit or demerit of whatever presents itself in nature or art as an object of admiration, whether and how far it is in reality beautiful, and of its fitness to awaken in us the emotions that we experience in view thereof. If we are able to observe, compare, discriminate, form opinions and conclusions well and correctly, on these matters, our taste is good; otherwise bad. Whether it be the one or the other, will depend not entirely on native endowment, not altogether on the degree to which the judgment is cultivated and developed in respect to other matters, but quite as much on the culture and training of the mind with respect to the specific objects of taste, viz., the beauties of nature and art. Men of strong minds, good understanding, and sound judgment in other matters, are not necessarily men of good taste. Like every other faculty of the mind, taste requires cultivation.

Taste and good Taste. — It is necessary to distinguish between taste, and good taste. Many writers use the terms indifferently, as when we say such a one is a man of taste, meaning of good taste, or such a one has no taste whatever, meaning that he is a man of bad taste. Strictly speaking, the savage who rejoices in the disfigurement of his person by tattooing, paint, and feathers, is a man of *taste*, as really as the Broadway dandy, or the Parisian exquisite. He has his faculty of judging in such matters, and exercises it — his standard of judging, and comes up to it. He is a man of taste, but not of correct taste. He has his own notions, but they do not agree with ours. He violates all the rules and principles by which well-informed minds are guided in such matters. He shocks our notions of fitness and propriety, excites in us emotions of disgust, or of the ludicrous, and, on the whole, we vote him down as a man of no authority in such matters.

As related to Sensibility. — Thus far we have spoken of taste only as related to the judgment. It is necessary to consider also its relation to the *sensibility*. Taste and sensibility are very often confounded. They are, in reality, quite distinct. Sensibility, so far as we are at present concerned with it, is the mind's *capability of emotion* in view of the beautiful or sublime. Taste is its *capability of judging*, in view of the same. Viewed as acts, rather than as states or powers of the mind, sensibility is the feeling awakened in view of a beautiful object; taste is the judgment or opinion formed respecting it. In the case already supposed, I stand before a fine statue or painting. It moves me, attracts me, fills me with delight and admiration. In this, it is not directly and immediately my taste, but my sensibility, that is affected and brought into play. I begin to judge of the object before me as a work of art, to form an opinion respecting its merits and demerits; and, in so doing, my taste is exercised.

The two not always proportional. — Not only are the two principles distinct, but not always do they exist in equal proportion and development in the same mind. Persons of the liveliest sensibility are not always, perhaps not generally, persons of the nicest taste. The child, the uneducated peasant, the negro, are as highly delighted with beautiful forms and beautiful colors as the philosopher, but could not tell you so well why they were moved, or what it was, in the object, that pleased them; neither would they discriminate so well the truly beautiful from that which is not worthy of admiration. If there may be sensibility without taste, so, on the other hand, a high degree of taste is not always accompanied with a corresponding degree of sensibility. The practised connoisseur is not always the man who enjoys the most at sight of a fine picture. The skillful musician has much better taste in music than the child that listens, with mingled wonder and delight, to his playing; but we have only to glance at the countenance of each, to see at once which feels the most.

Sensibility not inconsistent with Taste. — I should not, however, infer from this, that a high degree of sensibility is inconsistent with a high degree of taste. This was Mr. Stewart's opinion. The feeling, he would say, will be likely to interfere with the judgment, in such a case. Doubtless, where the feeling is highly wrought upon and excited, it may, for the time, interfere with the cool and deliberate exercise of the judgment. Yet, nevertheless, if sensibility be wanting, there will not be likely to be much taste. If I feel no pleasure at sight of a beautiful landscape or painting, I shall not be likely to trouble myself much about its comparative merits or defects. It is useless, in such a case, to inquire what pleases me, or why I am pleased, when, in truth, nothing pleases me. There is no motive for the exercise of judgment in such a case, neither is there an opportunity for its action. The very foundation for such an exercise is wanting. A lively sensibility is the basis of a correct taste, the ground on which it must rest, the spring and life of its action. The two are related somewhat as genius and learning, which are not always found in equal degree, yet are by no means inconsistent with each other. There may be a high degree of mental strength and activity, without corresponding acquisitions; yet there can hardly be learning without some degree of mental power and activity. There may be sensibility without much taste, but hardly much taste without sensibility. Taste is, in a great measure, acquired, cultivated, an art; sensibility, a native endowment. It may be developed, strengthened, educated, but not acquired. Genius produces, sensibility admires, taste judges or decides. Their action is reciprocal. If taste corrects and restrains the too ready or too extravagant sensibility, the latter, on the other hand, furnishes the ground and data upon which, after all, taste must rely in its decisions.

Cultivation of Taste. — We have investigated, with some care, as was proposed, the nature of that power of the mind which takes cognizance of the beautiful. On the cultivation of this power, a few words must be said in this connection. Taste is an intellectual faculty, a perceptive power, a matter of judgment, and, as such, both admits and requires cultivation. No forms of mental activity depend more on education and exercise, for their full development, than that class to which we give the general name of judgment, and no form of judgment more than that which we call taste. The mind uncultivated, untrained, unused to the nice perception of the beautiful, can no more judge correctly, in matters of taste, than the mind unaccustomed to judge of the distance, magnitude, or chemical properties of bodies, can form correct decisions upon these subjects. It must be trained by art, and strengthened by exercise. It must be made familiar with the laws, and conversant with the forms of beauty. It must be taught to observe and study the beautiful, in nature and in art, to discriminate, to compare, to judge. The works in literature and in art which have received the approbation of time, and the honorable verdict of mankind, as well as the objects in nature which have commanded the admiration of the race, must become familiar, not by observation only, but by careful study. Thus may taste be cultivated.

Historical Sketch.

View of Plato. — Among the ancients, *Plato* was, perhaps, the first to distinguish the idea of the beautiful from other kindred ideas, and to point out its affinity with the true and the good, thus recognizing in it something immutable and eternal. In making the good and the beautiful identical, however, he mistakes the true character and end of art. Previously to Plato, and even by him, art and the beautiful were treated only in connection with ethics and politics; æsthetics, as a distinct department of science, was not known to the ancients.

Of Aristotle. — *Aristotle* has not treated of the beautiful, but only of dramatic art. Poetry, he thinks, originates in the tendency to imitate, and the desire to know. Tragedy is the imitation of *the better.* Painting should represent, in like manner, not *what is,* but what *ought to be.* In this sense, may be understood his profound remark, that *poetry is more true than history.*

Plotinus and Augustine. — After Aristotle, *Plotinus* and *Augustine* alone, among the ancients, have treated of the beautiful. The work of Augustine is not extant. It is known that he made beauty consist in unity and fitness of parts, as in music. The treatise of Plotinus is regarded as at once beautiful and profound. Material beauty is, with him, only the expression or reflection of spiritual beauty. The soul alone, the mind, is beautiful, and in loving the beautiful, the soul loves its own image as there expressed. Hence, the soul must, itself, be beautiful, in order to comprehend and feel beauty. The tendency of this theory is to mysticism.

Longinus and Quintilian. — Longinus, and Quintilian, treat of the sublime, only with reference to eloquence and oratory; so, also, Horace, of art, as having to do with poetry.

Bacon. — Among the moderns, *Bacon* recognizes the fine arts as among the sciences, and poetry as one of the three chief branches of human knowledge, but nowhere, that I am aware, treats of the beautiful, distinctly, as such.

School of Leibnitz. — It was the school of *Leibnitz* and *Wolf* in Germany that first made the beautiful a distinct science. Baumgarten, disciple of Wolf, first conceived this idea. Like Plato, however, he makes the beautiful too nearly identical with the good and with morals.

School of Locke. — In England, the school of *Locke* have much to say of beauty. Shaftesbury and Hutcheson, while they do not clearly distinguish between the beautiful and the good, adopt the theory of unity in variety, as already explained. Hogarth falls into the same class, his idea of beauty being represented by the waving line. Burke does not distinguish sufficiently between the sublime and the terrible.

French Encyclopedists. — In France, the *Encyclopedists* coincide, essentially, with the school of Locke, and treat of the beautiful, chiefly in its moral aspect.

The later Germans. — In Germany, again, *Winckelman*, an artist, and not a philosopher, seizing the spirit of the Greek art, ascribes, as Plato had done, the idea of beauty to

God, from whom it passes into sensible things, as his mani festations.

In opposition to this ideal and divine aspect, *Lessing* takes a more practical view, regarding the beautiful from the stand-point of the *real.* *Herder* and *Goethe* contribute, also, much to the science of æsthetics. All these do little more than prepare the way for *Kant*, who goes more profoundly into the philosophy of the matter. He makes beauty a *subjective* affair, a play of the imagination.

Schiller makes it the joint product of the reason and the sensibility, but still a *subjective* matter, as Kant.

Schelling and Hegel. — *Schelling* develops the spiritual or ideal theory of beauty. *Hegel* carries out this theory and makes a complete science of it, classifies and analyzes the arts. His work is regarded as the first complete discussion of the philosophy of the fine arts. It is characterized by strength, clearness, depth, power of analysis, richness of imagination.

Theory of Jouffroy. — *Jouffroy*, in France, among the later writers, has treated fully, and in an admirable manner, of the philosophy of the beautiful. His theory is derived from that of Hegel, with some modifications. It is essentially the theory last presented in the discussion of the subject in the preceding section, viz., the expression of the spiritual or invisible element under sensible forms. No writer is more worthy of study than Jouffroy. His work is clear, strong, and of admirable power of analysis.

Cousin. — Among the eclectics, *Cousin*, in his treatise on the true, the beautiful, and the good, has many just observations, with much beauty and philosophic clearness of expression.

M'Dermot. — In English, beside the works already referred to, must be noticed the treatise of *M'Dermot* on Taste, in which the nature and objects of taste are fully and well discussed.

CHAPTER IV.

IDEA AND COGNIZANCE OF THE RIGHT.

§ I. — Idea of Right.

The Idea of Right a Conception of the Mind. — Among the conceptions which constitute the furniture of the mind, there is one, which, in many respects, is unlike all others, while, at the same time, it is more important than all others; that is, the notion or idea of *right.*

Universally prevalent. — When we direct our attention to any given instance of the voluntary action of any intelligent rational being, we find ourselves not unfrequently pronouncing upon its character as a *right* or *wrong* act. Especially is this the case when the act contemplated is of a marked and unusual character. The question at once arises, is it right? Or, it may be, without the consciousness of even a question respecting it, our decision follows instantly upon the mental apprehension of the act itself — this thing is right, that thing is wrong. Our decision may be correct or incorrect; our perception of the real nature of the act may be clear or obscure; it may make a stronger or weaker impression on the mind, according to our mental habits, the tone of our mental nature, and the degree to which we have cultivated the moral faculty. There may be minds so degraded, and natures so perverted, that the moral character of an act shall be quite mistaken, or quite overlooked in many cases; or, when perceived, it shall make little impression on them. Even in such minds, however, the *idea* of right and wrong still finds a place, and the understanding applies it, though not perhaps always correctly, to particular instances of human conduct. There is no reason to believe that any mind possessing ordinary endowments, that degree of reason and intelligence which nature usually bestows, is destitute of this idea, or fails altogether to apply it to its own acts, and those of others.

The Question and its different Answers. — But here an important question presents itself: *Whence come* these ideas and perceptions; their origin? How is it, why is it, that we pronounce an act right or wrong, when once fairly apprehended? How come we by these notions? The fact is admitted; the explanations vary. By one class of writers our ideas of this nature have been ascribed to *education* and *fashion;* by another, to *legal restriction*, human or divine. Others, again, viewing these ideas as the offspring of nature, have assigned them either to the operation of a *special sense*, given for this specific purpose, as the eye for vision; or to the joint action of certain associated emotions; while others regard them as originating in an exercise of *judgment*, and others still, as *natural intuitions* of the mind, or reason exercised on subjects of a moral nature.

Main Question. — The main question is, are these ideas *natural*, or *artificial and acquired?* If the latter, are they the result of education, or of legal restraint? If the former, are they to be referred to the *sensibilities*, as the result of a special sense or of association, or to the *intellect*, as the result of the faculty of judgment or as intuitions of reason?

1. *Education.* — Come they from *Education and Imitation?* — So Locke, Paley, and others, have supposed. Locke was led to take this view, by tracing, as he did, all simple ideas, except those of our own mental operations, to sensation, as their source. This allows, of course, no place for the ideas of right and wrong, which, accordingly, he concluded, cannot be natural ideas, but must be the result of education.

Objection to this View. — Now it is to be conceded that education and fashion are powerful instruments in the culture of the mind. Their influence is not to be overlooked in estimating the causes that shape and direct the opinions of men, and the tendencies of an age. But they do not account for the *origin* of any thing. This has been ably and clearly shown by Dugald Stewart, in answer to Locke; and it is a sufficient answer. Education and imitation both *presuppose* the existence of moral ideas and distinctions; the very things to be accounted for. How came they who first taught these distinctions, and they who first set the example of making such distinctions, to be themselves in possession of these ideas? Whence did *they* derive them? Who taught *them*, and set *them* the example? This is a question not answered by the theory now under consideration. It gives us, therefore, and can give us, no account of the origin of the ideas in question.

2. *Legal Enactment.*—Do we then derive these ideas from *legal restriction and enactment?* So teach some able writers. Laws are made, human and divine, requiring us to do thus and thus, and forbidding such and such things, and hence we get our ideas originally of right and wrong.

Presupposes Right.—If this be so, then, previous to all law, there could have been no such ideas, of course. But does not law *presuppose* the idea of right and wrong? Is it not built on that idea as its basis? How, then, can it originate that on which itself depends, and which it presupposes? The first law ever promulgated must have been either a just or an unjust law, or else of no moral character. If the latter, how could a law which was neither just nor unjust, have suggested to the subjects of it any such ideas? If the former, then these qualities, and the ideas of them, must have existed *prior* to the law itself; and whoever made the law and conferred on it its character, must have had already, in his own mind, the idea of the right and its opposite. It is evident that we cannot, in this way, account for the *origin* of the ideas in question. We are no nearer the solution of the problem than before.

In opposition to the views now considered, we must regard the ideas in question, as, directly or indirectly, the work of nature, and the result of our constitution. The question still remains, however, in which of the several ways indicated, does this result take place?

2. *Special Sense.* — Shall we attribute these ideas to a *special sense?* This is the view taken by Hutcheson and his followers. Ascribing, with Locke, all our simple ideas to sensation, but not content with Locke's theory of moral distinctions as the result of education, he sought to account for them by enlarging the sphere of sensation, and introducing a new sense, whose specific office is to take cognizance of such distinctions. The tendency of this theory is evident. While it derives the idea of right and its opposite from our natural constitution, and is, so far, preferable to either of the preceding theories, still, in assigning them a place among the sensibilities, it seems to make morality a mere *sentiment*, a matter of feeling merely, an impression made on our sentient nature — a mere subjective affair — as color and taste are impressions made on our organs of sense, and not properly qualities of bodies. As these affections of the sense do not exist independently, but only relatively to us, so moral distinctions, according to this view, are merely subjective affections of our minds, and not independent realities.

Hume and the Sophists. — Hume accedes to this general view, and carries it out to its legitimate results, making morality a mere relation between our nature and certain objects, and not an independent quality of actions. Virtue and vice, like color and taste, the bright and the dull, the sweet and the bitter, lie merely in our sensations.

These skeptical views had been advanced long previously by the Sophists, who taught that man is the measure of all things, that things are only what they seem to us.

Ambiguity of the term Sense. — It is true, as Stewart has

observed, that these views do not necessarily result from Hutcheson's theory, nor were they, probably, held by him; but such is the natural tendency of his doctrine. The term *sense*, as employed by him, is, in itself, ambiguous, and may be used to denote a *mental perception;* but when we speak of *a* sense, we are understood to refer to that part of our constitution which, when affected from without, gives us certain sensations. Thus the sense of hearing, the sense of vision, the sense of taste, of smell, etc. It is in this way that Hutcheson seems to have employed the term, and his illustrations all point in this direction. He was unfortunate, to say the least, in his use of terms, and in his illustrations; unfortunate, also, in having such a disciple as Hume, to push his theory to its legitimate results.

If, by a special sense, he meant only a direct perceptive power of the mind, then, doubtless, Hutcheson is right in recognizing such a faculty, and attributing to it the ideas under consideration. But that is not the proper meaning of the word *sense*, nor is that the signification attached to it by his followers.

No Evidence of such a Faculty. — But if he means, by sense, what the word itself would indicate, some adaptation of the sensibilities to receive impressions from things without, analogous to that by which we are affected through the organs of sense, then, in the first place, it is not true that we have any such special faculty. There is no evidence of it; nay, facts contradict it. There is no such *uniformity* of moral impression or sensation as ought to manifest itself on this supposition. Men's eyes and ears are much alike, in their activity, the world over. That which is white, or red, to one, is not black to another, or green to a third; that which is sweet to one, is not sour, or bitter, to another. At least, if such variations occur, they are the result only of some unnatural and unusual condition of the organs. But it is otherwise with the operation of the so-called special sense. While all men have probably, some idea of right and wrong, there is the greatest possible variety in its application to particular instances of conduct. What one approves as a virtue, another condemns as a crime.

No Need of it. — Nor, secondly, have we any need to call in the aid of a special sense to give us ideas of this kind. It is not true, as Locke and Hutcheson believed, that all our ideas, except those of our own mental operations, or consciousness, are derived ultimately from sensation. We have ideas of the true and the beautiful, ideas of cause and effect, of geometrical and arithmetical relations, and various other ideas, which it would be difficult to trace to the senses as their source; and which, equally with the ideas of right and wrong, would require, in that case, a special sense for their production.

4. *Association.* — Shall we, then, adopt the view of that class of ethical writers who account for the origin of these ideas by *the principle of association?* Such men as Hartley, Mill, Mackintosh, and others of that stamp, are not lightly to be set aside in the discussion of such a question. Their view is, that the moral perceptions are the result of certain combined antecedent emotions, such as gratitude, pity, resentment, etc., which relate to the dispositions and actions of voluntary agents, and which very easily and naturally come to be transferred, from the agent himself, to the action in itself considered, or to the disposition which prompted it; forming, when thus transferred and associated, what we call the moral feelings and perceptions. Just as avarice arises from the original desire, not of money, but of the things which money can procure — which desire comes, eventually, to be transferred, from the objects themselves, to the means and instrument of procuring them — and, as sympathy arises from the transfer to others of the feelings which, in like circumstances, agitate our own bosoms, so, in like manner, by the principle of association, the feelings which naturally arise in view of the conduct of others, are transferred from the agent to the act, from the enemy or the

benefactor, to the injury or the benefaction, which acts stand afterward, by themselves, as objects of approval or condemnation. Hence the disposition to approve all benevolent acts, and to condemn the opposite; which disposition, thus formed and transferred, is a part of conscience. So of other elementary emotions.

Makes Conscience a mere Sentiment. — It will be perceived that this theory, which is indebted chiefly to Mackintosh for its completeness, and scientific form, makes conscience wholly a matter of sentiment and feeling; standing, in this respect, on the same ground with the theory of a special sense, and liable, in part, to the same objections. Hence the name *sentimental* school, often employed to designate, collectively, the adherents of each of these views. While the theory, now proposed, might seem then to offer a plausible account of the manner in which our moral *sentiments* arise, it does not account for the origin of our *ideas* and *perceptions* of moral rectitude. Now the moral faculty is not a mere sentiment. There is an intellectual perception of one thing as right, and another as wrong; and the question now before us is, Whence comes that perception, and the idea on which it is based? To resolve the whole matter into certain transferred and associated emotions, is to give up the inherent distinction of right and wrong as qualities of actions, and make virtue and vice creations of the sensibility, the play and product of the excited feelings. To admit the perception and idea of the right, and ascribe their origin to antecedent emotion, is, moreover, to reverse the natural order and law of psychological operation, which bases emotion on perception, and not perception on emotion. We do not first admire, love, hate, and then perceive, but the reverse.

Further Objections. — The view now under consideration, while it seems to resolve the moral faculty into mere feeling, thus making morality wholly a relative affair, makes conscience, itself, an acquired, rather than a natural faculty, a secondary process, a transformation of emotions, rather than itself an original principle. It does it, moreover, the further injustice of deriving its origin from the purely *selfish* principles of our nature. I receive a favor, or an injury; hence I regard, with certain feelings of complacency, or the opposite, the man who has thus treated me. These feelings I come gradually to transfer to, and associate with, the act in itself considered, and this with other acts of the same nature; and so, at last, I come to have a moral faculty, and pronounce one thing right, and another wrong.

At Variance with Facts. — This view is quite inadmissible; at variance with facts, and the well-known laws of the human mind. The moral faculty is one of the earliest to develop itself. It appears in childhood, manifesting itself, not as an acquired and secondary principle, the result of a complicated process of associated and transferred emotion, requiring time for its gradual formation and growth, but rather as an original instinctive principle of nature.

Sympathy. — Adam Smith, in his "Theory of Moral Sentiments," has proposed a view which falls properly under the general theory of association, and may be regarded as a modification of it. He attributes our moral perceptions to the feeling of *sympathy.* To adopt the feelings of another is to approve them. If those feelings are such as would naturally be awakened in us by the same objects, we approve them as morally proper. Sympathy with the gratitude of one who has received a favor, leads us to regard the benefaction as meritorious. Sympathy with the resentment of an injured man, leads us to regard the injurer as worthy of punishment, and so the sense of demerit originates; sympathy with the feelings of others respecting our own conduct gives rise to self-approval and sense of duty. Rules of morality are merely a summary of these sentiments.

This View not sustained by Consciousness. — Whatever credit may be due to this ingenious writer, for calling attention to a principle which had not been sufficiently taken into account by preceding philosophers, we cannot but regard it as an insufficient explanation of the present case. In the first place, we are not *conscious* of the element of sympathy in the decisions and perceptions of the moral faculty. We look at a given action as right or wrong, and approve of it, or condemn it *on that ground*, because it *is* right or wrong, not because we sympathize with the feelings awakened by the act in the minds of others. If the process now supposed intervened between our knowledge of the act, and our judgment of its morality, we should know it and recognize it as a distinct element.

No imperative Character. — Furthermore, sympathy, like other emotions, has no *imperative* character, and, even if it might be supposed to suggest to the mind some idea of moral distinctions, cannot of itself furnish a foundation for those feelings of *obligation* which accompany and characterize the decisions of the moral faculty.

The Standard of Right. — But more than this, the view now taken makes the standard of right and wrong *variable*, and dependent on the feelings of men. We must know how others think and feel, how the thing affects them, before we can know whether a given act is right or wrong, to be performed or avoided. And then, furthermore, our feelings must agree with theirs; there must be sympathy and harmony of views and feelings, else the result will not follow. If any thing prevents us from knowing what are the feelings of others with respect to a given course of conduct, or if for any reason we fail to sympathize with those feelings, we can have no conscience in the matter. As those feelings vary, so will our moral perceptions vary. We have no fixed standard. There is no place left for right, as such, and absolutely. If no sympathy, then no duty, no right, no morality.

Result of the preceding Inquiries. — We have, as yet, found no satisfactory explanation of the origin of our moral ideas and perceptions. They seem not to be the result of education and imitation, nor yet of legal enactment. They seem to be natural, rather than artificial and acquired. Yet we cannot trace them to the action of the sensitive part of our nature. They are not the product of a special sense, nor yet of the combined and associated action of certain natural emotions, much less of any one emotion, as sympathy. And yet they are a part of our nature. Place man where you will, surround him with what influences you will, you still find in him, to some extent at least, indications of a moral nature; a nature modified, indeed, by circumstances, but never wholly obliterated. Evidently we must refer the ideas in question, then, to the intellectual, since they do not belong to the sensitive part of our nature.

5. *Judgment.* — Are they then the product and operation of the faculty of judgment? But the judgment does not *originate* ideas. It compares, distributes, estimates, decides to what class and category a thing belongs, but creates nothing. I have in mind the idea of a triangle, a circle, etc. So soon as certain figures are presented to the eye, I refer them at once, by an act of judgment, to the class to which they belong. I affirm that to be a triangle, this, a circle, etc.; the judgment does this. But judgment does not furnish my mind with the primary idea of a circle, etc. It deals with this idea already in the mind. So in our judgment of the beauty and deformity of objects. The perception that a landscape or painting is beautiful, is, in one sense, an act of judgment; but it is an act which presupposes the idea of the beautiful already in the mind that so judges. So also of moral distinctions. Whence comes the *idea* of right and wrong which lies at the foundation of every particular judgment as to the moral character of actions? This is the question before us, still unanswered; and to this there remains but one reply.

6. *These Ideas intuitive.* — The ideas in question are *intuitive;* suggestions or perceptions of *reason.* The view now proposed may be thus stated: It is the office of reason

to discern the right and the wrong, as well as the true and the false, the beautiful and the reverse. Regarded subjectively, as conceptions of the human mind, right and wrong, as well as beauty and its opposite, truth and its opposite, are simple ideas, incapable of analysis or definition; *intuitions of reason.* Regarded as objective, right and wrong are realities, qualities absolute, and inherent in the nature of things, not fictitious, not the play of human fancy or human feeling, not relative merely to the human mind, but independent, essential, universal, absolute. As such, reason recognizes their existence. Judgment decides that such and such actions do possess the one or the other of these qualities; are right or wrong actions. There follows the sense of obligation to do or not to do, and the consciousness of merit or demerit as we comply, or fail to comply, with the same. In view of these perceptions emotions arise, but only as based upon them. The emotions do not, as the sentimental school affirm, originate the idea, the perception; but the idea, the perception, gives rise to the emotion. We are so constituted as to feel certain emotions in view of the moral quality of actions, but the idea and perception of that moral quality must *precede*, and it is the office of reason to produce this.

First Truths. — There are certain simple ideas which must be regarded as first truths, or first principles, of the human understanding, essential to its operations, ideas universal, absolute, necessary. Such are the ideas of personal existence, and identity, of time and space, as conditions of material existence; of number, cause, and mathematical relation. Into this class fall the ideas of the true, the beautiful, the right, and their opposites. The fundamental maxims of reasoning and morals find here their place.

How awakened. — These are, in a sense, intuitive perceptions; not strictly innate, yet connate; the foundation for them being laid in our nature and constitution. So soon as the mind reaches a certain stage of development they present themselves. Circumstances may promote or retard their appearance. They depend on opportunity to furnish the occasion of their springing up, yet they are, nevertheless, the natural, spontaneous development of the human soul, as really a part of our nature as are any of our instinctive impulses, or our mental attributes. They are a part of that native intelligence with which we are endowed by the author of our being. These intuitions of ours, are not themselves the foundation of right and wrong; they do not make one thing right and another wrong; but they are simply the reason why we so regard them. Such we believe to be the true account of the origin of our moral perceptions.

§ II. — Cognizance of the Right.

The Cognition distinguished from the Idea of Right. — Having, in the preceding section, discussed the *idea* of the right, in itself considered, as a conception of the mind, we proceed now to consider *the action of the mind as cognizant of right.* The theme is one of no little difficulty, but, at the same time, of highest importance.

Existence of this Power. — After what has been already said, it is hardly necessary to raise the preliminary inquiry, as to the *existence* of a moral faculty in man. That we do possess the power of making moral distinctions, that we do discriminate between the right and the wrong in human conduct, is an obvious fact in the history and psychology of the race. Consciousness, observation, the form of language, the literature of the world, the usages of society, all attest and confirm this truth. We are conscious of the operation of this principle in ourselves, whenever we contemplate our own conduct, or that of others. We find ourselves, involuntarily, and as by instinct, pronouncing this act to be right; that, wrong. We recognize the obligation to do, or to have done, otherwise. We approve, or condemn. We are sustained by the calm sense of that self-approval, or cast down by the fearful strength and bitterness of that remorse. And what we find in ourselves, we observe, also, in others. In like circumstances, they recognize the same distinctions, and exhibit the same emotions. At the story or the sight of some flagrant injustice and wrong, the child and the savage are not less indignant than the philosopher. Nor is this a matter peculiar to one age or people. The languages and the literature of the world indicate, that, at all times, and among all nations, the distinction between right and wrong has been recognized and felt. The τὸ δίκαιον and το καλόν of the Greeks, the *honestum* and the *pulchrum* of the Latins, are specimens of a class of words, to be found in all languages, the proper use and significance of which is to express the distinctions in question.

Since, then, we do unquestionably recognize moral distinctions, it is clear that we have a moral faculty.

Questions which present themselves. — Without further consideration of this point, we pass at once to the investigation of the subject itself. Our inquiries relate principally to the *nature* and *authority* of this faculty. On these points, it is hardly necessary to say, great difference of opinion has existed among philosophers and theologians, and grave questions have arisen. What *is* this faculty as exercised; a judgment, a process of reasoning, or an emotion? Does it belong to the rational or sensitive part of our nature: to the domain of intellect, or of feeling, or both? What is the value and correctness of our moral perceptions, and especially of that verdict of *approbation* or *censure*, which we pass upon ourselves and others, according as the conduct conforms to, or violates, recognized obligation? Such are some of the questions which have arisen respecting the nature and authority of conscience.

I. *The Nature of Conscience.* — What is it? A matter of *intellect*, or of *feeling*; a *judgment*, or an *emotion?*

A careful analysis of the phenomena of conscience, with a

view to determine the several elements, or mental processes, that constitute its operation, may aid us in the solution of this question.

Analysis of an Act of Conscience.

Cognition of Right. — Whenever the conduct of intelligent and rational beings is made the subject of contemplation, whether the act thus contemplated be our own or another's, and whether it be an act already performed, or only proposed, we are cognizant of certain ideas awakened in the mind, and of certain impressions made upon it. First of all, the act contemplated strikes us as *right* or *wrong.* This involves a double element, an *idea*, and a *perception* or *judgment.* The *idea* of right and its opposite are, in the mind, simple ideas, and, therefore, indefinable. In the act contemplated, we *recognize* the one or the other of these simple elements, and pronounce it, accordingly, a right or wrong act. This is simply a *judgment*, a perception, an exercise of the understanding.

Of Obligation. — No sooner is this idea, this cognition, of the rightness or wrongness of the given act, fairly entertained by the mind, than another idea, another cognition, presents itself, given along with the former, and inseparable from it, viz., that of *obligation* to do, or not to do, the given act: the *ought*, and the *ought not* — also simple ideas, and indefinable. This applies equally to the future and to the past, to ourselves and to others: I ought to do this thing; I ought to *have done* it yesterday. He ought, or ought not to do, or to have done it. This, like the former, is an intellectual act, a perception or cognition of a truth, of a reality, for which we have the same voucher as for any other reality or apprehended fact, viz., the reliability of our mental faculties in general, and the correctness of their operation in the specific instance. It is a conviction of the mind inseparable from the perception of right. Given, a clear perception of the one, and we cannot escape the other.

Of Merit and Demerit. — There follows a third element, logically distinct, but chronologically inseparable, from the preceding: the cognition of merit or demerit in connection with the deed, of good or ill desert, and the consequent approval or disapproval of the deed and the doer. No sooner do we perceive an action to be right or wrong, and to involve, therefore, an obligation on the part of the doer, than there arises, also, in the mind, the idea of merit or demerit, in connection with the doing; we regard the agent as deserving of praise or blame, and in our own minds do approve or condemn him and his course, accordingly. This approval of ourselves and others, according to the apprehended desert of the act and the actor, constitutes a process of trial, an inner tribunal, at whose bar are constantly arraigned the deeds of men, and whose verdict it is no easy matter to set aside. This mental approval may be regarded by some as a matter of feeling, rather than an intellectual act. We speak of *feelings* of approval and of condemnation. To approve and condemn, however, are, properly, acts of the judgment. The feelings consequent upon such approval or disapproval are usually of such a nature, and of such strength, as to attract the principal attention of the mind to themselves, and, hence, we naturally come to think and speak of the whole process as a matter of feeling. Strictly viewed, it is an intellectual perception, an exercise of judgment, giving sentence that the contemplated act is, or is not, meritorious, and awarding praise or blame accordingly.

This completes the process. I can discover nothing in the operation of my mind, in view of moral action, which does not resolve itself into some one of these elements.

These Elements intellectual. — Viewed in themselves, these are, strictly, intellectual operations; the recognition of the right, the recognition of obligation, the perception of good or ill desert, are all, properly, acts of the intellect. Each of these cognitive acts, however, *involves a corresponding action of the sensibilities.* The perception of the right awakens, in the pure and virtuous mind, feelings of pleasure, admiration, love. The idea of obligation becomes, in its turn, through the awakened sensibilities, an impulse and motive to action. The recognition of good or ill desert awakens feelings of esteem and complacency, or the reverse; fills the soul with sweet peace, or stings it with sharp remorse. All these things must be recognized and included by the psychologist among the phenomena of conscience. These emotions, however, are based on, and grow out of, the intellectual acts already named, and are to be viewed as an incidental and subordinate, though by no means unimportant, part of the whole process. When we speak of conscience, or the moral faculty, we speak of a *power*, a faculty, and not *merely* a feeling or susceptibility of being affected. It is a cognitive power, having to do with realities, recognizing real distinctions, and not merely a passive play of the sensibilities. It is simply the mind's power of recognizing a certain class of truths and relations. As such, we claim for it a place among the strictly cognitive powers of the mind, among the faculties that have to do with the perception of truth and reality.

Importance of this Position. — This is a point of some importance. If, with certain writers, we make the moral faculty a matter of mere feeling, overlooking the intellectual perceptions on which this feeling is based, we overlook and leave out of the account, the chief elements of the process. The moral faculty is no longer a cognitive power, no longer, in truth, a faculty. The distinctions which it seems to recognize are merely *subjective ;* impressions, feelings, to which there may, or may not, be a corresponding reality. We have at least no evidence of any such reality. Such a view subtracts the very foundation of morals. Our feel ings vary; but right and wrong do not vary with our feelings. They are objective realities, and not subjective phenomena. As such, the mind, by virtue of the natural powers with which it is endowed by the Creator, recognizes them

The power by which it gives this, we call the *moral faculty;* just as we call its power to take cognizance of another class of truths and relations, viz., the beautiful, its *æsthetic* faculty. In view of these truths and relations, as thus perceived, certain feelings are, in either case, awakened, and these emotions may, with propriety, be regarded as pertaining to, and a part of, the phenomena of conscience, and of taste; the full discussion of either of these faculties will include the action of the sensibilities; but in neither case will a true psychology resolve the faculty into the feeling. The mathematician experiences a certain feeling of delight in perceiving the relation of lines and angles, but the power of perceiving that relation, the faculty by which the mind takes cognizance of such truth, is not to be resolved into the feeling that results from it.

Result of Analysis. — As the result of our analysis, we obtain the following elements as involved in, and constituting, an operation of the moral faculty:

(1.) The mental perception that a given act is right or wrong.

(2.) The perception of obligation with respect to the same, as right or wrong.

(3.) The perception of merit or demerit, and the consequent approbation or censure of the agent, as doing the right or the wrong thus perceived.

(4.) Accompanying these intellectual perceptions, and based upon them, certain corresponding emotions, varying in intensity according to the clearness of the mental perceptions, and the purity of the moral nature.

II. *Authority of Conscience.* — Thus far we have considered the *nature* of conscience. The question arises now as to its *authority* — the reliableness of its decisions.

If conscience correctly discerns the right and the wrong, and the consequent obligation, it will be likely to judge correctly as to the deserts of the doer. If it mistake these points, it may approve what is not worthy of approval, and condemn what is good.

What Evidence of Correctness. — How are we to know, then, whether conscience judges right? What voucher have we for its correctness? How far is it to be trusted in its perceptions and decisions? Perhaps we are so constituted, it may be said, as invariably to judge that to be right which is wrong, and the reverse, and so to approve where we should condemn. True, we reply, this may be so. It may be that I am so constituted, that two and two shall *seem* to be four, when in reality they are five; and that the three angles of a triangle shall *seem* to be equal to two right angles, when in reality they are equal to three. This may be so. Still it is a presumption in favor of the correctness of all our natural perceptions, that they are the operation of original principles of our constitution. It is not probable, to say the least, that we are so constituted by ·he great Author of our being, as to be habitually deceived. It may be that the organs of vision and hearing are absolutely false; that the things which we see, and hear, and feel, through the medium of the senses, have no correspondence to our supposed perceptions. But this is not a probable supposition. He who denies the validity of the natural faculties, has the burden of proof; and proof is of course impossible; for the simple reason, that, in order to prove them false, you must make use of these very faculties; and if their testimony is not reliable in the one case, certainly it is not in the other. We must then take their veracity for granted; and we have the right to do so. And so of our moral nature. It comes from the Author of our being, and if it is uniformly and originally wrong, then he is wrong. It is an error, which, in the nature of the case, can never be detected or corrected. We cannot get beyond our constitution, back of our natural endowments, to judge, *à priori*, and from an external position, whether they are correct or not. Right and wrong are not, indeed, the creations of the divine will; but the faculties by which we perceive and approve the right, and condemn the wrong, are from him; and we must presume upon their general correctness.

Not infallible. — It does not follow from this, however, nor do we affirm, that conscience is infallible, that she never errs. It does not follow that our moral perceptions and judgments are invariably correct, because they spring from our native constitution. This is not so. There is not one of the faculties of the human mind that is not liable to err. Not one of its activities is infallible. The reasoning power sometimes errs; the judgment errs; the memory errs. The moral faculty is on the same footing, in this respect, with any and all other faculties.

Its Value not thus destroyed. — But of what use, it will be said, is a moral faculty, on which, after all, we cannot rely? Of what use, we reply, is *any* mental faculty, that is not absolutely and universally correct? Of what use is a memory or a judgment, that sometimes errs? We do not wholly distrust these faculties, or cast them aside as worthless. A time-keeper may be of great value, though not absolutely perfect. Its authorship and original construction may be a strong presumption in favor of its general correctness; nevertheless its hands may have been accidentally set to the wrong hour of the day.

Actual Occurrence of such Cases. — This is a spectacle that not unfrequently presents itself in the moral world — a man with his conscience pointing to the wrong hour; a strictly conscientious man, fully and firmly persuaded that he is right, yet by no means agreeing with the general convictions of mankind; an hour or two before, or, it may be, as much behind the age. Such men are the hardest of all mortals to be set right, for the simple reason, that they are conscientious. "Here is my watch; it points to such an hour; and my watch is from the very best maker. I cannot be mistaken." And yet he is mistaken, and egregiously so. The truth is, conscience is no more infallible than any other mental faculty. It is simply, as we have seen, a power of perceiving and judging, and its operations, like all other perceptions and judgments, are liable to error.

Diversity of Moral Judgment. — And this which we have just said, goes far to account for the great diversity that has long been known to exist in the moral judgments and opinions of men. It has often been urged, and with great force, against the supposed existence of a moral faculty in man, as a part of his original nature, that men think and act so differently with respect to these matters. Nature, it is said, ought to act uniformly; thus eyes and ears do not give essentially conflicting testimony, at different times, and in different countries, with respect to the same objects. Certain colors are universally pleasing, and certain sounds disagreeable. But not so, it is said, with respect to the moral judgments of men. What one approves, another condemns. If these distinctions are universal, absolute, essential; and if the power of perceiving them is inherent in our nature, men ought to agree in their perception of them. Yet you will find nothing approved by one age and people, which is not condemned by some other; nay, the very crimes of one age and nation, are the religious acts of another. If the perception of right and wrong is intuitive, how happens this diversity?

This Diversity accounted for. — To which I reply, the thing has been already accounted for. Our ideas of right and wrong, it was stated, in discussing their origin, depend on circumstances for their time and degree of development. They are not irrespective of opportunity. Education, habits, laws, customs, while they do not originate, still have much to do with the development and modification of these ideas. They may be by these influences aided or retarded in their growth, or even quite misdirected, just as a tree may, by unfavorable influences, be hindered and thwarted in its growth, be made to turn and twist, and put forth abnormal and monstrous developments. Yet nature works there, nevertheless, and in spite of all such obstacles, and unfavorable circumstances, seeks to put forth, according to her laws, her perfect and finished work. All that we contend is, that nature, under favorable circumstances, develops in the human mind, the idea of moral distinctions, while, at the same time, *men may differ much in their estimate of what is right, and what is wrong*, according to the circumstances and influences surrounding them. To apply the distinction of right and wrong to particular cases, and decide as to the morality of given actions, is an office of judgment, and the judgment may err in this, as in any other of its operations. It may be biassed by unfavorable influences, by wrong education, wrong habits, and the like.

Analogy of other Faculties. — The same is true, substantially, of all other natural faculties and their operations. They depend on circumstances for the degree of their development, and the mode of their action. Hence they are liable to great diversity and frequent error. Perception misleads us as to sensible objects, not seldom; even in their mathematical reasonings, men do not always agree. There is the greatest possible diversity among men, as to the retentiveness of the memory, and as to the extent and power of the reasoning faculties. The savage that thinks it no wrong to scalp his enemy, or even to roast and eat him, is utterly unable to count twenty upon his fingers; while the philosopher, who recognizes the duty of loving his neighbor as himself, calculates, with precision, the motions of the heavenly bodies, and predicts their place in the heaven, for ages to come. Shall we conclude, because of this diversity, that these several faculties are not parts of our nature?

General Uniformity. — We are by no means disposed to admit, however, that the diversity in men's moral judgments is so great, as might, at first, appear. There is, on the contrary, a general uniformity. As to the great essential principles of morals, men, after all, do judge much alike, in different ages and different countries. In details, they differ;

in general principles, they agree. In the application of the rules of morality to particular actions, they differ widely, according to circumstances; in the recognition of the right and the wrong, as distinctive principles, and of obligation to do the right as known, and avoid the wrong as known, in this they agree. It must be remembered, moreover, that men do not always act according to their own ideas of right. From the general neglect of virtue, in any age or community, and the prevalence of great and revolting crimes, we cannot safely infer the absence, or even the perversion, of the moral faculty.

Precisely in what the Diversity consists.—It is important to bear in mind, throughout this discussion, the distinction between the *idea* of right, in itself considered, and the *perception* of a given act as right; the one a simple conception, the other an act of judgment; the one an idea derived from the very constitution of the mind, connate, if not innate, the other an application of that idea, by the understanding, to particular instances of conduct. The former, the *idea* of moral distinctions, may be universal, necessary, absolute, unerring; the latter, the *application* of the idea to particular instances, and the decision that such and such acts are, or are not, right, may be altogether an incorrect and mistaken judgment. Now it is precisely at this point that the diversity in the moral judgments of mankind makes its appearance. In recognizing the distinction of right and wrong, they agree; in the application of the same to particular instances in deciding *what* is right and *what* is wrong—a simple act of the judgment, an exercise of the understanding, as we have seen—in this it is that they differ. And the difference is no greater, and no more inexplicable, with respect to this, than in any other class of judgments.

Conscience not always a safe Guide.—I have admitted that conscience is not infallible. Is it, then, a safe guide? Are we, in all cases, to follow its decisions? Since liable to err, it cannot be, in itself, I reply, in all cases, a safe guide. We cannot conclude, with certainty, that a given course is right, simply because conscience approves it. This does not, of necessity, follow. The decision that a given act is right, or not, is simply a matter of judgment; and the judgment may, or may not, be correct. That depends on circumstances, on education partly, on the light we have, be it more or less. Conscientious men are not always in the right. We may do wrong conscientiously. Saul of Tarsus was a conscientious persecutor, and verily thought he was doing God service. No doubt, many of the most intolerant and relentless bigots have been equally conscientious, and equally mistaken. Such men are all the more dangerous, because doing what they believe to be right.

It is, nevertheless, to be followed. — What, then, are we to do? Shall we follow a guide thus liable to err? Yes, I reply, follow conscience; but see that it be a right and well-informed conscience, forming its judgments, not from impulse, passion, prejudice, the bias of habit, or of unreflecting custom, but from the clearest light of reason, and especially of the divine word. We are responsible for the judgments we form in morals, as much as for any class of our judgments; responsible, in other words, for the sort of conscience we have. Saul's mistake lay, not in acting according to his conscientious convictions of duty, but in not having a more enlightened conscience. He should have formed a more careful judgment; have inquired more diligently after the right way. To say, however, that a man ought not to do what conscience approves, is to say that he ought not to do what he sincerely believes to be right. This would be a very strange rule in morals.

Conscience not exclusively intellectual. — I have discussed, as I proposed, the *nature* and *authority* of conscience. In this discussion I have treated of the moral faculty as an intellectual, rather than an emotional power. I would not be understood, however, as implying that con science has not also an emotional character. Every intellectual act, and faculty of action, partakes more or less of this character, is accompanied by feeling, and these feelings are in some degree peculiar, it may be, to the particular faculty or act of mind to which they relate. The exercise of imagination involves some degree of feeling, either pleasurable or painful, and that often in a high degree; so also the æsthetic faculty. It is peculiarly so with the exercise of the moral faculty. As already stated, in our analysis of an act of conscience, it is impossible to view our past conduct as right or wrong, and to approve or condemn ourselves accordingly, without emotion; and these emotions will vary in intensity, according to the clearness and force of our intellectual conception of the merit or demerit of our conduct.

These feelings constitute an important part of the phenomena of moral action, and consequently of psychology; as they belong, however, to the department of *sensibility*, rather than of *intellect*, their further discussion is not here in place. They will be considered in connection with other emotions in the subsequent division of the work.

INTELLECTUAL FACULTIES.

SUPPLEMENTARY TOPICS.

SUPPLEMENTARY TOPICS.

CHAPTER I.

INSTINCT. — THE INTELLIGENCE OF THE BRUTE AS DISTINGUISHED FROM THAT OF MAN.

Closely connected with the philosophy of human intelligence is the science of *instinct*, or the intelligence of the brute — a subject of interest not merely in its relations to psychology, but to some other sciences, as natural history, and theology.

We work at a Disadvantage in such Inquiries. — With regard to this matter, it must be confessed, at the outset, that we work, in some respects, in the dark, in our inquiries and speculations concerning it. It lies wholly removed from the sphere of consciousness. We can only observe, compare, and infer, and our conclusions thus derived must be liable, after all, to error. The operations of our own minds we know by the clearest and surest of all sources of knowledge, viz., our own consciousness; the operation of brute intelligence must ever be in great measure unknown and a mystery to us. How far the two resemble each other, and how far they differ, it is not easy to determine, not easy to draw the dividing line, and say where brute intelligence stops and human intelligence begins.

Method proposed. — Let us first define instinct, the term usually applied to denote brute intelligence, and ascertain, if possible, what are its peculiar characteristics; we may then be able to determine wherein it differs from intelligence in man.

Definition. — I understand, by instinct, a law of action, governing and directing the movement of sentient beings — distinct, on the one hand, from the mere blind forces of matter, as attraction, etc., and from reason on the other; a law working to a given end by impulse, yet blindly — the subject not knowing why he thus works; a law innate, inherent in the constitution of the animal, not acquired but transmitted, the origin of which is to be found in the intelligent author of the universe. These I take to be the principal characteristics of that which we term instinct.

Instinct a Law. — It is a *law of action.* In obedience to it the bee constructs her comb, and the ant her chambers, and the bird her nest; and in obedience to it, the animal, of whatever species, seeks that particular kind of food which is intended and provided for it. These are merely instances of the operation of that law. The uniformity and universality which characterize the operations of this principle, show it to be a law of action, and not a merely casual occurrence.

Works by Impulse. — It is a law *working by impulse,* not mechanical or automatic, on the one hand, nor yet rational on the other. The impelling or motive force, in the case supposed, is not that of a weight acting upon machinery, or any like mechanical principle, nor yet the reflex action of a nerve when irritated, or the spasmodic action of a muscle. It is not analogous to the influence of gravitation on the purely passive forms of matter. Nor yet is it that higher principle which we term reason in man. The bird constructs her nest as she does, and the bee her cell, in obedience to some blind yet powerful and unfailing *impulse* of her nature, guiding and directing her movements, prompting to action, and to this specific form of action, with a restless yearning, unsatisfied until the end is accomplished. Yet the creature does not herself understand the law by which she works. The bee does not know that she constructs her comb at that precise angle which will afford the greatest content in the least space, does not know why she constructs it at that precise angle, could give no reason for her procedure, even were she capable of understanding our question. It is not with her a matter of reflection, nor of reason, at all, but merely of blind, unthinking, yet unerring impulse.

As innate. — This law is *innate*, *inherent* in the constitution of the animal, *not acquired*. It is not the result of education. The bird does not learn to build her nest, nor the bee her comb, nor the ant her subterranean chambers, by observing how the parent works and builds. Removed from all opportunities of observation or instruction, the untaught animal still performs its mission, constructs its nest or cell, and does it as perfectly in solitude as among its fellows, as perfectly on the first attempt as ever after. Whatever intelligence there is involved in these labors and constructions, and certainly the very highest intelligence would seem, in many instances, to be concerned in them, is an intelligence transmitted, and not acquired, the origin of which is to be sought, ultimately, not in the creature itself, but in the Author of all intelligence, the Creator of the universe. The intelligence is that not of the creature, but of the Creator.

Manifests itself irrespective of Circumstances. — It is to be further observed, with respect to the principle under consideration, that it often manifests its peculiar tendencies prior to the development of the appropriate organs. The young calf butts with its head before its horns are grown. The instinctive impulse manifests itself, also, under circumstances which render its action no longer needful. The beaver caught and confined in a room, constructs its dam, as aforetime, with whatsoever materials it can command, although, in its present circumstances, such a structure is of no possible use. These facts evidently indicate the presence and action of an impulse working blindly, without reflection, without reason, without intelligence, on the part of the animal.

Indications of Contrivance. — On the other hand, there

are instances of brute action which seem to indicate contrivance and adaptation to circumstances. The bee compelled to construct her comb in an unusual and unsafe position, steadies it by constructing a brace of wax-work between the side that inclines and the nearest wall of the hive. The spider, in like manner, whose web is in danger, runs a line, from the part exposed to the severest strain or pressure, to the nearest point of support, in such a manner as to secure the slender fabric. A bird has been known, in like manner, to support a bough, which proved too frail to sustain the weight of the nest, and of her young, by connecting it, with a thread, to a stronger branch above.

These Facts do not prove Reason. — Facts of this nature, however interesting, and well authenticated, must be regarded rather as exceptions to the ordinary rule, the nearest approach which mere instinct has been known to make toward the dividing line that separates the brute from the human intelligence. They do not, in themselves, prove the existence of reason, of a discriminating and reflecting intelligence, on the part of the animal; for the same law of nature that impels the creature to build its nest or its comb, under ordinary circumstances, in the ordinary manner, may certainly be supposed to be capable of inducing a change of operation to meet a sudden exigency, and one liable at any time to occur. It is certainly not more wonderful, nor so wonderful, that the bee should be induced to brace her comb, or the spider her web, when in danger, as that either should be able to construct her edifice originally, at the precise angle employed. It must be remembered, moreover, that, in the great majority of cases, brute instinct shows no such capacity of adaptation to circumstances.

The Question before us. — We are ready now to inquire how far that which we call instinct in the brute, differs from that which we call intelligence in man. Is it a difference in *kind*, or only in *degree?* A glance at the history of the doctrine may aid us here.

Early Views. — From Aristotle to Descartes, philosophers took the latter view. They ascribed to the brute a degree of reason, such as would be requisite in man, were he to do the same things, and proceeding on this principle, they attributed to animals an intelligence proportioned to the wants of their nature and organization. This principle, it need hardly be said, is an assumption. It is not certain that the same action proceeds from the same principle in man, and in the brute; that whatever indicates and involves intelligence and reason, in the one case, as its source, involves the same in the other. This is a virtual *petitio principii.* It assumes the very point in question. It may be that what man does by virtue of an intelligent, reflecting, rational soul, looking before and after, the brute does by virtue of entirely a different principle, a mere unintelligent impulse of his nature, a blind sensation, prompting him to a given course. This is the question to be settled, the thing to be proved or disproved. And if the view already given of the character of brute instinct, is correct, the position now stated as possible, may be regarded as virtually established.

View of Descartes. — Descartes, perceiving the error of preceding philosophers, went to the opposite extreme, and resolved the instinct and action of the brute into mere mechanism, a principle little different from that by which the weight moves the hands of the clock. The brute performs the functions of his nature and organization, just as the puppet moves hither and thither by springs hidden within, of which itself knows nothing. The bird, the bee, the ant, the spider, are so organized, such is the hidden mechanism of their curious nature, that at the proper times, and under the requisite conditions, they shall build, each, its own proper structure; and perform, each, its own proper work and office. So doing, each moves automatically, mechanically.

Locke and his Disciples. — Differing, again, from this view, which certainly ascribes too little, as the opposite theory ascribes too much to the brute, Locke, Condillac, and their disciples in France and England, took the ground that the actions of the brute which seem to indicate intelligence, are to be ascribed to the power of habit, and to the law of association. The faculties of the brute, as indeed of man, resolve themselves ultimately into impressions from without. Nothing is innate. The dog scents his prey, and the beaver builds his dam, and the bird migrates to a warmer clime, from the mere force of habit, unreflecting, unintelligent. But how, it may occur to some one to ask, happens such a habit to be formed in the first place? How happens the poor insect, just emerging from the egg, to find in himself all requisite appliances and instruments for capturing his prey? How happens the bee always, throughout all its generations, to hit upon the same contrivance for storing its honey, and not only so, but to select out of a thousand different forms, and different possible angles, always the same one? And so of the ant, the spider, etc. And if this is a matter of education, as it certainly is not, then how came the first bee, the first ant, spider, or other insect, to hit upon so admirable an expedient?

The Scotch Philosophers. — On the other hand, Reid, Stewart, and the Scotch philosophers generally, departing widely from the merely mechanical view, have ascribed to instinct some actions which are properly automatic and involuntary, as the shutting of the eyelid on the approach of a foreign body, the action of the infant in obtaining its food from the mother's breast, and certain other like movements of the animal organization, which, according to recent discoveries in physiology, are to be attributed, rather to the simple reflex action of the nerves and muscles. This is not properly instinct.

Question returns. — Among these several views, where then, lies the truth? Unable to coincide with the merely mechanical theory of Descartes, or with the view which resolves all into mere habit and association, with Locke and Condillac, shall we fall back upon the ancient, and for a long time universally prevalent, view which makes instinct only a lower degree of that intelligence which, in man becomes reason and reflection? This we are hardly prepared to do. The well-known phenomena and laws of instinct, its essential characteristics as developed in the preceding pages, seem to point to a difference in kind and not merely in degree.

Reasons for this Opinion.—1. *The Brute incapable of high Cultivation.* — To recapitulate briefly the points of difference: If instinct in the brute were of the same nature with intelligence in man, if it were, properly speaking, *intelligence*, the same in kind, differing only in degree, then, it ought, as in man, to be capable of cultivation to an indefinite extent, capable of being elevated, by due process of training, to a degree very much superior to that in which it first presents itself. Now, with certain insignificant exceptions, such is certainly not the case. No amount of training or culture ever brings the animal essentially above the ordinary range of brute capacity, or approximates him to the level of the human species.

2. *Brute does not improve by Practice.* — On this theory the brute ought, moreover, to improve by practice, which, for the most part, certainly he does not. The spider lays out its lines as accurately and constructs its web as well, and the bee her comb, and the bird her nest, on the first attempt, as after the twentieth or the fiftieth trial. There is no progress, no improvement. Its skill, if such it may be called, is a fixture. There is nothing of the nature of *science* about it, for it is of the essential nature of all intelligent action to improve.

3. *Does not adapt itself to Circumstances.* — If it were of the nature of intelligence, it ought uniformly and invariably to adapt itself to changing circumstances, and not to keep on working blindly in the old way, when such procedure is no longer of use. It is not intelligence, but mere blind impulse, in the beaver, that leads him to build his dam on a dry floor or the pavement of a court-yard.

4. *Opposite View proves too much.* — It is furthermore to be noticed, that the theory under consideration, while it ascribes to the brute only a lower degree of intelligence, in reality places him, in some respects, far beyond man in point of intellect. If the instinct of the brute be intelligence at all, it is intelligence which leaves his prouder rival, man, in many cases, quite in the shade. No science of man can vie with the mathematical precision of the spider or the bee in the practical construction of lines and planes that shall enclose a given angle. The engineer must take lessons of the ant in the art of running lines and parallels. To the same humble insect belongs the invention of the arch and of the dome in architecture. Many of the profoundest questions and problems of science are in like manner virtually solved by those creatures that possess, it is claimed, only a *lower degree* of intelligence than man. The facts are inconsistent with the theory. The theory either goes too far, or not far enough. If instinct is intelligence at all, it is intelligence, in some respects at least, *superior* to man's.

For reasons now stated, we must conclude that the intelligence of the brute differs in *kind*, and not in *degree* merely, from that of man.

Faculties wanting in the Brute. — If now the inquiry be raised, what are the specific faculties which are wanting in the brute, but possessed by man, in other words, where runs the dividing line which marks off the domain of instinct from that of intellect, we reply, beginning with the differences which are most obvious, the brute is, in the first place, not a *moral* and *religious* being. He has no moral nature, no ideas of right and justice, none of accountability, and of a higher power. He is, moreover, not an *æsthetic* being. He has no taste for beauty, nor appreciation of it. The horse, with all his apparent intelligence, looks out upon the most enchanting landscape as unmoved by its beauty as the carriage which he draws. He has no idea, no cognizance of the beautiful. The faculty of original conception, which furnishes man with ideas of this nature, seems to be wanting in the brute. He is, furthermore, not a *scientific* being. He does not understand the principles by which he himself works. He makes no progress or improvement, accordingly, in the application of those principles, but works as well first as last. He learns nothing by experience. Certain grand rules and principles do indeed lie at the foundation of his work, but they have no *subjective* existence in the brute himself. Now the faculties which constitute man a scientific being are those which, in the present treatise, we have grouped together under the title of *reflective*. These seem to be wanting in the brute. He never classifies, nor analyzes, never forms abstract conceptions, never generalizes, judges, nor reasons, never reflects on what is passing around him ; never, in the true sense of the word, *thinks*.

Further Deficiency. — Here many, perhaps most, who have reflected upon the matter at all, would place the dividing line between man and the brute, denying him the possession of reason and reflection, the higher intellectual powers, but allowing him the other faculties which man enjoys. We must go further, however, and exclude imagination from the list of brute faculties. Having no idea of the beautiful, nor any power of forming abstract conceptions, the *ideals*, according to which imagination shapes its creations, are wholly wanting, and imagination itself, the faculty of the ideal, must also be wanting.

The Power to perceive and remember. — But has the brute the power of perception and memory, the only two distinct remaining faculties of the human mind ? If we distinguish, as we must, the physical from the strictly intellectual element, in perception by the senses, the capacity to receive impressions of sense, from the capacity to *understand* and *know* the object, as such, from which the impressions proceed, while we must admit the former, we should question the existence of the latter in the brute. To know or understand the objects of sense, to distinguish them as such, from each other, and from self as the perceiving sub ject, is an attribute of intelligence in its strict and proper sense, an attribute of mind. If the brute possesses it, he possesses as really a mind, though not of so high an order, as man.

The dividing Line. — Now it is just here that we are compelled to place the line of division between the brute and man, between instinct and intellect. The brute has senses, as man; in some respects, indeed, more perfect than his. Objects external make impressions upon his senses; his eye, his ear, his various organs of sense, respond to these impressions. In a word, he has sensations, and those sensations are accompanied, as all sensations in their nature are, and must be, with consciousness, that is, they are felt. But this does not necessarily involve what we understand by consciousness in its higher sense, or *self-consciousness.* The brute has, we believe, no knowledge of himself as such, no *self-consciousness*, properly speaking; does not distinguish between self as perceiving, and the object as perceived, has no conception of self as a separate existence distinct from the objects around him, has, strictly speaking, no ideas, no thoughts, no intelligent comprehension of objects about him; has *sensations*, but no *perceptions* in the true sense of the word, since perception involves the distinction of subject and object, or self-consciousness. These distinctions are lost to the brute, blindly merged in the one simple consciousness of physical sensation. He feels, but does not think, does not understand. Sensation takes the place of understanding and reason with him. It is his guide. To the impressions thus received, his nature blindly responds, he knows not how or why. He is so constituted by his wise and benevolent Maker, that sensation being awakened, the impulses of his nature at once spring into play, and prompt irresistibly to action, and to such action as shall meet the wants of the being. There is no need for intelligence to supervene, as with man. The brute feels and *acts.* Man feels, *thinks*, and acts. The Creator has provided, for, the former, a substitute which takes the place of intellect, and secures by blind, yet unerring impulse, the simple ends which correspond to his simpler necessities, and his humbler sphere.

Man's Superiority. — Herein lies man's mastership and dominion over the brute. He has what the brute has not, intellect, mind, the power of thought, the power to understand and know. Just so far as he fails to grasp this high prerogative, just so far as he is governed by sensation and its corresponding impulses, rather than by intelligence and reason, just in such degree he lays aside his superiority, and sinks to the sphere of the brute. Thus, in infancy and early life, there is little difference. Thus, many savage and uneducated races never rise far above the brute capacity, are mere creatures of sensation, impulse, instinct.

In one Respect inferior. — In one respect, indeed, man, destitute of intelligence or failing to govern himself by its precepts, sinks *below* the brute. He has not the substitute for intelligence which the brute has, has not instinct to guide him, and teach him the true and proper bounds of indulgence, but giving way to passion and inclination, without restraint, presents that most melancholy spectacle on which the sun, in all his course, ever looks down, a man under the dominion of his own appetites, incapable of self-government, lost to all nobleness, all virtue, all self-respect.

Memory in the Brute. — It may still be asked, does not the brute *remember?* It is the office of memory to replace or represent what has been once felt or perceived. It simply reproduces, in thought, what has once passed before the mind. It originates nothing. Whatever, then, of intelligence was involved in the original act of perception and sensation, so much and no more is involved in the replacing those sensations and perceptions. If in the original act there was nothing but simple sensation, without intellectual apprehension of the object, without self-consciousness or distinction of subject from object, then, of course, nothing more than this will be subsequently reproduced. Mere images or phantasms of sensible objects may reappear, as shadows flicker and dance upon the wall, or as such images flit before us in our dreams. The memory of the brute is, probably, of this nature, rather a sort of dream than a distinct conception of past events. What was not clearly apprehended at first, will not be better understood now. Failing, in the first in-tance, to distinguish self from the object external, as the source of impressions, there can be no *recognition* of that distinction when the object reappears, if it ever should, in conception. The essential element of memory, which connects the object or event of former perception with *self* as the percipient, must, in such a case, be wanting.

The Brute associates rather than remembers. — What is usually called memory in the brute, is not, however, so much his capacity of conceiving of an absent object of sense, as his recognition of the object when again actually present to his senses. The dog manifests pleasure at the appearance of his master, and the horse chooses the road that leads to his former home. This is not so much memory as association of ideas or rather of feelings. Certain feelings and sensations are associated, confusedly blended, with certain objects. The reappearance of the objects, of course, reawakens the former feelings. Thus, the whip is associated with the sensation experienced in connection with it. So, too, a horse which has once been frightened by some object beside the road, will manifest fear on subsequently approaching the same place, although the same object may no longer be there. The surrounding objects which still remain, and which were associated with the more immediate object of fear in the first instance, are sufficient to awaken, on their reappearance, the former unpleasant sensations.

A being endowed with intelligence and reason would connect the recurring object, in such a case, with his own former experience as the perceiving subject, would recall the time and the circumstances of the event and its connection with his personal history. This would be, properly, an act of memory.

But there is no reason to suppose that such a process takes place with the brute. We have no evidence of any thing more, in his case, than the recurrence of the associated conception or sensation, along with the recurrence of the object which formerly produced it. Given, the object *a*, accompanied with surrounding objects *b*, *c*, *d*, and there is produced a given sensation, *y*. Given, again, at some subsequent time, the same object *a*, or any one of the associate objects *b*, *c*, *d*, and there is at once awakened a lively conception of the same sensation *y*.

Summary of Results. — This is, I think, all we can, with any certainty, attribute to the brute. He has sensations, and so far as mere sense is concerned, perceptions of objects, as connected with those sensations, but not perception in the true sense as involving intellectual apprehension. These sensations and confused perceptions recur, perhaps, as images or conceptions, in the absence of the objects that gave rise to them, and as thus reappearing, constitute what we may call the memory of the brute; but not, as with us, a memory which connects the object or event with his own former history, and the idea of a personal self as the percipient. Let the object, however, reappear, and the previous sensation associated therewith, is reawakened.

This, I am aware, is not the view most commonly entertained of brute intelligence. We naturally conceive of the brute as possessing faculties similar to our own. The brute, in turn, were he capable of forming such a conception, would, probably, conceive of man, as endowed with capacities like his own. In neither case is this the right conception.

CHAPTER II.

MIND AS AFFECTED BY CERTAIN STATES OF THE BRAIN AND NERVOUS SYSTEM.

Statement. — There are certain mental phenomena connected with the relation which the mind sustains to the nervous organism, and depending intimately on the state of that organism, which seem to require the notice of the psychologist, though often overlooked by him; I refer to the phenomena of sleep, dreams, somnambulism, and insanity. So far as the activity of the mind is involved in these states or phenomena, they become proper objects of psychological inquiry. They present many problems difficult of solution, yet not the less curious and interesting, as phases of mental activity hitherto little understood.

View sometimes taken by Physiologists. — It becomes the more important for the psychologist to investigate these phenomena, inasmuch as views and theories little accordant with the true philosophy of the mind have sometimes been put forth by physiologists, in attempting to explain the phenomena in question. They have viewed the cerebral apparatus as competent of itself to produce the phenomena of thought, as *self-acting*, in the absence of the higher principle of intelligence which usually governs its operations, carrying on by a sort of automatic action, the processes usually ascribed to the mind or spiritual principle, while consciousness and volition are entirely suspended. Consciousness, in fact, is nothing but sensation, and thought a mere function of the brain. This is downright materialism, a doctrine utterly subversive of the very existence of that which we call mind or soul in man. If the cerebral organization is competent of itself during sleep to carry on those operations which in waking moments are ascribed to the spiritual element of our being, if thought is a function of the brain, as digestion is of the stomach, what need and what evidence of any thing more than merely cerebral action at any time? What, in fact, is the mind itself but cerebral activity, and what is man, with all his higher powers, but a mere animated organism?

It becomes important, then, to account for the phenomena under consideration in some way more consistent with all just and true notions of the nature and philosophy of mind.

Distinction of normal and abnormal States. — Of these phenomena, while all may be regarded as intimately connected with and dependent on the state of the brain and nervous system, some seem to proceed from a normal, others from an abnormal and disordered state of the nervous and particularly the cerebral organism. Of the former class, are sleep and dreams; of the latter, somnambulism, the mesmeric state, so called, and the various forms of disordered mental action, or insanity.

§ I. — Sleep.

Meaning of the Term. — What is sleep? Will the name itself afford any solution of this problem? Like most names of familiar things, we find the word descriptive of some particular circumstance or phase, some one prominent characteristic of the thing in question, rather than a *definition* — much less an explanation — of the thing itself.

The word sleep, from *schlafen*, as the Latin *somnus* from *supinus*, refers to the supine condition and appearance of the body when in this state; the relaxing of the muscles, the falling back or sinking down of the frame, if unsupported. This is the first and most obvious effect to the eye of an observer, of the condition of sleep as regards the body. Further than this the word gives us no light.

1. *Sleep involves primarily Loss of Consciousness.* — What then, further than this, is sleep? If we observe somewhat closely, and with a view to scientific arrangement, the different aspects or phenomena that present themselves as constituting that state of body and mind which we call sleep, the primary and most obvious fact, I apprehend, is *loss of consciousness*, of *the me.* Not perhaps of all consciousness, for we seem still to exist, but of self-consciousness, of the me as related to time, and place, and external circumstance. We *lose ourselves*, as a common but most exact expression describes it.

We are not at the Time aware of this Loss. — Of course, sleep consisting primarily in loss of consciousness, we are not conscious of the fact that we sleep, for this would be a *consciousness* that we were unconscious. Illustrations of this fact are of frequent occurrence. You are of an evening getting weary over your book. You are vaguely conscious of that weariness, amounting even to drowsiness; you find it difficult to follow the course of thought, or even to keep the line, but have no idea that you are at length actually asleep for the moment, till the sudden fall of the book awakens you. Nay, one who has been vigorously nodding for five minutes will, on recovering himself, stoutly deny that he has really been asleep at all; the truth is, he was not *conscious* of it; we never are, directly.

This results from what? — This loss of consciousness results from the inactivity of the bodily senses. It is these that afford us the data for a knowledge of self in relation to external things. In sleep these avenues of communication with the external world are shut up, and we silently drop off, and, as it were, float away from all *conscious* connection with it. We no longer recognize our relations to time and space, nor even to our own bodies, which, as material, come under those relations; for it is by the senses alone that we get these ideas. So far as consciousness of these relations is concerned, we exist in sleep as in death, out of the laws and limits of time and space, and irrespective of the body and of all material existence. Mental action, however, doubtless goes on, and we are conscious of thought and of the feeling of the moment, but of nothing further. All self-consciousness is gone.

An Affection primarily of the nervous System. — Sleep, then, would seem to be primarily an affection of the nervous system; not of the reproductive — that goes on as usual, and even with increased vigor; nor yet of the muscular — that is still capable of action; but only of the nervous. That gets weary; by continued use, its vital active force is exhausted, it needs rest, becomes inactive, gradually drops off, and so there results this loss of consciousness, of which I have spoken. It is strictly, then, the nervous system, and not the whole body that sleeps.

Different Senses fall Asleep successively. — The different senses become inactive and fall asleep, not all at once, but successively. First, sight goes. The eye-lids droop, and close. Taste and smell probably next. Touch, and hearing, are among the last to give way. Hence, noises so easily disturb us, when falling asleep. Hence, too, we are most easily awaked by some one repeating our name, or by some one touching us. These senses are also the first to waken. One sense may be asleep and another awake. You may still hear what one is saying that sits near you, when already the eye is asleep. So in death, one *hears* when no longer able to see or to speak.

2. *Loss of personal Control.* — Accompanying this loss of self-consciousness is the loss of *personal control, i.e.*, the control of the will over the bodily organization. This follows from the inactivity of the senses and of the nervous system, for it is only through that, and not by direct agency of the will, that we, at any time, exert voluntary power over the body. When that system becomes exhausted, and its force is spent, so that it can no longer furnish the motive power, nor execute the commands of the higher intelligence,

the will no longer maintains its empire over the physical organization, its little realm of matter, its control is suspended, its sceptre falls, and it realizes for the time the story of the enchanted palace on which a magic spell had fallen, suddenly arresting the busy tide of life, and sealing up, on the instant, the senses of king, courtiers, and attendants, in the unbroken sleep of ages.

Indications of approaching Sleep. — One of the first indications, accordingly, of the approach of sleep, is the relaxing of the muscles, the drooping of the eye-lid, the dropping of the head and of the arm, the sinking down of the body from an erect to a supine position. If in church, the head seeks the friendly support of the pew in front, fortunate if it can secure itself there from the still further demands of gravitation.

Analogous Cases. — In respect to the point now under consideration, the loss of control over the physical frame, the phenomena of sleep closely resemble those of intoxication, and of fainting; and for the same reason, in either case, *i. e.*, the inactivity of the nervous system, which is the medium of voluntary power over the body. That inactivity of the nervous system is produced in the one case by natural, in the other by unnatural causes, but the direct effect is the same as regards the loss of voluntary power. The same effects are also produced in certain diseases, and eventually by death.

3. *Loss of Control over the Mind.* — Analogous to this is the loss of voluntary control over the mental operations, which is in fact, so far as the mind is concerned, the essential feature and characteristic of sleep. Mental action still goes on, there is reason to suppose; in many cases we know that it does; but the thoughts come and go at their own pleasure, without regulation or control. It is not in our power to arrest a certain thought, and fix our minds upon it for the time, to the exclusion of others, as we can do in the waking moments, and which constitutes, in fact, the chief

control and power we have over our thoughts, nor can we dismiss, and throw off, an unpleasant train of thought, a disagreeable impression, however much we may desire to be rid of it. We are at the mercy of our own thoughts and casual associations, which, in the ungoverned, spontaneous play of the mind's own inherent energy, and guided only by its own native laws, produce the wildest and strangest phantasmagoria, having to us all the semblance of reality, while we are, in truth, mere passive spectators of the scene.

Faculties of Mind not suspended in Sleep. — It has been supposed by some that the faculties of the mind are, in part or wholly, suspended in sleep, especially the higher faculties more immediately dependent on the will. So long as mental activity goes on, however, — and there is no evidence that it ever entirely ceases in sleep — so long there is thought, and so long must that thought and activity be exerted in some particular direction, and on some particular object. We cannot conceive of the mind as acting or thinking, and not exercising any of its faculties, for what is a faculty of the mind but its capacity of acting in this or that way or mode, and on this or that class of subjects. It may be perception, or conception, or memory, or imagination, or judgment, or reasoning, or any other faculty that is for the moment active; it *must* be some one of the known faculties of the mind, unless, indeed, we suppose some new faculties to be then developed, of whose existence we are at other times unconscious.

Mental Action modified by certain Causes in Sleep. — The faculties will, however, be materially modified in their action during sleep, by the causes already named; chiefly these two: 1st. the entire suspension of voluntary control over the train of thought; 2d. the loss of personal consciousness as regards especially the bodily organization, and its present relations to time, and space, and all sensible objects. In consequence of the *former*, our thoughts will come and go all unregulated and disconnected; there will be no coherence; the slightest analysis will suffice for the associating principle; we shall be hurried on and borne away on the rushing tide of thought, as a frail passive leaf swept on the bosom of the rapids; we shall whirl hither and thither as in the dance of the witches; we shall waken in confusion, and seek to recover the reins of self-control, only to lose them again and be swept on in the fearful dance.

Want of Congruity owing to what. — In consequence of the *latter* cause — the loss of sensational consciousness and of our relations to sensible objects — there will be an entire want of fitness and congruity in our mental operations. The laws of time, and space, and personal identity, will be altogether disregarded, and we shall not be conscious of the incongruity, nor wonder at the strangest and most contradictory combinations. Here, there, everywhere, now this and now that. The scene is in the valley of the Connecticut, and anon on the Ural mountains, or the desert of Arabia, and we do not notice the change as any thing at all remarkable. Now we are walking up the aisle of the church, in garments all too scanty for the proprieties of the occasion, and now it is a wild bull that is racing after us, and the transition from one to the other is instantaneous. Why should it not be, for it is by the senses alone that we are brought into conscious relation to the external world, and so made cognizant of the laws of time and space, and those senses being now locked in oblivion, what are time and space to us?

The Causes now named a sufficient Explanation of the Phenomena. — The causes already named will sufficiently account for the strange and distorted action of the various mental faculties as exercised in sleep. Memory, *e.g.*, will give us the past with *variations* ad libitum; things will appear to us, and events will seem to transpire, and forms and faces familiar will look out upon us, not as they really are, or ever were. We talk with a former friend, without the thought once occurring to us that he has been dead these many years. Impression there is, feeling, idea, fancy, association of all these, but hardly memory, or even imagination, much less judgment or reasoning. So it would seem at first. A closer inspection, however, will show us that there is in reality, in this spontaneous play of the mind, the exercise of all these faculties, only so modified by causes now named as to present strange and uncouth results.

Mental Faculties not immediately dependent on the Will. — If any of the mental faculties can be shown to be entirely dependent on the will for their activity and operation, so as to have no power to act except by its order or permission, then it would follow that when the will is no longer in possession of the throne, when its sway is for the time suspended as in sleep, the faculties thus dependent on it must lie inactive. But with regard to most if not all mental operations, we know the reverse to be true. They are capable of *spontaneous*, as well as voluntary action. Nay, some of them, it would seem, are not subject, in any case, directly to its control. It is not at our option whether to remember or forget, whether to perceive surrounding objects, whether such or such a thought shall, by the laws of association, follow next in the train of ideas and impressions. Some mental operations are more closely connected with and admit of a more direct interference on the part of the will than others, but it cannot be shown, I think, that any faculty is so far dependent on the will as not to be capable of action, irrespective of its demands. Indeed, facts seem to show that where once a train of mental action has been set in operation by the will, that action goes on, for a time, even when the will is withdrawn, or held in abeyance, as in sleep, or profound reverie.

Whence this Suspension of Power of the Will. — The question may occur, whence arises this suspension of the power of the will over the mental operations in sleep? What produces it? Does it, like the loss of voluntary power over the physical frame, result from the inactivity of the nervous apparatus? The fact that it always accompanies this, and is found in connection with it, that whatever produces the latter seems to be the occasion, also, of the former, as in the case of disease, delirium, mesmeric influence, stupefying drugs, inebriation, etc., and that the degree of the one, whether partial or complete, is in proportion to the degree of the other—these facts seem to me to favor the idea now suggested.

Summary of Results. — These, then, seem to be the principal phenomena of sleep: loss of sensational consciousness, loss of voluntary power over the body, loss of voluntary power over the operations of the mind.

Exhaustion of the nervous System. — Sleep, then, appears to be primarily an affection of the nervous system, the result of its exhaustion. By the law of nature, it cannot continue always active; repose must succeed to effort. Hence, the more rapid the exhaustion of the nervous system, from any cause, the more sleep is demanded. This we know to be the fact. The more sensitive the system, as in childhood, or with the gentler sex, as in men of great sensibility also, poets, artists, and others, the more sleep. On the other hand, those sluggish natures which allow nothing to excite or call into action the nervous system, sleep from precisely the opposite cause; not the exhaustion of nervous activity, but its absolute non-existence. If both our systems, the animal and the vegetative or nutritive, should sleep at once, says Rauch, there would be nothing to awaken us. That would be death. "In sleep, every man has a world of his own," says Heraclitus; "when awake, all men have one in common." Sleeping and waking, it has been beautifully said by another, are the ebb and flood of mind and matter on the ocean of our life.

§ II. — Dreams.

Resumè of previous Investigation. — It has been shown in the preceding section, that sleep is primarily and chiefly an affection of the nervous system, in which, through exhaustion, the senses become inactive, and, as it were, dead, while, at the same, the nutritive system and the functions essential to life go on; that in consequence of this inactivity of the sensorium, there results, 1. Loss of consciousness, so far, at least, as regards all connection with, and relation to, external things; 2. Loss of voluntary power over the physical and muscular frame; 3. Loss of voluntary control over the operations of the mind; the mind still remaining active, however, and its operations going on, uncontrolled by the will.

We are now prepared to take up, more particularly, that specific form of mental activity in sleep, called dreaming; a state which admits of easy explanation on principles already laid down.

A Dream, what. — What, then, is a *dream?* I reply, it is any mental action in sleep, of which, for any reason, we are afterward *conscious.* This is not the case with all, perhaps, with most mental action during sleep. Senses and the will are inactive, then, for the most part, and whatever thoughts and impressions may be wrought out in the laboratory of the mind, whatever play of forces and wondrous alchemy may there be going on, when the controlling principle that presides over and directs its operations is withdrawn, are, for the most part, never subsequently reported. Let the sensitivity be partially aroused, however, let some disturbing cause come in to prevent entire loss of sensibility, or let the conceptions of the mind present themselves with more than usual vividness and force of impression, and what we then think may afterward be remembered. This is the philosophy of dreams. What is thus remembered of our thoughts in sleep, we call a dream, more especially applying the term to such of our thoughts and conceptions in sleep, as have some degree of coherence and connection between themselves, so as to constitute a sort of unity.

Sources of our Dreams. — Our dreams take shape and character from a variety of circumstances. They are not altogether accidental nor unaccountable; and even when we cannot trace the connection, there is reason to suppose that such connection exists between the dream, and the state of the body, or of the mind, at the time, as, if known, would account for the shape and complexion of the dream. The principal sources, or, perhaps, it were more correct to say, modifying influences of our dreams are, 1, Our present bodily sensations, and especially the internal state of the physical system, and, 2, Our previous waking thoughts, dispositions, and prevalent states of mind.

Illustrations of the first. — As to the first of these modifying causes, instances of its operation will probably occur to every one from his own experience. You find yourself on a hard bed, or, it may be, have thrown yourself into some uncomfortable position, and you dream of broken bones or of the rack. The band of your robe buttons tightly about the neck, and you dream of hanging. You have taken a late supper of food highly seasoned and indigestible, and in your dreams a black bear very heavy and huge, quietly seats himself on your chest, or, as a military officer once dreamed, under similar circumstances, the prince of darkness sits cross-legged over your stomach, with the Bunker Hill monument in his lap. The instance related by Mr. Stewart, of the gentleman, who, sleeping with bottles of hot water at his feet, dreamed that he was walking along the burning crater of Mount Ætna, is in point here. Here the bodily sensation of heat upon the soles of the feet suggests the idea of a situation in which such a sensation would be likely to occur, and this idea blending with the sensation which is permanent and real, assumes, also, the character of reality, and the dream shapes itself accordingly. So when a window falls, or some sudden noise is heard, if it do not positively awaken you so far as to make known the real cause, you hear the sound, the sensorium partially aroused, mistakes it, perhaps, for the sound of a gun, and instantly you are in the midst of a battle at sea, or a fight with robbers. To such an extent are our dreams modified by sensible impressions of this sort, that it is possible, by skillful management, to shape and direct, to some extent, at least, the dreams of another as you will. An instance is related of an officer who was made, in this way, in his sleep, to go through with all the minutia of a duel, even to the firing of the pistol which was placed in his hand, at the proper moment, the noise of which awoke him. This was simply an *acted* dream.

Latent Disease. — Not unfrequently, some physical disorder, incipient or latent, of which we may not be aware in our waking moments, makes itself felt in the state of sleep, when the system is more susceptible of internal impressions, and thus modifies the dreams. In such cases, the dreams may serve as a sort of *index* of the state of the physical system, and somewhat, doubtless, of the apparently prophetic character of certain dreams may be accounted for in this way.

The second Source.—A second source, if not of our dreams themselves, at least of the peculiar shape and character which they assume, is to be found in our previous thoughts, and prevalent mental occupations and dispositions. We fall asleep, and mental action goes on much as before, in whatever direction and channel it had already received an impulse. Whatever has made the deepest impression on us through the day, has longest or most intently occupied us, *repeats* itself the moment we lose our consciousness of surrounding objects. The mind goes on with the new and strange spectacle, or with the unfinished problem, and unsolved intricate study of the day or of the night hour; and not seldom is the train of thought resumed and pursued to some purpose. On waking in the morning, we find little difficulty in completing a demonstration or solving a difficulty which had appeared insurmountable when we left it the previous night. Now the truth is, we did not leave it the previous night. It occupied us in our sleep. The brain was busy with it, it may be, all the night. It is solved in the morning, not because the mind is fresher then, but because it has been at work upon it through the night. Sometimes we are conscious of this on waking, and can dimly recall the severe continuous mental toil which went on while we slept. Usually, I suppose, we have no consciousness of it, and our only evidence of it is the well-known law and habit of the mind, to run in its worn and latest channels, together with the often observed fact that the difficulty previously felt is, somehow, strangely solved.

Further Illustration of the same Principle.—Condorcet is not the only mathematician who has received, in sleep, suggestions which led to the right solution of a problem that he had been obliged to leave unfinished on retiring for the night; nor is Franklin the only statesman who has, in dreams, reached a satisfactory conclusion respecting some intricate political movement. However this may be, there can be no reasonable doubt that our previous mental occupation, our prevalent state and disposition of mind, our habits of thought and habits of feeling, determine and shape the complexion of our dreams. They have a *subjective* connection, are by no means so disconnected with us and our real history, so much a matter of hap-hazard, as one may suppose. It was not without reason that President Edwards took notice of his dreams as affording an index of the state of his heart, and his real native propensities. They are the vane that shows which way the mind is set. Who will say that the dreams of Lady Macbeth, those dreams of a guilty conscience, are not among the most truthful of the portraitures of the great master dramatist?

Native Talent then shows itself.—Not only our native disposition and prevalent cast of thought betray themselves in dreams, but, as a certain writer has remarked, our native talents show out in those moments of spontaneous mental action. Talents which have had no opportunity to develop themselves, owing to our education and professional pursuits, take their chance and their time when we sleep, and we are poets, artists, orators, whatever nature designed, whatever the trammelled mind longs, but longs in vain, to be in our waking moments.

Incoherency of Dreams. — The *incoherency* of our dreams has been sufficiently accounted for in what I have previously said. It is not, I think, owing chiefly, as Upham supposes, to our loss of voluntary power and control over our thoughts during sleep, though it is quite true that we have no such control. The truth is, we are not at the time *aware* of any such incoherency. It cannot, of course, be owing then to our loss of voluntary power, since no increase of such power would enable us to repair a defect which we are unconscious of, but is owing entirely to another cause already mentioned, viz., that in sleep we lose our *relation* to things around us, lose our place, and our time, and hence, retain no standard of judging as to what is, and what is not, consentaneous and fit, self-consistent and coherent.

Apparent Reality. — Nothing is more remarkable in dreams than their apparent *reality*. The scenes, actions, and incidents, all stand out with peculiar distinctness, are projected as images into the air before us, and have not at all the semblance of any thing merely subjective. This has been, by some, ascribed to the fact that there is nothing to distract or call off the attention from the conceptions of the mind in dreams; we are wholly in them, and hence they appear as realities. I do not find, however, that in proportion as my attention in waking moments is wholly absorbed in any train of thought, those conceptions manifest any such tendency to project themselves, so to speak, into objective reality. They are still mere conceptions, only more vivid. I am inclined, therefore, to attribute the seeming reality of dreams to another source. We are accustomed to regard every thing as *objective*, which is out of the reach and control of our will, which comes and goes irrespective of us and our volition. Now, such we find to be the prime law of cerebral action in sleep. Of course, then, we are deceived into the belief that these conceptions over which we have no control, are not conceptions, but *perceptions*, realities.

Estimate of Time. — Nothing has seemed to some writers more mysterious than the entire disproportion between the *real* and *apparent* time of a dream. I refer to the fact that our dreams occupy frequently such very minute portions of time, while they seem to us to stretch over such long continued periods. An instance is related of an officer confined in the prisons of the French Revolution, who was awakened by the call of the sentry changing guard, fell asleep again, witnessed, as he supposed, a very long and very horrible procession of armed and bloody warriors, defiling on horseback down a certain street of Paris, occupying some hours in their passage, then awoke in terror in season to hear distinctly the response of the sentry to the challenge given before the dream began. The mind in such cases, say some, operates more rapidly than at other times. There is no evidence of that. Mr. Stewart has suggested, I think, the right explanation. As our dreams seem to us real, and we have no means of estimating time otherwise than by the apparent succession of events, the conceptions of the brain, that is, our dreams, seem to us to take up just so much time in passing as the *events themselves* would occupy were they real. This is perfectly a natural result, and it fully accounts for the apparent anomaly in question.

Prophetic Aspect. — Are dreams sometimes *prophetic*, and how are such to be accounted for? Cicero narrates a remarkable instance of what would seem to be a prophetic dream. I refer to the account of the two Arcadians who came to Megara and occupied different lodgings. The one of these appeared twice, in a dream, to the other, first imploring help, then murdered, and informing his comrade that his body would be taken out of the city early in the morning, by a certain gate, in a covered wagon. Agitated by the dream, the other repairs at the designed time to the appointed place, meets the wagon, discovers the body, arrests the murderer, and delivers him to justice.

Other Instances of the like Nature. — Another instance, perhaps equally striking, is narrated in the London *Times.* A Mr. Williams, residing in Cornwall, dreamed thrice in the same night that he saw the Chancellor of England killed, in the vestibule of the House of Commons. The dream so deeply impressed him that he narrated it to several of his acquaintance. It was subsequently ascertained that on the evening of that day the Chancellor, Mr. Perceval, was assassinated according to the dream. Now, this was certainly a remarkable coincidence. Was it any thing more? Was it merely an accidental thing — a matter of chance — that the dream should occur as it did, and should tally so closely with the facts? But these are not singular instances. Many such are on record.

Case related by Dr. Moore. — Dr. Moore, author of an interesting work on the use of the body in relation to the mind, narrates the following, as coming under his own observation. A friend of his dreamed that he was amusing himself, as he was in the habit of doing, by reading the epitaphs in a country church-yard, when a newly made grave attracted his attention. He was surprised to find on the stone the name, and date of death, of an intimate friend of his, with whom he had passed that very evening in conversation. Nothing more was thought of the dream, however, nor, perhaps, would it ever have recurred to mind, had he not received intelligence, some months afterward, of the death of this friend, which took place at the very date he had, in his dream, seen recorded on the tombstone.

Case related by Dr. Abercrombie. — The case mentioned

by Dr. Abercombie is another of these remarkable coincidences. Two sisters sleeping in the same room adjoining that of a sick brother, the one awakens in affright, having dreamed that the watch had stopped, and that on mentioning it to her sister, the latter replied, "Worse than that has happened, for ——'s breath has stopped also." On examination the watch was found going and the brother in a sound sleep. The next night the dream was repeated precisely as before with the same result. The next morning as one of the sisters had occasion to take the watch from the writing-desk she was surprised to find it had stopped, and at the same moment was startled by a scream from the other sister in the chamber of the sick man, who had, at that moment, expired

Additional Cases.—Another instance of a similar nature is related, but I know not on how good authority. The sister of Major Andrè, it is said, dreamed of her absent brother, one night, as arrested and on trial before a court martial. The appearance of the officers, their dress, etc., was distinctly impressed on her mind; the room, the relative position of the prisoner and his judges, were noticed; the general nature of the trial, and its result, the condemnation of her brother. She woke deeply impressed. Her fears were shortly afterward confirmed by the sad intelligence of her brother's arrest, trial, and execution, and, what is remarkable, the facts corresponded to her dream, both as respects the time of occurrence, the place, the appearance of the room, position, and dress of the judges, etc. Washington and Knox were particularly designated, though she had never seen them.

Another instance is related of a man who dreamed that the vessel in which his brother was an officer, and, in part, owner of the cargo, was wrecked on a certain island, and the vessel lost, but the hands saved. He was so impressed that he went directly and procured an extra insurance of five thousand dollars on his brother's portion of the property. By the next arrival news came that the vessel was wrecked, at the time and place of which the man had dreamed, and the mariners saved.

Coincidences.—Now it is perfectly easy to call all these things *coincidences.* They certainly are. But is it certain, or it is probable, that they are *mere* coincidences? To call them coincidences, and pass them off as if they were easily and fully accounted for in that way, is but a shallow concealment of our ignorance under a certain show of philosophy. It is but a conjecture at the best; a conjecture, moreover, which explains nothing, but leaves the mystery just as great as before; a conjecture which is by no means the most probable of all that might be made, but, on the contrary, one of the most improbable of all, as it seems to me. Mark, the cases I have now mentioned do not come under any of the laws or conditions laid down as giving rise or modification to our dreams. They are not suggested, so far as it appears, by any present bodily sensation on the part of the dreamer, nor was there any reason in the nature of the case why any such event, much less conjunction of events, should be apprehended by the dreamer in his waking moments. It was not the simple carrying out of his waking thoughts. Doubtless many dreams regarded as prophetic, may be explained on these principles. They are the result of our present sensations or impressions, or of the excited and anxious state of mind and train of thought during the day. But not so in the cases now cited.

Not necessary to suppose them Supernatural.—Shall we believe, then, that dreams are sometimes prophetic? We have no reason to doubt that they *may* be so. Are they, in that case, *supernatural* events? No doubt the future may be supernaturally communicated in dreams. No doubt it has been, and that not in a few cases, as every believer in the sacred Scriptures must admit. But this is not a necessary supposition. A dream may be prophetic, yet not supernatural. Some law, not fully known to us, may exist, by virtue of which the nervous system, when in a highly excited state, becomes susceptible of impressions not ordinarily received, and is put in communication, in some way to us mysterious, with scenes, places, and events, far distant, so as to become strangely cognizant of the coming future. Can any one show that this is impossible? Is it more improbable than that the cases recorded are mere chance coincidences? Is it not quite as likely to be so, as that the event should correspond, in so many cases and so striking a manner, with the previous dream, and yet there be *no cause, whatever*, for the correspondence? Is it not as reasonable, even, as to suppose direct divine interposition to reveal the future, the possibility of which interposition I by no means deny, but the reason for which does not become apparent? Is it not possible that there may be some natural law or agent of the sort now intimated, some as yet unexplained, but partially known, condition of the physical system, when in a peculiarly sensitive state, of which the *modus operandi* is not yet understood, but the existence of which is indicated in cases like those now described? That this is the true explanation, I by no means affirm; I make the suggestion merely to indicate what, it seems to me, may be a *possible* solution of the problem.

Possible Modes of accounting for the Facts.—Evidently there are only these four possible solutions. 1. To deny the facts themselves, *i. e.*, that any such dreams occurred, or at least, that they were verified in actual result. 2. To call them accidental coincidences. 3. To admit a supernatural agency. 4. To explain them in the way suggested. Our choice lies, as it seems to me, between the second and the last of these suppositions.

§ III. — Somnambulism.

Relation to the magnetic State.—Somnambulism or sleep-walking, is called, by some writers, *natural magnetic sleep.* They suppose it to differ from the state ordinarily called mesmeric, chiefly in this, that the former is a natural, and the latter an artificial process.

Resemblance of this to other cognate Phenomena. — We shall have occasion, as we proceed, to notice the very close resemblance between dreaming, somnambulism, mesmerism, and insanity, all, in fact, closely related to each other, characterized each and all by one and the same great law, and passing into each other by almost imperceptible gradations.

Method proposed. — It will be to the purpose, first to describe the phenomena of somnambulism, then to inquire whether they can be accounted for.

Description. — The principal phenomena of somnambulism are the following: The subject, while in a state of sound sleep, and perfectly unconscious of what he does, rises, walks about, finds his way over dangerous, and, at other times, inaccessible places, speaks and acts as if awake, performs in the dark, and with the eyes closed, or even bandaged, operations which require the closest attention and the best vision, perceives, indeed, things not visible to the eye in its ordinary waking state, perhaps even things absent and future, and when awakened from this state, is perfectly unconscious of what has happened, and astonished to find himself in some strange and unnatural position.

An Instance narrated. — A case which fell under the observation of the Archbishop of Bordeaux, when a student in the seminary, is narrated in the French Enclycopedia. A young minister, resident there, was a somnambulist, and to satisfy himself as to the nature of this strange disease, the Archbishop went every night into his room, after the young man was asleep. He would arise, take paper, pen, and ink, and proceed to the composition of sermons. Having written a page in a clear legible hand, he would read it aloud from top to bottom, with a clear voice and proper emphasis. If a passage did not please him, he would erase it, and write the correction, plainly, in its proper place, over the erased line or word. All this was done without any assistance from the eye, which was evidently asleep; a piece of pasteboard interposed between the eye and the paper produced no interruption or inconvenience. When his paper was exchanged for another of the same size, he was not aware of the change, but when a paper of a different size was substituted, he at once detected the difference. This shows that the sense of tact or feeling was active, and served as a guiding sense.

Other Cases of a similar Nature. — Similar cases, almost without number, are on record, in which much the same phenomena are observed. In some instances it is remarked that the subject, having written a sentence on a page, returns, and carefully dots the i's, and crosses the t's. These phenomena are not confined to the night. Persons have fallen into the magnetic state, while in church, during divine service, have gone home with their eyes closed, carefully avoiding obstacles in their way, as persons or carriages passing; and have been sent, in this state, of errands to places several miles distant, going and returning in safety.

An amusing incident is on record of a gentleman who found that his hen-roost was the scene of nightly and alarming depredations, which threatened the entire devastation of the premises, and what was strange, a large and faithful watch-dog gave no alarm. Determined to ascertain the true state of the case, he employed his servants to watch. During the night the thief made his appearance, was caught, after much resistance, and proved to be the *gentleman himself*, in a state of sound sleep, the author of all the mischief.

A remarkable Instance. — Another case is also related, which presents some features quite remarkable. In a certain school for young ladies, I think in France, prizes had been offered for the best paintings. Among the competitors was a young and timid girl who was conscious of her inferiority in the art, yet strongly desirous of success. For a time she was quite dissatisfied with the progress of her work, but by and by began to notice, as she resumed her pencil in the morning, that something had been added to the work since she last touched it. This was noticed for some time, and quite excited her curiosity. The additions were evidently by a superior hand, far excelling her own in skill and workmanship. Her companions denied, each, and severally, all knowledge of the matter. She placed articles of furniture against her door in such a way that any one entering would be sure to awaken her. They were undisturbed, but still the mysterious additions continued to be made. At last, her companions concluded to watch without, and make sure that no one entered her apartment during the night, but still the work went on. At length it occurred to them to watch her movements, and now the mystery was explained. They saw her, evidently in sound sleep, rise, dress, take her place at the table, and commence her work. It was her own hand that, unconsciously to herself, had executed the work n a style which, in her waking moments, she could not approach, and which quite surpassed all competition. The picture, notwithstanding her protestations that it was not er painting, took the prize.

The Question. — How is it now, that in a state of sleep, vith the eye, probably, fast closed, and the room in darkness, his girl can use the pencil in a manner so superior to any hing that she can do in the day time, with her eyes open, nd in the full possession and employment of her senses and er will?

Several Things to be accounted for. — Here are, in fact, everal things to be accounted for. How is it that the somambulist rises and moves about in a state of apparently ound sleep? How is it that she performs actions requirg often a high degree of intelligence, and yet without pparent consciousness? How is it that she moves fearessly and safely, as is often the case, over places where he could not stand for a moment, in her waking state, ithout the greatest danger? How is it that she can see ithout the eye, and perform actions in utter darkness, reuiring the nicest attention, and the best vision, and not only do them, but in such a manner as even to surpass what can be done by the same person in any other state, under the most favorable circumstances?

First, the Movement. — As to the first thing — the movement and locomotion in sleep — it may be accounted for in two ways. We may suppose it to be wholly automatic. This is the view of some eminent physiologists. The conscious soul, they say, has nothing to do with it, no knowledge of it. The will has nothing more to do with it, than it has with the contraction of a muscle, or irritation in an amputated limb.

Objection to this View. — For reasons intimated already, we cannot adopt the automatic theory. It seems to us subversive of all true science of the mind. The body is self-moved in obedience to the active energy of the nervous organism, and this organism again, acts only as it is acted upon by the mind that animates, pervades, and controls that organism. In the waking state, this mental action, and the consequent nervous and muscular activity, are under the control of the will. In sleep, this control is, for the time, suspended, and the thoughts come and go as it may chance, subject to no law but that of the associative principle. The mind, however, is still active, and the thoughts are busy in their own spontaneous movement. To this movement, the brain and nervous system respond. That the brain itself thinks, that the nerves and muscles act, and the limbs move automatically, without the energizing activity of the mind, is a supposition purely gratuitous, inconsistent with all the known facts and evident indications of the case, and at war with all just notions of the relation of body and mind.

Another Theory. — Another, and much more reasonable supposition is, that the will, which ordinarily in sleep loses control both over the mind and the body, in the state of somnambulism regains, in some way, and to some extent its power over the latter, so that the body rises and moves about in accordance with the thought and feeling that hap pen, at the moment, to be predominant in the mind. There is no control of the will over those thoughts and suggestions: they are spontaneous, undirected, casual, subject only to the ordinary laws of association; but for the time, whether owing to the greater vividness and force of these suggestions and impressions, or to the disturbed and partially aroused state of the sensorial organism, the will, acting in accordance with these suggestions of the mind, so far regains its power over the bodily organism, that locomotion ensues. The dream is then simply acted out. The body rises, the hand resumes the pen, and the appropriate movements and actions corresponding to the conceptions of the mind in its dream, are duly performed.

The second Point of Inquiry. — This virtually answers the second question, how the somnambulist can perform actions requiring intelligence, yet without apparent consciousness.

There is, doubtless, consciousness at the time — there must be; the thought and feeling of the moment are known to us at the moment. Not to be conscious of thought and feeling, is, not to think and feel. That the acts thus performed are not subsequently remembered, is no evidence that they were not objects of consciousness at the time of their occurrence. This is absence of memory, and not of consciousness.

Not remembered. — Why they are not subsequently remembered, we may, or may not, be able to explain. Not improbably, it may be owing to the partial inactivity of the senses, and the consequent failure to perceive the actual relations of the person to surrounding objects. But to whatever it may be owing, it does not prove that the mind is, for the time, unconscious of its own activity, for that is impossible.

Third Question. — As to the third question, how the somnambulist can safely move where the waking person cannot, as along the edge of precipices, and on the roofs of houses, the explanation is simple and easy. The eye is closed. The sense of touch is the only guide. Now the foot requires but a space of a few inches for its support, that, given it knows nothing further, asks nothing beyond. It is the eye that informs us at other times of the danger beyond, and so creates, in fact, the present danger. You walk safely on a two-inch plank one foot from the ground. The same effort of the muscles will enable you to walk the same plank one hundred feet from the ground, if you do not know the difference. This the somnambulist, with closed eye, and trusting to the sense of feeling alone, does not recognize.

A Question still to be answered. — But the most difficult question remains. How is it that the sleep-walker in utter darkness, reads, writes, paints, runs, etc., better even than others can do, or even than he himself can do at other times and with open eyes. How can he do these things without seeing? and how see in the dark and with the organs of vision fast locked in sleep. The facts are manifest. Not so ready the explanation. I can see how the body can move and with comparative safety, and even how the cerebral action may go on in sleep, without subsequent remembrance. But to read, to write, to paint, to run swiftly when pursued through a dark cellar, without coming in contact with surrounding objects, are operations requiring the nicest power of vision, and how there can be vision without the use of the proper organ of vision, is not to me apparent. It does not answer this question to say that the action is automatic. That would account for one's seeing, but not *without eyes.* The movement from place to place, according to the same theory, is also automatic; that accounts for a person's walking in sleep, but not for his walking *without legs.* Nor does it solve the difficulty to say that in sleep the life of the soul is merged in that of the body; doubtless, but how can the body see without the eye, or the eye without light?

Theory of a general Sense. — The only theory that seems to offer even a plausible solution is that advanced by some German psychologists, and by Rauch in this country, of a *general sense.* The several special senses, they say, are all resolvable into one general sense as their source, viz., that of feeling. They refer us in illustration to the ear of the crab, to the eye of the fly and the snail, to the scent of flies, in which cases, respectively, we find no *organ* of hearing, or vision, or smell, but simply an expansion of the general nerve of sensation, or some filament from it, connecting with a somewhat thinner and more delicate membrane than the ordinary skin. This shows that our ordinary way of perceiving things is not the only way; that special organs of vision, etc., are not needed in order to all perception, much less to sensation. It has been found by experiment that bats, after their eyes have been entirely removed, will fly about as before, and avoid all obstacles just as before. In these cases, it is contended, perception is merely *feeling heightened*, the exercise of the general sense into which the special senses are severally merged. And this, it is said, may be the case with the somnambulist.

Remarks on this Theory. — There is doubtless truth in the general statement now advanced. I do not see, however, that it accounts for all that requires explanation in the case. It explains, perhaps, how, without the organ of vision, a certain dim, confused perception of objects might be furnished by the general sense, but not for a *clearer* vision and a *nicer* operation than the waking eye can give. This, to me, remains yet unexplained. Is there an inner consciousness, a hidden soul-life not dependent on the bodily organization, which at times comes forth into development and manifests itself when the usual relations of body and soul are disturbed and suspended? So some have supposed, and so it may be for aught we know to the contrary, but this is only to solve one mystery by supposing another yet greater.

Must admit what. — Whatever theory we adopt, or even if we adopt none, we must admit, I think, in view of the facts in the case, that in certain disordered and highly excited states of the nervous system, as, *e. g.*, when weakened by disease, so that ordinary causes affect it more powerfully than usual, *it can, and does sometimes, perceive what, under ordinary circumstances, is not perceptible to the eye, or to the ear; nay, even dispenses with the use of eye and ear, and the several organs of special sense.* This occurs, as we have seen, in somnambulism, or natural magnetic sleep. We meet with the same thing also in even stranger forms, in the mesmeric state, and in some species of insanity.

The mental Process obvious. — So far as regards the purely mental part of the phenomena, the operations of the mind in somnambulism, there is nothing which is not easily explained. In somnambulism, as indeed in all these states so closely connected — sleep, dreams, the mesmeric process, and even insanity — *the will loses its controlling power over the train of thought, and, consequently, the thought or feeling that happens to be dominant gives rise to, and entirely shapes, the actions that may in that state be performed.* This dominant thought or feeling, in the case of the somnambulist, is, for the most part, probably, the result of previous causes; a continuation of the former mental action, which, when the influence of the will is suspended and the senses closed, by a sort of inherent activity keeps on in the same channel as before. Of such action, the soul is itself probably conscious at the moment, but afterward no recollection of it lingers in the mind.

§ IV.—Disordered Mental Action.

Relation to other mental Phenomena. — Closely allied to somnambulism, dreaming, etc., are certain forms of disordered mental condition commonly termed insanity; having this one element in common with the former, the loss or suspension of all voluntary control over the train of thought. This must be regarded as the characteristic feature and essential ground-work of the various phenomena in all these various states.

Classification. — The forms of disordered mental action are various, and admit of some classification. Some are transient, others permanent, arising from some settled disorder of the intellect, or the sensibilities.

I. *Transient Forms.* — Of these, some are artificially produced, as by exciting drugs, stimulants, intoxicating drinks, etc., others by physical and natural causes, as disease, etc.

Delirium, artificial. — The most common of these forms of disordered mental action is that transient and artificial state produced by intoxicating drugs and drinks. This is properly called delirium, and takes place whenever total or even partial inebriation occurs, whether from alcoholic or narcotic stimulants, as the opium of the Chinese, and the Indian hemp or *hachish* of the Hindoos. The same effects, substantially, are produced, also, by certain plants, as the deadly night-shade and others, and also by aconite. In all these cases the effect is wrought primarily, it would seem, upon the blood, which is brought into a poisonous state, and thus deranges the action of the nerves and the brain. The *hachish* or Indian hemp, which, in the East, is used for purposes of intoxication more generally, perhaps, than even opium, or alcoholic drinks, may serve as an illustration of the manner in which these various stimulants affect the senses. At first the subject perceives an increased activity of mind; thoughts come and go in swift succession and pleasing variety; the imagination is active — memory, fancy, reason, all awake. Gradually this mental activity increases and *frees itself from voluntary control;* attention to any special subject becomes difficult or even impossible; ideas, strange and wonderful, come and go at random with no apparent cause and by no known law of suggestion; these absorb the attention until the mind is at last given up to them, and there is no further consciousness of the external things, while, at the same time, the patient is susceptible, as in the magnetic state, of influence and impression from without. How closely, in many respects, this resembles the state of the mind in somnambulism, mesmerism, and ordinary dreaming, I need not point out. The mental excitement produced by opium is perhaps greater, and the images that throng the brain, and assume the semblance of reality, are more numerous and real. The subsequent exhaustion and reaction in either case are fearful. For illustration of this the reader is referred to the Confessions of an Opium Eater, by the accomplished De Quincey.

Delirium of Disease. — The ordinary *delirium of disease* is essentially of the same nature with that now described, differing rather in its origin, or producing cause, than in its effects. It comes on often in much the same way; increased mental activity shows itself; attention is fixed with difficulty; strange images, and trains of thought at once singular and uncontrolled by the will, come and go; the mind at last is possessed by them and loses all control over its own movements. Every thing now, which the mind conceives, assumes the form of reality. It has no longer conceptions but perceptions. Figures move along the walls and occupy the room. They are as really *seen*, that is, the *sensation* is the same, as in any case of healthy and actual vision; only the effect is wrought from within outward, from the sensorium to the optic nerve and retina, instead of the reverse, as in actual vision. Voices are heard also, and various sounds, in the same manner; the producing cause acting from within outward, and not from without inward.

Differs from Dreaming. — This state differs from dreaming in that the subject is not necessarily asleep, and that it involves a greater and more serious disorder of the faculties, as well as of longer continuance. The illusions are perhaps also more decided, and more vividly conceived as external and real entities. Like dreams, and unlike the conceptions of the magnetic state, these ideas and illusions may be subsequently recalled, and in many cases are so; the mind, however, finding it difficult still to believe that they were *fictions*, and not actual occurrences.

In dreaming, the things which we seem to see and hear are changes produced in the sensorium by cerebral or other influences. In delirium, the sensorium itself is disordered and produces false appearances, spectres, etc.

Mania. — That form of disordered mental action termed *mania*, differs from that already described in that, along with the derangement of the intellect, there is more or less emotional disorder. The patient is strongly excited on any thing that at all rouses the feelings. There may be much or little intellectual derangement accompanying this excitement. The two forms, in fact, pass into each by a succession of almost indefinable links. The main element is the same in each, *i. e.*, loss of voluntary control over the thoughts and feelings. Each is produced by physical causes, and is of transient duration.

Power of Suggestion. — In all these forms of delirium now described, whether artificial or natural, the mind is open to suggestions from without, and these become often controlling ideas. Hence it is of imperative necessity that the attendant should be on his guard as to what he says or does in the presence of the patient. An instance in point is related by Dr. Carpenter, in which a certain eminent physician lost a number of his patients in fever by their jumping from the window, a fact accounted for at once, when we come to hear that he was stupid enough to caution the attendants, *in the hearing of his patients*, against the possibility of such an event.

II. *Permanent Forms.* — I proceed next to notice those more permanent forms of mental disorder, commonly termed *insanity*, a term properly applied to designate those cases of abnormal mental activity in which there seems to be either some settled disorder of the intellect, as, *e. g.*, when the brain has been weakened by successive attacks of mania, epilepsy, etc., or else some permanent tendency to disordered emotional excitement.

Disorder of the Intellect. — Where the intellectual faculties are disordered, the chief elementary feature of the case is the same as in those already noticed, viz., *Loss of voluntary control over the mental operations* — the psychological ground-work, as we have seen, of all the various forms of abnormal mental action which have as yet come under our notice.

Memory affected. — In the cases now under consideration, the memory is the faculty that in most cases gives the first signs of failure, particularly that form of memory which is strictly voluntary, viz., recollection. In consequence of this, past experience is placed out of reach, cannot be made available, and therefore reasoning and judgment are deficient. The thoughts lose their coherency and connection, as they are thus cut loose from the fixtures of the past, to which the laws of association no longer bind them; they come and go with a strange automatic sort of movement, over which the mind feels that it has little power. Gradually this little fades away; the will no longer exercises its former and rightful control over the mental activities; its sway is broken, its authority gone; the mind loses control of itself, and, like a vessel broken from her moorings, swings sadly and hopelessly away into the swift stream of settled insanity. The mind still retains its full measure of activity, perhaps greatly increased; but it acts as in a *dream.* All its conceptions are realities to it, and the actually real world, as it mingles with the dream and shapes it, is but vaguely and imperfectly apprehended through the confused media of the mind's own conceptions. All this may be, and often is, realized, where there is entire absence of all emotional excitement.

Not easily cured. — The condition now described is much less open to medical treatment than the mental states previously mentioned. Indeed, where there is insanity resulting from settled cerebral disorder, there is very little hope of cure. Nature may in time recover herself; she may not. This depends on age, constitution, predisposing causes, and a variety of circumstances not altogether under human control.

Disordered Action of the Sensibilities. — Another form of insanity is that which consists in, or arises from, not any primary disorder of the intellectual faculties, but a tendency to disordered *emotional* excitement. Sometimes this is general, extending to all the emotions. These cases require careful treatment. The patient is like a child, and must be governed mildly and wisely, is open to argument and motives of self-control. In other cases, some one emotion is particularly the seat and centre of the disturbance, while the others are comparatively tranquil. In such cases the exaggerated emotion may prompt to some specific action, as suicide, or murder, etc. This is termed *impulsive* insanity. The predominant idea or impulse tyrannizes over the mind, and, by a sort of irresistible fatality, drives it on to the commission of crime. The patient may be conscious of this impulse, and revolt from it with horror; there may be no pleasure or desire associated with the deed, but he is unable to resist. He is like a boat in the rapids of Niagara. So fearful the condition of man wher reason is dethroned, and the will no longer master

MENTAL PHILOSOPHY.

DIVISION SECOND.

THE SENSIBILITIES.

THE SENSIBILITIES.

PRELIMINARY TOPICS.

CHAPTER I.

NATURE, DIFFICULTY, AND IMPORTANCE OF THIS DEPARTMENT OF THE SCIENCE.

Previous Analysis. — In entering upon the investigation of a new department of our science, it may be well to recur, for a moment, to the analysis and classification of the powers of the mind which has been already given in the introduction to the present volume. The faculties of the mind were divided in that analysis, it will be remembered, into three grand departments, the Intellect, the Sensibilities, and the Will; the first comprising the various powers of *thinking* and *knowing*, the second of *feeling*, the third of *willing*. The first of these main divisions has been already discussed in the preceding pages. Upon the second we now enter.

Difference of the two Departments. — This department of mental activity differs from the former, as feeling differs from thinking. The distinction is broad and obvious. No one can mistake it who knows any thing of his own mental operations. Every one knows the difference, though not every one may be able to explain it, or tell precisely in what it consists. But whether able to define our meaning or not, we are perfectly conscious that to think and to feel are different acts, and involve entirely different states of mind.

The common language of life recognizes the distinction, alike that of the educated and of the uneducated, the peasant and the man of science. The literature of the world recognizes it.

Relation of the two. — As regards the relation of the two departments to each other, the intellect properly precedes the sensibility. The latter implies the former, and depends upon it. There can be no feeling — I speak, of course, of mental feeling, and not of mere physical sensation — without previous cognizance of some object, in view of which the feeling is awakened. Affection always implies an object of affection, desire, an object of desire; and the object is first apprehended by the intellect before the emotion is awakened in the mind. When we love, we love something, when we desire, we desire something, when we fear, or hope, or hate, there is always some object, more or less clearly defined, that awakens these feelings, and in proportion to the clearness and vividness of the intellectual conception or perception of the object, will be the strength of the feeling.

Strength of Feelings as related to Strength of Intellect. — The range and power of the sensibilities, then, in other words, the mind's capacity of feeling, depends essentially upon the range and vigor of the intellectual powers. Within certain limits, the one varies as the other. The man of strong and vigorous mind is capable of stronger emotion than the man of dwarfed and puny intellect. Milton, Cromwell, Napoleon, Webster, surpassed other men, not more in clearness and strength of intellectual perception, than in energy of feeling. In this, indeed, lay, in no small degree, the secret of their superior power. In the most eloquent passages of the great orators of ancient or modern times, it is not so much the irresistible cogency and unrelenting grasp of the terrible logic, that holds our attention, and casts its spell over us, as it is the burning indignation that exposes the sophistries, and tears to shreds the fallacies of an opponent, and sweeps all argument and all opposition before it like a devouring fire. The orations of Demosthenes, of Burke, of Webster, furnish numerous examples of this.

Influence of the Feelings on the Intellect. — On the other hand, it is equally true that the state of the intellect in any case depends not a little on the nature and strength of the mind's capacities of feeling. A quick and lively sensibility is more likely to be attended with quickness and strength of intellectual conception; imagination, perception, fancy, and even reasoning, are quickened, and set in active play, by its electric touch.

A man with sluggish and torpid sensibilities, is almost of necessity a man of dull and slugglish intellect. A man without feeling, if we can conceive so strange a phenomenon, would be a man, the measure of whose intellectual capacity would be little above that of the brutes.

Importance of this Department of the mental Faculties. — Such being the nature of the sensibilities, the *importance* of this department of mental activity becomes obvious at a glance. The springs of human action lie here. We find here a clue to the study of human nature and of ourselves. To understand the complicated and curious problem of human life and action, to understand history, society, nations, ourselves, we must understand well the nature and philosophy of the sensibilities. Here we find the motives which set the busy world in action, the causes which go to make men what they are in the busy and ever changing scene of life's great drama. It is the emotions and passions of men which give, at once, the impulse, and the direction, to their energies, constitute their character, shape their history and their destiny. A knowledge of man and of the world is emphatically a knowledge of the human heart.

Extract from Brown. — The importance of this part of our nature is well set forth in the following passage from Dr. Thomas Brown:

"We might, perhaps, have been so constituted, with respect to our intellectual states of mind, as to have had all the varieties of these, our remembrances, judgments, and creations of fancy, without our emotions. But without the emotions which accompany them, of how little value would the mere intellectual functions have been! It is to our vivid feelings of this class we must look for those tender regards which make our remembrances sacred, for that love of truth and glory, and mankind, without which to animate and reward us in our discovery and diffusion of knowledge, the continued exercise of judgment would be a fatigue rather than a satisfaction, and for all that delightful wonder which we feel when we contemplate the admirable creations of fancy, or the still more admirable beauties of the unfading model, that model which is ever before us, and the imitation of which, as has been truly said, is the only *imitation* that is itself *originality*. By our other mental functions, we are mere spectators of the machinery of the universe, living and inanimate; by our *emotions*, we are admirers of nature, lovers of man, adorers of God. * * *

Less attractive Aspects. — "In this picture of our emotions, however, I have presented them in their fairest aspects; there are aspects which they assume, as terrible as these are attractive; but even terrible as they are, they are not the less interesting objects of our contemplation. They are the enemies with which our mortal combat, in the warfare of life, is to be carried on; and of these enemies that are to assail us, it is good for us to know all the arms and all the arts with which we are to be assailed; as it is good for us to know all the misery which would await our defeat, as well as all the happiness which would crown our success, that our conflict may be the stronger, and our victory, therefore, the more sure.

"In the list of our emotions of this formidable class, is to be found every passion which can render life guilty and miserable; a single hour of which, if that hour be an hour of uncontrolled dominion, may destroy happiness forever, and leave little more of virtue than is necessary for giving all its horror to remorse. There are feelings as blasting to every desire of good that may still linger in the heart of the frail victim who is not yet wholly corrupted, as those poisonous gales of the desert, which not merely lift in whirlwinds the sands that have often been tossed before, but wither even the few fresh leaves, which on some spot of scanty verdure, have still been flourishing amid the general sterility."

Difficulty of the Study. — With regard to the difficulty attending the study of this part of our nature, a word seems necessary in passing. It has been supposed to constitute a peculiar difficulty in the way of the successful investigation of this department of mental activity, that the sensibilities are, in their very nature, of such an exciting character, as to preclude the calm, dispassionate observation and reflection so necessary to correct judgment. At the moment of exercising any lively emotion, as hope, fear, anger, etc., the mind is in too great perturbation to be in any condition for accurate self-observation, and when the excitement has subsided, the important moment has already passed. Mr. Stewart has particularly noticed this difficulty in his Introduction to the Active and Moral Powers, and quotes Hume to the same effect.

Not peculiar to this Department of the Science. — The difficulty in question, however, is one which, in reality, pertains to all mental science, and not to this department of it alone; and so Hume, in the passage cited by Mr. Stewart, seems to intend. It is true that while we are under the influence of any exciting emotion, we are in no mood, and in no suitable state to observe, with critical eye, the workings of our own minds; neither are we in any condition to do so when engaged in the less exciting, but not less absorbing *intellectual* occupation of reasoning, or imagining, or remembering. The moment we begin to observe ourselves as thus engaged, the mind is no longer employed as before, the experiment which we wish to observe is interrupted, and instead of reasoning, imagining, or remembering, we are only observing ourselves. Our only resource, in either case, is to turn back and gather up, as well as we can from *memory*, the data of our mental activity and condition while thus and thus employed. And this we can do with regard to the action of the sensibilities, as well as of the intellect, provided only the degree of emotion and excitement is not so great as to interfere with the present consciousness, and so with the subsequent recollection of what was passing in our own minds.

Sources of Information. — Nor are we dependent entirely on self-observation. Our sources of information are twofold, the observation of our own minds, and of others. From the latter source we may learn much of the nature of this department of mental action. The sensibilities of others are more open to our inspection, and less readily mistaken, than their intellectual states. Nor do we meet, in this case, with the same difficulty; for however excited and incapable of self-inspection, at the moment, the subject of any strong emotion or passion may be, the spectator, at least, is able to observe the effect of that passion, and note its phenomena, with calm and careful eye.

CHAPTER II.

ANALYSIS AND CLASSIFICATION OF THE SENSIBILITIES.

Certain Distinctions may be noticed. — Including, under the term sensibility, according to the definition already given, whatever is of the nature of *feeling*, in distinction from thought or cognition, and limiting the term also to feelings strictly *mental*, in distinction from merely physical sensation, it is obvious that there are certain leading distinctions still to be observed in this class of our mental states, certain great and strongly marked divisions or differences, by which we shall do well to be guided in our arrangement and classification of them. Our feelings are many and various; it is impossible to enumerate or classify them with perfect precision; yet there are certain points of resemblance and difference among them, certain groups or classes into which they naturally divide themselves.

A general Distinction indicated.—One general distinction lies at the outset, patent and obvious, running through all forms and modes of sensibility, namely, the difference of *agreeable* and *disagreeable.* Every feeling is, in its very nature, and of necessity, one or the other, either pleasing or painful. In some cases the distinction is much more strongly marked than in others; sometimes it may be hardly perceptible, and it may be difficult to determine, so slight is the degree of either, whether the feeling under consideration partakes of the character of pleasure or pain; sometimes there is a blending of the two elements, and the same emotion is at once pleasing and painful to the mind that experiences it. But I cannot conceive of a feeling that is neither agreeable or disagreeable, but positively indifferent. The state of indifference is not an exercise of sensibility, but a simple *want* of it, as the very name denotes by which we most appropriately express this state of mind, *i. e., apathy* (*α παθος*).

Simple Emotions. — Passing this general and obvious distinction, we find among our sensibilities a large class which we may denominate *simple emotions.* These comprise the joys and sorrows of life in all their varieties of modification and degree, according as the objects which awaken them differ. Under this class fall those general states of the mind which, without assuming a definite and obvious form, impart a tinge and coloring of joyousness or sadness to all our activity. Under this class, also, must be included the more specific forms of feeling, such as the grief or sorrow we feel at the loss of friends, sympathy with the happiness or sorrow of others, the enjoyment arising from the contemplation or persuasion of our own superiority, and the chagrin of the reverse, the enjoyment of the ludicrous, of the new and wonderful, of the beautiful, to which must be added the satisfaction resulting from the consciousness of right action, and those vivid feelings of regret in view of the wrong, which, in their higher degree, assume the name of remorse, and fall like a chill and fearful shadow over the troubled path of earthly life. These all are simple emotions, and all, moreover, are but so many forms of joy and sorrow, varying as the objects vary which give rise to them.

Further Difference of instinctive and rational Emotion. — It will be observed, however, that of these several specific forms of simple emotion, some are of a higher order than the others. Such are those last named in the series, the feelings awakened in view of the ludicrous, in view of the new and wonderful, in view of the beautiful, and in view of the right, or, in general, the æsthetic and moral emotions. These, as seeming to possess a higher dignity, and to involve a higher degree of intellectual development, we may denominate the *rational*, in distinction from the other simple emotions, which, to mark the difference, we may term *instinctive.*

Emotions of a complex Character. — Passing on in our analysis, we come next to a class of emotions differing from that already considered, in being of a complex character. It is no longer a simple feeling of delight and satisfaction in the object, or the reverse, but along with this is blended the wish, more or less definite and intense, of good or ill, to the object which awakens the emotion. The feeling assumes an active form, becomes objective, and travels out from itself and the bosom that cherishes it, to the object which calls it forth. In this desire of good or ill to the object, the simple element of joy or sorrow, the subjective feeling, is often merged and lost sight of; yet it ever exists as an essential element of the complex emotion.

Further Subdivision of this Class. — Of this class are the feelings usually denominated *affections*, which may be further subdivided into *benevolent* and *malevolent*, according as they seek the good or the ill of their respective objects. As the *simple emotions* are all but so many modes and forms of the feeling of *joy*, and its opposite, *sorrow*, so the *affections* are but so many different modifications of the one comprehensive principle of *love*, and its opposite, *hate.*

Various Objects of Affection. — The affections vary as the objects vary on which they rest. Of the benevolent class, the more prominent are, love of kindred, of friends, of benefactors, of home and country. Of the malevolent affections, so called, the more important are the feeling of resentment in view of personal injury, of indignation at the wrongs of others, the feeling of jealousy, and the like.

The Passions. — These various affections, both malevolent and benevolent, when they rise above the ordinary degree, and become impatient of restraint, imperious, no longer under the control of reason and sober reflection, but themselves assuming the command of the whole man, and impelling him toward the desired end, regardless of other and higher interests, become the *passions* of our nature, with which no small part of the self-conflict and self-discipline of this our mortal life is to be maintained.

The Desires. — There is still another class of emotions, differing essentially in their nature from each of the two leading divisions already mentioned, that is, our *desires.* These are of two sorts. Those which are founded in the physical nature and constitution of man — as the desire of food, of muscular exertion, of repose, of whatever is adapted to the animal nature and wants — are usually denominated *appetites:* those, on the other hand, which take their rise from the nature and wants of the mind, rather than of the body, may be termed *rational*, in distinction from *animal* desires or appetites. Of these the more important are the desire of happiness, of knowledge, of power, of society, of the esteem of others.

As joy has its opposite, sorrow, and love its opposite, hate, so also desire has its opposite, aversion; and the objects of aversion are as numerous as the objects of desire. The desire of wealth has its counterpart, the aversion to poverty and want; the desire of life and happiness stands over against the aversion to suffering and death. The two are, so to speak, the positive and negative poles of feeling.

Hope and Fear. — There is yet another and important class of our emotions, having not a little to do with the happiness or misery of life, casting its lights and shadows over no small part of our little path from the cradle to the grave, our *hopes* and our *fears*. These, however important in themselves, are, nevertheless, but modifications of the principles of desire and aversion, and are, therefore, to be referred to the same general division of the sensibilities. Hope is the desire of some expected good, fear the aversion to some anticipated evil.

Summary of Classes. — To the three comprehensive classes now named, *Simple Emotions*, *Affections*, and *Desires* may be referred, if I mistake not, the various sensibilities of our nature; or, if the analysis and classification be not complete and exhaustive, it is at least sufficiently minute for our present purpose.

Historical Sketch of the leading Divisions of the Sensibilities adopted by different Writers.

Important to know the Principles of Division adopted by others. — The discussion of the present topic would be incomplete without a glance at the *history* of the same. It is of service, having obtained some definite results and conclusions of our own, to know also what have been the views and conclusions of others upon the same matter. As with regard to the intellectual powers, so also with respect to the sensibilities, different principles of division and classification have been adopted by different writers. Our limits will allow us to glance only at the more important of these.

General Principles of Classification. — Of those who have written upon the sensibilities, some have placed them in contrast to each other, as hope and fear, love and hate, etc., making this the principle of division; others have classed them as personal, social, etc.; others as relating to time, the past, the present, and the future; others as instinctive and rational; while most who have had occasion to treat of this part of our mental constitution, have considered it with reference solely or mainly to the science of ethics or morals, and have adopted such a division and arrangement as best suited that end, without special regard to the psychology of the matter.

Of the Greek Schools. — Among the Greeks, the Academicians included the various emotions under the four principal ones, fear, desire, joy, and grief, classing despair and aversion under grief, while hope, courage, and anger were comprised under desire.

To denote the *passivity* of the mind, as acted upon, and under the influence of emotion, the Greeks named the passions in general, πάθος, suffering, whence our terms pathos, pathetic, etc., whence also the Latin *passio* and *patior*, from which our word *passion.* The Stoics, in particular, designated all emotions as παθη, diseases, regarding them as disorders of the mind.

Hartley's Division. — Among the moderns, *Hartley* divides the sensibilities into the two leading classes of *grateful* and *ungrateful* ones; under the former, including love, desire, hope, joy, and pleasing recollection; under the latter, the opposites of these emotions, hatred, aversion, fear, grief, displeasing recollection.

Distinction of primitive and derivative. — Certain other English writers, as *Watts* and *Grove*, derive all the emotions ultimately from the three principal ones, admiration, love, and hatred, which they term the *primitive* passions, all others being *derivative*.

Division of Cogan. — *Cogan*, whose treatise on the passions is a work of much interest, divides the sensibilities into *passions*, *emotions*, and *affections*; by the first of these terms designating the first impression which the mind receives from some impulsive cause; by the second, the more permanent feeling which succeeds, and which betrays itself by visible signs in the expressions of the countenance and the motions of the body; while by affections, he denotes the less intense and more durable influence exerted upon the mind by the objects of its regard. The passions and affections are, by this author, further divided into those which spring from *self-love* and those which are derived from the *social principle*.

Classification of Dr. Reid. — *Dr. Reid* divides the active principles, as he terms them, into three classes, the *mechanical*, the *animal*, and the *rational*, including, under the first, our instincts and habits, under the second, our appetites, under the third, our higher principles of action.

Of Stewart. — *Dugald Stewart* makes two classes, the *instinctive* or *implanted*, and the *rational* or *governing* principles, under the former including *appetites*, *desires*, and *affections*, under the latter, *self-love* and the *moral faculty*. The desires are distinguished from the appetites, in that they do not, like the former, take their rise from the body, nor do they operate, periodically, after certain intervals, and cease after the attainment of their object. Under the title of affections, are comprehended all those principles of our nature that have for their object the communication of good or of ill to others.

Of Brown. — *Dr. Brown* divides the sensibilities, to which he gives the general name of *emotions*, with reference to their relation to *time*, as *immediate*, *retrospective*, and *prospective*. Under the former, he includes, as involving no moral feeling, cheerfulness and melancholy, wonder and its opposite, feelings of beauty and the opposite, feelings of sublimity and of the ludicrous; as involving moral feeling, the emotions distinctive of vice and virtue, emotions of love and hate, of sympathy, of pride and humility. Under *retrospective* emotion he includes anger, gratitude, regret, satisfaction; under *prospective* emotion, all our desires and fears.

Of Upham.—Prof. Upham divides the sensibilities into the two leading departments, the *natural* and the *moral*, the former comprehending the *emotions* and the *desires*, the latter, the *moral sentiments* or *conscience*. Under the class of desires, he includes our instincts, appetites, propensities, and affections.

Of Hickok.—Dr. Hickok classes the sensibilities under the departments of *animal*, *rational*, and *spiritual* susceptibility; the former comprehending instincts, appetites, natural affections, self-interested feelings, and disinterested feelings; the second, æsthetic, scientific, ethic, and theistic emotions; while the latter or spiritual susceptibility differs from each of the others, in not being, like them, constitutional, but arising rather from the personal disposition and character.

Remarks on the foregoing Divisions.—Our limits forbid, nor does the object of the present work require, a critical discussion of these several plans of arrangement.

It is but justice to say, however, that no one of these several methods of arrangement is altogether satisfactory. They are not strictly scientific. The method of Cogan, for example, derives all our sensibilities ultimately from the two principles of self-love, or desire for our own happiness, and the social principle, or regard for the condition and character of others; which again resolve themselves, according to this author, into the two cardinal and primitive affections of *love* and *hate*. This division strikes us at once as arbitrary, and, therefore, questionable; and, also, as *ethical* rather than *psychological*. There are many simple emotions which cannot properly be resolved into either of these two principles. On the other hand, the psychological distinction between the emotions and desires is overlooked in this arrangement. The same remarks apply substantially to several of the other methods noticed.

Objection to Stewart's Division. — The arrangement of Mr. Stewart is liable to this objection, that the principle of self-love, and also the moral faculty, which he classes by themselves as *rational* principles, in distinction from the other emotions as *implanted* or *instinctive* principles, are as really implanted in our nature, as really constitutional or instinctive, as any other. Appetite, moreover, is but one form or class of desires; self-love is but another, *i. e.*, the desire of our own happiness.

To Upham's Division. — The division of Mr. Upham is still more objectionable on the same ground. The *natural* and the *moral* sentiments, into which two great classes he divides the sensibilities, are distinct neither in fact nor in name; the moral sentiments, so called, are as really and truly *natural*, founded in our constitution, as are our desires and affections; nor is the term natural properly opposed to the term moral as designating distinct and opposite things. The terms instinctive and rational, which Mr. Stewart employs, though not free from objection, much more accurately express the distinction in view, could such a distinction be shown to exist.

Difference of ethical and psychological Inquiry. — In a work, the main object of which is to unfold the principles of ethical science, it may be desirable to single out from the other emotions, and place by themselves, the principle of self-love, together with the social principle and the moral sentiments, as having more direct reference to the moral character and conduct. In a strictly psychological treatise, however, in which the aim is simply to unfold, and arrange in their natural order, the phenomena of the human mind, such a principle of classification is evidently inadmissible. The different operations and emotions of the mind must be studied and arranged, not with reference to their *logical* or *ethical* distinctions, but solely their *psychological* differences. Viewed in this light, the moral sentiments, so far as they are of the nature of feeling or sensibility at all, and not rather of intellectual perception, are simple emotions, and do not inherently differ from any other feelings of the same class. The satisfaction we feel in view of right, and the pain in view of wrong past conduct, differ from the pain and pleasure we derive from other sources, only as the *objects* differ which call forth the feelings. They are essentially of the same class, the difference is specific rather than generic. They are modifications of the one generic principle of joy and sorrow, and differ from each other not so much as each differs from a *desire*, or an affection of love or hate.

Objection to Brown's Arrangement. — The classification of Dr. Brown, if not ethical, is, perhaps, equally far from being psychological. The relation of the different emotions to *time* is an accidental, and not an essential difference, and it is, moreover, a distinction wholly inapplicable to far the larger portion of the sensibilities, viz., those which he calls immediate emotions, or "those which arise without involving necessarily *any notion* of time." This is surely *lucus a non lucendo*

SENSIBILITIES.

PART FIRST.

SIMPLE EMOTIONS.

SIMPLE EMOTIONS.

CHAPTER I.

INSTINCTIVE EMOTIONS.

Previous Analysis.—It will be recollected that in the analysis which has been given of the sensibilities, they were arranged under three generic classes, viz., Simple Emotions, Affections, and Desires, all, however, having this in common, that they are in themselves agreeable or disagreeable, as states of mind, according as the object which awakens them is viewed as either good or evil.

Nature of simple Emotions.—Of these, the *simple emotions*, which are first to be considered, comprise, it will be remembered, that large class of feelings which, in their various modifications and degrees, constitute the joys and sorrows of life. They may be comprised, with some latitude of meaning, under the general terms joy and sorrow, as modifications of that comprehensive principle or phase of human experience. They are awakened in view of an object regarded as good or as evil; an object, moreover, of present possession and present enjoyment or suffering; in which last respect they differ from *desires*, which have respect always to some good, or apparent good, *not* in present possession, but viewed as attainable.

Division of simple Emotions.—Of these simple emotions, again, some may be called *instinctive*, as belonging to the *animal* nature, and, to some extent, common to man with the brutes, in distinction from others of a higher order, involving or presupposing the exercise of reason and the reflective powers.

It is of the former class that we are to treat in the present chapter.

§ I.—Of that General State of the Mind known as Cheerfulness; and its opposite, Melancholy.

Nature of this Feeling.—There is a state of mind, of which every one is at times conscious, in which, without any immediately exciting cause, a general liveliness and joyousness of spirit, seldom rising to the definiteness of a distinct emotion, a subdued under-current of gladness, seems to fill the soul, and flow on through all its channels. It is not so much itself joy, as a disposition to be joyful; not so much itself a visible sun in the heavens, as a mild, gently-diffused light filling the sky, and bathing all objects in its serene loveliness and beauty. It has been well termed "a sort of perpetual gladness."

Prevalence at different Periods of Life.—There are those, of fortunate temperament, with whom this seems to be the prevailing disposition, to whom every thing wears a cheerful and sunny aspect. Of others, the reverse is true. In early life this habitual joyousness of spirit is more commonly prevalent; in advanced years, more rarely met with. Whether it be that age has chilled the blood, or that the sober experience of life has saddened the heart, and corrected the more romantic visions of earlier years, as life passes on we are less habitually under the influence of this disposition. It is no longer the prevailing frame of the mind. In the beautiful language of another, "We are not happy, without knowing why we are happy, and though we may still be susceptible of joy, perhaps as intense, or even more intense, than in our years of unreflecting merriment, our joy must arise from a cause of corresponding importance; yet even down to the close of extreme old age there still recur occasionally some gleams of this almost instinctive happiness, like a vision of other years, or like those brilliant and unexpected corruscations which sometimes flash along the midnight of a wintry sky, and of which we are too ignorant of the circumstances that produce them, to know when to predict their return."

The opposite Feeling. — Corresponding to this general state of mind now described, is one of quite the opposite character — that habitual disposition to sadness which is usually called melancholy. Like its opposite, cheerfulness, it is rather a frame of mind than a positive emotion, and, like its opposite, it exists, often, without any marked and definite cause to which we can attribute it. It is that state in which subsiding grief, or the pressure of any severe calamity now passing away, leaves the mind, the grey and solemn twilight that succeeds a partial or total eclipse. It is, with many persons, the habitual state of mind, through long periods, perhaps even the greater part, of life. Not unfrequently it occurs that minds, of the rarest genius and most delicate sensibility, are subject to that extreme and habitual depression of spirits which casts a deep gloom over the brightest objects, and renders life itself a burden. This state of habitual gloom and despondency, itself usually a form of disease, the result of some physical derangement, deepens sometimes into a fixed and permanent disorder of the mind, and constitutes one of the most pitiable and hopeless forms of insanity. Such was the case with the melancholy, but most amiable and gentle Cowper.

Element of poetic Sensibility. — In its milder forms, the state of mind which I describe, constitutes, not unfrequently, an element of what is termed poetic genius, a melancholy arising from some sad experience of the troubles and conflicts of life, and from sympathy with the suffering and sorrowing world, the great sad heart of humanity — a melancholy that, like the plaint of the Æolian harp, lends sweetness and richness to the music of its strain. Such are many of the strains of Tennyson; such the deep under-current of Milton's poetry; such, preëminently, the spirit and tone of John Foster, one of the truest and noblest specimens of poetic genius, although a writer of prose. A quick and lively sensibility, itself an inseparable concomitant of true genius, is not unfrequently accompanied with this gentler form of melancholy. The truly great soul that communes with itself, with nature, and with eternal truth, is no stranger to this subdued yet pleasing sadness. It is this to which Milton pays beautiful tribute in the *Il Penseroso*, and which he thus invokes:

"But hail, thou goddess, sage and holy,
Hail, divinest Melancholy!
Come, pensive nun, devout and pure,
Sober, steadfast, and demure,
All in a robe of darkest grain
Flowing with majestic train,
And sable stole of Cyprus lawn
Over thy decent shoulders drawn.
Come, but keep thy wonted state,
With even step and musing gait,
And looks commercing with the skies,
Thy rapt soul sitting in thine eyes."

Not inconsistent with Wit.—It should be remarked that the disposition of which we speak is not inconsistent with the occasional and even frequent prevalence of feelings of directly the opposite nature. A prevailing tendency to sadness is not unfrequently associated with an almost equally prevailing tendency to emotions of the ludicrous. The same liveliness of sensibility which prepares the soul to feel keenly whatever in life is adapted to awaken sad and sober reflections, also disposes it to notice quickly the little incongruities of character, the foibles and follies of mankind, in which a duller eye would detect nothing absurd or comical. It is, moreover, the natural tendency of the mind to spring back, like the bow unstrung, from one extreme of feeling to its opposite, and seek relief from its sadness in the lighter sallies of wit. And so we have the melancholy Cowper singing John Gilpin, and the author of the Night Thoughts, in conversation, a jovial and witty man.

§ II. — Sorrow at Loss of Friends.

Differs from Melancholy. — Beside the general states of mind already described, and which can hardly be called distinct emotions, there are certain specific forms of joy and sorrow which claim our attention. Prominent among these is the grief we feel at any great and sudden bereavement or calamity, as, for example, the loss of friends. This is a state of mind closely allied, indeed, to the melancholy of which I have spoken, but differs from it in that it springs from a more obvious and immediate cause, and is at once more definite and more intense. After a time, when the first bitterness of anguish is past, and the mind recovers itself in a measure from the violence of the shock it has received, and which, for the time, like a sudden blow, seemed to stagger all its energies, when other causes begin to operate, and other scenes and cares demand its attention, its sorrow, at first violent and irrepressible, gradully subsides into that calmer but more permanent form which we have already described as melancholy.

Effects of Grief upon the Mind in the first Shock of any Calamity. — When the loss is very great, especially if it comes suddenly to us — and what bereavement, however long anticipated and feared, does not at last overtake us suddenly? — the mind is at first, in a manner, stupefied and amazed, unable to realize its loss, and looks helplessly about it for relief. To this succeeds a state of mental anguish, more or less intense, in proportion to the liveliness of the sensibilities, and the strength of the previous attachment. In many cases the sorrow is uncontrollable, and finds relief in tears, or in those more violent expressions of anguish in which the burdened heart of man in all ages has been wont to indicate its grief, as the rending of the garments, the beating of the breast, the tearing of the hair, and other like demonstrations of utter and hopeless sorrow. The mind in such a state resigns itself passively to the violence of its emotion, and is swept on by the rushing current that overflows its banks. It is Rachel mourning for her children, and refusing to be comforted. It is David going to the chamber over the gate, and exclaiming, as he goes, "O Absalom, my son! my son!"

Subsequent State of Mind. — When the first violence of grief has subsided, and reflection succeeds to passion, the mind begins to recall the circumstances of its loss, and sets itself to comprehend the greatness and reality of the calamity that has befallen it. It dwells with interest and satisfaction on all the worth and virtues of the departed, magnifies all that was good, excuses or overlooks all that was faulty, recalls the words, the tones, the looks, and gathers up the slightest memento of the former history, with the same sacred regard and reverence with which it treasures in the funeral urn the ashes of the dead. A sacredness and dignity invest the character, and the life, when once the angel death has set his seal upon them.

Silence of deep Grief. — The deepest sorrow is not always, perhaps not usually, the most violent and demonstrative. It is when the first sudden passion of grief is passed and the soul retires within herself to meditate upon her loss, calmly gathering her mantle about her to hide from the observation of others those tears and that sorrow which are sacred, it is then that the deepest sorrow, and the heaviest darkness gather about the burdened spirit. The truest, deepest grief is ever silent. It shrinks from human observation. It finds no words for expression, wishes none. It is a veiled and silent goddess, whose rites and altars are hidden from the eye of day. It is the nature of joy to communicate itself. It is the nature of sorrow, whatever may be the occasion whence it springs, to retire within itself. It seeks its chamber that it may weep there.

Effect of Time in assuaging Sorrow. — The effect of time in softening and allaying the violence of grief, is known to every one. The manner in which this effect is produced is worthy of attention. A recurrence to the laws of suggestion may explain this. It will be recollected that among the secondary or subjective laws which regulate the suggestion of our thoughts, the interval of time which has elapsed since the occurrence of any event holds an important place. That which has taken place but recently is more likely to recur again to mind than events of remoter date. On the first occurrence of any calamity, or bereavement, every thing tends to remind us of our loss, and this constant suggestion of it has a powerful effect in keeping alive our sorrow. As time passes on, however, the objects which once suggested only that which we had lost, become associated with, and so suggest other objects and occurrences; or, if they still remind us of our loss, the remembrance is mingled with that of other scenes and events which have since transpired, and other feelings which have since agitated our hearts. Thus time is constantly mingling other ingredients in the cup of our grief. The law of *the most recent* still holds in suggestion, and thus the very principle that formerly reminded us continually of our loss, now shuts it out, by interposing between it and us what has since transpired. The thought of the past comes up less frequently, and when it recurs, is mingled with so many other associated objects, and experiences, that it no longer awakens emotions of unmitigated grief. Gradually other objects interest us, other plans and duties engage us, other emotions agitate the heart, as successive waves beat on the same troubled shore, and render fainter, at each return, the traces which former billows had impressed upon its sands.

Thus time, the *great consoler*, assuages our sorrows, and the unbroken darkness that once hung over the mind, and shrouded all its thoughts and purposes, gives place, at length, to a chastened and subdued sadness, that suffuses the past with a soft and mellow radiance. We are ever moving on, swiftly, steadily, in the current of events, and objects whose fearful magnitude, once, from their very nearness, engrossed our whole attention as we passed into their deep shadow, gradually diminish as they recede, until their dark outline is barely discernible on the distant horizon.

§ III. — Sympathy with the Happiness and Sorrow of Others.

In what Manner awakened. — Closely allied to the emotions of joy and sorrow awakened by our own personal experience of good and of evil, is the sympathy we feel with the joys and sorrows of others in similar circumstances. Joy is contagious. So also is grief. We cannot behold the emotions of others, without, in some degree, experiencing a corresponding emotion. Nor is it necessary to be eye-witnesses of that happiness, or sorrow. The simple description of any scene of happiness or of misery affects the heart, and touches the chords of sympathetic emotion. We picture the scene to ourselves, we fancy ourselves the spectators, or, it may be, the actors and the sufferers; we imagine what would be our own emotions in such a case, and in proportion to the liveliness of our power of conception, and also of our power of feeling, will be our sympathy with the real scene and the real sufferers.

Nature of this Principle. — The sympathy thus awakened, whether with the joy or the sorrow of others, is a simple emotion, distinct in its nature from both the affections and the desires, and it is, moreover, instinctive, rather than rational — a matter of impulse, a principle implanted in our nature, and springing into exercise, as by instinct, whenever the occasion presents itself, rather than the result of reason and reflection. It is a susceptibility which we possess, to some extent, at least, in common with the brutes, who are by no means insensible to the distresses or to the happiness of their fellows. It is a susceptibility which manifests itself in early life, before habits of reflection are formed, and under circumstances which preclude the supposition that it may be the result of education, or in any manner an acquired and not an original and implanted principle. So far from being the result of reflection, reason and reflection are often needed to check the emotion, and keep it within due bounds. There are times when sympathy, for example, with the distresses of others, would stand in the way of efficient and necessary action, and when it is needful to summon all the resources of reason to our aid, in the stern and resolute performance of a duty which brings us into conflict with this instinctive principle of our nature. The judge is not at liberty to regard the tears of the heart-broken wife or child, when he rises to pronounce the stern sentence of violated law upon the wretched criminal. The kind-hearted surgeon must for the time be deaf to the outcries of his patient, and insensible to his sufferings, or his ministrations are at an end.

Usual Limitation of the Term. — The term sympathy is more frequently used to denote the emotion awakened by the sufferings of others, than our participation in their joys. There can be no doubt, however, of the tendency of our nature to each of these results, and that it is, in fact, but one and the same principle under a twofold aspect. Nor does the word itself more properly belong to, and more truly express, the one, than the other of these aspects. We as readily rejoice with those who do rejoice, as we weep with those who weep, and in either case our feeling is *sympathy* (*συνπαθος*).

This Limitation accounted for. — The reason why the term is more frequently applied to denote participation in the sorrows of others, is obvious on a little reflection. Such, and so benevolent, are the arrangements of a kind Providence, that happiness is the prevalent law of being, and sorrow the exception to that general rule. It is diffused as the sunshine, and the gentle air, over all things that breathe, and even inanimate objects, by a sort of sympathetic gladness, reflected from our own minds, seem to share in the general joy. Calamity and sorrow, at least in their more marked and definite forms, come, like storm and tempest in nature, more seldom, and, when they do occur, are the more remarkable and stand out more impressively from the common experience of life, from their very rarity.

More Need of Sympathy with Sorrow. — There is doubtless, also, more occasion for sympathy with the sorrows of others, when those sorrows do occur, than with their joys, and this may be another reason for the more frequent use of the term in this connection. Sorrow *needs* sympathy, as joy does not. It leans for support on some helping and friendly arm. Joy is, in its nature, strong and self-sustaining, sorrow the reverse. It is a wise and kind provision of the Author of our nature, by which there is implanted in our constitution an instinctive sympathy with sorrow and suffering in all their forms, even when we ourselves are not directly the objects on which the calamity falls.

Remark of Dr. Brown. — It is well remarked by Dr. Brown that "we seem to sympathize less with the pleasures of others than we truly do, because the real sympathy is lost in that constant air of cheerfulness which it is the part of good manners to assume. If the laws of politeness required of us to assume, in society, an appearance of sadness, as they now require from us an appearance of some slight degree of gayety, or, at least, of a disposition to be gay, it is probable that we should then remark any sympathy with gladness, as we now remark particularly any sympathy with sorrow; and we should certainly, then, use the general name to express the former of these, as the more extraordinary, in the same way as we now use it particularly to express the feelings of commiseration. Joy," remarks the same writer, "may be regarded as the common dress of society, and real complacency is thus as little remarkable as a well-fashioned coat in a drawing-room. Let us conceive a single ragged coat to appear in the brilliant circle, and all eyes will be instantly fixed on it. Even beauty itself, till the buzz of astonishment is over, will, for the moment, scarcely attract a single gaze, or wit a single listener. Such, with respect to the general dress of the social mind, is *grief*. It is something for the very appearance of which we are not prepared.".

Not true that we sympathize only with Sorrow. — These reasons sufficiently account for the almost exclusive attention paid by moralists to this part of our sympathetic nature, as well as for the almost exclusive use of the term itself to denote participation in the sorrows, rather than in the joys of others. It is not necessary to infer from this circumstance, as some have done, that our sympathies are only with sorrow, that we do not experience a corresponding emotion in view of the happiness of others, a view as unfavorable to our nature as it is remote from truth.

Distinction of Terms. — Sympathy, as usually employed, to denote a fellowship with the sufferings of others, is synonymous with the more specific term *commiseration*, and this again is interchangeable with the terms pity and compassion. So far as use establishes a difference between these terms, it is perhaps this: we more frequently employ the word compassion where there is an ability and a disposition to relieve the suffering; we pity and we commiserate what it is out of our power to remedy.

Strength of this Feeling. — The emotion of sympathy, especially in that form more specially under consideration, is probably one of the strongest and most marked in its effects upon the mind, of any of the feelings of which we are susceptible. When fully aroused, it amounts even to a passion. When the object that awakens it is exposed to imminent danger, and there is need of instant and efficient exertion to avert the danger, and bring that relief which, if it comes at all, must come speedily, then there is no prudent calculation of consequences, no deliberation, no hesitation, no fear, but, regardless of every danger, the sympathizer, forgetful of himself, and thinking only of the object to be accomplished, plunges into the sea or into the flames, faces the wild beast, or the more savage human foe, seizes the assassin's arm, or rushes desperately between the murderous weapon and its victim. This boldness and energy of action are, indeed, the result of sympathy, rather than the direct exercise of the emotion itself, but they show how powerful is the feeling from which they spring.

Irrespective of moral Qualities. — It is worthy of note, moreover, that the emotion of which we speak, is, in great measure, irrespective of the moral qualities of the sufferer. He may be a criminal on the rack or the gallows, the most hardened and abandoned of men, and the suffering to which he is exposed may be the just punishment of his crimes, still it is impossible for any one whose heart is not itself hardened against all human suffering, to regard the miserable victim with other than feelings of compassion. That must be a hard heart that could witness the agony of even its worst enemy, in such a case, without pity for the sufferer.

Design of this Principle. — If we inquire, now, for what end this feeling was implanted in our nature, its final cause is obvious. It is a benevolent arrangement, the design of which is twofold: — first, to prevent undue suffering, by keeping in check the excited passions that would otherwise prompt to the infliction of immoderate and unjust punishment when the object of our resentment is in our power; secondly, to secure that relief to the sufferer which, in circumstances of peril, might fail to be afforded were it not for the pressure and impulse of so strong and sudden an emotion.

Adaptation to Circumstances. — A further and incidental benefit resulting from the possession of a lively sensibility to the joys and sorrows of others, has been noticed by Cogan, in his treatise on the passions, viz., that it disposes the mind to accommodate itself readily to the tastes, manners, and dispositions of those with whom we have occasion to associate. A mind of quick and ready sympathy easily enters into the feelings and understands the conduct of others under given circumstances, and is able to adapt itself to the same, easily, and by a sort of instinct. It places itself at once in the same position, and governs itself accordingly.

Sympathy not to be traced to Self-love as its Origin.— The question has arisen, whether sympathy, which, of all the sensibilities, would seem to lie at the furthest remove from all admixture of selfishness, is not, after all, to be traced ultimately to the principle of self-love. Those philosophers who regard this principle as the main-spring of all human action, and the parent source of all the various emotions that agitate the human heart, are at some pains to show that even the feeling of pity may be traced to the same origin. It was the theory of Hobbes, that the sentiment of pity at the calamities of others springs from the imagination, or fiction as he terms it, of a similar calamity befalling ourselves. Adam Smith also maintains that it is only from our own experience that we can form any idea of the sufferings of others, and that the way in which we form such an idea is by supposing ourselves in the same circumstances with the sufferer, and then conceiving how we should be affected. All this is very true. It is in this way, doubtless, that we get the idea of what another is suffering. But the *idea* of what he suffers is one thing, and our *sympathy* with that suffering is another. One is a conception, and the other is the feeling awakened by that conception. Moreover, it does not follow, as Mr. Stewart has well shown in his criticism upon this theory, that the sympathy in this case arises from our conceiving or believing, for the moment, those sufferings to be really our own. The feeling which arises on the contemplation of our own real or fancied distress, is quite another feeling in its character, from that of pity or compassion. The two emotions are readily distinguished. The mere uneasiness which we feel at the sight of another's suffering, and the desire which we naturally feel to be rid of that uneasiness, are not the chief elements in compassion. If they were, the sure and simple remedy would be to run away from the distress which occasions the uneasiness, to put it as quickly as possible out of sight and out of mind. Such an emotion, prompting to such a course, might well be termed selfish. But this is not the true nature of sympathy. It is not a mere unpleasant sensation produced by observing the sufferings of another, though such a sensation, doubtless, is produced in a sensitive mind, and accompanies, or may even be said to form a part of, the emotion which we term sympathy; there is, over and above this feeling of uneasiness, a *fellowship* of sorrow and of suffering, a bearing of that suffering with him, as *his*, and not as our own, a pain *for him*, and not for ourselves, the result and urgent prompting of which is the impulse, the strong irrepressible desire to relieve, not ourselves from uneasiness, but the sufferer from that which occasions his distress.

What follows from this Theory. — If compassion for others were the offspring of fear for ourselves, then, as Butler has well said, the most fearful natures ought to be the most compassionate, which is far from being the case. It may be added, also, that if sympathy is, in any respect, a *selfish* principle, then they who are most completely and habitually governed by selfish considerations ought, for the same reason, to be the most keenly alive to the sufferings of others, which is little less than a contradiction in terms.

CHAPTER II.

RATIONAL EMOTIONS.

§ I. — Emotions of Joy or Sadness arising from the Contemplation of our own Excellence or the Reverse.

Nature and Objects of this Emotion. — Among those susceptibilities which, while implanted in our nature, and springing into exercise by their own spontaneous energy, imply in their operation the exercise of the reflective powers, and in general, of the higher intellectual faculties, and which on that account, we designate as *rational*, in distinction from the *instinctive* emotions, a prominent place is due to those vivid feelings of pleasure, and pain, with which we contemplate any real or supposed excellence, or defect, in ourselves. The direct object of the emotions now under consideration, is self in some form or aspect. The immediate cause of these emotions is some real or fancied excellence which we possess, or, on the other hand, some real or imagined deficiency. This excellence or deficiency may pertain to our intellectual or to our moral qualities and attainments, or even to our circumstances and condition in life, to any thing, in short, which is *ours*, and which distinguishes us from our fellows. The quality contemplated may be a real possession and attainment, or it may exist only in our imagination and conceit. And so, also, of the defect; that, too, may be real, or imaginary. In either case, vivid feelings are awakened in the mind. It is impossible to contemplate ourselves either as possessing or as lacking any desirable quality without emotion, pleasing or painful, and that in a high degree.

In what Manner awakened. — These emotions are awakened in either of two ways: by the simple contemplation of the supposed excellence, or defect, in *themselves* considered, as pertaining to us; or, more frequently, by *the comparison of ourselves with others* in these respects. It is to the feelings awakened, in the latter case, by the perceived superiority or inferiority of ourselves to others, as the result of such comparison, that the terms pride and humility are ordinarily applied. These terms are relative, and imply, always, some process of comparison. There may be, however, the painful consciousness of defect, or the pleasing consciousness of some high and noble attainment, when the relation which we sustain to others, as regards these points, forms no part of the object of contemplation. The comparison is not of ourselves with others, but only of our present with our former selves. We are satisfied and delighted at our own progress and improvement, or humbled and cast down at our repeated failure, and manifest deficiency.

Not the same with moral Emotion. — The emotions now under consideration must not be confounded with the satisfaction which arises in view of moral worthiness, and the regret and disapprobation with which we view our past conduct as morally wrong. The emotions of which we now speak, are not of the nature of moral emotion, however closely allied in some respects. It is not the verdict of an approving or condemning conscience that awakens them. They have no reference to the right as such. The object is viewed, not in the light of obligation or duty, but merely as a *good*, a thing agreeable and desirable. Thus viewed, its possession gives us pleasure, its absence, pain.

Not blame-worthy in itself. — In the simple emotion thus awakened, the satisfaction and pleasure with which we regard our own intellectual and moral attainments, or even our external circumstances, there is nothing blamable or unworthy of the true man. It is simply the working of nature. The susceptibility to such emotion is part of our constitution, implanted and inherent. As Dr. Brown has well remarked, it is impossible to desire excellence, and not to rejoice at its attainment; and if it is culpable to feel pleasure at attainments which have made us nobler than we were before, it must, of course, have been culpable to desire such excellence.

In what Cases the Emotion becomes culpable.—It is only when the emotion exists in an undue degree, or with regard to unworthy objects, when the supposed excellence upon which we congratulate ourselves really does not exist, or, when existing, we are disposed to set ourselves up above others on account of it, and perhaps to look down upon others for the lack of it, or even to make them feel by our manner and bearing what and how great the difference is between them and us; it is only under such forms and modifications, that the feeling becomes culpable and odious. These it not unfrequently assumes. They are the states of mind commonly denoted by the term *pride*, as the word is used in common speech; and the censure usually and very justly attached to the state of mind designated by that term, must be understood as applicable to the disposition and feelings now described, and not to the simple emotion of pleasure in view of our own real or supposed attainments. That which we condemn in the proud man is not that he excels others, or is conscious of thus excelling, or takes pleasure even in that consciousness, but that, comparing himself with others, and feeling his superiority, he is disposed to think more highly of himself than he ought, on account of it, and more contemptuously of others than he ought; and especially if he seeks to impress others with the sense of that superiority.

Different Forms which this Disposition assumes.—This he may do in several ways. He may be fond of displaying his superiority, and of courting the applause and distinction which it brings. Then he is the *vain* man. He may make much of that which really is worth little, and plume himself on what he does not really possess. Then he is the *conceited* man. He may look with contempt upon and treat with arrogance his inferiors. Then he is the *haughty* man. Or he may have too much pride to show in this way his own pride; too much self-respect to put on airs, and court attention by display; too much sense to rate himself very far above his real worth; too much good breeding to treat others with arrogance and hauteur. In that case he contents himself with his own high opinion and estimate of himself, and the enjoyment of his own conscious superiority to those around him. He is simply the proud man then, not the vain, the conceited, or the arrogant. The difference, however, is not so much that he thinks less highly of himself, and less contemptuously of others in comparison, but that he does not so fully show what he thinks. The superiority is felt, but it is not so plainly manifested.

The Disposition, as thus manifested, reprehensible. — Of this disposition and state of mind in any of its manifestations as now described, it is not too much to say that it is worthy of the censure which it commonly receives. It is not merely unamiable and odious, but morally reprehensible. Especially is this the case where the superiority consists, not in mental or moral endowments and attainments, but in adventitious circumstances, such as beauty or strength of person, station in society, wealth, or the accident of birth — circumstances which imply no necessary worth in the possessor, no real and inherent superiority to those on whom he looks down. In such a case, pride is purely contemptible.

Incompatible with the highest Excellence. — The highest excellence is ever incompatible with the disposition to think highly of our present attainments and excellence, and to place ourselves above others in comparison. Emotions of pleasure may indeed arise in our minds, as we view the unmistakable evidences of our own improvement. But the noblest nature is that which looks neither at itself, to mark its own acquirements, nor yet at others below itself, to mark its own superiority, but whose earnest gaze is fixed only on that which is above and superior to itself — the beau ideal ever floating before it of an excellence not yet attained — in comparison with which all present attainments seem of little moment. The truly great and noble mind is ever humble, and conscious of its own deficiencies.

§ II. — Enjoyment of the Ludicrous.

Properly an Emotion. — Among the sources of rational enjoyment which the constitution of our nature affords, must be reckoned the feeling awakened by the perception of the *ludicrous.* We class this among the emotions, inasmuch as it is a matter of feeling, and of pleasurable feeling, differing in its nature not more from the intellectual faculties, on the one hand, than from the affections and desires, on the other. It is a species of joy or gladness, a pleasurable excitement of feeling, awakened by a particular class of objects. Whatever else may be true of the feeling in question, the character of agreeableness is inseparable from it. It falls, therefore, properly into that class of feelings which comprises the various modifications of joy and sorrow, and which we have denominated simple emotions.

Why rational. — We term it *rational,* rather than instinctive, inasmuch as it implies, if I mistake not, the exercise of the higher intellectual faculties. It is the prerogative of reason. The brute nature has no perception, and of course no enjoyment, of the ludicrous. The idiot has none. The uncultivated savage nature has it only in a slight degree. In this respect the feeling under consideration is quite analogous to the enjoyment of the beautiful and sublime, and also to the feeling awakened in view of right or wrong action, the approbation or disapprobation of our past conduct. All these, though founded in our nature and constitution, are rational rather than instinctive, as implying the exercise of those faculties which more peculiarly distinguish man from the lower orders of being.

In what Way to be defined.—To define precisely the emotion of the ludicrous would be as difficult as to give an exact definition of any other feeling. We must content ourselves, as in all such cases, by determining the circumstances or conditions which give occasion for the feeling. Though we cannot define the emotion itself, we can carefully observe and specify the various objects and occasions that give rise to it.

The Question stated.— Views of Locke and Dryden.—Under what circumstances, then, is the feeling of the ludicrous awakened? What is that certain peculiarity, or quality, of a certain class of objects, which constitutes what we call *the ludicrous*, objectively considered? Various answers have been given to this question, by writers not unaccustomed to the careful observation of mental phenomena. Mr. Locke's definition of wit is to this effect, that it consists in "putting those ideas together with quickness and variety, wherein can be found any resemblance or congruity, whereby to make up pleasant pictures and agreeable visions in the fancy." This, it has been justly remarked, is too comprehensive, since it includes the entire range of eloquence and poetry. It comprends the sublime and the beautiful as well as the witty. It applies to the most facetious passages of Hudibras; it applies equally well to the most eloquent passages of Burke or Webster, and to many of the finest passages of Paradise Lost. Still more comprehensive is Dryden's definition, who says of wit, that it is a propriety of thoughts and words, or thoughts and words eloquently adapted to the subject, a definition which, it has been jocosely remarked, would include at once Blair's Sermons, Campbell's Pleasures of Hope, Cæsar's Commentaries, the Philippics of Cicero, and the funeral orations of Bossuet, as peculiarly witty productions. It should in justice be remarked, however, that neither Dryden nor Locke, in their use of the term wit, seem to have had in mind what we now understand by it, viz., facetiousness, or the mirth-provoking power, but rather to have employed the word in that more general sense, in which it was formerly almost exclusively used, to denote smartness and vigor of the intellectual powers, good sense, sound judgment, quickness of the apprehension, more particularly as these qualities are exhibited in discourse or in writing.

Definition of Johnson. — Johnson comes nearer the mark when he defines wit as "a kind of *concordia discors*, a combination of dissimilar images, a discovery of occult resemblances in things apparently unlike." Not much removed from this, if not indeed derived from it, is the definition of wit given by Campbell, in his Philosophy of Rhetoric — "that which excites agreeable surprise in the mind, by the strange assemblage of related images presented to it." To this, also, applies the same objection as to the preceding definitions, that it includes too much, the beautiful and sublime not less than the ludicrous, eloquence as well as wit.

Of Hobbes. — Hobbes defines laughter, which, so far as relates to the mind, is merely the expression of the feeling of the ludicrous, to be "a sudden glory, arising from a sudden conception of some eminency in ourselves, by comparison with the infirmity of others, or our own former infirmity." There can be little doubt, I think, that the object which excites laughter, always present itself to the mind as in some sense its inferior; and in so far, the definition involves an essential element of the ludicrous. The person laughing is always, for the time being, superior, in his own estimation at least, to the person or thing laughed at. It is some awkwardness, some blunder, some defect of body, mind, or manner, some lack of sharpness and sense, or of courage, or of dignity, some perceived incongruity between the true character or position of the individual and his present circumstances, that excites our laughter, and constitutes the ludicrous.

Objections to this Theory. — It is not true, however, that the laughter, or the disposition to laugh, arises from the simple conception of our own superiority, or the inferiority of the object contemplated, even in the cases supposed; for if that were so, then wherever and whenever we discover such superiority, the feeling of the ludicrous ought to be awakened, and the greater the superiority, the stronger the tendency to mirth; which is far from being the case. We are not disposed to laugh at the misfortunes of others, however superior our own condition may be to theirs in that very respect. My estate may be better than my neighbor's, or my health superior to his, but I am not disposed to laugh at him on that account. On the theory of Hobbes, no persons ought to be so full of merriment, even to overflowing, as the proud, self-conceited, and supercilious, who are most deeply impressed with the idea of their own vast superiority to people and things in general. The fact is precisely the reverse. Such persons seldom laugh, and when they do, the smile that plays for a moment on the face is of that cold and disdainful nature which is far removed from genuine and hearty merriment. It has little in it, as it has been well said, "of the *full glorying and eminency* of laughter," but is rather like the smile of Cassius.

> "He loves no plays,
> As thou dost, Antony; he hears no music;
> Seldom he smiles; and smiles in such a sort,
> As if he mocked himself, and scorned his spirit,
> That could be moved to smile at any thing."

We cannot then resolve the ludicrous into the simple perception of some inferiority of the object or person thus regarded, to ourselves, since there are many kinds of inferiority which do not, in the least, awaken the sense of the ludicrous, while, at the same time, those who are most impressed by the consciousness of their superiority are not usually most disposed to mirth.

Incongruity the essential Element. — If we are required now to specify in what consists the essential character of the ludicrous, and of wit which may be regarded as the exciting or producing cause of the same, we should detect it in *the grouping, or bringing together in a sudden and unexpected manner, ideas or things that are in their nature incongruous.* The *incongruity* of the objects thus brought into juxtaposition, and the *surprise* felt at the *novel* and *unexpected* relation thus discovered, are, it seems to me, the true essential elements in the idea of the ludicrous. If we examine closely the different objects that give rise to this emotion, we shall find, I think, always something incongruous, and consequently unusual and unexpected, in the relations presented, whether of ideas or of things. It may be the result of accident, or of awkwardness, or of mental obtuseness, or of design; it matters not in what mode or from what source the thing proceeds; whenever these conditions are answered, the sense of the ludicrous is awakened.

Relation of Surprise to the ludicrous. — Surprise is an essential concomitant of the ludicrous. This is the state of mind into which we are thrown by the occurrence of any thing new, strange, out of the usual course, and, therefore, unexpected. Whatever is incongruous, is likely to be unusual, and of course unexpected, and hence strikes the mind with more or less surprise. Not every thing that surprises us, however, is witty. The sudden fall of a window near which we are sitting, or the unexpected discharge of a musket within a few paces of us, may cause us to start with surprise, but would not strike us probably as particularly facetious. We are surprised to hear of the death of a friend, or of some fearful accident, attended with loss of life to many, but there is no mirthfulness in such surprise. It is only that form of surprise which is awakened by the perception of the incongruous, and not the surprise we feel in general at any thing new and strange, that is related to the ludicrous. It is rather a concomitant, therefore, than strictly an element of the emotion we are now considering.

Novelty as related to Wit. — How much novelty and suddenness add to the effect of wit, every one knows. A story however witty, once heard, loses its freshness and zest, and, often repeated, becomes not merely uninteresting, but irksome, and at length intolerable. In the same manner, and for the same reason, a witticism which we know to have been premeditated produces little effect, as compared with the same thing said in sudden repartee, and on the spur of the moment. That a man should have studied out some curious relations and combinations of things in his closet, does not surprise us so much, as that he should happen to conceive of these relations at the very moment when they would meet the exigency of the occasion. The epithets which we most commonly apply to any witty production or facetious remark, indicate the same thing; we call it lively, fresh, sparkling, full of vivacity and zest — terms borrowed, perhaps, from the choicer wines, which will not bear exposure but lose their flavor and life when once brought to the air.

Even the Incongruous not always ludicrous. — We come to this result, then, in our own attempted analysis, that the incongruity of the ideas or objects brought into relation with each other constitutes the essential characteristic, the invariable element of the ludicrous, the effect being always greatly heightened by the surprise we feel at the novel and unexpected combinations thus presented. It must be remarked, however, that even the incongruous and unexpected fail to awaken the sense of the ludicrous, when the object or event contemplated is of such a nature as to give rise to other and more serious emotions. When the occurrence, however novel and surprising in itself, or even ludicrous, is of such a nature as to endanger the life, or seriously injure the well-being of ourselves or of others, in the one case fear, in the other compassion, are at once awakened, and all sense of the ludicrous is completely at an end. The graver passion is at variance with the lighter, and banishes it from the mind. Should we see a well dressed and portly man, of some pretension and bearing, accidentally lose his footing and sprawl ingloriously in the gutter, our first impulse undoubtedly would be to laugh. The incongruity of his present position and appearance with his general neatness of person and dignity of manner would appeal strongly to the sense of the ridiculous. Should we learn, however, that in the fall he had broken his leg, or otherwise seriously injured himself, our mirthfulness at once gives place to pity.

Discovery of Truth not allied to the ludicrous. — It is for a similar reason that the discovery of any new and important truth in science, however strange and unexpected, never awakens the feeling of the ludicrous. Its importance carries it over into a higher sphere of thought and feeling. Kepler's law of planetary motion must have been at first a strange and wonderful announcement; the chemical identity of charcoal and the diamond presents, in a new and strange relation, objects apparently most unlike and incongruous; yet, in all probability, neither the astronomer, nor the chemist, who made and announced these discoveries, were regarded by the men of the time as having done any thing peculiarly witty. We look at the importance of the results in such cases, and whatever of oddity or incongruity there may be in the ideas or objects thus related, fails to impress the mind in the presence of graver emotions.

Various Forms of the ludicrous. — The incongruity that awakens the feeling of the ludicrous may present itself in many diverse forms. It may relate to *objects*, or to *ideas.* In either case, the grouping or bringing together of the incongruous elements may be *accidental*, or it may be *intentional.* If accidental, it passes for a blunder; if intentional, it takes the name of wit.

Accidental and intentional grouping of Objects incongruous. — Of the *accidental* grouping of *objects* that are incongruous, we have an instance in the case already supposed, of the well-dressed and dignified gentleman unexpectedly prostrate in the mud. If in place of the dignified gentleman we have the dandy, or the Broadway exquisite, fresh from the toilet, the incongruity is so much the greater, and so much the greater our mirth. Let the hero of the scene, for instance, be such a one as Hotspur so contemptuously describes as coming to parley with him after battle :—

"When I was dry with rage and extreme toil,
Breathless and faint, leaning upon my sword,
Came there a certain lord, neat, trimly dressed,
Fresh as a bridegroom; and his chin, new-reaped,
Showed like a stubble-land at harvest home.
He was perfumed like a milliner;
And 'twixt his finger and his thumb he held
A pouncet box, which ever and anon
He gave his nose, and took 't away again;

– imagine such a character, with all his finery, floundering in the mud, and the ludicrousness of the scene would be such as to set at naught all attempts at gravity, even on the part of those who seldom smile.

When the incongruous objects are purposely brought into relation for the sake of exciting mirth, the wit may be *at the expense of others*, in which case we have either the practical joke, or simple buffoonery, imitating the peculiarities and incongruities of others; or the joker may play off his wit *at his own expense*, and act the clown or the fool for the amusement of observers.

Accidental grouping of incongruous Ideas. — When the incongruity is that not of *objects*, but of *ideas* brought into new and unexpected relation, and when this is the result of accident or awkwardness, rather than of design, we have what is termed a *blunder* or a *bull.* In such a case there is always involved some inconsistency between the thing meant, and the thing said or done. There is an apparent congruity, but a real incongruity of the related ideas. An instance of this occurs in the anecdote related by Sydney Smith, of a physician, who, being present where the conversation turned upon an English nobleman of rank and fortune, but without children, remarked, with great seriousness, that to be childless was a misfortune, but he thought he had observed that it was *hereditary* in some families. Of this nature is most of the wit which we call Irish; the result of accident rather than design — a blunder, a bull. It is said that during the late rebellion in Ireland, the enraged populace, on a certain occasion, vented their wrath against a famous banker, by solemnly resolving to burn all his bank-notes which they could lay hands on; forgetting, in their rage, that this was only to make themselves so much the poorer, and him so much the richer. The instance given by Mr. Mahan is also in point, of two Irishmen walking together through the woods, the foremost of whom seizing a branch, as he passed along, and holding it for a while, suddenly let it fly back, whereby his companion behind was suddenly reduced to a horizontal position, but on recovering himself, congratulated his associate on having held back the branch as long as he did, since it must otherwise have killed him.

Intentional grouping of incongruous Ideas. — The *intentional* grouping of incongruous ideas, for the purpose of exciting the feeling of the ludicrous, is more properly denominated *wit.* This, again, may assume diverse forms. Where the ideas are entirely dissimilar, but have a name or sound in common, which similarity of mere sound or name is seized upon as the basis of comparison, the wit takes the name of a *pun.* The more complete the incongruity of the two ideas, thus brought into strange and unexpected relation, under cover of a word, the more perfect the pun, and the more ludicrous the effect. This kind of wit is deservedly reckoned as inferior. "By unremitting exertions," says a quaint writer, "it has been at last put under, and driven into cloisters, from whence it must never again be suffered to emerge into the light of the world." One invaluable blessing, adds the same author, produced by the banishment of punning is, an immediate reduction of the number of wits.

The Burlesque. — When the wit is employed in debasing what is great and imposing, by applying thereto figures and phrases that are mean and contemptible, it takes the name of *burlesque.* The pages of Hudibras afford abundant illustrations of this form of the ludicrous. The battle of Don Quixote and the wind-mills is a burlesque on the ancient tournaments

The Mock-Heroic. — The mock-heroic, by a contrary process, provokes the sense of the ridiculous by investing what is inconsiderable and mean with high-sounding epithets and dignified description. The battle of the mice and frogs is an instance of this.

The double Meaning. — Beside the varieties of intentional incongruity of ideas already mentioned, there are certain less important forms of witticism, which can perhaps hardly be classed under any of the foregoing divisions. The whole tribe of *double entendres*, or double meanings, where one thing is said and another thing is meant, or at least where the apparent and honest is not the only or the real meaning; *satire*, which is only a modification of the same principle, drawn out into somewhat more extended and dignified discourse, and which, under the form of apparent praise, hides the shafts of ridicule and invective ; *sarcasm*, which conveys the intended censure and invective in a somewhat more indirect and oblique manner ; — these are all but various modes of what we have called intentional incongruity of ideas.

This Principle, in what Respects of dangerous Tendency.— Of the value of this principle of our nature, I have as yet said nothing. To estimate it at its true worth, is not altogether an easy thing. On the one hand, there can be little doubt that, carried to excess, it becomes a dangerous principle. The tendency to view all things, even perhaps the most sacred, in a ludicrous light, and to discover fanciful and remote relations between objects and ideas the most diverse and incongruous, must exert an unhappy influence on the general tone and character of both the mind and the heart. Where wit, or the disposition to the ludicrous, becomes the predominant quality of the mind, impressing the other and nobler faculties into its lawless service, it must be to the detriment of the mind's highest energies and capacities; to the detriment especially of that sincerity and honesty of purpose, and that earnest love of truth, which are the foundation of all true greatness. I speak in this of the excess and abuse of wit; I speak of the *mere* wit.

Of use to the Mind. — On the other hand, the tendency to the ludicrous has its uses in the economy and constitution of our nature, and they are by no means to be overlooked. It gives a lightness and buoyancy, a freshness and life, to the faculties that would otherwise be jaded in the weary march and routine of life. It is to the mind what music is to the soldier on the march. It enlivens and refreshes the spirits. A hearty laugh doeth good like a medicine. A quick and keen perception of the ludicrous, when not permitted to usurp undue control, but made the servitor of the higher powers and propensities, and keeping its true place, not in the fore-front, but in the background of the varied and busy scene, is to be regarded as one of the most fortunate mental endowments.

Wit often associated with noble Qualities. — There is no necessary connection, no connection of any sort, perhaps, between wisdom and dullness, although a great part of mankind have always persisted in the contrary opinion. The laughter-loving and laughter-provoking man is by no means a fool. He who goes through the world, such as it is, and sees in all its caprices, and inconsistencies, and follies, and absurdities, nothing to laugh at, much more justly deserves the suspicion of a lack of sense. "Wit," it has been justly remarked, "is seldom the only eminent quality which resides in the mind of any man; it is commonly accompanied by many other talents of every description, and ought to be considered as a strong evidence of a fertile and superior understanding. Almost all the great poets, orators, and statesmen of all times, have been witty."

Wit as an Instrument for correcting Folly. — There is one important use of the faculty under consideration, to which I have not as yet alluded. I refer to its power as an instrument for keeping in check the follies and vices of those who are governed by no higher principle than a regard to the good opinion of society, and a fear of incurring the ridicule of an observing and sharp-sighted world. To such, and such there are in multitudes, "*the world's dread laugh*" is more potent and formidable than any law of God or man. There are, moreover, many lighter foibles and inconsistencies of even good men, for which the true and most effective weapon is ridicule.

Remarks of Sydney Smith. — I cannot better conclude my remarks upon this part of our mental constitution, than by citing some very just observations of Sydney Smith — himself one of the keenest wits of the age.

"I have talked of the *danger* of wit; I do not mean by that to enter into common-place declamation against faculties, because they *are* dangerous; wit is dangerous, eloquence is dangerous, a talent for observation is dangerous, every thing is dangerous that has energy and vigor for its characteristics; nothing is safe but mediocrity. * * * But when wit is combined with sense and information; where it is softened by benevolence, and restrained by strong principle; when it is in the hands of a man who can use it and despise it, who can be witty and something much *better* than witty, who loves honor, justice, decency, good nature, morality, and religion, ten thousand times better than wit; wit is *then* a beautiful and delightful part of our nature."

§ III. — Enjoyment of the New and Wonderful.

Surprise and Ennui. — Of that form of surprise which arises in view of the incongruous, and which accompanies the feeling of the ludicrous, I have already had occasion to speak, in treating of that emotion. Of the feeling of sur prise in general, its nature, and occasions, and also of that feeling to which it stands opposed, and which for want of a better term we may call *ennui*, I am now to speak.

Definition and nature of Surprise. — Surprise may be defined as the feeling awakened by the perception of whatever is new and wonderful. It is, in itself considered, an agreeable emotion, rather than otherwise. Variety and novelty are usually pleasing; our nature demands them, and is gratified at their occurrence. Monotony, the unbroken thread, and ever-recurring routine of ordinary life and duty, weary, and, after a time, disgust us. Upon this listlessness and lethargy of the mind, a new and unexpected event, as the arrival of a friend, or the reception of some unlooked-for intelligence, breaks in with an agreeable surprise. Hence the eagerness of men, in all ages and all nations, to hear or see some new thing. It is only when the new event or intelligence is of the nature of positive evil, when the news is of some misfortune, real or imagined, when the experience of present, or the fear of future suffering, is the direct and natural result of the occurrence, that the surprise becomes a painful emotion. And even in such cases, I am not quite sure that there is not in the first excitement of the mind upon the reception of bad news, as of the death of a friend, or the calamity of a neighbor, something for the moment, of the nature of pleasure mingling with the pain. We deeply regret the occurrence, but are pleased to have heard the news. The thing grieves us, but not the hearing of it. It is not the surprise that pains us, but the thing at which we are surprised. Surprise, like every other form of mental excitement, is not, in itself, and within due bounds, disagreeable, but the reverse.

How awakened. — This emotion is awakened, as already stated, in view of any thing unforeseen and unexpected. We naturally anticipate, to some extent, the course of the future. We presume it will be substantially as the past. We expect the recurrence of what has often and usually occurred, and whenever any thing breaks in on this established order of events, we are surprised at the interruption in the ordinary train of sequences. Hence the new and the strange always excite surprise.

Differs from Wonder. — Surprise differs from wonder, in that the latter involves an *intellectual* element, the effort of the mind to satisfy itself of the cause and proper explanation of the new and strange phenomenon. Surprise is purely a matter of sensibility, of feeling, and not of intellect. The mind is wholly passive under this emotion. It may lead to action, as may any other emotion, but, like every other emotion, it is, in itself, an influence exerted upon the mind, and not by it, something passively received, and not actively put forth.

From Astonishment. — It differs from astonishment in that the latter expresses a higher degree of mental excitement, as in view of some occurrence exceedingly remarkable and strange, or of some object whose magnitude and importance fills the mind.

Design of this Principle. — The end to be accomplished by this provision of our nature is sufficiently obvious. Our attention is thereby called to whatever is out of the ordinary course, and which, from the circumstance that it is something unusual, may be supposed to require attention, and we are put on our guard against the approaching danger, or roused to meet the present emergency. Surprise is the alarm-bell that calls all our energies into action, or at least warns them to be in present readiness for whatever service may be needed. The same principle operates also as a stimulus to exertion in the ordinary affairs of life. We seek new things, we are weary with the old, and this simple law of our nature is often one of the strongest incitements to effort.

The opposite Feeling. — The opposite of surprise is that uneasy feeling, of which we are conscious, from the constant recurrence of the same objects in unvaried sequence; as, for instance, from the continued repetition of the same sound, or series of sounds, the uniform succession of the same or similar objects in the landscape, and the like. Every one knows how tedious becomes a perfectly straight and level road, with the same objects occurring at regular intervals, and with nothing to break the dead monotony of the scene. The most rugged passes of the Alps would be a relief in exchange, both to body and mind. The repetition of the same song, or the same succession of musical sounds, however pleasing in themselves, becomes in like manner, after a time, intolerable. For want of a better term, for I am not sure that we have in our own language any one word that exactly expresses the feeling now under consideration, we may borrow of the French the somewhat expressive term *ennui*, by which to designate this form of the sensibility.

Use of Ennui. — There can be little doubt that this feeling subserves a valuable purpose in the constitution and economy of our nature. It is the needed motive and stimulus to action, without which we should settle down often into a sluggish indifference and contentment with things as they are, instead of pressing forward to something worthier and better.

§ IV. — Enjoyment of the Beautiful and Sublime.

The Enjoyment, as distinguished from the intellectual Perception of the Beautiful. — Of the *idea* of the beautiful, and of the action of the mind as *cognizant* of it, in so far as regards the intellectual faculties, I have already treated in another connection. But it is not the intellect alone that comes under the influence of the beautiful. What the sense perceives, what the taste and judgment recognize and approve, the sensibility is quick to feel. Emotion is awakened. No sooner is a beautiful object perceived in nature or art, than we are conscious of lively sensations of pleasure. So strong and so universal are these feelings, that many writers have been led to speak of beauty itself, as if it were an emotion, a merely subjective matter, an affair of feeling merely. The incorrectness of this view has been already shown, and we need not enter upon the discussion anew.

The term Admiration. — The feeling awakened by the perception of the beautiful, like some other feelings of which we are conscious, has not a name that precisely designates it; hence the expression — ambiguous, and, therefore, objectionable — emotions of beauty, employed by certain writers to denote the feeling in question. The word *admiration*, though often used in a somewhat wider sense, perhaps more nearly expresses the emotion to which I refer, than any other word in our language. We are surprised at what is new and strange. We admire what is beautiful and sublime. The feeling is one of pure and unalloyed pleasure, mingled with more or less of wonder or surprise, in case the object contemplated is one which is new to us, or one of rare and surpassing beauty. As the beautiful has its opposite — the deformed or ugly — so the feeling which it awakens stands contrasted with an opposite emotion, viz., *disgust.*

In connection with this form of sensibility, there are some questions requiring consideration.

Whether the Emotion is immediate. — It is a question somewhat debated, whether the emotions awakened by the beautiful and sublime are immediate, or reflective; whether they spring up at once on perception of the object, or only as the result of reflection and reasoning. Those who maintain that beauty consists in utility, or in order and proportion, fitness, unity with variety, etc., must, of course, regard the emotions awakened by it as not immediate, since, according to their theory, time must be allowed for the understanding to convince itself, in the first place, that the object *is* useful, etc. The qualities constituting the beauty must be first apprehended by the mind as existing in the object, before there can be emotion, and to do this is the work of reflection. If, however, beauty is but the expression of the invisible under the visible and sensible forms, then all that is necessary to produce emotion is simply the perception of the object thus expressive, since the moment it is perceived, it is perceived as expressing something, and thus, appealing to our own spiritual nature, awakens immediate emotion.

How to be decided. — The question must be decided by the observation of facts, and the result will constitute an additional argument in favor of one, or the other, of the general views of the beautiful now named. What then are the facts in the case, as given by consciousness, and observation?

Testimony of Consciousness. — So far as I can judge, no sooner do we find ourselves in presence of a beautiful object than we are conscious of emotions of pleasure. There is no previous cross-questioning of the object to find out whether it is adapted to this or that useful end, or whether the rules of order, and proportion, are observed in its construction. Before we have time to think of these things, the sensibility has already responded to the appeal which beauty ever makes to our sensitive nature, and the first distinct fact of which we are conscious is an emotion of pleasure.

Effect of Repetition. — Consciousness assures us, moreover, that the pleasure is usually quite as vivid at the first sight of a beautiful object as ever after, which would indicate that it is not the result of reflection. In truth, repetition is found, in most cases, to weaken the emotion, and familiarity may even destroy it. Yet every repetition adds to our opportunity for observation and reflection, and strengthens our conviction of the utility, the order, the fitness, the proportion, of that which we observe.

Critical Reflection subsequent to Emotion. — It seems evident, moreover, that whatever reflections of this nature we may choose to indulge, are uniformly subsequent to the first emotion of pleasure and delight, to the first impression made upon us by the beauty of the object — after-thoughts readily to be distinguished from those first impressions — and that they are usually the result of a special volition to inform ourselves as to these matters; whereas the emotion is spontaneous and involuntary. Doubtless a pleasure arises from the perception of the qualities referred to, but it is a pleasure of another kind from that which arises in view of the beautiful, as such. We must think, then, that the emotions awakened by the beautiful are immediate, not reflective.

Further Question. — Closely allied to the preceding is the question, Which precedes the other, the emotion which a beautiful object awakens, or the judgment of the mind that the object is beautiful. Logically, doubtless, the two things may be distinguished, but not, perhaps, in order of time. No sooner is the object perceived, than it is both perceived and felt to be beautiful. The emotion awakened and the mental affirmation, "That is beautiful," are both immediate on the perception of the object, synchronous events, so far as concerns at least our ability to distinguish between them in point of time.

Logically, Emotion precedes. — In point of logical relation, the emotion, I think, must be allowed the precedence, although so high an authority as Kant decides otherwise. Had we no emotion in view of the beautiful, we should not know that it was beautiful. As, universally, sensation is the indispensable condition of perception, and logically, at least, its antecedent, so here the feeling of the beautiful is the condition and source of the perception of the beautiful. The object strikes us as being so, moves us, affects us, produces on us the impression, and hence we say, "That is beautiful." Had we no susceptibility of emotion in view of the beautiful, it may be seriously questioned whether we should ever have the perception or impression that any given object is beautiful.

The Beautiful as distinguished from the Sublime. — There is still another point deserving attention. In discussing the æsthetic emotions, we have spoken as yet only of the feeling awakened by the *beautiful.* How do these emotions differ — in degree merely — or in nature?

The Opinion that they differ only in Degree.—Some have maintained that sublimity is only a higher *degree* of what we call beauty. A little stream playing among the hills and tumbling over the rocks is beautiful; a little further on, as it grows larger, and swifter, and stronger, it becomes sublime. If this be so, it is a very simple matter: the surveyor's chain, or a ten foot pole, will, at any time, give us the difference, and enable us to determine at once whether a river or a mountain is merely pretty, or sublime.

Different Emotions excited by each.—If they differ in *kind*, however, and not merely in quantity, it may not be so easy to tell just what the difference is. We can best detect it, perhaps, by observing carefully the difference of the emotions excited in us by the two classes of objects. I contemplate an object, which, in common with all the world, I call beautiful. What emotion does that object awaken in me? An emotion of pleasure and delight, for which I can find, perhaps, no better name than admiration. I contemplate now another object which men call sublime. What now are my emotions? Admiration there may be, but not, as before, a calm, placid delight; far otherwise. An admiration mingled with awe, a sense of greatness and of power in the object now oppresses me, and I stand as before some superior being, or element, in whose presence I feel my comparative feebleness and insignificance.

The Sublime conveys the Idea of superior Power.—Accordingly we find that the objects which men call sublime are invariably such as are fitted to awaken such emotions. They are objects which convey the idea of superior force and power—something grand in its dimensions or in its strength—something vast and illimitable, beyond our comprehension and control. The boundless expanse of the ocean, the prairie, or the pathless desert, the huge mass of some lofty mountain, the resistless cataract, the awful crash of the thunder, as it rolls along the trembling firmament, the roar of the sea in a storm when it lifteth up its waves on high, the movements of an army on the battle-field — these, and such as these, are the objects we call sublime. The little may be beautiful, it is never sublime. Nor is the merely great always so, but only when it conveys the idea of superior power. Montmorenci is beautiful, Niagara is sublime. A Swiss valley, nestling among the hills, is beautiful; the mountains that tower above it through the overhanging clouds into the pure upper sky, and in the calm, serene majesty of their strength stand looking down upon the slumbering world at their feet, and all the insignificance of man and his little affairs, are sublime.

The Sublime and the Beautiful associated. — Nor is the sublime always unassociated with the beautiful. Niagara is not more sublime than beautiful. The deep emerald hue of the waters as they plunge, the bow on the mist, the foam sparkling in the abyss below, are each among the most beautiful objects in nature. The sublime and the beautiful are often mingled thus, distinct elements, but conjoined in the same object. The highest æsthetic effect is produced by this combination. The beauty tempers the sublimity; the sublimity elevates and ennobles the beauty. It is thus at Niagara. It is thus when the sunrise flashes along the summits of the snowy Alps.

The Beautiful tranquilizes, the Sublime agitates. — The beautiful pleases us; so, in a sense, does the sublime. Both produce agreeable emotions. Yet they differ. In the enjoyment of the beautiful there is a calm, quiet pleasure; the mind is at rest, undisturbed, can at its leisure and sweet will admire the delicacy and elegance of that which fills it with delight. But in the perception of the sublime it is otherwise. The mind is agitated, is in sympathy with the stir, and strife, and play of the fierce elements, or is oppressed with the feeling of its own insignificance, as contrasted with the stern majesty and strength of what it contemplates. Hence the sublime takes a deeper hold on the mind than the merely beautiful, awes it, elevates it, rouses its slumbering energies, quickens the slow course of thought, and makes it live, in brief moments, whole hours and days of ordinary life. The beautiful charms and soothes us; the sublime subdues us and leads us captive. The one awakens our sympathy and love, the other rouses in us all that is noble, serious, and great in our nature.

Relation of the Sublime to Fear. — The relation of the sublime to fear has been noticed by several writers. Mendelssohn, Ancillon, Kant, Jouffroy, Blair, have spoken of it, as well as Burke. The latter was not far from right in his theory of fear as an element of the sublime. It were better to say *awe* than fear, for the boldest and stoutest hearts are fully susceptible of it; and it were better to speak of it as an element of our emotion in view of the sublime, than as an element of the sublime itself.

Cultivation of æsthetic Sensibility. — I cannot, in this connection, entirely pass without notice a topic requiring much more careful consideration than my present limits will permit — the cultivation of the æsthetic sensibility — of a love for the beautiful.

This Culture neglected. — The love of the beautiful is merely one of the manifold forms of the sensibility, and, in common with every other feeling and propensity of our nature, it may be augmented, quickened, strengthened to a very great degree by due culture and exercise. It is an endowment of nature, but, like other native endownents, it may be neglected and suffered to die out. This, unfortunately, is too frequently the case with those especially who are engaged in the active pursuits of life. The time and the attention are demanded for other and more important matters, and so the merely beautiful is passed by unheeded. It admits of question, whether it is not a serious defect in our systems of education, that so little attention is paid to the culture of the taste, and of a true love for the beautiful. The means of such a culture are ever at hand. The great works and the most perfect models in art are not, indeed, accessible to all. Not every one can cross the seas to study the frescoes of Raphael and Michael Angelo. But around us in nature, along our daily paths, are the works of a greater Artist, and no intelligent and thoughtful mind need be unobservant of their beauty. Nor is there danger, as some may apprehend, that we shall carry this matter to excess. The tendencies of our age and of our country are wholly the reverse. The danger is rather that in the activity and energy of our new life, the higher culture will be overlooked, and the love of the beautiful die out.

Value of this Principle. — The love of the beautiful is the source of some of the purest and most exquisite pleasures of life. It is the gift of God in the creation and endowment of the human soul. Nature lays the foundation for it among her earliest developments. The child is, by nature, a lover of the beautiful. Nor is it in early life alone that this principle has its natural and normal developments. On the contrary, under favorable circumstances, it grows stronger and more active as the mind matures, and the years pass on. Happy he who, even in old age, keeps fresh in his heart this pure and beautiful fountain of his youth; who, as days advance, and shadows lengthen, and sense grows dull, can still look, with all the admiration and delight of his childish years, on whatever is truly beautiful in the works of God or man.

§ V. — Satisfaction in View of Right Conduct, and Remorse in View of Wrong.

The Feeling, as distinguished from the Perception of Right. — In the chapter on the Idea and Cognizance of the Right, the notion of right, in itself considered, and also the mind's action as cognizant of the right, so far at least as concerns the *intellectual* faculties thus employed, were fully discussed. It is not necessary now to enter again upon the investigation of these topics. But, as in the cognizance of the beautiful, so in the cognizance of the right, not only is the intellect exercised, but the sensibility also is aroused. As consequent upon the perceptions of the intellect, *emotion* is awakened; and that emotion is both definite and strong. It is peculiar in its operation. No emotion that stirs the human bosom is more uniform in its development, more strongly marked in its character, or exerts a deeper and more permanent influence on the happiness and destiny of man, than the satisfaction with which he views the virtuous conduct of a well-spent hour or a well-spent life, and the regret, amounting sometimes to remorse, with which, on the contrary, he looks back upon the misdeeds and follies of the past. Of all the forms of joy and sorrow that cast their lights and shadows over the checkered scene and pathway of human existence, there are none which, aside from their ethical relations, are of deeper interest to the psychologist, or more worthy his careful study, than the emotions to which I now refer.

The moral Faculty not resolvable into moral Feeling.—So deeply have certain writers been impressed with the importance of this part of our nature, that they have not hesitated to resolve the moral faculty itself into the emotions now under consideration, and to make the recognition of moral distinctions ultimately a mere matter of feeling. This, whether regarded ethically, or psychologically, is certainly a great mistake, fatal in either case to the true science whether of morals or of mind. Right and wrong, as also the beautiful and its opposite, are not mere conceptions of the human mind. They have an actual objective existence and reality, and, as such, are cognized by the mind, which perceives a given act to be right or wrong, and, as such, obligatory or the opposite, and approves or condemns the deed, and the doer, accordingly. So far the intellect is concerned. But the process does not stop here. Sensibility is awakened. The verdict and calm decisions of the judgment are taken up by the feelings, and made the basis and occasion of a new form of mental activity. It is with this excitement of the sensibility in view of conduct as right or wrong, that we are now concerned, and while we can by no means resolve all our moral perceptions and judgments into this class of emotions, we would still assign it an important place among the various forms of mental activity.

Not limited to our own Conduct. — The emotion of which we speak is not limited to the occasions of our own moral conduct; it arises, also, in view of the moral actions of others. A good deed, an act of generosity, magnanimity, courage, by whomsoever performed, meets our approbation, and awakens in our bosoms feelings of pleasure. If the act is one of more than ordinary heroism and self-sacrifice, we are filled with admiration. Instances of the opposite excite our displeasure and disgust. No small part of the interest with which we trace the records of history, or the pages of romance, arises from that constant play of the feelings with which we watch the course of events, and the development of character, as corresponding to or at variance with the demands of our moral nature.

A good Conscience an Object of universal Desire. — But it is chiefly when we become ourselves the actors, and the decisions of conscience respect our own good or evil deeds, that we learn the true nature and power of the moral emotions. A good conscience, it has been said, is the only object of universal desire, since even bad men wish, though in vain, for the happiness which it confers. It would perhaps be more correct to say that an accusing conscience is an object of universal dread. But in either case, whether for approval or condemnation, very great is its power over the human mind.

Sustaining Power of a good Conscience. — We all know something of it, not only by the observation of others, but by the consciousness of our own inner life. In the testimony of a good conscience, in its calm, deliberate approval of our conduct, lies one of the sweetest and purest of the pleasures of life; a source of enjoyment whose springs are beyond the reach of accident or envy; a fountain in the desert making glad the wilderness and the solitary place. It has, moreover, a sustaining power. The consciousness of rectitude, the approval of the still small voice within, that whispers in the moment of danger and weakness, "*You are right*," imparts to the fainting soul a courage and a strength that can come from no other source. Under its influence the soul is elevated above the violence of pain, and the pressure of outward calamity. The timid become bold, the weak are made strong. Here lies the secret of much of the heroism that adorns the annals of martyrdom and of the church. Women and children, frail and feeble by nature, ill fitted to withstand the force of public opinion, and shrinking from the very thought of pain and suffering, have calmly faced the angry reproaches of the multitude, and resolutely met death in its most terrific forms, sustained by the power of an approving conscience, whose decisions were, to them, of more consequence than the applause or censure of the world, and whose sustaining power bore them, as on a prophet's chariot of fire, above the pains of torture and the rage of infuriated men.

Power of Remorse. — Not less is the power of an accusing conscience. Its disapprobation and censure, though clothed with no external authority, are more to be dreaded than the frowns of kings or the approach of armies. It is a silent constant presence that cannot be escaped, and will not be pacified. It embitters the happiness of life, cuts the sinews of the soul's inherent strength. It is a fire in the bones, burning when no man suspects but he only who is doomed to its endurance; a girdle of thorns worn next the heart, concealed, it may be, from the eye of man, but giving the wearer no rest, day nor night. Its accusations are not loud, but to the guilty soul they are terrible, penetrating her inmost recesses, and making her to tremble as the forest trembles at the roar of the enraged lion, as the deep sea trembles in her silent depths, when her Creator goeth by on the wings of the tempest, and the God of glory thundereth. The bold bad man hears that accusing voice, and his strength departs from him. The heart that is inured to all evil, and grown hard in sin, and fears not the face of man, nor the law of God, hears it, and becomes as the heart of a child.

How terrible is remorse! that worm that never dies, that fire that never goes out. We cannot follow the human soul beyond the confines of its present existence. But it is an opinion entertained by some, and in itself not improbable, that, in the future, conscience will act with greatly increased power. When the causes that now conspire to prevent its full development and perfect action, shall operate no longer; when the tumult of the march and the battle are over; when the cares, the pleasures, the temptations, the vain pursuits, that now distract the mind with their confused uproar, shall die away in the distance, and cease to be heard, in the stillness of eternity, in the silence of a purely spiritual existence, the still small voice of conscience may perhaps be heard as never before. In the busy day-time we catch, at intervals, the sound of the distant ocean, as a low and gentle murmur. In the still night, when all is hushed, we hear it beating, in heavy and constant surges, on the shore. And thus it may be with the power of conscience in the future.

SENSIBILITIES.

PART SECOND.

THE AFFECTIONS.

THE AFFECTIONS.

CHAPTER I.

BENEVOLENT AFFECTIONS.

Character of the Affections as a Class. — Of the three generic classes into which the sensibilities were divided, viz., Simple Emotions, Affections, and Desires, the first alone has, thus far, engaged our attention. We now approach the second. It will be remembered that, in our analysis of the sensibilities, the Affections were distinguished from the Simple Emotions, as being of a complex character, involving, along with the feeling of delight and satisfaction in the object, or the reverse, the wish, more or less definite and intense, of good or ill to the object that awakens the emotion. The feeling thus assumes an active and transitive form, going forth from itself, and even forgetting itself, in its care for the object.

How divided. — The affections, it will also be remembered, were further divided into the *benevolent* and *malevolent*, according as they seek the good or the ill of the object on which they fasten. As the simple emotions are but so many forms of *joy* and *sorrow*, so, likewise, the affections are but so many modifications of the principle of *love* and its opposite, *hate*.

Effects upon the Character in their marked Development. — When these give tone to the general character of an individual, he becomes the philanthropist or misanthropist, the man of kind and gentle disposition, or the hater of his race, according as the one or the other principle predominates.

Roused to more than ordinary activity, breaking away from the restraints of reason, and the dictates of sober judgment, assuming the command of the soul, and urging it on to a given end, regardless of other and higher interests, these affections assume the name of *passions*, and the spectacle is presented of a man driven blindly and madly to the accomplishment of his wishes, as the ship, dismantled, drives before the storm ; or else, in stern conflict with himself and the feelings that nature has implanted in his bosom, controlling with steady hand his own restless and fiery spirit.

Relation to the simple Emotions.—The relation which the affections, as a class, bear to the simple emotions, deserves a moment's attention. The one class naturally follows and grows out of the other. What we enjoy, we come naturally to regard with feelings of affection, while that which causes pain, naturally awakens feelings of dislike and aversion. So love and hate succeed to joy and sorrow in our hearts, as regards the objects contemplated. The simple emotions precede and give rise to the affections.

Enumeration.—The benevolent affections, to which we confine our attention in the present chapter, assume different forms, according to their respective objects.

The more prominent are, *love of kindred*, *love of friends*, *love of benefactors*, *love of home and country*. Of these we shall treat in their order.

§ I.—Love of Kindred.

Includes what.—Under this head we may include the *parental*, the *filial*, and the *fraternal* affection, as modifications of the same principle, varying according to the varying relations of the parties concerned.

Does not grow out of the Relations of the Parties.—That the affection *grows out* of the relations sustained by the parties to each other, I am not prepared to affirm, although some have taken this view; I should be disposed rather to regard it as an implanted and original principle of our nature; still, that it is very much influenced and augmented by those relations, and that it is manifestly adapted to them, no one, I think, can deny.

But adapted to that Relation.—How intimate and how peculiar the relation, for example, that subsists between parent and child, and how deep and strong the affection that binds the heart of the parent to the person and well-being of his offspring. The one corresponds to the other; the affection to the relation; and the duties which that relation imposes, and all the kind offices, the care, and attention which it demands, how cheerfully are they met and fulfilled, as prompted by the strength and constancy of that affection. Without that affection, the relation might still exist, requiring the same kind offices, and the same assiduous care, and reason might point out the propriety and necessity of their performance, but how inadequate, as motives to action, would be the dictates of reason, the sense of propriety, or even the indispensable necessity of the case, as compared with that strong and tender parental affection which makes all those labors pleasant, and all those sacrifices light, which are endured for the sake of the helpless ones confided to its care. There was need of just this principle of our nature to meet the demands and manifold duties arising from the relation to which we refer; and in no part of the constitution of the mind is the benevolence of the great Designer more manifest. What but love could sustain the weary mother during the long and anxious nights of watching by the couch of her suffering child? What but love could prompt to the many sacrifices and privations cheerfully endured for its welfare? Herself famished with hunger, she divides the last morsel among those who cry to her for bread. Herself perishing with cold, she draws the mantle from her own shoulders to protect the little one at her side from the fury of the blast. She freely perils her own life for the safety of her child. These instances, while they show the strength of that affection which can prompt to such privation and self-sacrifice, show, also, the end which it was designed to subserve, and its adaptation to that end.

This Affection universal. — The parental affection is universal, not peculiar to any nation, or any age, or any condition of society. Nor is it strong in one case, and weak in another, but everywhere and always one of the strongest and most active principles of our nature. Nor is it peculiar to our race. It is an emotion shared by man in common with the lower orders of intelligence. The brute-beast manifests as strong an affection for her offspring, as man under the like circumstances exhibits. The white bear of the arctic glaciers, pursued by the hunter, throws herself between him and her cub, and dies in its defence.

All these circumstances, the precise adaptation of the sensibility in question to the peculiar exigencies it seemed designed to meet, the strength and constancy of that affection, the universality of its operation, and the fact that it is common to man with the brute, all go to show that the principle now under consideration must be regarded as an instinctive and original principle, implanted in our nature by the hand that formed us.

Strengthened by Circumstances. — But though an original principle, and, therefore, not derived from habit or circumstance, there can be no doubt that the affection of which we speak is greatly modified, and strengthened, by the circumstances in which the parent and child are placed with respect to each other, and also by the power of habit. Like most of our active principles, it finds, in its own use and exercise, the law of its growth. So true is this, that when the care and guardianship of the child are transferred to other hands, there springs up something of the parent's love, in the heart to which has been confided this new trust. It seems to be a law of our nature that we love those who are dependent on us, who confide in us, and for whom we are required to exert ourselves. The more dependent and helpless the object of our solicitude, and the greater the sacrifice we make, or the toil we endure, in its behalf, the greater our regard and affection for it. If in the little group that gathers around the poor man's scanty board, or evening fireside, there is one more tenderly loved than another, one on whom his eye more frequently rests, or with more tender solicitude than on the others, it is that one over whose sick-bed he has most frequently bent with anxiety, and for whose benefit he has so often denied himself the comforts of life. By every sacrifice thus made, by every hour of toil and privation cheerfully endured, by every watchful, anxious night, and every day of unremitting care and devotion, is the parental affection strengthened. And to the operation of the same law of our nature is doubtless to be attributed the regard which is felt, under similar circumstances, by those who are not parents, for the objects of their care. But it may reasonably be doubted whether, in such case, the affection, although of the same nature, ever equals, in intensity and fervor, the depth and strength of a parent's love.

Strongest in the Mother. — The parental affection, though common to both sexes, finds its most perfect development in the heart of the mother. Whether this is the natural result of the principle already referred to, the care and effort that devolve in greater degree upon the mother, and awaken a love proportionably stronger, or whether it is an original provision of nature to meet the necessity of the case, we can but see in the fact referred to a beautiful adaptation of our nature to the circumstances that surround us.

Stronger in the Parent than in the Child. — The love of the parent for the child is stronger than that of the child for the parent. There was need that it should be so. Yet is there no affection, of all those that find a place in the human heart, more beautiful and touching than filial love. Nor, on the contrary, is there any one aspect of human nature, imperfect as it is, so sad and revolting as the spectacle sometimes presented, of filial ingratitude, a spectacle sure to awaken the indignation and abhorrence of every generous heart. When the son, grown to manhood, forgets the aged mother that bore him, and is ashamed to support her tottering steps, or leaves to loneliness and want the father whose whole life has been one of care and toil for him, he receives, as he deserves, the contempt of even the thoughtless world, and the scorn of every man whose opinion is worth regarding.

There have not been wanting noble instances of the strength of the filial affection. If parents have voluntarily incurred death to save their children, so, also, though perhaps less frequently, have children met death to save a parent.

Value of these Affections. — The parental and filial affections lie at the foundation of the social virtues. They form the heart to all that is most noble and elevating, and constitute the foundation of all that is truly great and valuable in character. Deprived of these influences, men may, indeed, become useful and honorable members of society — such cases have occurred — but rather as exceptions to the rule. It is under the genial influences of home, and parental care and love, that the better qualities of mind and heart are most favorably and surely developed, and the character most successfully formed for the conflicts and temptations of future life.

Not inconsistent with the manly Virtues. — Nor is the gentleness implied in the domestic affections inconsistent with those sterner qualities of character, which history admires in her truly great and heroic lives. Poets have known this, painters have seized upon it, critics have pointed it out in the best ideal delineations, both of ancient and of modern times. It softens the gloomy and otherwise forbidding character of stern Achilles; it invests with superior beauty, and almost sacredness, the aged Priam suing for the dead body of Hector; it constitutes one of the brightest ornaments with which Virgil knew how to adorn the character of the hero of the Æneid, while in the affection of Napoleon for his son, and in the grief of Cromwell for the death of his daughter, the domestic affection shines forth in contrast with the strong and troubled scenes of eventful public life, as a gentle star glitters on the brow of night.

§ II. — Love of Friends.

Much said in Praise of Friendship. — Among the benevolent affections that find a place in the human heart, friendship has ever been regarded as one of the purest and noblest. Poets and moralists have vied with each other in its praise. Even those philosophers who have derived all our active principles from self-love have admitted this to a place among the least selfish of our emotions. There can be no doubt that it is a demand of our nature, a part of our original constitution. The man who, among all his fellows, finds no one in whom he delights, and whom he calls his friend, must be wanting in some of the best traits and qualities of our common humanity, while, on the other hand, pure and elevated friendship is a mark of a generous and noble mind.

On what Circumstances it depends. — If we inquire whence arises this emotion in any given case, on what principles or circumstances it is founded, we shall find that, while other causes have much to do with it, it depends chiefly on the *more or less intimate acquaintance* of the parties. There must, indeed, be on our part some perception of high and noble qualities belonging to him whom we call our friend, and some appreciation, also, of those qualities. We must admire his genius, or his courage, or his manly strength and prowess, or his moral virtues, or, at least, his position and success. All these things come in to modify our estimate and opinion of the man, and may be said to underlie our friendship for him. Still, it is not so much from these circumstances, as from personal and intimate acquaintance, that friendship most directly springs. Admira tion and respect for the high qualities and noble character of another, are not themselves friendship, however closely related to it. They may be, and doubtless are, to some extent, the foundation on which that affection rests, but they are not its immediately producing cause. They may exist where no opportunity for personal acquaintance is afforded, while, on the other hand, a simple and long-continued acquaintance, with one whom we, perhaps, should not, in our own candid judgment, pronounce superior to other men, either in genius, or fortune, or the nobler qualities of the soul, may, nevertheless, ripen into strong and lasting friendship.

How Acquaintance leads to Friendship. — To what is this owing? Not so much, I suspect, to the fact that acquaintance reveals always something to admire, even in those whom we had not previously regarded with special deference — although this, I am willing to admit, may be the case — but rather to that simple law of mental activity which we call association. The friend whom we have long and intimately known, the friend of other, and earlier, and, it may be, happier years, is intimately connected with our own history. His life and our own have run side by side, or rather, like vines springing from separate roots, have intertwined their branches until they present themselves as one to the eye. It is this close connection of my friend with whatever pertains to myself, of his history with my history, and his life with my life, that contributes in great measure to the regard and interest I feel for him. He has become, as it were, a part of myself. The thought of him awakens in my mind pleasing remembrances, and is associated with agreeable conceptions of the walks, the studies, the sports, the varied enjoyments and the varied sorrows that we have shared together.

Regard for inanimate Objects. — The same principle extends also to inanimate objects, as places and scenes with which we have become familiar, the meadows through which we roamed in childhood, the books we read, the rooms we inhabited, even the instruments of our daily toil. These all become associated with ourselves, we form a sort of friendship for them. The prisoner who has spent long years of confinement in his solitary cell, forms a species of attachment for the very walls that have shut him in, and looks upon them for the last time, when at length the hour of deliverance arrives, not without a measure of regret. The sword that has been often used in battle is thenceforth, to the old soldier, the visible representative of many a hard-fought field, and many a perilous adventure. Uncouth and rusty it may be, ill-formed, and unadorned, in its plain and clumsy iron scabbard, but its owner would not exchange it for one of solid gold. It is not strange that the principle of association, which attaches us so closely even to inanimate objects, should enter largely as an element into the friendships we form with our own species.

Other Causes auxiliary. — I would by no means deny, however, that other causes may, and usually do, contribute to the same result. Mere acquaintance and companionship do not, of necessity, nor invariably, amount to friendship. There must be some degree of sympathy, and congeniality of thought and feeling, some community of interests, pursuits, desires, hopes, something in common between the two minds, or no friendship will spring up between them. Acquaintance, and participation in the same scenes and pursuits, furnish, to some extent, this common ground. But even where this previous companionship is wanting, there may exist such congeniality and sympathy between two minds, the tastes and feelings, the aims and aspirations of each may be so fully in unison, that each shall feel itself drawn to the other, with a regard which needs only time and opportunity to ripen into strong and lasting friendship.

Dissimilarity not inconsistent with Friendship. — Nor is it necessary, in order to true friendship, that there should be complete similarity or agreement. The greatest diversity even may exist in many respects, whether as to qualities of mind, or traits of character. Indeed, such diversity, to some extent, must be regarded as favorable to friendship, rather than otherwise. We admire, often, in others, the very qualities which we perceive to be lacking in ourselves, and choose for our friends those whose richer endowments in these respects may compensate in a measure for our own deficiencies. The strongest friendships are often formed in this way by persons whose characters present striking points of contrast. Such diversity, in respect to natural gifts and traits of character, is not inconsistent with the closest sympathy of views and feelings in regard to other matters, and therefore not inconsistent with the warmest friendship.

Limitation of the Number of Friends. — It was, perhaps, an idle question, discussed in the ancient schools of philosophy, whether true friendship can subsist between more than two persons. No reason can be shown why this affection should be thus exclusive, nor do facts seem to justify such a limitation. The addition of a new friend to the circle of my acquaintance does not necessarily detract aught from the affection I bear to my former friends, nor does it awaken suspicion or jealousy on their part. In this respect, friendship is unlike the love which exists between the sexes, and which is exclusive in its nature.

It must be admitted, at the same time, that there are limits to this extension, and that he who numbers a large circle of friends is not likely to form a very strong attachment for any one of them. Not unfrequently, indeed, a friendship thus unlimited is the mark, as Mr. Stewart suggests, of a cold and selfish character, prompted to seek the acquaintance of others by a regard to his own advantage, and a desire for society, rather than by any real attachment to those whose companionship he solicits. True and genuine friendship is usually more select in its choice, and is wholly disinterested in its character. A cold and calculating policy forms no part of its nature. It springs from no selfish or even prudential considerations. It burns with a pure and steady flame in the heart that cherishes it, and burns on even when the object of its regard is no longer on earth. Our friendships are not all with the living. We cherish the memory of those whom we no longer see, and welcome to the heart those whom we no longer welcome to our home and fireside.

Effect of adventitious Circumstances. — Reverses in life, changes in fortune, the accidents of health and sickness, of wealth and poverty, of station and influence, have little power to weaken the ties of true friendship once formed. They test, but do not impair its strength. True friendship only makes us cling the closer to our friend in his adversity; and when fortune frowns, and the sunshine of popular favor passes away, and "there is none so poor to do him reverence," whom once all men courted and admired, we still love him, who, in better days, showed himself worthy of our love, and who, we feel, is none the less worthy of it, now that we must love him for what he *is*, and not for what he has. That is not worthy the name of friendship, which will not endure this test.

Changes in moral Character. — Much more seriously is friendship endangered by any change of moral character and principle, on the part of either of the friends. So long as the change affects merely the person, the wealth, the social position, the power, the good name even, we feel that these are but the external circumstances, the accidents, the surroundings, and not the man himself, and however these things may vary, our friend remains the same. But when the change is in the heart and character of the man himself, when he whose sympathies and moral sentiments were once in unison with our own, shows himself to be no longer what he once was, or what we fondly thought him to be, there is no longer that community of thought and feeling between us that is essential to true and lasting friendship. Yet, even in such a case, we continue to cherish for the friend of former years a regard and affection which subsequent changes do not wholly efface. We think of him *as he was*, and not as he is; as he was in those earlier and better days, when the heart was fresh and unspoiled, and the feet had not as yet turned aside from the paths of rectitude and honor.

§ III. — Love of Benefactors.

As related to Friendship. — Closely allied to the affections we feel for our friends is the emotion we cherish towards our benefactors. Like the former, it is one of the forms of that principle into which all kindly affection ultimately resolves itself, namely, love, differing as the object differs on which it rests, but one in nature under all these varieties of form. The love which we feel for a benefactor, differs from that which we feel for a friend, as the latter again differs from that which we feel for a parent or a child. It differs from friendship, in that the motive which prompted the benefaction, on the part of the giver, may be simple benevolence, and not personal regard; while, on our part, the emotion awakened may be simple gratitude to the generous donor, a gratitude which, though it may lead to friendship, is not itself the result of personal attachment.

Nature of this Affection. — If we inquire more closely into the nature of this affection, we find that it involves, as do all the benevolent affections, a feeling of pleasure or delight, together with a benevolent regard for the object on which the affection rests. The pleasure, in this case, results from the reception of a favor. It is not, however, merely a pleasure in the favor received, as in itself valuable, or as meeting our necessities; it is, over and beyond this, a pleasure in the giver as a noble and generous person, and as standing in friendly relations to us. Such conceptions are always agreeable to the mind, and that in a high degree. The benevolent regard which we cherish for such a person, the disposition and wish to do him good in turn, are the natural result of this agreeable conception of him; and the two together, the pleasure, and the benevolent regard, constitute the complex emotion which we call gratitude.

Regards the Giver rather than the Gift. — If this be the correct analysis of the affection now under consideration, it is not so much the *gift*, as the *giver*, that awakens the emotion; and this view is confirmed by the fact that when, from any circumstances, we are led to suspect a selfish motive on the part of the donor, that the gift was prompted, not so much by regard to us, as by regard to his own personal ends, for favors thus conferred we feel very little gratitude. The gift may be the same in either case, but not the giver.

Modes of manifesting Gratitude. — Philosophers have noticed the different manner in which persons of different character, and mental constitution, are affected by the reception of kindness from others, and the different modes in which their gratitude expresses itself. Some are much more sensibly affected than others by the same acts of kindness; and even when gratitude may exist in equal degree, it is not always equally manifested. We naturally look, however, for some exhibition of it, in all cases, where favors have been conferred; its due exhibition satisfies and pleases us; its absence gives us pain, and we set it down as indicative of a cold and selfish nature.

A disordered Sensibility indicated by the Absence of this Principle. — One of the most painful forms of disordered sensibility — the insanity, not of the intellect, but of the feelings — is that which manifests itself in the entire indifference and apathy with which the kindest attentions are received, or even worse, the ill-concealed and hardly-suppressed hatred which is felt even for the generous benefactor. A case of this sort is mentioned by Dr. Bell, the accomplished superintendent of the MacLean Asylum for the insane, as coming under his notice, in which the patient, a lady, by no means wanting in mental endowments, seemed utterly destitute and incapable of natural affection. Having, on one occasion, received some mark of kindness from a devoted friend, she exclaimed, "I suppose I ought to love that person, and I should, if it were possible for me to love any one; but it is not. I do not know what that feeling is." A more sad and wretched existence can hardly be conceived than that which is thus indicated — the deep night and winter of the soul, a gloom unbroken by one ray of kindly feeling for any living thing, one gleam of sunshine on the darkened heart. Happily such cases are of rare occurrence. The kindness of men awakens a grateful response, in every human heart, whose right and normal action is not hindered by disorder, or prevented by crime.

Disorder of the moral Nature. — Is it not an indication of the imperfect and disordered condition of our moral nature, that while the little kindnesses of our fellow men awaken in our breasts lively emotions of gratitude, we receive, unmoved, the thousand benefits which the great Author of our being is daily and hourly conferring, with little gratitude to the giver of every good and perfect gift?

§ IV. — Love of Home and Country.

Its proper Place. — Among the emotions which constitute our sensitive nature, the love of home and of country, or the patriotic emotion, holds a prominent rank. It falls into that class of feelings which we term affections, inasmuch as it involves not only an emotion of pleasure, but a desire of good towards the object which awakens the feeling.

Founded on the Separation of the Race. — The affection now to be considered implies, as its condition, the separation of the human race into families, tribes, and nations, and of its dwelling-places into corresponding divisions of territory and country, a division founded not more in human nature than in the physical conditions and distributions of the globe, broken as it is into different countries, by mountain, river, and sea. No one can fail to perceive, in this arrangement, a design and provision for the distribution of the race into distinct states and nations. To this arrangement and design the nature of man corresponds. To him, in all his wanderings, there is no place like home, no land like his native land. It may be barren and rugged, swept by the storms, and overshadowed by the frozen hills, of narrow boundary, and poor in resources, where life is but one continued struggle for existence with an inhospitable climate, unpropitious seasons, and an unwilling soil; but it is his own land, it is his father-land, and sooner than he will see its soil invaded, or its name dishonored, he will shed the last drop of blood in its defence.

Other Causes auxiliary.—The strong tendency to rivalry, and war, between different tribes, tends, doubtless, to keep alive the patriotic sentiment, by binding each more closely to the soil, which it finds obliged to defend at the sacrifice of treasure, and of life. The great diversity of language, manners, and customs, which prevails among different nations, must also tend very strongly to separate nations still more widely from each other, and bind them more closely to their own soil, and their own institutions.

Effect of Civilization. — Such are some of the causes which give rise to the patriotic sentiment. Civilization tends, in a measure, doubtless, to diminish the activity of these causes. In proportion as society advances, as national jealousies and rivalries diminish, as wars become less frequent, as nations come to understand better each other's manners, laws, and languages, and to learn that their interests, apparently diverse, are really identical, this progress of civilization and culture, removing, as it does, in great measure, the barriers that have hitherto kept nations asunder, must tend, it would seem, to weaken the influence of those causes which contribute to keep alive the patriotic feeling. And such we believe to be the fact. It is in the early period of a nation's existence, the period of its origin and growth, of its weakness and danger, that the love of country most strongly developes itself. It is then that sacrifices are most cheerfully made, and danger and toil most readily met, and life most freely given, for the state whose foundations can no other way be laid. As the state, thus founded in treasure and in blood, and vigilantly guarded in its infancy, gains maturity and strength, becomes rich, and great, and powerful, comes into honorable relation with the surrounding states and nations, the love of country seems not to keep pace with its growth in the hearts of the people, but rather to diminish, as there is less frequent and less urgent occasion for its exercise.

National Pride. — There is, however, a counteracting tendency to be found in the national pride which is awakened by the prosperity and power of a country, and especially by its historic greatness. The citizen of England, or of France, at the present day, has more to defend, and more to love, than merely his own home and fireside, the soil that he cultivates, and the institutions that guarantee his freedom and his rights. The past is intrusted to him, as well as the present. The land whose honor and integrity he is determined to maintain, at all hazard and personal sacrifice, is not the England, or the France, of to-day merely, but of the centuries. He remembers the glories of the empire, the armies, and the illustrious leaders that have carried his country's flag with honor into all lands, the monarchs that, in succession, from Clovis and Charlemagne, from Alfred and Harold the dauntless, have sat in state upon the throne that claims his present allegiance, the generations that have contributed to make his country what it now is; and he feels that not merely the present greatness and power of his country, but all its former greatness and glory, are intrusted to his present care and keeping.

Depends upon Association. — If we inquire more closely into the philosophy of the matter, we shall find, I think that the principle of *association* is largely concerned as the immediately producing cause of the emotion now under consideration. We connect with the idea of any country the history and fortunes, the virtues and vices of its inhabitants, of those who, at any time, recent or remote, have passed their brief day, and acted their brief part, within its borders, and whose unknown dust mingles with its soil. They have long since passed away, but the same hills stand, the same rivers flow along the same channels, the same ocean washes the ancient shores, the same skies look down upon those fields and waters, and with these aspects and objects of nature we associate all that is great and heroic in the history of the people that once dwelt among those hills, and along those shores. Every lofty mountain, every majestic river, every craggy cliff and frowning headland along the coast, stand as *representative* objects, sacred to the memory of the past, and the great deeds that have been there performed. How much this must add to the force and power of the patriotic emotion is obvious at a glance.

Same Principle concerned in the Love of Home. — In like manner, by the same principle of association, we connect our own personal history with the places where we dwell, and the country we inhabit. They become, in a measure, identified with ourselves. To love the home of our childhood, and our native land, is but to love our former selves, since it is here that our little history lies, and whatever we have wrought of good or ill.

An original Principle. — With respect to the character of this emotion, while it is doubtless awakened and strengthened by the law of association, still I cannot but regard it as an original provision and principle of our nature, springing up instinctively in the bosom, showing itself essentially the same under all conditions of society, and in all ages and countries. It waits not for education to call it forth, nor for reason and reflection to give it birth; while at the same time, reason and reflection doubtless contribute largely to its development and strength.

Strongest where it might be least expected. — It has been frequently observed, by those who have made human nature their study, that the patriotic feeling is not confined to the inhabitants of the most favored climes and countries, but, on the contrary, is often most strongly developed in nations less populous, and in countries little favored by nature. The inhabitants of wild, mountainous regions, of sterile shores, of barren plains, manifest as strong a love of home and country, as any people on the globe. It is thus with the Swiss among their mountain fastnesses, and with the poor Esquimaux of northern Greenland, where, beyond the arctic circle, cold and darkness reign undisturbed the greater part of the year. Even in those dreary realms, and in those bosoms little refined, the voice of nature is heard, and the love of home and of country is strong. Even beggars have been known to die of nostalgia, or home-sickness.

CHAPTER II.

MALEVOLENT AFFECTIONS.

As distinguished from the Benevolent. — The affections have already been distinguished from other forms of the sensibility, by the circumstance that they involve, along with the feeling of pleasure or pain, some feeling of kindness or the opposite, toward the object; in the one case we term them benevolent, in the other, malevolent affections. Of the former, I have treated in the preceding chapter; of the latter, I am now to speak.

Resentment the generic Name. — These affections may be comprised under the general name *resentment*, as that which underlies and constitutes the basis of them all. Envy, jealousy, revenge, etc., may be regarded as but so many modifications, or perversions, of this general principle. As the benevolent affections are all so many forms of love, going forth toward diverse objects, and varying as the objects vary, so the malevolent affections are so many forms of the opposite principle, *i. e.*, aversion, varying, likewise, with the objects.

Founded in Nature. — As the benevolent, so likewise the malevolent or irascible feelings are, as to their principle, instinctive; they have their foundation in our nature. They are, as such, universally exhibited under the appropriate circumstances; they are early in their development, showing themselves often prior to the exercise of the reflecting and reasoning powers; they are, also, to some extent, common to man with the brutes.

Capable, however, of rational Exercise and Control. — While we pronounce them instinctive, however, we would by no means imply that they are not capable of being deliberately and intelligently exercised, or that they are not in fact, frequently so exercised. What instinct originally teaches, reason and reflection, when, at a later date, they come into play, may sanction and confirm. On the other hand, they may repress and forbid what instinct prompts. In the former case, the emotion, affection, passion, is none the less an instinctive principle in its nature and origin, although it has now passed from the domain of mere instinct to the higher sphere of reason and intelligence. What was done in the first instance from sudden impulse, blindly, without thought, is now done deliberately and intelligently. This may be the case with all our instinctive principles of action, as well as with those now particularly under consideration. Instinct and reason, or intelligence, though *distinguished* from, are not necessarily *opposed* to each other, in the sense that one and the same mental act may not proceed, now from one, now from the other, of these principles. The love which I cherish for my friends, or my kindred, may be purely instinctive, it may be strictly rational, a matter of reflection, the result of deliberate purpose.

Existence of such a Principle denied by some. — The existence of such a principle as resentment, among the original and constitutional elements of our nature, has been called in question by some writers. It has been thought derogatory to the divine character, that the Creator should implant the principle of resentment in the human heart. He commands us to love, and not to hate, and what he expressly forbids, he cannot have made provision for in the very constitution of the mind. Such a principle, it is also maintained, is altogether unnecessary. This is the ground taken by Mr. Winslow, in his work on moral philosophy.

The Question at Issue. — There is certainly much force in the view thus presented. The question before us, however, is not, what we might, à priori, have *supposed* the nature of man to be, nor, what it *ought* to be, but simply, what *is* that nature as a matter of fact? Whether such a principle as resentment is *necessary* in a well-constituted mind, is not now the question; nor yet whether the Creator could consistently implant such a principle within us; nor, again, what may be the moral character of such a principle; but simply, Is there such a principle among the native elements of human character? If it be found there, we may conclude, either, that the Creator has placed it there for some wise purpose, or else, that the nature with which man comes into the world is no longer an adequate expression of the will of the Creator concerning him, but has, in some way, lost its original purity and integrity.

Existence of such a Principle. — Now that there are certain irascible feelings which find a place, under certain circumstances, in the human bosom, whenever the fitting occasion calls them forth, can hardly be denied; nor yet that they have their foundation in the nature of man. We have the same evidence of this, that we have of the existence of any other original and native principle. It manifests itself universally, uniformly, under all the varieties of social condition, among all nations, in all ages of the world. It developes itself at an early period of life, before education or example can have come in to account for its existence. Reason may subsequently control and restrain it, or it may fail to do so; but the principle exists before it can be either indulged or restrained. When the occasion which calls it forth is some injury or evil inflicted upon ourselves, the feeling takes the name of *resentment;* when others are the objects of that injustice, the feeling awakened is more properly termed *indignation.* We resent our own wrongs, we are indignant at those of others. The principle is, in either case, the same, and is as truly a part of our nature, as gratitude for favors received, or sympathy with the sorrows of the afflicted.

Term Malevolent, how employed. — The term *malevolent,* as used to designate this class of affections, is, it must be confessed, liable to serious objection. It has come into use as a convenient term, in place of, and for the want of, something better, to mark the distinction between the feelings now under consideration, and those of the opposite character, already considered; and as we call those *benevolent,* so we call these *malevolent,* merely by way of contrast, and not as implying any thing *criminal* in the character of the emotions themselves. The term, however, is unfortunate, as seeming to involve a meaning not intended. The moral character of the affections thus designated, is an open question, to be decided upon its own merits, and not to be considered as settled, one way or the other, by the use of the term now under consideration. This question we shall presently discuss. For the present, we have to consider, more particularly, the several forms in which the malevolent or irascible feeling presents itself.

Nature of Resentment. — *Resentment* is the feeling awakened in view of injury received. It is precisely the opposite of gratitude, which is the feeling awakened by benefits conferred. As, in the latter case, there springs up at once in the heart an affectionate regard for the generous donor, so, in the former there is awakened, at once a feeling of resentment against those who have done us the wrong. It is an instinctive emotion. No sooner are we conscious of the injury than we are conscious also of the feeling of resentment.

Design of this Principle. — The design of this principle of our nature is evident. It arms us against those sudden dangers and assaults, which no foresight can anticipate, nor prudence prevent, and which, when they occur, require instant action, and prompt redress. In such cases, reason and reflection would come to our aid too late; were we left to their counsels, however wise those counsels might be, we should already have suffered the injury from which they would seek to protect us. Something is needed that shall prompt to speedier action; some watchman vigilant and armed, ready on the first approach of danger to strike his alarm-bell, and summon the garrison to action. This we have in the principle of resentment. Were it not for this principle, moreover, a cautious and timid policy might often prevail over the sense of justice, and honor, and right, or a selfish policy might keep us back from interfering, at our own peril, for the protection of the injured, and the punishment of the aggressor. Instinct sets us right in such matters, before reason has time to act.

Necessary to the Punishment of Crime. — The malevolent feeling, at least in the form now under consideration, seems to be, in some degree, necessary for the punishment of crime, and the protection of society. It may be doubted whether, without it, we should act with sufficient energy, and promptness, for the redress of wrong, when that wrong is not inflicted upon ourselves. Nature has guarded against this danger, by planting in the human bosom an innate sense of justice, a hatred of wrong and injury wantonly inflicted, and a quick resentment against the perpetrator, which leads us to seek his detection and punishment, silences the plead ings of compassion in his behalf, and arms us to inflict the merited blow. That is but a weak and short-sighted benevolence, that is incapable of hatred of crime, and criminals; and that, under the flimsy pretence of compassion for the unfortunate, and humanity, would shield from justice, and due punishment, those who strike at the highest interests of society, and put in jeopardy all that is most dear and sacred to man. There are cases, in which compassion becomes malice aforethought, and stern resentment is the only true benevolence. It is one of the sublimest and most glorious attributes of deity, as portrayed in the Scriptures, that with the highest benevolence he combines the stern, inflexible hatred of wrong, so that, while it can with truth be said, "God is love," it can with equal truth be affirmed, "our God is a consuming fire."

Liable to abuse. — While, however, the principle now considered has its uses, and must be regarded as a most important provision of nature for the necessities of our race, it must also be conceded that it is a principle liable to abuse, and requiring to be kept in careful check. Especially in its sudden and instinctive action, upon the reception of personal harm or danger, are we liable to be carried to extremes, and indulge a resentment out of proportion to the merits of the case.

A Check on excessive Resentment. — Against this excessive resentment of injuries, real or imaginary, nature has provided a check needful and salutary, in the indignation with which any such manifestation is sure to be regarded by others, and the loss of that sympathy, otherwise on our side, but now turned in favor of the object of our too great resentment. The wise and prudent man will carefully avoid such a result, and this prudence will act as a powerful curb on his anger. To the man of virtuous and honorable sentiments there is also another restraint, hardly less powerful, upon the exercise of the malevolent feeling in any undue degree, and that is, the feeling of self-degradation and humiliation which such a man must feel, in consequence of his excessive resentment, when the heat of passion cools, and the moments of calmer reflection ensue. Even as exercised within due bounds, the malevolent affection is, from its very nature, a painful one. Not only the first emotion on the reception of injury or insult is one of a disagreeable nature, but the wish or desire, which instantly follows and accompanies it, of inflicting in return some ill upon the aggressor, is also a feeling which disturbs and disquiets the mind, and inflicts a species of suffering upon the mind that cherishes it, that may not improperly be termed its own punishment. And this again may be regarded, and doubtless is, to some extent, a check upon the indulgence of the malevolent affection.

Violent Exhibitions of this Feeling, where found.— It is accordingly in natures uncultivated and rude, little accustomed to self-control, and the restraints of reason and religion, that we naturally look for the violent and excessive outbursts of passion. A regard for our own happiness, a due sense of our own dignity and moral worth, and a decent respect for the opinions of those about us, whose approbation and sympathy we desire, contribute, if not to diminish the strength, at least to repress the manifestation, in any considerable degree, of the feeling of resentment, in those who have arrived at years of discretion, and have profited by the lessons of experience. The child is angry with the stone against which he strikes his foot, and vents his resentment for any injury upon the unconscious instrument, which was the means of its infliction. The savage tears from his flesh the arrow that has wounded him, and breaks it into fragments. This is undoubtedly the instinct of nature, untaught by reason and reflection. It is probably the first impulse of every man, on the reception of any injury, and before he has time to reflect on the folly of such a course, to express in some manner his resentment against the immediate instrument of his suffering.

Deliberate Form of Resentment. — When the first impulse has passed, and time gives opportunity for reflection, this instinctive resentment dies away, or gives place to a deliberate and rational form of the same emotion. Thus affected, the mind casts about it to ascertain the real extent of its injury, and the best means of redress; it distinguishes between the conscious agent, and the unconscious instrument, of its wrong, between the intentional injury and the unintentional, and, it may be, accidental harm; it takes into view the circumstances of the case, and the probable motives of the doer, and graduates its resentment accordingly.

Illustration of deliberate Resentment. — The law of retaliation which prevails among savage tribes, and which demands blood for blood, life for life, and exacts the fearful penalty with a justice inexorable and sure, though often long delayed, and which never loses sight of its victim, though years, and broad lands, and wide waters intervene, affords an illustration of deliberate in distinction from instinctive resentment. The law of honor, so called, as it exists among civilized nations, also illustrates the same principle.

Pointed out by Butler and others. — The distinction which we have indicated between the instinctive and deliberate form of this emotion, was clearly pointed out by Butler, though by no means original with him, as some writers have supposed; it is quite too obvious and important a distinction to have escaped the notice of earlier, and even of ancient philosophers, nor is it at all peculiar to this one affection, but common to all the sensibilities, as I have already said.

Modifications of the general Principle. — There are certain modifications of the malevolent affection, which require a passing notice in this connection. I refer to those emotions commonly known as *envy*, *jealousy*, and *revenge*. These are all but different forms of the same general principle, varying as the different circumstances and objects vary which call them forth.

Nature of Envy. — *Envy* is that form of resentment which too often, and too easily, finds a place in the human bosom, when another is more fortunate, more successful, more honored and esteemed, than ourselves. Especially is this the case, when the fortunate one is from our own circle of companionship, and our own rank in life, and when the honors and distinctions, or the wealth and power, that fall to his lot are such as we might ourselves have aspired to reach. We never, I suspect, envy those whose condition is, and originally was, very far removed from our own. The peasant envies not the lord of the realm, nor the beggar the king, but rather his fellow-peasant, or fellow-beggar, whose hut is warmer, and whose ragged garment not so ragged, as his own. It is the passion of a weak and narrow mind, a mean and degrading emotion, the opposite of every thing noble and generous.

Nature of Jealousy. — *Jealousy* is that form of the malevolent affection which has relation more particularly, though not exclusively, to the attachment which exists between the sexes, and which is awakened by the supposed rivalry of another. It is one of the most painful of the malevolent affections, and, when thoroughly roused, one of the strongest and most powerful principles of our nature. It is the peculiarity of this passion, that the object of its suspicion, and resentment, is, at the same time, the object of the heart's deepest love, and, it may be, adoration ; the strength and bitterness of the passion being in proportion to the fervor and earnestness of that affection. In the character of Othello, we have a fine delineation of the working and development of this trait of human character, as in Cassius we have a portraiture of the corresponding affection of envy.

Nature of Revenge. — *Revenge* is resentment in its most deliberate form, planned and carried into execution, not for the prevention of crime or injury, nor yet with reference to the ends of justice, but for the simple gratification of personal hatred. As such, and springing from such a motive, it is usually excessive in degree, and malicious in character. It is a dark and deadly passion, not more dangerous to society than degrading to the bosom that harbors it. It has not one redeeming quality to recommend it. It is neither the mark of a noble and generous, nor yet of a manly and brave spirit. It is the offspring of fear, rather than of courage. It usually seeks to accomplish, by secret and unlawful means, what it is ashamed or afraid to do openly, and by fair and honorable measures. It is a passion closely allied to those which may be supposed to reign in the bosom of a fiend.

Qualifying Remark. — I have spoken of envy, jealousy, and revenge, as modifications or different forms of the general principle of resentment, or the irascible propensity. There is, however, one important respect in which they all differ from the parent principle from which they spring. The latter, resentment, while founded in our nature, may, in exercise, be either instinctive or deliberate, as already shown; the former imply, I suspect, always some degree of deliberation, some element of choice. They are natural, in so far as there is a tendency in our nature to the exercise of these feelings under given circumstances, and, inasmuch as the principle from which they spring is founded in our nature, as one of its original elements; but they are not, like that principle, sometimes instinctive in their operation, but always, on the contrary, involve, as it seems to me, some process of thought, reflection, deliberation, choice.

Moral Character of the malevolent Affections. — It has been a question, much discussed, whether the class of feelings under consideration, in the present chapter, has *any moral character*, and if so, *what?* The question pertains, perhaps, more properly, to moral than to mental science; but we cannot pass it entirely without notice in this connection. So far as regards those forms of the malevolent emotion last considered, envy, jealousy, and revenge, there can be little doubt. Their exercise involves, as already stated, something of reflection and choice. They are not instinctive, but voluntary in their operation, capable, therefore, of control, and if not subjected to the stern dominion of reason, if not checked and subdued by the higher principles that should ever govern our conduct, we are reprehensible. Their indulgence in any form, and to any degree, must be regarded as blameworthy. They are *perversions* of that principle of resentment, which, for wise reasons, nature has implanted in our bosoms. Their tendency is evil, and only evil. They are *malevolent* in the full and proper sense of that term.

Of simple Resentment. — As to the primary principle of resentment in its simple and proper form, in so far as its operation is deliberate and voluntary, rather than purely instinctive, implying the exercise of reflection and reason, it must possess, in common with all other mental acts of that nature, some moral character. Within due limits, and on just occasions, it is a virtue; when it passes those limits, when it becomes excessive, or is uncalled for, by the circumstances of the case, it becomes a vice.

Of Resentment as instinctive. — The question before us properly relates to that form of resentment which is purely instinctive, unaccompanied by the exercise of reason and the reflective powers. Has such an emotion, strictly speaking, any moral character? How far are we responsible for its exercise? It seems to be a principle of manifest justice, and accordant with the common sense of mankind, that a man should be held responsible only for his rational and voluntary acts, for such things as it lies in his power to do, or not to do, according as he chooses. But that which is purely instinctive, is certainly not of this character. It may be in my power to repress the feeling of resentment that arises in my bosom on the reception of manifest injustice and wrong; I may refuse to harbor such a feeling; I may struggle to rise above it; but the feeling itself is instinctive, and I can no more prevent its first awakening and impulse, than I can prevent the involuntary contraction of the muscles upon the incision of the surgeon's knife.

Views of others — Upham, Reid, Chalmers. — Such is the view now generally entertained, we believe, by psychologists. "Instinctive resentment," says Mr. Upham, "has no moral character." "A moral character attaches only to the voluntary form of resentment." The same may be said of other affections, and of the sensibilities generally. In so far as they are purely instinctive, they have no moral character.

Dr. Reid, in his Active Powers of the Human Mind, holds this language, "Nothing in which the will is not concerned can justly be accounted either virtuous or immoral." The practice of all criminal courts, and all enlightened nations, he adds, is founded upon this principle; insomuch, "that if any judicature in any nation should find a man guilty, and the object of punishment, for what they allow to be altogether involuntary, all the world would condemn them as men who knew nothing of the first and most fundamental rules of justice."

Dr. Chalmers claims for the principle now under consideration a place among the primary and universal moral judgments of mankind. "It is in attending to these popular, or rather universal decisions, that we learn the real principles of moral science. And the first, certainly, of these popular, or rather universal decisions is, that nothing is moral or immoral that is not voluntary.

"That an action, then, be the rightful object either of moral censure or approval, it must have had the consent of the will to go along with it. It must be the fruit of a volition, else it is utterly beyond the scope, either of praise for its virtuousness, or of blame for its criminality. If an action be involuntary, it is as unfit a subject for any moral reckoning, as are the pulsations of the wrist."

(Sketches of Moral and Mental Philosophy, Chapter V. *On the Morality of the Emotions.*)

SENSIBILITIES.

PART THIRD.

THE DESIRES.

DESIRES.

CHAPTER I.

NATURE AND CLASSIFICATION OF DESIRES.

General Character of Desire. — What we enjoy we love, and what we enjoy and love, becomes, when no longer present, or when, although yet present, its future absence is regarded as probable, an object of *desire.* In the latter case it is perhaps more properly the continuance of the loved object, rather than the object itself, that is desired. Strictly speaking, we desire only that which is not in possession, and which is regarded as good and agreeable. More frequently the objects of desire are those things which, in some measure, we have actually enjoyed, and learned by experience how to prize. In many cases, however, we learn in other ways than by our own experience the value of an object; we gather it from observation, from the testimony of others, partly, perhaps, from imagination; and in such cases what is known or supposed to be agreeable and a good thing, though never, perhaps, actually enjoyed by ourselves, may be an object of desire. Thus I may desire wealth, or power, long before they come into my possession to be enjoyed. The felicities which await the righteous in the future may be distinct and definite objects of desire, while yet we are pilgrims on the earth, and have not seen "the land that is very far off." Even in the cases supposed, however, we have enjoyed, to some extent, if not the very same, yet similar objects; we have experienced something, though it may be on a small scale, of the advantages which wealth and power confer, while in our enjoyment of earthly happiness there is doubtless something on which the imagination can build its more glorious anticipations of the future, and it is this enjoyment and realization of a present or a past good, that constitutes the foundation of our desires. If we had never enjoyed aught, it may be doubted whether we should ever desire aught.

Law of the Sensibility. — The great law of the sensibility, then, may be thus stated, as regards the order and relation of the several classes of emotion to each other: I *enjoy*, I *love*, I *desire*; and the reverse, I *suffer*, I *dislike*, I cherish *aversion*. That such is the order or law of mental operation has been ably shown by Damiron in his Cours de Philosophie, and also, before him, by Jouffroy.

Conditions of Desire. — Desire is a feeling simple and indefinable. We can merely specify the conditions which it observes, and the occasions on which it is awakened. These conditions or occasions are the two already mentioned; the previous enjoyment, in some degree, of an agreeable object, and the present or contemplated absence of that object. Where these conditions are fulfilled, desire springs up at once in the mind, a desire proportioned to the degree of that previous enjoyment, and the strength of the affection thereby awakened in our minds for the object of our regard.

Opposite of Desire, Aversion. — The opposite of desire is aversion, the feeling that arises in view of an object not as agreeable but as disagreeable, not as a good but as an ill. This, too, like desire, is based upon some measure of experience; we have suffered somewhat of real or imagined ill, which, while it continues, is an object of dislike or hatred, and regarded as something which, though now absent, may possibly be realized in the future, becomes an object of aversion. Aversion, as well as its opposite, desire, finds its object in the future, while its basis lies in the past.

It will not be necessary to treat particularly of our aversions as a distinct class of emotions, since they are, for the most part, simply the counterparts of our desires, the desire of life, or happiness, having its equivalent in the aversion which we feel to suffering, and to death; so of other desires.

Desire always preceded by Emotion. — With regard to the nature of desires, it may further be remarked that while they imply always an object, an agreeable object, and that an absent one; while they imply, also, some previous enjoyment of that now absent object, or, at least, some knowledge of its existence and adaptation to our wants, as the foundation on which they rest, they do not take their rise immediately from the simple perception or intellectual contemplation of that absent object, as presented again merely to thought or imagination, but always some emotion or affection is first awakened by such thought or perception, and the desire succeeds to, and springs out of, that emotion. The mere perception of the object which formerly pleased me, does not, of itself, awaken in me immediately a desire for the object, but first an emotion or affection, and from that arises the desire.

Permanence of the Desires. — The greater permanence which our desires seem to possess, as compared with other simple emotions and affections, and which has been sometimes regarded as a distinguishing characteristic of this class of feelings, is owing, probably, not so much to the nature of desire, in itself considered, as to the fact that the object desired is always an absent object, and so long as it so remains, the desire for it is likely to continue. Were our desires always gratified as soon as they are definitely known, they would be no more permanent than any other state of mind.

Desire a motive Power. — The desires, it is to be noticed, moreover, are, in their nature, motive powers, springs of action to the mind. They are, if not the only, at least the chief source of mental activity. They prompt and excite the mind to action. The faculties, both physical and mental, are, in a manner, subject to their control. The intellect itself leads not to action; nor do the emotions; they agitate the mind, but it is only as they awaken desire, and that desire fixes upon a definite object, possible, but not in possession, that mind and body are both aroused to go forth for the attainment of the absent object of desire.

Classification of Desires. — Our desires may be classed according to their objects. These are of two sorts or classes: those which pertain to the physical nature and constitution, and those which relate to the wants of the mind rather than of the body. The desires, accordingly, may be classed as twofold — the *animal*, and the *rational;* the former having their source in the physical constitution of man, the latter in the nature and wants of the mind, rather than of the body. Of the former class are the desire of food, of sex, of exertion, of repose, of whatever, in a word, is adapted to the animal nature and wants. Of the latter class, the more prominent are the desire of happiness, of knowledge, of power, of society, of the esteem of others.

In connection with our desires are to be considered also those emotions which are known under the name of hope and fear, and which, as was stated in our previous analysis of the sensibilities, are to be regarded rather as modifications of desire, than as distinct principles or modes of mental activity.

CHAPTER II.

DESIRES ARISING FROM THE PHYSICAL CONSTITUTION.

Nature of Appetite as compared with other Forms of Desire. — These are usually called *appetites*, in distinction from those desires which are founded in the nature of the mind. They are, however, properly, a class of desires, though not always so ranked by philosophical writers. They are feelings which arise always in view of some good, real, or supposed, which has its adaptation to the wants of our nature, but which is not in present possession. This absence creates a longing for the object, which longing, so far as it relates to the mind at all, and not merely to the muscular sensation — as of hunger, etc. — is purely a *desire*. It differs from the other desires, in the respect mentioned, that it takes its rise from the constitution and wants of the body, rather than of the mind. It is not, however, on this account, the less a mental state, a psychological phenomenon.

Ambiguity of the Term. — The term *appetite* is ambiguous; sometimes denoting the uneasy physical sensations, as hunger, thirst, etc., which are conditions of the muscular and nervous systems, and not states of the mind; sometimes the mental condition which results from this, and which is properly called desire. It is only with the latter that psychology has to do; the former fall within the province of physiology.

Enumeration of the more important, and the End accomplished by each. — The desires, of the class to which we now refer, are various, comprehending all those which immediately relate to, and arise from, the various bodily wants. The more important are the desire of food, and of sex, to which may be added the desire of action, and of repose.

The constitution of our physical system is such as to lay the foundation of these desires. They pertain to our animal nature, and, as such, have a most important part to perform in the economy of life. They all relate, directly or indirectly, to the continuance of life, whether that of the individual, or of the species. Each of the appetites, or animal desires, as we prefer to call them, has its own specific object to accomplish, with reference to this general end. The desire of food looks to the preservation of individual life and vigor, by repairing the waste which the physical system is continually undergoing. The desire of muscular exertion and repose has the same general design. The desire of sex has for its object the preservation of the species.

Importance of these Principles. — Not only has each of these desires a specific end to accomplish, but it is an end which, so far as we can see, would not otherwise be accomplished. Reason might suggest the expediency of taking food to sustain the system, or of resting at intervals from exertion, in order to recruit our exhausted energies; but were it not for the desires that nature has implanted in us demanding positive gratification, and reminding us when we transgress those laws which govern our physical being, how often, in the pressure of business, should we neglect the due care of the body, and deprive ourselves of needed food, or needed rest, or needed muscular exertion. Were it not for the demands of appetite, how imperfectly should we judge either as to the proper proportion, or the proper quantity, and quality, of that refreshment which the body needs, and which food, and rest, and muscular exercise supply. And the same may be said of the other animal desires. They are necessary to the economy of life, by supplying a motive which would not otherwise exist, and thus securing a result not otherwise obtained. The principles to which we refer, are not, therefore, to be regarded as of little importance because relating to the wants of the body, and common to man with the animal races, generally; on the contrary, they are of the highest importance and value; a due regard to them is essential to the highest well-being, and the neglect or abuse of them brings its own sure and speedy punishment. To be ashamed of our animal nature, is to be ashamed of ourselves, and of the constitution that God gave us; to think lightly of it, is to despise the divine wisdom and benevolence. It is no part of an intelligent and rational nature to contemn the casket that contains all its treasure. Even were that casket worthless in itself, it would be valuable for the office it performs; much more when it is itself a piece of rare workmanship, curiously and wonderfully wrought.

Not selfish.—The appetites are not to be regarded as essentially selfish, in their nature. They relate, indeed, to our own personal wants; so do all our desires, and, in some measure, all our sensibilities. But when exercised within due bounds, they are not inconsistent with the rights and happiness of others, but the rather promotive of these results; and, therefore, not in the proper sense of the term are they *selfish* propensities. Their ultimate aim is not the securing of a certain amount of enjoyment to the individual by their gratification, but the securing of a certain end, not otherwise reached, by means of that enjoyment. They are to be set down as original and implanted principles of our nature, rather than as selfish and acquired propensities.

Dangerous Tendency.—I would, by no means, however, overlook the fact that the animal desires are of dangerous tendency when permitted to gain any considerable control over the mind, and that they require to be kept within careful bounds. They are liable to abuse. When suffered to become predominant over other and higher principles of action, when, from subjection and restraint, they rise to the mastery, and govern the man, then sinks the man to the level of the brute, and there is presented that saddest spectacle of all that the sun beholds in his course about the earth, a mind endowed with capacity of reason and intelligence, but enslaved to its own base passions. There is no slavery so degrading as that, none so hopeless. The most earnest efforts, the best and most sincere purposes and resolutions are too often made in vain, and the mind, struggling, to little purpose, with its own propensities, and its own vitiated nature, is swept on by the fearful current of its ungoverned, and now ungovernable, appetites, as the ship over which neither sail nor helm have any further power, is swept along in swift and ever lessening circles by the fatal maëlstrom.

Curious Law of our Nature.—It seems to be the law of our nature, that while our active principles gain strength by exercise, the degree of enjoyment or of suffering which they are capable of affording, diminishes by repetition. This has been clearly stated by Mr. Stewart. It follows from this, that while by long and undue indulgence of any of the animal desires, the gratification originally derived from such indulgence is no longer capable of being enjoyed, the desire itself may be greatly increased, and constantly increasing, in its demands. It is hardly possible to conceive a condition more wretched and miserable, than that of a mind compelled thus to drain the bitter dregs of its cup of pleasure, long since quaffed, and to repeat, in endless round, the follies that no longer have power to satisfy, even for the brief moment, the poor victim of their enchantment. The drunkard, the glutton, the debauchee, afford illustrations of this principle.

Acquired Appetites.—Beside the natural appetites of which I have hitherto spoken, and which are founded in the constitution of the physical system, there are certain appetites which must be regarded as artificial and acquired, such as the desire, so widely and almost universally prevalent, in countries both savage and civilized, for narcotic and stimulating drugs of various kinds, and for intoxicating drinks.

CHAPTER III.

DESIRES ARISING FROM THE CONSTITUTION OF THE MIND

§ I. — Desire of Happiness.

Propriety of the Designation Self-love. — Among that class of desires that have their foundation in the mental rather than in the physical constitution, one of the most important is the *desire of happiness*, or, as it is frequently called, *self-love*. The propriety of this designation has been called in question. "The expression," says Mr. Stewart, "is exceptionable, for it suggests an analogy (where there is none, in fact) between that regard which every rational being must necessarily have to his own happiness, and those benevolent affections which attach us to our fellow-creatures. There is surely nothing in the former of these principles analogous to the affection of *love*; and, therefore, to call it by the appellation of *self-love*, is to suggest a theory with respect to its nature, and a theory which has no foundation in truth."

This Position questionable. — I apprehend that in this remark, Mr. Stewart may have gone too far. The regard which we have for our own happiness certainly differs from that which we entertain for the happiness of others, as the objects differ on which, in either case, the regard is fixed. That the emotion is not essentially of the same *nature*, however, psychologically considered, is not so clear. Love or affection, as it has been defined in the preceding chapters, is the enjoyment of an object, mingled with a wish or desire of good to the same. Love of friends is the pleasure felt in, and the benevolent regard for, them. Love of self, in like manner, is the enjoyment of, and the desire of, good to self. Whoever, then, enjoys himself, and wishes his own good, exercises self-love; and the essential ingredient of this affection is the desire for his own happiness. Not only, then, is there an *analogy* between the two principles, the desire of our own happiness, and the regard which we feel for others, but *something more* than an analogy; they are essentially of the same nature so far as regards the mental activity exercised in either case, and the term love as properly designates the one, as the other, of these states of mind. I may love myself, as truly as I love my friend, nor is it the part of a rational nature to be destitute of the principle of self-love.

Not to be confounded with Selfishness. — There is more force in the objection, also urged by Mr. Stewart, against the phrase *self-love*, used to denote the desire of happiness, that it is, from its etymology, liable to be confounded, and in fact, often is confounded, with the word *selfishness*, which denotes a very different state of mind. The word selfishness is always used in an unfavorable sense, to denote some disregard of the happiness and rights of others; but no such idea properly attaches to self-love, or the desire of happiness, which, as Mr. Stewart justly remarks, is inseparable from our nature as rational and sensitive beings.

Views of Theologians. — Misled, perhaps, by the resemblance of the words, many theological writers, both ancient and modern, have not only represented self-love as essentially sinful, but even as the root and origin of evil, the principle of original sin.

So Barrow expressly affirms, citing Zuingle as authority. English moralists have sometimes taken the same view, and the earlier American divines very generally held it.

Self-love not criminal. — It can hardly be that a principle, which seems to belong to our nature as intelligent and rational beings, should be essentially criminal in it nature. The mistake, doubtless, arises from overlooking the distinction, already indicated, between self-love and selfishness.

The love of self, carried to the extreme of disregarding the happiness of others, and trespassing upon the rights of others, in the way to self-gratification, is indeed a violation of the principles of right, and is equally condemned by nature, speaking in the common sense and reason of man, and by divine revelation. But neither reason, nor the divine law, forbid that regard to our own happiness which self-love, in its true and proper sense, implies, and which exists, it may safely be affirmed, in every human bosom in which the light of intelligence and reason has not gone out in utter darkness. The sacred Scriptures nowhere forbid this principle. They enjoin upon us, indeed, the love of our neighbor; but the very command to love him as myself, so far from forbidding self-love, implies its existence as a matter of course, and presents that as a standard by which to measure the love I ought to bear to others.

Opinion of Aristotle. — Much more correct than the opinions to which I have referred, is the view taken by Aristotle in his Ethics, who speaks of the good man as necessarily a lover of himself, and, in *the true sense, preëminently* so. "Should a man assume a preëminence in exercising justice, temperance, and other virtues, though such a man has really *more true self-love* than the multitude, yet nobody would impute his affection to him as a crime. Yet he takes to himself the fairest and greatest of all goods, and those the most acceptable to the ruling principle in his nature, which is, properly, himself, in the same manner as the sovereignty in every community is that which most properly constitutes the state. He is said, also, to have, or not to have, the command of himself, just as this principle bears sway, or as it is subject to control; and those acts are considered as most voluntary which proceed from this legislative or sovereign power. Whoever cherishes and gratifies this ruling part of his nature, is *strictly and peculiarly a lover of himself*, but in quite a different sense from that in which self-love is regarded as a matter of reproach." (Ethic.

Nic., lib. ix., cap. viii.) This view appears to me eminently just.

That man is not, in the true and proper sense, a self-lover who seeks his present at the expense of his future and permanent well-being, or who tramples upon the rights and happiness of others, intent only upon his gratification. The glutton, the drunkard, the debauchee, are not the truest lovers of self. They stand fairly chargeable, not with too much, but *too little* regard for their own happiness and well-being.

Not the only original Principle. — But while the desire of happiness is a principle which has its foundation in the constitution of the mind, and which is characteristic of reason and intelligence, it is by no means to be regarded as the only original principle of our nature. Certain moralists have sought to resolve all other active principles into self-love, making this the source and spring of all human conduct, so that, directly or indirectly, whatever we do finds its origin and motive in the love of self. According to this view, I love my friends, my kindred, my country, only because of the intimate connection between their well-being and my own; I pity and relieve the unfortunate only to relieve myself of the unpleasant feelings their condition awakens; I sacrifice treasure, comfort, health, life itself, only for the sake of some greater good that is to be thus and only thus procured; even the sense of right, and the obligations of a religious nature, which bind and control me, find their chief strength, as principles of action, in that regard for my own happiness which underlies all other considerations.

Such a View indefensible. — This is a view not more derogatory to human nature than inconsistent with all true psychology. That the principle under consideration is one of the most powerful springs of human conduct, that it enters more largely than we may ourselves, at the time, be aware, into those motives and actions that wear the appearance of entire disinterestedness, I am disposed to admit nor would I deny that our sense of right, and of religious obligation, finds a strong support in that intimate and inseparable connection which exists between duty and happiness. The Scriptures constantly appeal to our love of happiness as a motive to right action. Their rewards and promises on the one hand, and their warnings and threatenings on the other, all rest on this assumed law of human nature, that man everywhere and always desires his own well-being. But that this is the only and ultimate ground of human action, that all the benevolent affections, all honor, and virtue, all sense of duty and right, all religious emotion and religious principle resolves itself into this, neither reason, nor revelation, nor the closest observation of the human mind, do either teach or imply.

This Desire, in what Sense rational. — *Stewart's View.* — We have spoken, thus far, of the desire of happiness as a rational principle. Is it, in such a sense, peculiar to a rational and intelligent nature? Does it so imply and involve the exercise of reason, that it is not to be found except in connection with, and as the result of, that principle? If so, it can hardly be called an original and implanted, or, at least, an *instinctive* principle. And such is the view taken by Mr. Stewart, in his Philosophy of the Active and Moral Powers The desire of happiness implies, in his estimation, a deliberate and intelligent survey of the various sources of enjoyment, a looking before and after, to ascertain what will, and what will not, contribute to ultimate and permanent well-being; and this it is the part of reason to perform.

Not exclusively so. — That the desire of happiness, as exercised by a rational nature, involves something of this process, some general idea of what constitutes happiness, of what is good on the whole and not merely for the present, some perception of consequences, some comprehensive view and comparison of the various principles of action and courses of conduct, as means to this general end, may, indeed, be admitted. And, so far as the exercise of self-love is of the nature now indicated, it is certainly a rational rather than an instinctive act. But I see no reason why one and the same emotion, or mental activity of any sort, may not be, at one time, the result of reflection, at another, of impulse; now deliberate and rational, and now, instinctive in its character. We know this to be the case, for example, with the affections, both benevolent and malevolent. A principle of action may be none the less instinctive, and originally implanted in man's nature, from the fact that, when he arrives at years of discretion, his reason confirms and strengthens what nature had already taught, or even adopts it as one of its own cardinal principles. It is not necessary, in order to *all* desire of good, that I should know, completely and comprehensively, in what good consists, and I may still desire my own happiness, according to the measure of my knowledge and capacity, when I simply know that I am happy at the present moment.

Desire of continued Existence. — Closely analogous to the principle now under consideration, if not, indeed, properly a form or modification of it, is the desire of *continued existence.* No desire that finds a place in the human bosom, perhaps, is stronger or more universal than this. Life is valued above all other possessions; riches, honors, place, power, ease, are counted as of little worth in comparison. There are, indeed, occasions when life is willingly sacrificed, rather than to incur dishonor and reproach, or for the defence of the innocent and helpless who depend on us for protection, or for some great and good cause that demands of the good and true man such service as may cost life. Even in such cases, the importance of the interests which demand and receive such a sacrifice, show the value we attach to that which is laid upon the altar.

Increases with Age. — The desire of continued existence seems to increase, as age advances, and life wears away. We always value that the more of which we have but little. It is a striking proof of the divine benevolence, that, in a world so full of care, and toil, and sorrow, as the present is, and must be, to the multitude of its inhabitants, there are few so miserable as not to regard continued existence as a boon to be purchased at any price.

§ II. — Desire of Knowledge.

An original Principle. — Among the various principles that enter into the composition of our nature, and are the motive powers of the human mind, awakening and calling forth its energies, and impelling it to action, the desire of knowledge holds an important place. From its early manifestation, before reason and reflection have as yet, to any extent, come into play, and from its general, if not universal existence, we infer that it is one of those principles originally implanted in our nature by the great Author of our being.

Not Curiosity. — The desire of knowledge, though often spoken of as synonymous with *curiosity*, is not altogether identical with it. Curiosity has reference rather to the novelty and strangeness of that which comes before the mind. It is the feeling awakened by these qualities, rather than the general desire to know what is yet unknown. It is of more limited application, and while it implies a desire to understand the object in view of which it is awakened, implies also some degree of wonder, at the unusual and unexpected character of the object as thus presented. While, then, curiosity is certainly a most powerful auxiliary to the desire of learning, and stimulates the mind to exertions it might not otherwise put forth, it is hardly to be viewed as identical with the principle under consideration.

Manifested in early Life. — The desire of knowledge is never, perhaps, more strongly developed than in early life, and never partakes more fully of the character of curiosity than then. To the child, all things are new and strange. He looks about him upon a world as unknown to him as he is to it, and every different object that meets his eye is a new study, and a new mystery to him. The desire to acquaint himself with the new and unknown world around him, keeps him constantly employed, constantly learning.

In later Years. — As he grows up, and the sphere of his intellectual vision enlarges, every step of his progress only opens new and wider fields to be explored, beyond the limits of his previous investigations. If there is less of childish curiosity, there is more of earnest, manly, irrepressible desire and determination to know. His studies assume this or that direction, according to native taste and temperament, early associations, or the force of circumstances; he becomes a student of science, or a student of letters, or of art, or of the practical professions and pursuits of life; but turn in what direction and to what pursuits he will, the desire to know still lives within him, as a sacred lamp ever burning before the shrine of truth.

Explains the Love of Narrative. — Every one has remarked the eagerness with which children listen to stories, histories, and fables. This is owing not more to the love of the ideal, which is usually very strongly developed in early life, than to the desire of knowing what presents itself to the mind as something new and unknown, yet with the semblance of reality. Nor does this love of narrative forsake us as we grow older. We have still our romances, our histories, our poems, epic and tragic, to divert us amid the graver cares of life; and the old man is, perhaps, as impatient as the child, to go on with the story, and comprehend the plot, when once his interest and curiosity are awakened.

A benevolent Provision. — We cannot but regard it as a benevolent provision of the Creator, so to constitute the human mind, that not only knowledge itself, but the very process of its acquisition, should be a pleasure. And when we consider how great is the importance to man of this desire of knowledge, and how great is the progress of even the humblest mind, from the dawn of its intelligence, on to the period of its full maturity and strength; how, under the influence of this desire, the mind of a Newton, a Kepler, a Bacon, a Descartes, a Leibnitz, moves on, from the slow and feeble acquisitions of the nursery, to the great and sublime discoveries that are to shed a light and glory, not only on the name of the discoverer, but on the path of all who come after him, we can hardly attach too high an importance to this part of our mental constitution.

A rational, though an instinctive Principle. — The desire of knowledge, like many of the active principles which have already fallen under our notice, is capable of rational exercise and control, while, at the same time, an implanted and instinctive principle. It operates, at first, rather as a blind impulse, impelling the mind to a given end; when reason assumes her sway of the mind and its restless energies, what was before a mere impulse and instinct of nature, now becomes a deliberate and rational purpose.

Moral Character. — As to moral character, it may, or may not, pertain to the exercise of the principle under consideration. The desire of knowledge is not of necessity a virtuous affection of the mind. Characteristic as it is of a noble and superior nature, more elevated and excellent, as it certainly is, than the merely animal desires and impulses, it is not inseparably connected with moral excellence.

As rationally exercised, it is laudable and virtuous, provided we seek knowledge with proper motives, and for right ends; otherwise, the reverse. Inasmuch, however, as we are under obligation to act in this, as in all other matters, from pure motives, and for right ends, the mere absence of such a motive, the desire and pursuit of knowledge in any other manner, and from other motives, becomes blame worthy.

§ III. — Desire of Power.

A native Principle. — The desire of power must be regarded as an original principle of our nature. Like the desire of happiness, and of knowledge, it is both early in its development, and powerful in its influence over the mind. It is also universally manifest.

In what Manner awakened. — Of the idea of power or cause, and of the manner in which the mind comes, in the first instance, to form that idea, I have already spoken, under the head of original conception. We see changes taking place in the external world. We observe these changes immediately and invariably preceded by certain antecedents. The idea of cause is thus suggested to the mind, and cause implies power of one thing over another to produce given effects. We find, also, our own volitions attended with corresponding effects upon objects external, and thus learn, still further, that we ourselves possess power over other objects. The idea thus awakened in the mind, there springs up, also, in connection with the idea, an activity of the sensibilities. The power which we find ourselves to have over objects about us affords us pleasure; what we enjoy we love, and what we love we desire; and so there is awakened in the mind a strong and growing desire for the possession of power.

Pleasure of exerting Power. — The pleasure which we derive from producing, in any instance, a manifest effect, and from the consciousness that we have in ourselves the power to produce like effects whenever we will, is one of the highest sources of enjoyment of which nature has made us capable. It is, to a great extent, the spring and secret of the constant activity of which the world is full. It shows itself in the sports of childhood, and in the graver pursuits of maturer years. The infant, when it finds that it can move and control its own little limbs, the boy learning the art of such athletic sports as he perceives his fellows practise, the man when he finds that he can control the action of his fellow-man, and bend the will of others to his own, are each, and perhaps equally, delighted at the acquisition of this new power; and the pleasure is generally in proportion to the novelty of the acquisition, and the apparent greatness of the effect produced.

Strength and Influence of this Principle.—The love of power is one of the strongest of the ruling principles of the human mind. It has its seat in the deepest foundations of our nature. I can *do* something; I can do what others do; I can do more than they; such is the natural order and progression of our endeavors, and such also the measure and increase of our delight. What, but the love of power, leads to those competitions of strength with strength, which mark the athletic games and contests of all nations, civilized and savage? What, but the love of power, impels the hunter over the pathless mountains, and deserts, in quest of those savage denizens and lords of nature, whose strength is so far superior to his own? What, but the love of power, leads the warrior forth, at the head of conquering armies, to devastate and subdue new realms?

Seen also in other Pursuits.—And in the peaceful pursuits of life, how largely does the same impulse mingle with the other, and perhaps more apparent, motives of human action? The man of science, as he watches the nightly courses of the stars, or resolves the stubborn compounds of nature into their simple and subtle elements, as he discovers new laws, and unlocks the secrets that have long baffled human inquiry, derives no small part of his gratification from the consciousness of that power which he thus exercises over the realm of matter subjected to his will. And when, in like manner, the orator, on whose words depend the lives of men, and the fate of nations, stands forth to accuse or defend, to arouse the slumbering passions, and inflame the patriotism, the courage, the resentment of his audience, or to soothe their anger, allay their prejudice, awaken their pity or their fears, how does the consciousness of his power over the swaying, agitated multitude before him, mingle with the emotions that swell his bosom, and augment the fierce delight of victory?

Auxiliary to desire of Knowledge. — The desire of power is accessory to, and in some cases, perhaps, the foundation of certain other principles of action. It is especially auxiliary to the desire of knowledge, inasmuch as every new acquisition of truth is an accession of power to the mind, and is, therefore, on that account, as well as for its own sake, desirable. As a general thing, the more we know, the more and the better we can do. Every mental acquisition becomes, in some sense, an instrument to aid us in further and larger acquisitions. We are enabled to call to our aid the very forces and elements of nature which our discoveries have, in a manner, subjected to our sway, and to conform our own conduct to those established laws which science reveals. The mind is thus stimulated, in all its investigations, and toilsome search for truth, by the assurance that every increase of knowledge is, in some sense, an increase, also, of power. Hence the aphorism so current, and generally attributed to Bacon, which affirms that knowledge *is* power.

Auxiliary also to love of Liberty. — The *love of liberty*, according to some writers, proceeds also, in part, at least, from the desire of power, the desire of being able to do whatever we like. Whatever deprives us of liberty trenches upon our power. In like manner, writers upon morals have noticed the fact that the *pleasure of virtue* is in a measure due to the same source. When evil habits predominate and acquire the mastery, we lose the power of self-control, the mind is subjected to the baser passions, and this loss of power is attended with the painful consciousness of degradation. On the other hand, to the mind that is bent on maintaining its integrity, though it be by stern and determined conflict with the evil influences that surround it, and its own natural propensities to a course of sinful indulgence, every fresh struggle with those adverse influences becomes a pledge of final success, and the hour of victory, when it comes at last, as come it will, is an hour of triumph and of joy.

§ IV. — Certain Modifications of the Desire of Power; — as, the Desire of Superiority, and of Possession.

General Statement. — There are certain desires to which the human mind is subject, and which seem to have a foundation in nature, which, though frequently regarded as distinct principles of action, are more properly, perhaps, to be viewed as but modifications of the principle last considered. I refer to the *desire of superiority*, and *the desire of possession;* or, as they are more succinctly termed, ambition and avarice.

The Desire to excel, universal. — The desire to excel is almost universal among men. It shows itself in every condition of society, and under all varieties of character and pursuit. It animates the sports of childhood, and gives a zest to the sober duties and realities of life. It penetrates the camp, the court, the halls of legislation, and of justice; it enters alike into the peaceful rivalries of the school, the college, the learned professions, and into those more fearful contests for superiority which engage nations in hostile encounter on the field of strife and carnage. What have we, under all these manifestations, but the desire of superiority, and what is that but the desire of power in one of its most common forms?

Not peculiar to Man. — This is a principle not peculiar to human nature, but common to man with the brute. The lower animals have also their rivalries, their jealousies, their contests for superiority in swiftness, and in strength, and he is the acknowledged leader who proves himself superior in these respects to his fellows.

Not the same with Envy. — The desire to excel, or the principle of emulation, is not to be confounded with envy, with which it is too frequently, but not necessarily, associated. Envy is pained at the success of a rival; a just and honorable emulation, without seeking to detract from the well-merited honors of another, strives only to equal and surpass them. This distinction is an important one, and has been very clearly pointed out by *Mr. Stewart*, and also by *Bp. Butler*, and, still earlier, by *Aristotle.* "Emulation," says Butler, "is merely the desire of superiority over others, with whom we compare ourselves. To desire the attainment of this superiority by the particular means of others being brought down below our own level, is the distinct notion of envy." To the same effect, Aristotle, as quoted by Stewart: "Emulation is a good thing, and belongs to good men; envy is bad, and belongs to bad men. What a man is emulous of he strives to attain, that he may really possess the desired object; the envious are satisfied if nobody has it."

Not malevolent of Necessity. — Dr. Reid has classed emulation with the malevolent affections, as involving a sentiment of ill-will toward the rival; but, as Mr. Stewart very justly remarks, this sentiment is not a *necessary* concomitant of the desire of superiority, though often found in connection with it; nor ought emulation to be classed with the affections, but with the desires, for it is the desire which is the active principle, and the affection is only a concomitant circumstance.

View maintained by Mr. Upham. — Mr. Upham denies emulation a place among the original and implanted principles of our nature, on this ground. All our active principles, he maintains, from instinct upward, are subordinate to the authority and decisions of conscience, as a faculty paramount to every other. But the desire of superiority he supposes to be utterly inconsistent with the law of subordination. Whenever man perceives a superior, he perceives one with whom, by this law of his nature, if such it be, he is brought into direct conflict and collision, and as he is surrounded by those who, in some respect, are his superiors, he is really placed in a state of perpetual warfare and misery; nor can he regard even the Supreme Being with other feelings than those of unhallowed rivalry. A principle that would lead to such results, he concludes, cannot be founded in the constitution of our nature. He accordingly resolves the desire of superiority into the principle of imitativeness.

The Correctness of this View called in Question. — It is difficult to perceive the force of this reasoning. The desire of superiority, it is sufficient to say, whatever be its origin, leads to no such results. As actually manifest in human character and conduct, it does not show itself to be inconsistent with due subordination to authority, nor does it involve man in necessary and perpetual conflict with his fellows, nor does it present the Supreme Being as an object of unhallowed rivalry. We have only to do with facts, with the phenomena actually presented by human nature; and we do not find the facts to correspond with the view now given. Nor can we perceive any reason, in the nature of the case, why the desire in question *should* lead, or be supposed to lead, to such results. The desire of superiority does not necessarily imply the desire to be superior to every body, and every thing, in the universe. It may have its natural and proper limits; and such we find to be the fact.

Actual Limitations of this Principle. — We desire to excel not, usually, those who are far above us in rank and fortune, but our fellows and companions; our rivals are mostly those who move in the same sphere with ourselves. The artist vies with his brother artist, the student with his fellow student, and even where envy and ill-will mingle, as they too often do, with the desire, still, the object of that envy is not every one, indiscriminately, who may happen to be superior to ourselves, but only our particular rival in the race before us. The child at school does not envy Sir Isaac Newton, or the illustrious Humboldt, but the urchin that is next above himself in the class. The desire of superiority, like every other desire of the human mind, looks only at what is possible to be accomplished, at what is probable, even; it aims not at the clouds, but at things within our reach, things to be had for the asking and the striving. But whatever view we take of the matter, the desire of superiority certainly exists as an active principle in the human mind; nor do we see any reason why it should not be admitted as an original principle founded in the constitution of our nature, or, at least, as one of the forms and modifications of such a principle, viz., the love of power.

This Principle requires Restraint. — I would by no means deny, however, that the desire now under consideration is one which is liable to abuse, and which requires the careful and constant restraints of reason and of religious principle. The danger is, that envy and ill-will, toward those whom we regard as rivals and competitors with us, for those honors and rewards which lie in our path, shall be permitted to mingle with the desire to excel. Indeed, so frequently are the two conjoined, that to the reflecting and sensitive mind, superiority itself almost ceases to be desirable, since it is but too likely to be purchased at the price of the good-will, and kind feeling, of those less fortunate, or less gifted, than ourselves.

Another Form of the same Desire. — *The desire of possession* may be regarded, also, as a modification of the desire of power. That influence over others which power implies, and which is, to some extent, commanded by superiority of personal strength or prowess, by genius, by skill, by the various arts and address of life, or by the accident of birth and hereditary station, is still more directly and generally attainable, by another, and perhaps a shorter route — the possession of wealth. This, as the world goes, is the key that unlocks, the sceptre that controls, all things. Personal prowess, genius, address, station, the throne itself, are, in no inconsiderable degree, dependent upon its strength, and at its command. He who has this can well afford to dispense with most other goods and gifts of fortune; so far, at least, as concerns the possession of power. He may be neither great, nor learned, nor of noble birth; neither elegant in person, nor accomplished in manners, distinguished neither for science, nor virtue; he may command no armies, he may sit upon no throne; yet with all his deficiencies, and even his vices, if so he have wealth, he has power. Unnumbered hands are ready to task their skill at his bidding, unnumbered arms, to move and toil and strive in his service, unnumbered feet hasten to and fro upon his errands. He commands the skill and labor of multitudes whom he has never seen, and who know him not. In distant quarters of the globe, the natives of other zones and climes hasten upon his errands; swift ships traverse the seas for him; the furs of the extreme North, the rich woods and spices of the tropics, the silks of India, the pearls and gems of the East — whatever is costly, and curious, and rare, whatever can contribute to the luxury and the pride of man — these are his, and for him. No wonder that he who desires power, should desire that which is one of the chief avenues and means to the attainment of power, and that what is valued, at first, rather as an instrument than as an end, should presently come to be regarded and valued for its own sake.

A twofold Aspect — Covetousness, Avarice. — There are, if I mistake not, two forms which the desire of possession assumes. The one is the simple desire of acquiring, that there may be the more to spend; the other of accumulating, adding to the heaps already obtained — which may be done by keeping fast what is already gotten, as well as by getting more. The one is the desire of getting, which is not inconsistent with the desire of spending, but, in fact, grows out of that in the first instance; the other is the desire of increasing, and the corresponding dread of diminishing, what is gotten, which, when it prevails to any considerable degree, effectually prevents all enjoyment of the accumulated treasure, and becomes one of the most remarkable and most odious passions of our perverted nature. The term *covetousness* answers somewhat nearly to the one, *avarice* to the other, of these forms of desire. It must be added, also, that it seems to be the natural tendency of the primitive and milder form of this principle, to pass into the other and more repulsive manifestation. He who begins with desiring wealth as a means of gratifying his various wants, too frequently ends with desiring it for its own sake, and becomes that poorest and most miserable of all men, the miser.

The inordinate love of Money not owing wholly to Association. — Whence arises that inordinate value which the miser attaches to money, which, in reality, is but the mere representative of enjoyment, the mere means to an end? Why is he so loth to part with the smallest portion of the representative medium, in order to secure the reality, the end for which alone the means is valuable? Is it that, by the laws of association, the varied enjoyments which gold has so often procured, and which have a fixed value in our minds, are transferred with all their value to the gold which procured them? Doubtless this is, in some measure, the case, and it may, therefore, in part, account for the phenomenon in question. The gold piece which I take from my drawer for the purchase of some needful commodity, has, it may be, an increased value in my estimation, from the recollection of the advantages previously derived from the possession of just such a sum. But why should such associations operate more powerfully upon the miser, than upon any other person? Why are we not *all* misers, if such associations are the true cause and explanation of avarice? Nay, why is not the spendthrift the most avaricious of all men, since he has more frequently exchanged the representative medium for the enjoyment which it would procure, and has, therefore, greater store of such associations connected with his gold?

The true Explanation. — Dr. Brown, who has admirably treated this part of our mental constitution, has suggested, I think, the true explanation of this phenomenon.

So long as the gold itself is in the miser's grasp, it is, and is felt to be, a permanent possession; when it is expended, it is usually for something of a transient nature, which perishes with the using. It seems to him afterward as so much utter loss, and is regretted as such. Every such regretted expenditure increases the reluctance to part with another portion of the treasure. There is, moreover, another circumstance which heightens this feeling of reluctance. The enjoyment purchased is one and simple. The gold with which it was purchased is the representative, not of that particular form of enjoyment alone, but of a thousand others as well, any one of which might have been procured with the same money. All these possible advantages are now no longer possible. Very great seems the loss. Add to this the circumstance that the miser, in most cases, probably, has accumulated, or set his heart upon accumulating, a certain round sum, say so many thousands or hundreds of thousands. The spending a single dollar breaks that sum, and, therewith, the charm is broken, and he who was a millionaire before that unlucky expenditure, is a millionaire no longer. It is mainly in these feelings of regret, which attend the necessary expenses of the man who has once learned to set a high value upon wealth, that avarice finds, if not its source, at least its chief strength and aliment.

Odiousness of this Vice. — There is, perhaps, no passion or vice to which poor human nature is subject, that is, in some respects, more odious and repulsive than this. There is about it no redeeming feature. It is pure and unmingled selfishness, without even the poor apology that most other vices can offer, of contributing to the present enjoyment and sensual gratification of the criminal. The miser is denied even this. He covets, not that he may enjoy, but that he may refrain from enjoying.

Strongest in old Age. — "In the contemplation of many of the passions that rage in the heart with greatest fierceness," says Dr. Brown, "there is some comfort in the thought that, violent as they may be for a time, they are not to rage through the whole course of life, at least if life be prolonged to old age; that the agitation which at every period will have some intermissions, will grow gradually less as the body grows more weak, and that the mind will at last derive from this very feebleness a repose which it could not enjoy when the vigor of the bodily frame seemed to give to the passion a corresponding vigor. It is not in avarice, however, that this soothing influence of age is to be found. It grows with our growth and with our strength but it strengthens also with our very weakness. There are no intermissions in the anxieties which it keeps awake; and every year, instead of lessening its hold, seems to fix it more deeply within the soul itself, as the bodily covering around it slowly moulders away. * * * The heart which is weary of every thing else is not weary of coveting more gold; the memory which has forgotten every thing else, continues still, as Cato says in Cicero's dialogue, to remember where its gold is stored; the eye is not dim to gold that is dim to every thing beside; the hand which it seems an effort to stretch out and fix upon any thing, appears to gather new strength from the very touch of the gold which it grasps, and has still vigor enough to lift once more, and count once more, though a little more slowly, what it has been its chief and happiest occupation thus to lift and count for a period of years far longer than the ordinary life of man. When the relations or other expectant heirs gather around his couch, not to comfort, nor even to seem to comfort, but to await, in decent mimicry of solemn attendance, that moment which they rejoice to view approaching; the dying eye can still send a jealous glance to the coffer near which it trembles to see, though it scarcely sees, so many human forms assembled; and that feeling of jealous agony, which follows and outlasts the obscure vision of floating forms that are scarcely remembered, is at once the last misery and the last consciousness of life."

§ V. — Desire of Society.

A natural Principle. — There can be little doubt that the desire of society is one of the original principles of our nature. It shows itself at a very early period of life, and under all the diverse conditions of existence. Its universal manifestation, and that under circumstances which preclude the idea of education or imitation in the matter, proves it an implanted principle, having its seat in the constitution of the mind.

Manifested by Animals of every Species. — The child rejoices in the company of its fellows. The lower animals manifest the same regard for each other's society, and are unhappy when separated from their kind. Much of the attachment of the dog to his master may, not improbably, be owing to the same source. The beast of labor is cheered and animated by his master's presence, and the patient ox as he toils along the furrow, or the highway, moves more willingly when he hears the well-known step and voice of his owner trudging by his side. Every one knows how much the horse is inspirited by the chance companionship, upon the way, of a fellow-laborer of his own species. Horses that have been accustomed to each other's society on the road, or in the stall, frequently manifest the greatest uneasiness and dejection when separated; and it has been observed by those acquainted with the habits of animals, that cattle do not thrive as well, even in good pasture, when solitary, as when feeding in herds.

Social Organizations of Animals. — Accordingly we find most animals, when left to the instinct of nature, associating in herds, and tribes, larger or smaller, according to the habits of the animal. They form their little communities, have their leaders, and, to some extent, their laws, acknowledged and obeyed by all, their established customs and modes of procedure — in which associations, thus regulated, it is impossible not to recognize the essential feature and principle of what man, in his political associations of the same nature, calls the *state.* What else are the little communities of the bee, and the ant, and the beaver, but so many busy cities, and states, of the insect and animal tribes?

The social State not adopted because of its Advantages merely. — It may be said that man derives advantages from the social state, and adopts it for that reason. Unquestionably he does derive immense advantages from it; but is that the reason he desires it? Is the desire of society consequent upon the advantages, experienced or foreseen, which accrue from it, or are the advantages consequent upon the desire and the adoption of the state in question? Is it matter of expediency and calculation, of policy and necessity, or of native instinct and implanted constitutional desire? What is it with the lower animals? Has not nature provided in their very constitution for their prospective wants, and, by implanting in them the desire for each other's society, laid the foundation for their congregating in tribes and communities? Is it not reasonable to suppose that the same may be true of man? The analogy of nature, the early manifestation of the principle prior to education and experience, the universality and uniformity of its operation, and the fact that it shows itself often in all its strength under circumstances in which very little benefit would seem to result from the social condition, as with the savage races of the extreme North, and with many rude and uncultivated tribes of the forest and the desert — all these circumstances go to show that the desire of society is founded in the nature of man, and is not a mere matter of calculation and policy.

Man's Nature deficient without this Principle. — And this is a sufficient answer to the theory of those who, with Hobbes, regard the social condition of man as the result of his perception of what is for his own interest, the dictate of prudence and necessity. The very fact that it is for his interest would lead us to expect that some provision should be made for it in his nature; and this is precisely what we find to be the case. Were it otherwise, we should feel that, in one important respect, the nature of man was deficient, inferior even to that of the brute. But the truth is, the whole history of the race is one complete and compact contradiction of the theory of Hobbes, and shows, with the clearness of demonstration, that the *natural* condition of man is not that of seclusion, and isolation from his fellows, but of society and companionship.

Strength of this Principle. — So strongly is this principle rooted in the very depths of our nature, that when man is for a length of time shut out from the society of his fellow men, he seeks the acquaintance and companionship of brutes, and even of insects, and those animals for whom, in his usual condition, he has a marked repugnance, as a relief from utter loneliness and absolute solitude. Mr. Stewart relates the instance of a French nobleman, shut up for several years a close prisoner in the Castle of Pignerol, during the reign of Louis XIV., who amused himself, in his solitude, by watching the movements of a spider, to which he at length became so much attached, that when the jailor, discovering his amusement, killed the spider, he was afflicted with the deepest grief. Silvio Pellico, in his imprisonment, amused himself in like manner. Baron Trench sought to alleviate the wretchedness of his long imprisonment, by cultivating the acquaintance or friendship of a mouse, which in turn manifested a strong attachment to him, played about his person, and took its food from his hand. The fact having been discovered by the officers, the mouse was removed to the guard-room, but managed to find its way back to the prison door, and, at the hour of visitation, when the door was opened, ran into the dungeon, and manifested the greatest delight at finding its master. Being subsequently removed and placed in a cage, it pined, refused all sustenance, and in a few days died. "The loss of this little companion made me for some time quite melancholy," adds the narrator.

Case of Silvio Pellico.—How strongly is the desire for society manifested in these words of Silvio Pellico, when forbidden to converse with his fellow-prisoner. "I shall do no such thing. I shall speak as long as I have breath, and invite my neighbor to talk to me. If he refuse, I will talk to my window-bars. I will talk to the hills before me. I will talk to the birds as they fly about. I *will* talk."

Facts of this nature clearly indicate that the love of society is originally implanted in the human mind.

Illustrated from the History of Prison Discipline.—The same thing is further evident from the effects of entire seclusion from all society, as shown in the history of prison discipline. For the facts which follow, as well as for some of the preceding, I am indebted to Mr. Upham.

The legislature of New York some years since, by way of experiment, directed a number of the most hardened criminals in the State prison at Auburn, to be confined in solitary cells, without labor, and without intermission of their solitude. The result is thus stated by Messrs. Beaumont and Tocqueville, who were subsequently appointed commissioners by the French government to examine and report on the American system of prison discipline. "This, trial from which so happy a result had been anticipated, was fatal to the greater part of the convicts; in order to reform them, they had been subjected to complete isolation; but this absolute solitude, if nothing interrupts it, is beyond the strength of man; it destroys the criminal, without intermission, and without pity; it does not reform, it kills. The unfortunates on whom this experiment was made, fell into a state of depression so manifest that their keepers were struck with it; their lives seemed in danger if they remained longer in this situation; five of them had already succumbed during a single year; their moral state was no less alarming; one of them had become insane; another, in a fit of despair, had embraced the opportunity, when the keeper brought him something, to precipitate himself from his cell, running the almost certain chance of a mortal fall. Upon those, and similar effects, the system was finally judged." The same results substantially have followed similar experiments in other prisons. It is stated by Lieber, that in the penitentiary of New Jersey, ten persons are mentioned as having been killed by solitary confinement. Facts like these show how deeply-rooted in our nature is the desire of society, and how essential to our happiness is the companionship of our fellow-beings.

§ VI. — Desire of Esteem.

An important and original Principle. — Of the active principles of our nature, few exert a more important influence over human conduct, few certainly deserve a more careful consideration, than the regard which we feel for the approbation of others. The early period at which this manifests itself, as well as the strength which it displays, indicate, with sufficient clearness, that it is an original principle, founded in the constitution of the mind.

Cannot be regarded as an acquired Habit. — When we see children of tender age manifesting a sensitive regard for the good opinion of their associates, shrinking with evident pain from the censure of those around them, and delighted with the approbation which they may receive; when, in maturer years, we find them — children no longer — ready to sacrifice pleasure and advantage in every form, and to almost any amount, and even to lay down life itself to maintain an honorable place in the esteem of men, and to preserve a name and reputation unsullied — and these things we do see continually — we cannot believe that what shows itself so early, and so uniformly, and operates with such strength, is only some acquired principle, the result of association, or the mere calculation of advantage, and a prudential regard to self-interest. In many cases we know it cannot be so.

It is not the dictate of prudence, or the calculation of ad vantage, that influences the little child; nor is it the force of such considerations that induces the man of mature years to give up ease, fortune, and life itself, for the sake of honor and a name. Even where the approbation or censure of those who may pass an opinion, favorable, or unfavorable, upon our conduct, can be of no benefit or injury to us, that approbation is still desired, that censure is still feared. We prefer the good opinion of even a weak man, or a bad man, to his disesteem; and even if the odium which, in that case, we may chance to incur in the discharge of duty, is felt to be unjust and undeserved, and our consciousness of right intention and right endeavor sustains us under all the pressure of opinion from without, it is impossible, nevertheless, not to be pained with even that unjust and undeserved reproach. We feel that, in losing the confidence and esteem of others, we incur a heavy loss.

Want and wretchedness may drive a man to desperate and reckless courses; yet few, probably, can be found, so wretched and desperate, who, in all their misery, would not prefer the good opinion and the good offices of their fellow-man.

Accounted for neither by the selfish nor the associative Principle. — It can hardly be, then, a *selfish* and prudential principle — this strong desire of esteem; nor yet can it be the result of association, as some have inferred; since it shows itself under circumstances where a selfish regard for one's own interests could not be supposed to operate, and with a power which no laws of association can explain.

Hume's Theory. — Hardly better is it accounted for on the principle which Hume suggests, that the good opinion of others confirms our good opinion of ourselves, and hence is felt to be desirable. Doubtless there is need enough, in many cases, perhaps in most, of some such confirmation. Nor would I deny that this may be one element of the pleasure which we derive from the esteem of others. Dr.

Brown, in his analysis of the principle under consideration, has very justly included this among the components of the pleasure thus derived. But it by no means accounts for the origin, nor explains the nature, of this desire. It is rather an incidental circumstance than the producing cause.

This Principle as it relates to the Future. — Perhaps in no one of its aspects is the desire of esteem more remarkable, than when it relates to the future — the desire to leave a good name behind us, when we are no longer concerned with the affairs of time. It would seem as if the good or ill opinion of men would be of no moment whatever to us, when once we have taken our final departure from the stage of life. We pass to a higher tribunal, and the verdict of approving or reproving millions, the applause of nations, the condemnation of a world in arms against us, will hardly break the silence or disturb the deep repose of the tomb. These approving and condemning voices will die away in the distance, or be heard but as the faint echo of the wave that lashes some far-off shore.

Yet, though the honors that may then await our names will be of as little moment to us, personally, as the perishing garlands that the hand of affection may place upon our tombs, we still desire to leave a name unsullied at least, if not distinguished, even as we desire to live in the memory and affections of those who survive us.

How to be explained. — To what, then, can be owing this desire of the good opinion and esteem of those who are to come after us, and whose opinion, be it good or ill, can in no way affect our happiness? Philosophers have been sadly at a loss to account for it, especially those who trace the desire of esteem to a selfish origin. Some, with Wollaston and Smith, have referred it to the illusions of the imagination, by which we seem, to ourselves, to be present, and to witness the honors, and listen to the praises, which the future is to bestow. Such an illusion may possibly arise in some hour of reverie, some day-dream of the mind; but it is impossible to suppose that any one of sound mind should be permanently influenced by such an illusion, or fail to perceive, when reason resumes her sway, that it *is* an illusion, and that only.

Admits of Explanation in another Way. — If, however we regard the desire of the good opinion of others as an original principle of our nature, and not as springing from selfish considerations, it is easy to see how the same principle may extend to the future. If, irrespective of personal advantage, we desire the esteem of our fellow-men while we live, so, also, without regard to such advantage, we may desire their good opinion when we are no longer among them.

True, it is only a name that is transmitted and honored, as Wollaston says, and not the man himself. *He* does not live because his *name* does, nor is *he* known because his name is known. As in those lines of Cowley, quoted by Stewart:

"'Tis true the two immortal syllables remain;
But, O! ye learned men, explain
What essence, substance, what hypostasis
In five poor letters is?
In these alone does the great Cæsar live —
'Tis all the conquered world could give."

Yet reason as we may, it is no trait of a noble and ingenuous mind to be regardless of the opinions of the future. The common sentiment of men, even the wisest and the best, finds itself, after all, much more influenced by such considerations than by any reasoning to the contrary.

Not unworthy of a noble Mind. — Nor is it altogether unworthy of the ambition of a noble and generous mind to leave a good name as a legacy to the future; in the language of Mr. Stewart, "to be able to entail on the casual combination of letters which compose our name, the respect of distant ages, and the blessings of generations yet unborn. Nor is it an unworthy object of the most rational benevolence to render these letters a sort of magical spell for kindling the emulation of the wise and good whenever they shall reach the human ear."

Desire of Esteem not a safe Rule of Conduct. — I would by no means be understood, however, to present the desire of esteem as, on the whole, a safe and suitable rule of conduct, or to justify that inordinate ambition which too frequently seeks distinction regardless of the means by which it is acquired, or of any useful end to be accomplished. The mere love of fame is by no means the highest principle of action by which man is guided — by no means the noblest or the safest. It is ever liable to abuse. Its tendencies are questionable. The man who has no higher principle than a regard to the opinions of others is not likely to accomplish any thing great or noble. He will lack that prime element of greatness, *consistency* of character and purpose. His conduct and his principles will vary to suit the changing aspect of the times. He will, almost of necessity, also lack firmness and strength of character. It is necessary, sometimes, for the wise and good man to resist the force and pressure of public opinion. He must do that, or abandon his principles, and prove false at once to duty, and to himself. To do this costs much. It requires, and, at the same time, imparts, true strength. Such strength comes in no other way. That mind is essentially weak that depends for its point of support on the applause of man. In the noble language of Cicero, "To me, indeed, those actions seem all the more praiseworthy which we perform without regard to public favor, and without observation of man. The true theatre for virtue is conscience; there is none greater." The praise of man confers no solid happiness, unless it is felt to be deserved; and if it *be* so, that very consciousness is sufficient.

Disregard of public Opinion equally unsafe. — It must be confessed, however, that if a regard to the opinions of others is not to be adopted as a wise and safe rule of conduct, an entire disregard of public opinion is, on the other hand, a mark neither of a well ordered mind, nor of a virtuous character. "Contempta fama," says Tacitus, "contemnantur virtutes."

Accordingly we find that those who, from any cause, have lost their character and standing in society, and forfeited the good opinion of their fellow-men, are apt to become desperate and reckless, and ready for any crime.

CHAPTER IV.

HOPE AND FEAR.

Nature of these Emotions.—In the analysis of the sensibilities, which was given in a preceding chapter, *hope and fear* were classed as modifications of *desire and aversion*, having reference to the probability that the object which is desired or feared may be realized. Desire always relates to something in the future, and something that is agreeable, or viewed as such, and also something possible, or that is so regarded. Add to this future agreeable something the idea or element of *probability*, let it be not only something possible to be attained, but not unlikely to be, and what was before but mere desire, more or less earnest, now becomes *hope*, more or less definite or strong, according as the object is more or less desirable, and more or less likely to be realized. And the same is true of fear; an emotion awakened in view of any object regarded as disagreeable, in the future, and as more or less likely to be met.

As desire and aversion do not necessarily relate to different objects, but are simply counterparts of each other, the desire of any good implying always an aversion to its loss, so, also, hope and fear may both be awakened by the same object, according as the gaining or losing of the object becomes the more probable. What we hope to gain we fear to lose. What we fear to meet, we hope to escape.

The Strength of the Feeling dependent, in part, on the Importance of the Object. — The *degree* of the emotion, however, in either case, the readiness with which it is awakened, and the force and liveliness with which it affects the mind, are not altogether in proportion to the probability merely that the thing will, or will not, be as we hope or fear, but somewhat in proportion, also, to the importance of the object itself. That which is quite essential to our happiness is more ardently desired, than what is of much less consequence, though, perhaps, much more likely to be attained; and because it is more important and desirable, even a slight prospect of its attainment, or a slight reason to apprehend its loss, more readily awakens our hopes, and our fears, and more deeply impresses and agitates the mind, than even a much stronger probability would do in cases of less importance. What we very much desire, we are inclined to hope for, what we are strongly averse to, we are readily disposed to fear. Nothing is more desirable to the victim of disease than recovery, and hence his hope and almost confident expectation that he shall recover, when, perhaps, to every eye but his own, the case is hopeless. Nothing could be more dreadful to the miser than the loss of his treasure, and nothing, accordingly, does he so much fear. Poverty would be to him the greatest of possible calamities, and of this, accordingly, he lives in constant apprehension. Yet nothing is really more unlikely to occur. It is the tendency of the mind, in such cases, to magnify both the danger of the evil, on the one hand, and the prospect of good on the other.

Illustration from the case of a Traveller. — "There can be no question," says Dr. Brown, "that he who travels in the same carriage, with the same external appearances of every kind, by which a robber could be tempted or terrified, will be in equal danger of attack, whether he carry with him little of which he can be plundered, or such a booty as would impoverish him if it were lost. But there can be no question, also, that though the probabilities of danger be the same, the fear of attack would, in these two cases, be very different; that, in the one case, he would laugh at the ridiculous terror of any one who journeyed with him, and expressed much alarm at the approach of evening; — and that, in the other case, his own eye would watch, suspiciously, every horseman who approached, and would feel a sort of relief when he observed him pass carelessly and quietly along, at a considerable distance behind."

Uneasiness attending the sudden Acquisition of Wealth. — This tendency of the imagination to exaggerate the real, and conjure up a thousand unreal dangers, when any thing of peculiar value is in possession, which it is certainly possible, and it may be slightly probable, that we may lose, may, perhaps, account for the uneasiness, amounting often to extreme anxiety, that frequently accompanies the sudden acquisition of wealth. The poor cobbler, at his last, is a merry man, whistling at his work, from morning till night. Bequeath him a fortune, and he quits at once his last and his music; he is no longer the light-hearted man that he was; his step is cautious, his look anxious and suspicious; he grows care-worn and old. He that was never so happy in his life as when a poor man, now dreads nothing so much as poverty. While he was poor, there was nothing to fear, but every thing to hope, from the future; now that he is rich, there is nothing further to hope, but much to fear, since if the future brings any change in his condition, as it is not unlikely to do, it will, in all probability, be a change, not from wealth to still greater wealth, but from present affluence to his former penury.

The Pleasure of Hope surpasses the Pleasure of Reality. — It will, doubtless, be found generally true, that the pleasure of hope surpasses the pleasure derived from the realization of the object wished and hoped for. The imagination invests with ideal excellence the good that is still future, and when the hour of possession and enjoyment comes, the reality does not fully answer the expectation. Or, as in the case, already supposed, of the acquisition of wealth, there come along with the desired and expected treasure, a thousand cares and anxieties that were not anticipated, and that go far to diminish the enjoyment of the acquisition. From these, and other causes, it happens, I believe, not unfrequently, that those enjoy the most, who have really the least, whether of wealth, or of any other good which the mind naturally desires as a means of happiness; nor can we fail to see in this a beautiful provision of divine benevolence for the happiness of the great human family.

Influence on the Mind.—The influence of hope, upon the human mind, is universally felt, and recognized, as one of the most powerful and permanent of those varied influences, and laws of being, that make us what we are. It is limited to no period of life, no clime and country, no age of the world, no condition of society, or of individual fortune. It cheers us, alike, in the childhood of our being, in the maturity of our riper years, and in the second childhood of advancing age. There is no good which it cannot promise, no evil for which it cannot suggest a remedy and a way of escape, no sorrow which it cannot assuage. It is strength to the weary, courage to the desponding, life to the dying, joy to the desolate. It lingers with gentle step about the couch of the suffering, when human skill can do no more; and, upon the tombs of those whose departure we mourn, it hangs the unfading garland of a blessed immortality.

> "Angel of life! thy glittering wings explore
> Earth's loveliest bounds, and ocean's widest shore."

The same poet who sang so well the pleasures of hope, has depicted the influence of this emotion, on the mind which some great calamity has bereft of reason.

> "Hark, the wild maniac sings to chide the gale
> That wafts so slow her lover's distant sail;
> * * * * * *

Oft when yon moon has climbed the midnight sky
And the lone sea-bird wakes its wildest cry,
Piled on the steep, her blazing fagots burn
To hail the bark that never can return;
And still she waits, but scarce forbears to weep,
That constant love can linger on the deep."

It is, indeed, a touching incident, illustrative not more of the strength of this principle of our nature, than of the benevolence which framed our mental and moral constitution, that when, under the heavy pressure of earthly ills, reason deserts her empire, and leaves the throne of the human mind vacant, *Hope* still lingers to cheer even the poor maniac, and calmly takes her seat upon that vacant throne, even as the radiant angels sat upon the stone by the door of the empty sepulchre.

MENTAL PHILOSOPHY.

DIVISION THIRD.

THE WILL.

THE WILL

PRELIMINARY OBSERVATIONS.

Leading Divisions. — In our analysis and distribution of the powers of the mind, they were divided into three generic classes, viz., Intellect, Sensibility, and Will. Of these, the two former have been discussed in the preceding pages; it now remains to enter upon the examination of the third.

Importance and Difficulty of this Department. — This is, in many respects, at once the most important and the most difficult of the three. Its difficulty becomes apparent when we consider what questions arise respecting this power of the mind, and what diverse and conflicting views have been entertained, not among philosophers only, but among all classes of men, and in all ages of the world, concerning these matters. Its importance is evident from the relation which this faculty sustains to the other powers of the mind, and from its direct and intimate connection with some of the most practical and personal duties of life. Whatever control we have over ourselves, whether as regards the bodily or the mental powers, whatever use and disposition it is in our power to make of the intellectual faculties with which we are endowed, and of the sensibilities which accompany or give rise to those intellectual activities, and of the physical organization which obeys the behests of the sovereign mind, whatever separates and distinguishes us from the mere inanimate and mechanical forces of nature on the one hand, or the blind impulses of irrational brute instinct on the other; for all this, be it more or less, we are indebted to that faculty which we call the Will. And hence it happens that in this, as in many other cases, the most abstract questions of philosophy become the most practical and important questions of life. In every system of mental philosophy the Will holds a cardinal place. The system can no more be complete without it, than a steamship without the engines that are to propel her. As is the view taken of the Will, such is essentially the system.

Relation to Theology. — Nor is it to be overlooked that the doctrine of the Will is a cardinal doctrine of theology, as well as of psychology. Inasmuch as it has a direct and practical bearing upon the formation of character, and upon the moral and religious duties of life, it comes properly within the sphere of that science which treats of these duties, and of man's relation to his Maker. Hence every system of theology has to do with the Will; and according to the view taken of this faculty, such essentially is the system. If in psychology, still more in theology, is this the stand-point of the science.

Not, therefore, to be treated as a theological Doctrine. — Not, however, on this account, is the matter to be treated as theological and not strictly psychological. It is a matter which pertains properly and purely to psychology. It is for that science which treats of the laws and powers of the human mind to unfold and explain the activity of this most important of all the mental faculties. To this science theology must come for her data, so far as she has occasion to refer to the phenomena of the Will. The same may be said f ethical, as well as of theological science. In so far as they are concerned with the moral powers, and with the human will, they must both depend on psychology. Withn her proper sphere they stand, not as teachers, but as learners.

The more Care requisite on this Account. — For this reason all the more care is necessary, in the study and ex planation of the present theme. An error in this part of the investigation is likely to extend beyond the bounds of the science itself, into other and kindred sciences. The most serious consequences may flow from it, in other and wider fields of thought.

Sources of Information.—The sources of our information are essentially the same in this as in the preceding divisions of the science. They are twofold; the consciousness of what passes in our own minds, and the observation of others. Our single business is to ascertain facts, actua phenomena; not to inquire what might be, or what *ought* to be, according to preconceived notions and theories, but what *is*. This is to be learned, not by reasoning and logical argument, but by simple observation of phenomena. Having once ascertained these, we may infer, and conclude, and reason from them, as far as we please, and our conclusions will be correct, provided the data are correct from which we set forth, and provided we reason correctly from these principles.

Method to be pursued. — In treating of this department of mental activity, it will be our first business, then, to point out the well established and evident facts pertaining to the matter in hand, viewed simply as psychological phenomena, as modes in which the human mind manifests itself in action, according to the laws of its constitution. These being ascertained, we shall be prepared to consider some of the more difficult and doubtful matters respecting the will, on which the world has long been divided, and which can never be intelligently discussed, much less settled, without a clear understanding, in the first place, of the psychological facts in the case, about which there need be, and should be, no dispute.

CHAPTER I.

NATURE OF THE WILL.

What the Will is. — I understand, by the will, that power which the mind has of determining or deciding what it will do, and of putting forth volitions accordingly. The will is the *power* of doing this; willing, is the exercise of the power; volition, is the deed, the thing done. The will is but another name for the executive power of the mind. Whatever we do intelligently and intentionally, whether it implies an exercise of the intellect, or of the feelings, or of both, that is an act of the will. All our voluntary, in distinction from our involuntary movements of the body, and movements of mind, are the immediate results of the activity of the Will.

Condition of a Being destitute of Will. — We can, perhaps, conceive of a being endowed with intellect and sensibility, but without the faculty of will. Such a being, however superior he might be to the brutes in point of intelligence, would, so far as regards the capacities of action, be even their inferior, since his actions must be, as theirs, the result of mere sensational impulse, without even that unerring instinct to guide him, which the brute possesses, and which supplies the place of reason and intelligent will. To this wretched condition man virtually approximates when, by any means, the will becomes so far enfeebled, or brought under the dominion of appetite and passion, as to lose the actual control of the mental and physical powers.

Will not distinct from the Mind. — It must be borne in mind, of course, as we proceed, that the will is nothing but the mind itself willing, or having power to will, and not something distinct from the mind, or even a *part* of the mind, as the handle and the blade are distinct parts of the knife. The power to think, the power to feel, the power to will, are distinct powers, but the mind is one and indivisible, exercising now one, now another, of these powers.

§ I. — Elements involved in an Act of Will.

Proposed Analysis. — In order to the better understanding of the nature of this faculty, let us first analyze its operations, with a view to ascertain the several distinct stages or elements of the mental process which takes place. We will then take up these several elements, one by one, for special investigation.

Observation of an Act of Will. — What, then, are the essential phenomena of an act of the will? Let us arrest ourselves in the process of putting forth an act of this kind, and observe precisely what it is that we do, and what are the essential data in the case. I am sitting at my table. I reach forth my hand to take a book. Here is an act of my will. My arm went not forth self-moved and spontaneously, it was sent, was bidden to go; the soul seated within, animating this physical organism, and making it subservient to her will, moved that arm. Here, then, is clearly an act of will. Let us subject it to the test of observation.

The first Element. — First of all, then, there was evidently, in this case, *something to be done* — an end to be accomplished — a book to be reached. The action, both of body and of mind, was directed to that end, and but for that the volition would not have been put forth. It is to be observed, moreover, that the end to be accomplished, in this case, was a *possible* one — the book was, or was supposed to be, within my reach. Otherwise I should not have attempted to reach it.

A second Element. — I observe, furthermore, in the case under consideration, a motive, impelling or inducing to that end; a *reason why* I willed the act. It was curiosity, perhaps, to see what the book was, or it may have been some other principle of my nature, which induced me to put forth the volition.

A further Step in the Process. — But the motive does not, itself, produce the act. It is merely the *reason why* I produce it. It has to do not directly with the action, but with me. Its immediate effect terminates on me, and it is only indirectly that it affects the final act. The next step in the process, then, is to be sought, not in the final act, but in my mind as influenced by motive; and that step is my *choice.* Previous to my putting forth the volition to move my arm, there was a choice or decision to do so. In view of the end to be accomplished, and influenced by the motive, I *made up my mind* — to use a common but not inapt expression — to perform the act. The question arose, for the instant, Shall I do it? The very occurrence of a thing to be done, a possible thing, and of a motive for doing it, raises, of itself, the question, Shall it be done? The question may be at once decided in the affirmative, in the absence of reasons to the contrary, or, in the absence of reflection, so quickly decided, that, afterward, we shall hardly be conscious that it was ever before the mind. Or it may be otherwise. Reasons to the contrary suggest themselves — counter influences and motives — in view of which we hesitate, deliberate, decide; and that decision, in view of all the circumstances, is our *preference*, or *choice.* In most cases the process is so rapid as to escape attention; but subsequent reflection can hardly fail to detect such a process, more or less distinctly marked.

The final Stage of the Act. — We have reached now the point at which it is decided, in our own minds, what course to pursue. In the case supposed, I have decided to take up the book. The volition is not yet put forth. Nothing now remains, however, but to put forth the volition, and at once the muscular organism, if unimpeded and in health, obeys the will. The thing is done, and the experiment concluded.

Summary of Results. — I repeat now the experiment ten or a hundred times, but always with like results. I find always, where there is an act of the will, some end to be obtained, some motive, a choice, an executive volition. I conclude that these are the essential phenomena of all voluntary action.

Of these, the two former, viz., the end to be accomplished, and the motive, may be regarded as more properly *conditions* of volition, than constituent elements of it. Still, so intimately is the volition connected with one, at least, of these conditions, viz., the motive, that it claims special consideration. The ends to be accomplished by volition are as numerous as the infinite variety of human purposes and actions, and, of course, admit of no complete enumeration or classification. We confine our further attention, then, to these elements — the motive, the choice, the executive volition — and proceed to their more careful investigation as phenomena of the will.

§ II. — Investigation of these Elements.

The first of these Elements, Motive, always implied in Action. — I. The Motive — that which incites the mind to action — the reason why it acts, and acts as it does. We never act without some such incitement, some reason for acting; at least this is true of all our intelligent and voluntary actions, of which, alone, we now speak. It may be nothing more than mere present impulse, mere animal appetite or passion; even that is a motive, a reason why we act. We cannot conceive of any being having the power of voluntary action, and exerting that power without *any reason whatever* why he did it. The reason may, or may not, be clearly apprehended by his own mind — that is another question; but whether distinctly and clearly recognized as such, or not, by our own minds, a reason there always is for what we do.

In what Sense this Term employed.—Strictly speaking, the motive is not any and every influence which may bear upon the mind as an inducement to action, but only the *prevailing* inducement, that which *actually moves* or induces us to perform the proposed act. In this sense, there may be many different inducements, but only one motive. Such, however, is not the ordinary use of the term. That is usually called a motive which is of a nature to influence the mind, and induce volition, whether it is, in the given case, effective, or not. To avoid confusion, I adopt the general use.

Nature of Motives.—As to the nature of the motives from which we act, they are manifestly of two kinds, and widely distinct. There is desire, and there is the sense of moral obligation or duty;—the agreeable, and the right; each of these constitutes a powerful motive to action. We find ourselves, under the influence of these motives, acting, now from desire, now from sense of duty, now in view of what is in itself agreeable, and now in view of what is right; and the various motives which influence us and result in action, may be resolved into one or the other of these powerful elements.

These Elements distinguished.—These are quite *distinct* elements, never to be confounded with, nor resolved into each other. *Desire* is the feeling which arises in view of some good not in present possession, something agreeable, and to be obtained; it looks forward to that; its root and spring is that grand principle of our nature, the love of happiness. Its appeal is to that. Its strength lies in that. *Duty*, as we have already shown—that sense of obligation which is implied in the very idea of *right*—is quite another principle than that, not founded in that; springs not from self-love, or the desire of happiness; is, on the contrary, a simple, primitive, fundamental idea of the human mind, based in the inherent, essential, eternal nature of things. Given the right, the perception of right, and there is given, also along with it, the sense of *obligation.*

Their Action not always in Unison. — These two motives may act in different directions; they frequently do so. Desire impels me one way, duty another. Conflict then arises. Which shall prevail, desire or duty, depends on circumstances, on my character already formed, my habits of thought and feeling, my degree of self-control, my conscientiousness, the strength of my native propensities, the clearness with which, at the time, I apprehend the different courses of conduct proposed, their character and their consequences. Desire may prevail, and then I go counter to my sense of obligation. Remorse follows. I am wretched. I suffer penalty. Duty prevails, and I do that which I believe to be right, regardless of consequences. I suffer in property, health, life, external good, but am sustained by that approving voice within, which more than compensates for all such losses.

That there are these two springs or motives of human action, and that they are *distinct* from each other, is what I affirm, and what no one, I think, who reflects on what consciousness reveals, will be disposed to deny.

Motives of Duty not resolvable into Motives of Interest. — Should any still contend that this very approval of conscience, this peace and happiness which result from doing right, are, themselves, the motive to action, in the case supposed, and so, self-love, a desire of happiness, is, after all, the *only motive*, I reply, this is an assumption utterly without proof. Consciousness contradicts it. The history of the human race contradicts it. There is such a thing as doing right for its own sake, irrespective of good to ourselves. Every man is conscious of such distinction, and of its force as a motive of conduct. Every *virtuous* man is conscious of acting, at times, at least, from such a motive.

Coincidence of Desire and Duty. — It is only when desire and duty coincide, that the highest happiness can be reached, when we no longer desire and long for, because we no longer view as agreeable, that which is not strictly right.

This is a state never fully realized in this life. It implies perfection of character, and a perfect world.

Desires, as Motives of Action, further distinguished.—Desire, and the feeling of obligation, I have spoken of as motives of conduct. The former, again, is not always of one sort. Desire is, indeed, in itself, a simple element, springing from one source, but not always directed to the same object. We desire now one thing, now another. There are two classes, at least, of desires quite easy to be distinguished, the physical and the psychical, the one relating to the wants of the body, the other to the craving of the higher nature; the mere animal instincts, propensities, passions, looking to animal gratification; and the higher rational self-love, which seeks the true and permanent well-being, under the guidance of reason. Each of these furnishes a powerful motive, or class of motives, to human action. They are each, however, but different forms of *desire.*

The second Element, Choice, always involved in Volition. — II. CHOICE. — This is an essential element in volition, and next in order. As, setting aside such acts as are purely spontaneous and mechanical, we never, intelligently and purposely, do any thing without a volition to do it, so we never put forth volition without exercising *choice.* The act performed is not a *voluntary* act, unless it is something which I *choose* to do. True, my choice may be influenced by extraneous causes — may even be constrained — circumstances may virtually compel me to choose as I do, by shutting me up to this one course, as being either the only right, or the only desirable course. And these circumstances, that thus influence my decisions, may be essentially beyond my control, as they not unfrequently are. Yet, all things considered, it is my *choice* to do thus and not otherwise, and so long as I do choose, and am free to act accordingly, the act is voluntary.

The Position illustrated. — This may be illustrated by the case of the soldier who, in the bombardment of his native city, is ordered to point his piece in the direction of his own dwelling. To disobey, is death. To obey, is to put in jeopardy those who are dear to him. He hesitates, but finally chooses to obey orders. He aims his piece as directed, sadly against his inclination; yet, on the whole, it is his *choice* to do it. He prefers that to the certainty of dishonorable death, a death which would in no way benefit or protect those whom he wishes to save. A man, of his own accord, lies down upon the surgeon's operating table, and stretches out his arm to the knife. It is his choice — a hard choice, indeed, but, nevertheless, decidedly his choice. He prefers that to still greater suffering, or even death. In these cases — and they are only instances and illustrations of what, in a less marked and decided way, is continually occurring — we see the utmost strain and pressure of circumstances upon a man's choice, making it morally certain that he will decide as he does, shutting him up to that decision, in fact, yet his choice remaining unimpaired, and his act a *free* act; free, because he does as he, on the whole, and under the circumstances, chooses to do. He does the thing voluntarily.

Another Case supposed. — Suppose, now, the man were forcibly seized, and borne by sheer strength to the table, and placed upon it, and held there while the operation was performed. In that case, he no longer acts, is only acted upon, no longer chooses and wills to go there, nay, chooses and wills directly the contrary. The difference in the two cases, is the difference between a voluntary act, chosen reluctantly, indeed, and under the pressure of an exigency, but still *chosen*, and the passive suffering of an action which, so far from being voluntary, was, in no sense, an act of his own.

Choice always influenced by Circumstances. — Now, as regards the actual operation of things, our choices are, in fact, always influenced by circumstances, and these circumstances are various and innumerable; a thousand seen and unseen influences are at work upon us, to affect our decisions.

Were it possible to estimate aright all these influences, to calculate, with precision, their exact weight and effect, then our choice, under any given circumstances, might be predicted with unerring certainty. This can never be exactly known to man. Sagacity may approximate to it, and may, so far, be able to read the future, and predict the probable conduct of men in given circumstances. To the omniscient, these things *are* fully known, and to his eye, therefore, the whole future of our lives, our free choices and voluntary acts, lie open before they are yet known to ourselves.

Conclusion stated. — From what has been said, it appears that it is not inconsistent with the nature of choice, to be influenced, nay, decided by circumstances, even when those circumstances are beyond our control.

Diversity of Objects essential to Choice.—What is *implied* in an act of choice? Several things. In order to choice, there must, of course, be *diversity of objects* from which to choose. If there were but one possible course to be pursued, it were absurd to speak of choice. Hence, even in the cases just now supposed, there was a diversity of objects from which to choose — death, or obedience to orders, suffering from the surgery, or greater suffering and danger without it, and between these the man made his choice.

Liberty of Selection also essential. — As a further condition of choice, there is implied *liberty* of selection from among the different objects proposed. It were of no use that there should be different courses of conduct — different ends, or different means of attaining an end — proposed to our understanding, if it were not in our power to select which we pleased, if we were not free to go which way we will. Choice always implies that different actions and volitions are possible, and are, as such, submitted to our decision and preference. There can be no volition without choice, and no choice without liberty to choose. Whatever interferes, then, with that liberty, and diminishes or takes it away, interferes, also, with my choice, and diminishes or destroys that. The very *essence* of a voluntary act consists in its being an act of choice, or a free-will act. No tyranny can take this away, except such as destroys, also, all voluntary and responsible action. You may command me to burn incense on a heathen altar. The very command leaves it optional with me whether to obey. If I do not, the penalty is death. Very well — I may *choose* the penalty, rather than the crime, and no power on earth can *compel* me to choose otherwise. I die, but I die a *free* man. True, you may bind me, and by mechanical force urge me to the altar, and by superior strength of other arms, may cause my hand to put incense there, but it is not *my* act then ; it is the act of those who use me as a mere passive instrument; it is no more my act, than it would be the act of so much iron, or wood, or other instrument.

Deliberation implied. — Choice, moreover, implies deliberation, the balancing and weighing of inducements, the comparison and estimate of the several goods proposed, the several ends and objects, the various means to those ends; the exercise of reason and judgment in this process. I see before me different courses, different ends proposed to my understanding, am conscious of diverse inducements and reasons, some urging me in one direction, some in another. Native propensities impel me toward this line of conduct. Rational self-love puts in a claim for quite another procedure. Benevolence, and a sense of duty, it may be, conspire to urge me in still another direction. I am at liberty to choose. I must choose. I can go this way or that, must go in one or the other. I hesitate, deliberate, am at a loss.

Now there is no choice which does not virtually involve some process of this kind. It may be very rapid; so rapid as to escape detection, in many cases, so that we are hardly conscious of the process. In other cases, we are painfully conscious of the whole scene; we hesitate long, are in doubt and suspense between conflicting motives and interests. Desire and duty wage a fierce contest within us. Shall we choose the agreeable? Shall we choose the right? And then, again, which is really the agreeable, and which is truly the right?

Final Decision. — As the result of this deliberation, we finally decide, one way, or the other. This decision is our *preference*, our choice. Our minds, as we say, are made up what to do, what course to pursue. When the time comes, we shall act. Something may prevent our having our way, opportunity may not offer, or we may see fit, subsequently, to reconsider and revoke our decision. Otherwise, our choice is carried out in action.

Choice implies, then, these things: diversity of objects, liberty of selection, deliberation, decision, or preference.

The final Element. — III. Executive Volition. — In our investigation of the several elements or momenta of an act of the Will, we have as yet considered but two, viz., *motive* and *choice* — the first, more properly a *condition* of voluntary action, than itself a constituent part of it, yet still, a condition so indispensably connected with volition, as to require investigation in connection with the latter. It only remains now to notice the last stage of the process, the final element, which added, the process is complete — that is, the *executive act of the mind*, *volition* properly so called. When the objects to be attained have been presented, when the motives or inducements to action have been considered, when, in view of all, the choice or preference has been made, it still remains to put forth the volition, or the act will not be performed. This may never happen. Opportunity may never offer. But suppose it does. We *will*. This done, the bodily mechanism springs into play, obedient to the call and command of the soul.

Even now, the action does not of necessity correspond to the volition. Even now, we may be disappointed. Other wills may be in action in opposition to ours. Other arms may move in obedience to those other wills. Or we may find the thing too much for us to do, impracticable, beyond our strength and means, or disease may palsy the frame, so that it shall not obey the mandate of the spirit. Nevertheless the *volition* is complete. That depends not on the success of the exertion. We have *willed*, and with that our mental action ceases. What remains is physical, not psychological. If we succeed, if the volition finds itself answered in execution, then, also, the act once performed is thenceforth out of our power. It is done, and stands a permanent historic event, beyond our control, beyond our decision or revocation. Our power over it ceases in the moment of volition. Our connection with it may never cease. It moves on in its inevitable career of consequences, and, like a swift river, bears us along with it. We have no more to do with it, but it has to do with us; it may be to our sorrow, it may be, forever.

Such are, in brief, the main psychological facts, relating to the will, as they offer themselves to our consciousness and careful inspection.

CHAPTER II.

RELATION OF THE WILL TO OTHER POWERS OF THE MIND.

Activity of the Intellect in Volition. — It is a matter of some importance to ascertain the relation which the will sustains to the other mental powers. There can be no doubt that the activity of the will is preceded, in all cases by that of the intellect. I must first perceive some object presented to my understanding, before I can will its attainment. In the case already supposed, the book lying on my table is an object within the cognizance of sense, and to perceive it is an act of intellect. Until perceived, the will puts not forth any volition respecting it. Nor does the mere perception occasion volition. In connection with the perception of the book, ideas present themselves to the mind, curiosity is awakened, the mind is set upon a train of thought, which results in the desire and the volition to take the book. In all this the intellect is active. In a word, whatever comes in as a motive to influence the mind in favor of, or against a given course, must in the first instance address itself to the understanding, and be comprehended by that power, before it can influence the mental decisions. A motive which I do not comprehend is no motive; a reason which I do not perceive, or understand, is, to me, no reason.

Activity of the Sensibilities also involved. — But does volition immediately follow the action of the intellect in the case supposed? Do we first understand, and then will; or does something else intervene between the intellectual perception and the volition? Were there no *feeling* awakened by the intellectual perception, would there be any volition with regard to the object perceived? I think, I *feel*, I will; is not that the order of the mental processes? "We can easily imagine," says Mackintosh, "a percipient and thinking being without a capacity of receiving pleasure or pain. Such a being might perceive what we do; if we could conceive him to reason, he might reason justly; and if he were to judge at all, there seems no reason why he should not judge truly. But what could induce such a being to *will* or to *act?* It seems evident that his existence could only be a state of passive contemplation. Reason, as reason, can never be a motive to action. It is only when we superadd to such a being sensibility, or the capacity of emotion, or sentiment of desire and aversion, that we introduce him into the world of action."

Opinion of Locke. — To the same effect, Locke: "Good and evil, present and absent, it is true, work upon the mind, but that which immediately determines the will from time to time, to every voluntary action, is the uneasiness of *desire*, fixed on some absent good, either negative, as indolence to one in pain, or positive, as enjoyment of pleasure. That it is this uneasiness that determines the will to the successive voluntary actions, whereof the greatest part of our lives is made up, and by which we are conducted through different courses to different ends, I shall endeavor to show both from experience and the reason of the thing." Elsewhere again: "For good, though appearing and allowed ever so great, yet till it has raised desires in our minds, and thereby made us uneasy in its want, it reaches not our wills; we are not within the sphere of its activity."

Testimony of Consciousness. — The general opinion of philosophical writers is now in accordance with the views thus expressed. The intellect they regard as acting upon the will not directly, but through the medium of the sensibilities, the various emotions and desires which are awakened by the perceptions of the intellect. That this is the correct view, admits of little doubt. The question is best settled by an appeal to consciousness. In the case supposed, the perception of the book upon the table does not, of itself, directly influence my will. It is not until some feeling is aroused, my curiosity excited, or desire, in some form, awakened, that my will acts. The object must not only be perceived, but perceived as agreeable, and the wish to possess it be entertained, before the volition is put forth.

Whether this Rule applies in all Cases. — That this is so as regards a large class of our volitions, will hardly be denied. When the motive to action is of the nature of *desire*, it is the sensibility, and not the intellect, that is directly, concerned in shaping the action of the will. I first perceive the object to be agreeable; I next desire its possession, as such; then I will its attainment. The intellectual activity gives rise to emotion, and the latter leads to volition.

It may be supposed, however, that when the motive which influences the will is not of the nature of desire, but rather of a sense of obligation or duty, then the case is otherwise, the intellectual perception of the right, and of the obligation to do the right, being sufficient of themselves to lead the mind to action. But as the intellectual perception of the agreeable is followed by emotion or desire in view of the same, so the intellectual perception of the right is followed, in like manner, by a certain class of feelings or emotions, usually called moral sensibilities; and it is the *feeling*, in either case, and not the *knowing*, the sensibility, and not the intellect, that is directly in contact with the will. I know that I ought, and I feel that I ought, are states of mind closely connected, indeed, but not identical; and it is the latter which leads directly to volition.

Desire and Volition not always distinguished. — Another point requiring investigation, is the precise relation between volition and *desire*. Are they the same thing, and if not, wherein do they differ? It has been the custom of certain writers not to distinguish between desire and volition, as states of mind, or to regard them as differing, if at all, only in degree. Thus Condillac, and writers of the French school, as also Brown, Mill, and others, in Great Britain, have treated of volition as only a stronger degree of desire, which, again, is only a form of emotion. Even M'Cosh, in his treatise on moral government, while insisting on the distinction between emotions and desires, regards wishes, desires, and volitions, as belonging essentially to the same class of mental states. "Appealing to consciousness," says that able and elegant writer, "we assert that there is a class of mental states embracing wishes, desires, volitions, which cannot be analyzed into anything else. These mental states or affections are very numerous, and occupy a place in the human mind second to no other. They differ from each other in degree, and possibly even in some minor qualities, but they all agree in other and more important respects, and so are capable of being arranged under one head." And in a subsequent paragraph he remarks to the same effect, "Later mental inquirers are generally disposed to admit that the volition the positive determination to take a particular step, the resolution, for instance, to give a sum of money to take our friend to a warmer climate for the restoration of his health, is more than a mere emotion. But if we are thus to constitute a separate attribute to which to refer volition, it is worthy of being inquired whether we should not arrange, under the same head, wishes, desires, and the cognate states, as being more closely allied in their nature to volitions than to the common emotions."

The Difference generic. — It is on this latter point that we are compelled to join issue with the writer just quoted. A wish, a desire, are forms of *feeling;* a volition is not. The difference is generic, and not one of degree merely. A desire differs from any other form of feeling, not so much, not so radically, as it differs from a volition. A wish or desire may *lead* to volition, or it may not. We often wish or desire what we do not will. The object of our desires may not be within the sphere of our volitions, may not be possible of attainment, may not depend, in any sense, upon our wills. Or it may be something which reason and the law of right forbid, yet, nevertheless, an object of natural desire. And so, on the other hand, we may, from a sense of duty, or from the dictates of reason and prudence, will what is contrary to our natural inclinations, and our volitions, so fai from representing our desires, in that case, may be directly contrary to them.

Opinion of Reid. — Accordant with the view now expressed, are the following remarks of Dr. Reid: "With regard to our actions, we may desire what we do not will, and will what we do not desire, nay, what we have a great aversion to. A man a-thirst has a strong desire to drink, but, for some particular reason, he determines not to gratify his desire. A judge, from a regard to justice and the duty of his office, dooms a criminal to die, while, from humanity and particular affection, he desires that he should live. A man, for health, may take a nauseous draught for which he has no desire, but a great aversion. Desire, therefore, even when its object is some action of our own, is only an excitement to the will, but is not volition. The determination of the mind may be not to do what we desire to do."

Opinion of Locke. — To the same effect is the following from Locke: "This caution, of being careful not to be misled by expressions that do not enough keep up the difference between the *will* and several acts of the mind that are quite distinct from it, I think the more necessary, because I find the will often confounded with several of the affections, especially *desire*, and one put for the other, and that by men who would not willingly be thought not to have had very distinct notions of things, and not to have writ very clearly about them. This, I imagine, has been no small occasion of obscurity and mistake in this matter; and therefore is, as much as may be, to be avoided. For, he that shall turn his thoughts inward upon what passes in his mind when he *wills*, shall see that the *will* or power of *volition* is conversant about nothing, but that particular determination of the mind, whereby, barely by a thought, the mind endeavors to give rise, continuation, or stop to any action which it takes to be in its power. This well considered, plainly shows that the *will* is perfectly distinguished from *desire*, which, in the very same action may have quite a contrary tendency from that which our will sets us upon. A man whom I cannot deny, may oblige me to use persuasions to another, which, at the same time I am speaking, I may wish may not prevail on him. In this case, it is plain, the *will* and *desire* run counter. I will the action that tends one way, while my desire tends another, and that right contrary. Whence it is evident," he adds, "that *desiring* and *willing* are two distinct acts of the mind; and, consequently, that the *will*, which is but the power of *volition*, is much more distinct from *desire*."

Testimony of Consciousness. — The testimony of consciousness seems to be clearly in accordance with the views now expressed. We readily distinguish between our desires and our volitions. We are conscious of willing, often, what is contrary to our desires; the course which honor and duty approve, and which we resolutely carry out, is in disregard of many fond and cherished desires which still agitate the bosom. And even when our desires and volitions coincide, it requires but little reflection to discover the difference between them. It is a difference recognized in the common language of life, and in the writings and conversation of men who are by no means theorists or metaphysicians.

Further Illustrations of the Distinction.—Mr. Upham, who has very clearly and ably maintained the distinction now in question, refers us, in illustration, to the case of Abraham offering his son upon the altar of sacrifice, sternly, resolutely willing, in obedience to the divine command, what must have been repugnant to every feeling of the father's heart; to the memorable instance of Brutus ordering and witnessing the execution of his own sons, as conspirators against the State, the struggle between the strong will and the strong paternal feeling evidently visible in his countenance, as he stood at the dreadful scene; and the case of Virginius, plunging the knife into the bosom of a beloved daughter, whose dishonor could in no other way be averted. In all these, and many other similar cases, private interests and personal affections are freely and nobly sacrificed, in favor of high public interests, and moral ends; yet, to do this, the will must act in opposition to the current of natural feeling and desire.

CHAPTER III.

FREEDOM OF THE WILL.

Problems respecting the Will. — Our attention has thus far been directed to the psychological facts respecting the will, in itself considered, and also in its relations to the other mental powers. It becomes necessary now, in order to the more complete understanding of the matter, to look at some of the disputed points, the grand problems, respecting the human will, which have for ages excited and divided the reflecting world. The way is prepared for these more difficult questions, when once the simple facts, to which our attention has already been directed, are well understood. These questions are numerous, but, if I mistake not, they all resolve themselves virtually into the one general problem of the *freedom* of the will, or, at least, so link themselves with that as to admit of discussion in the same connection.

Freedom, what. — In approaching this much-disputed question, it is necessary to ascertain, in the first place, what is *meant* by freedom, and what by *freedom of the will*, else we may discuss the matter to no purpose. Various definitions of freedom have been given. It is a word in very common use, and, in its general application, not liable to be misunderstood. Every one who understands the ordinary language of life, knows well enough what freedom is. It denotes the opposite of restraint; the power to do what one likes, pleases, is inclined to do. My person is free, when it can come and go, do this or that, as suits my inclination Any faculty of the mind, or organ of the body, is free, *when its own specific and proper action is not hindered.* Freedom of motion, is power to move when and where we please.

Freedom of speech, is power to say what we like. Freedom of action, is power to do what we like.

Freedom of the Will, what. — What, then, is freedom of the *will?* What can it be but the power of exercising, without restraint or hindrance, its own specific and proper function, viz., the putting forth volitions, just such volitions as we please. This, as we have seen, is the proper office of the will, its specific and appropriate action. If nothing prevents or restrains me from forming and putting forth such volitions as I please, then my will is free; and not otherwise.

Freedom of the will, then, is *not* power to *do what one wills*, in the sense of executing volitions when formed; that is simple freedom of the limbs, and muscular apparatus, not of will — a freedom which may be destroyed by a stroke of paralysis, or an iron chain; — it is not a freedom of walking, if one wills to walk, or of singing, or flying, or moving the right arm, if one is so disposed. That is freedom, but not freedom of the *will.* My will is free, not when I can *do* what I *will* to do, but *when I can will to do* just what I please. Whatever freedom the will has, must lie within its own proper sphere of action, and not without it; must relate to that, and not to something else. This distinction, so very obvious, has, nevertheless, been sometimes strangely overlooked.

Is, then, the human will free, in the sense now defined? Let us first notice some presumptions in favor of its freedom; then the more direct argument.

§ I. — Presumptions in Favor of Freedom.

The general Conviction of Freedom a Presumption in its Favor. — 1. It is a presumption in favor of freedom that there is among men, a very general, not to say universal conviction of freedom. It is a prevalent idea, an established conviction and belief of the mind. We are conscious of this belief ourselves, we observe it in others. When we perform any act, or choose any course of conduct, we are impressed with the belief that we could have done or chosen differently, had we been so disposed. We never doubt or call in question this ability, in regard to the practical matters of life. The languages and the literature of the world bear witness to the universality of this belief. Now this general conviction and firm belief of freedom constitute, to say the least, a presumption, and a strong one, in favor of the doctrine. If men are free to do as they like, then they are free to *will* as they like, for the willing precedes the doing; and if they are not thus free, how happens this so general conviction of a freedom which they do not possess?

The Appeal to Consciousness. — The argument is sometimes stated, by the advocates of freedom, in a form which is liable to objection. The appeal is made directly to consciousness. We are *conscious*, it is said, of freedom, conscious of a power, when we do any thing, to do otherwise, to take some other course instead. Strictly speaking, we are conscious only of our present state of mind. I may *know* the past; but it is not a matter of consciousness; I may also know, perhaps, what *might have* been, in place of the actual past, but of this I am not conscious. When I experience a sensation, or put forth a volition, I am conscious of that sensation or volition; but I am not conscious of what never occurred, that is, of some other feeling or volition instead of an actual one. I may have a firm conviction, amounting even to knowledge, that at the moment of experiencing that feeling, or exercising that volition, it was possible for me to have exercised a different one; but it is a conviction, a belief, at most a knowledge, and not, properly, consciousness. I am conscious of the *conviction* that I am free, and that I can do otherwise than as I do; and this, in itself, is a presumption, that I have such a power; but I am not conscious of the power itself. It may be said, that if there were any restraint upon my will, to prevent my putting forth such volitions as I please, or to prevent my acting otherwise than

I do, I *should be* conscious of such restraint; and this may be very true; and from the absence of any such consciousness of restraint, I may justly infer that I am free; but this, again, is an *inference*, and not a *consciousness*. One thing, however, I am conscious of, that my *actual* volitions are such, and only such, as I please to put forth; and this leads to the conviction that it is in my power to put forth any volition that I may please.

Our moral Nature a Presumption in Favor of Freedom. — 2. It is a further presumption in favor of the entire freedom of the will, that man's moral nature seems to imply it. We approve or condemn the conduct of others. It is with the understanding that they acted freely, and could have done otherwise. We should never think of praising a man for doing what he could not help doing, or of blaming him for what it was utterly out of his power to avoid. So, also, we approve and condemn our own actions, and always with the understanding that these actions and volitions were free. There may be regret for that which was unavoidable, but never a sense of *guilt*, never *remorse*. The existence of these feelings always implies freedom of the will, the power to have done otherwise. Let any man select that period of his history, that act of his whole life, for which he blames himself most, and of which the recollection casts the deepest gloom and sadness over all his subsequent years, and let him ask himself why it is that he so blames himself for that course, and he will find, in every case, that it is because he knows that he might have done differently. Take away this conviction, and you take away the foundation of all his remorse, and of self-condemnation. The same thing is implied, also, in the feeling of obligation. It is impossible to feel under moral obligation to do what it is utterly and absolutely out of our power to do.

This View maintained by Mr. Upham. — "There are some truths," says Mr. Upham, "which are so deeply based in the human constitution, that all men of all classes receive them, and act upon them. They are planted deeply and immutably in the soul, and no reasoning, however plausible, can shake them. And, if we are not mistaken, the doctrine of the freedom of the will, as a condition of even the possibility of a moral nature, is one of these first truths. It seems to be regarded, by all persons, without any exception, as a dictate of common sense, and as a first principle of our nature, that men are morally accountable, and are the subjects of a moral responsibility in any respect, whatever, only so far as they possess freedom, both of the outward action, and of the will. They hold to this position, as an elementary truth, and would no sooner think of letting it go. than of abandoning the conviction of their personal existence and identity. They do not profess to go into particulars, but they assert it in the mass, that man is a moral being only so far as he is free. And such a unanimous and decided testimony, bearing, as it absolutely does, the seal and superscription of nature herself, is entitled to serious consideration."

Also by Dr. Reid. — Dr. Reid, also, takes essentially the same view. He regards it as a first principle, to be ranked in the same class with the conviction of our personal existence and identity, and the existence of a material world, "that we have some degree of power over our actions, and the determinations of our will." It is implied, he maintains, in every act of volition, in all deliberation, and in every resolution or purpose formed in consequence of deliberation. "It is not more evident," he says, "that mankind have a conviction of the existence of a material world, than that they have the conviction of some degree of power in themselves, and in others, every one over his own actions, and the determinations of his will — a conviction so early, so general, and so interwoven with the whole of human conduct, that it must be the natural effect of our constitution, and intended by the Author of our being to guide our actions."

Consequences of the Opposite. — 3. The consequences of the opposite view afford a presumption in favor of freedom.

If the will is not free, if all our liberty is merely a liberty to do what we will to do, or to execute the volitions which we form, but we have no power over the volitions themselves, then we have no power whatever to will or to act differently from what we do. This is *fatalism.* All that the fatalist maintains is, that we are governed by circumstances out of our own control, so that, situated as we are, it is impossible for us to act otherwise than as we do. From this follows, as a natural and inevitable consequence, the absence of all accountability and obligation. The foundation of these, as we have already seen, is freedom. Take this away, and you strike a fatal blow at man's moral nature. It is no longer possible for me to feel under obligation to do what I have absolutely no power to do, or to believe myself accountable for doing what I could not possibly avoid. Morality, duty, accountability, become mere chimeras, idle fancies of the brain, devices of the priest and the despot, to frighten men into obedience and subjection.

This View sustained by Facts. — These are not random statements. It is a significant fact, that those who have undertaken to deny accountability, and moral obligation, have, almost without exception, I believe, been advocates of the doctrine of necessity. Indeed, it seems impossible to maintain such views upon any other ground; while, on the other hand, the denial of the freedom of the will leads almost of necessity to such conclusions. "Remorse," says Mr. Belsham, "is the exquisitely painful feeling which arises from the belief that, in circumstances precisely the same, we might have chosen and acted differently. This *fallacious* feeling is superseded by the doctrine of necessity."

Equally plain, and to the same effect, are the following passages from the correspondence of Diderot, as quoted by Mr. Stewart: "Examine it narrowly, and you will see that the word liberty is a word devoid of meaning; that there are not, and that there cannot be, free beings; that we are only what accords with the general order, with our organization, our education, and the chain of events. These dispose of us invincibly. We can no more conceive of a being acting without a motive, than we can of one of the arms of a balance acting without a weight. The motive is always exterior and foreign, fastened upon us by some cause distinct from ourselves. * * * We have been so often praised and blamed, and have so often praised and blamed others, that we contract an inveterate prejudice of believing that we and they will and act freely. But if there is no liberty, there is no action that merits either praise or blame; neither vice nor virtue; nothing that ought either to be rewarded or punished. * * * The doer of good is lucky, not virtuous. * * * *Reproach others for nothing, and repent of nothing; this is the first step to wisdom.*"

These Opinions not to be charged upon all Necessitarians. — It is not to be supposed, of course, that all who deny the freedom of the will, adopt the views above expressed. Whether such denial, however, consistently followed out to its just and legitimate conclusions, does not lead to such results, is another question.

§ II. — The Direct Argument.

Another Mode of Argument. — Thus far we have considered only the presumptions in favor of the freedom of the will. We find them numerous and strong. The question is, however, to be decided not by presumptions for or against, but by direct argument based upon a careful inquiry into the psychological facts of the case. To this let us now proceed, bearing in mind, as we advance, what are the essential phenomena of the will, as already ascertained, and what is meant by freedom of the will as already defined.

The Will free unless its appropriate Action is hindered. — It is evident that, if we are right in our ideas of what freedom is, the will is strictly and properly free, provided nothing interferes with, and prevents, our putting forth such volitions as we please and choose to put forth. The specific and appropriate action of the will, as we have seen, is simply to put forth volitions. Whatever freedom it has, then, must lie within that sphere, and not without it, must relate to *that*, and not to *something else;* whatever restraint or want of freedom it has, must also be found within these limits. My will is free, when I can *will to do* just what I *please.*

Strength of Inclination, no Impediment. — If this be so, then it is clear, 1. That mere *strength of inclination* can by no means impair the freedom of the will. Be the inclination never so strong, it matters not. Nay, so far from interfering with freedom, it is an essential element of it. Freedom presupposes and implies inclination. One is surely none the less free because very strongly inclined to do as he likes, provided he *can do* what he wishes or prefers. This is as true of the action of the will as of any other action.

The Source of Inclination, of no Consequence to the present Inquiry. — 2. It is evident, furthermore, that freedom has nothing to do with the *source* of my inclinations, any more than with their strength. It makes no difference what causes my preference, or whether any thing causes it. I *have* a preference, an inclination, a disposition to do a given thing, and put forth a given volition — am disposed to do it, and *can* do it — then I am free, my will is free. It is of no consequence *how I came* by that inclination or disposition. The simple question is, Am I at liberty to follow it?

The Interference must be from without, and must affect the Choice. — It is evident, moreover, according to what has now been said, that if there be really any restraint upon the will, or lack of freedom in its movements, it must proceed from something extraneous, outside the will itself, something which comes in from without, and that in such a way as to *interfere, in some way, with my choice;* for it is there that the element of freedom lies. But whatever interferes with my choice, *interferes with my willing at all;* the act is no longer a *voluntary* act. Choice is essential to volition, the very element of it. In order to an act of will, as we have seen, there must be liberty to choose, deliberation, actual preference. Volition presupposes them, and is based on them. Whatever prevents them, prevents volition. Whatever places me in such a state of mind that I have no preference at all, no choice, as to any given thing, places me in such a state that I have also no volition as to that thing. The question of freedom is forestalled in such a case, becomes absurd. Where there is no volition, there is of course no freedom of volition, nor yet any want of freedom. Freedom of will is power to will as I like; but now I *have* no liking, no preference.

The Supposition varied. — But suppose now that I am not prevented from choosing, but only from carrying out my choice in actual volition; from willing, according to my choice. Then, also, the act is no longer properly a *volition*, an act of will, for one essential element of every such act, viz., *choice*, is wanting. I *have* a choice, indeed, but it is not here, not represented in this so-called volition, lies in another direction, is, in fact, altogether opposed to this, my so-called volition. There *can be* no such volition. The human mind is a stranger to any such phenomenon, and if it did occur, it would not be volition, not an act of the will, not a *voluntary* act. Whatever, then, comes in, either to prevent my choosing, or to prevent my exercising volition *according* to my choice, does, in fact, prevent my willing at all. If there *be* an act of the will, it is, in its very nature, a *free* act, and cannot be otherwise. Allow me to choose, and to put forth volition according to my choice, and you leave me *free*. Prevent this, and you prevent my willing at all.

The Limitation, as usually regarded, not really one. — Those who contend that the will is not free, *place the limitation back of the choice.* Choice is governed by *inclina-*

tion, they say, and inclination depends on *circumstances;* on education, habits, fashion, etc., things, in great measure, *beyond our control;* and while these circumstances remain the same, a man cannot choose otherwise than he does. To this I reply, that, as we have already seen, the will is strictly and properly free, *provided* nothing interferes with, and prevents, our putting forth such volitions as we *choose* to put forth. Is there, then, any thing in these circumstances which are supposed to control our choice, and to be so fatal to our freedom, is there in them any thing which really interferes with, or prevents our willing as we *choose?* Does the fact that I am inclined, and strongly so, to a given choice, prevent me from putting forth that choice in the shape of executive volition? So far from this, that inclination is the very circumstance that leads to my doing it. All that could *possibly* be contended, is that the supposed inclination to a given choice is likely to prevent my having some *other* and *different* choice. But that has nothing to do with the question of the freedom of my will, which depends, as we have seen, not on the power to choose *otherwise* than one is inclined, or than one likes, but *as* he likes. What force, I ask again, is there in any circumstance, or combination of circumstances, which go to mould and shape my inclinations and my disposition, and have no further power over me, what force in them, or what tendency, to prevent my *willing as I choose, as* I like, *as* I am inclined? Nay, if my will acts at all, it must, as I have shown, act in this way, and therefore act freely.

Freedom of Inclination not Freedom of Will. — But suppose I have no power to *like*, or to be inclined, differently from what I do like, and am now inclined? I reply, it matters not as to the present question. The supposition now made, takes away or limits, not the freedom of the will, it does not touch that; but the freedom of the *affections*. Can I like what I do not like — and can I put forth such volitions as I please or choose — are two distinct questions, and again

I repeat that the freedom of our will depends, *not* on our having this or that particular choice, but on our being able to carry out whatever choice we do make into our volitions; *not* on our being able to will otherwise than we choose, nor yet on our ability to choose otherwise than we do, but simply on our being able to will *as* we choose, whatever that choice may be.

Are the Sensibilities Free. — Have I, in reality, however, any freedom of the affections, any power *under given circumstances*, to be affected otherwise than I am, to feel otherwise than I do? I reply, the affections are not *elements* of the will, are not under its immediate control; are not strictly voluntary. It depends on a great variety of circumstances, what, in any given case, your affections or inclinations may be. You have no power of will *directly* over them. You can modify and shape them, only by shaping your own voluntary action so far as that bears upon their formation. *By shaping your* CHARACTER *which* IS *under your control*, you may, in a manner, at least, determine the nature and degree of the emotions which will arise, under given circumstances, in your bosom.

The two Questions entirely distinct. — But, however that may be, it has nothing to do,. I repeat, with the question now under discussion. The freedom of the affections, and the freedom of the will, are by no means the same thing. We have already seen that there may be a fixed and positive connection between my inclinations and my choice, and so my will, and yet my will be perfectly free. This is the main thing to be settled; and there seems to be no need of further argument to establish this point; and if this be so, it decides the question as to the freedom of the will.

Bearing of this View upon the divine Government. — The view now taken, leaves it open and quite in the power of Providence, so to shape circumstances, guide events, and so to array, and bring to bear on the mind of man, motives and inducements to any given course, as virtually to control and determine his conduct, by controlling and determining his *inclinations*, and so his choice; while, at the same time, the man is left perfectly free to put forth such volitions as he pleases, and to do as he *likes*. There can be no higher liberty than this. To this point I shall again revert, when the question comes up respecting the divine agency in connection with human freedom.

CHAPTER IV.

CERTAIN QUESTIONS CONNECTED WITH THE PRECEDING

§ I. — Contrary Choice.

The Question stated. — In the preceding chapters our attention has been directed to the psychological facts respecting the will, and also to the general question respecting the freedom of the will. Closely connected with this main question, and involved in its discussion, are certain inquiries of a like nature, which cannot wholly be passed by, and for the consideration of which the way is now prepared. One of these respects *the power of contrary choice.* Have we any such power? Is the freedom, which, as we have seen, belongs to the very nature of the will, *such* a freedom as allows of our choosing, under given circumstances, any otherwise than we do? When I put forth a volition, all other things being as they are, *can* I, at that moment, in place of that volition, put forth a different one in its stead?

Not identical with the preceding. — This question is not identical with that respecting the freedom of the will, for it has been already shown that there may be true freedom without any such power as that now in question. My will is free, provided I can put forth such volitions as I please, irrespective of the power to substitute other volitions and choices in place of the actual ones.

Such Power not likely to be exercised. — The question, however, is one of some importance, whether we have any such power or not. And whether we have it or not, one thing is certain — we are not likely to exercise it. If among the fixed and given things, which are to remain as they are, we include whatever inclines or induces the mind to choose and act as it does, then, power or no power to the contrary, the choice *will* be as it is, and would be so, if we were to try the experiment a thousand times; for choice depends on these preceding circumstances and inducements — the inclination of the mind — and if this is given, and made certain, the choice to which it will lead becomes certain also. A choice opposed to the existing inclination, to the sum total of the existing inducements to action, is not a choice at all; it is a contradiction in terms. The power of contrary choice, then, is one which, from the nature of the case, will never be put in requisition, unless something lying back of the choice, viz., inclination, be changed also.

But does such Power exist. — The question is not, however, whether such a power is likely to be employed, but whether it *exists;* not whether the choice *will be* thus and thus, but whether it *can be* otherwise. When, from various courses of procedure, all practicable, and at my option, I select or choose one which, on the whole, I will pursue, have I no *power*, under those very circumstances, and at that very moment, to choose some other course instead of that? *Can* my choice be otherwise than it is?

In what Sense there is such Power. — Abstractly, I suppose, it can. Power and inclination are two different things. The power to act is one thing, and the disposition to exert that power is another thing. *Logically*, one does not involve the other. The power may exist without the disposition, or the disposition without the power. There is *power*, logically, abstractly considered, to choose, even when inclination is wanting; you have only to supply the requisite inclination and the power is at once exerted, the choice is made, the act is performed. But the change of inclination does not *create any new power;* it simply puts in requisition a power already existing.

§ II. — Power to Do what we are not Disposed to Do.

The Question under another Form. — Closely analogous to the question last discussed, virtually, indeed, the same question under another form, is the inquiry, whether we can, at any moment, will or do what we are not, at that moment, inclined to do. Have I any such power or freedom as this, that *I* CAN *do what I am not* DISPOSED *or do not wish to do?* My disposition being to pursue a given course, is it really in my *power* to pursue a different one?

In order to determine this question, let us see what constitutes, or in what consists, the *power* of doing, in any case, what we *are* disposed to do; and then we may be able to judge whether that power still exists, in case the disposition is wanting.

In what Power consists. — It is admitted that I *can* do what I wish or am disposed to do. Now, in what consists that power? That depends on *what sort* of act it is that I am to put forth. Suppose it be a physical act. My power to do what I wish, in that case, consists in my having certain physical organs capable of doing the given thing, and under the command of my will. Suppose it be an intellectual act. My power, in that case, of doing what I like, depends on my having such mental faculties as are requisite for the performance of the given act, and these under control. So long, then, as I have the faculties, physical or mental, that are requisite to the performance of a given act, and those faculties are under the control of my will, so that I can exert them if I please, and when I please, so long my power of doing what I like is unimpaired, and complete, as, *e. g.*, the power of walking, or adding a column of accounts.

But suppose the Disposition wanting. — Suppose, now, the disposition to be wanting; does the power also disappear, or does it remain? I have the same faculties as before, and they are as fully under the control of the will as ever, and that constitutes all the power I ever had. I have the power, then, of doing what I have no inclination to do. Whatever I can do if I like, that also I *can* do, even if I do *not* like. In itself considered, the power to do a thing may be quite complete, and independent of the inclination or disposition to do or not to do.

Will it be put in Requisition? — But will this power be ever exercised? Certainly not, so long as the disinclination continues. In order to the doing of any thing, there must not only be *power* to do it, but *disposition*. If the latter be wanting, the former, though it may exist, will never be put forth.

Our Actions not consequently inevitable. — Have I, then, no power, that is really available, to do what I do not happen to be, at this moment, inclined to do? Am I shut up to the actual inclinations and choices of any given hour or moment? Am I under the stern rule of inevitable necessity and fate to do as I do, to choose as I choose, to be inclined as I am inclined? By no means. My inclinations are not fixed quantities. They may change. They depend, in part, on the intellectual conceptions: these may vary; in part on the state of the heart: divine grace may change the heart.

Actual Choices not necessary ones. — The actual choice of any given moment is by no means a necessary one. Another might have been in its stead. A different inclination is certainly possible and conceivable, and a different inclination *would* have led to a different choice. If, instead of looking at the advantage or agreeableness of a proposed course, and being influenced by that consideration, I had looked at the right, the obligation in the case, my choice would have been a different one, for I should have been influenced by a different motive. Two different objects were presented to my mind, *a* and *b*. As it is, I choose *a*, but *might* have chosen *b*, and *should*, had I been so inclined. Why did I choose *a*? Because, as the matter then presented itself to my mind, I was so inclined. But I might have taken a different view of the whole thing, and then my inclination and my choice would have been different. It was in my power to have thought, to have felt, to have acted differently. What is more, I not only *might*, but, perhaps, *ought* to have felt and acted differently. I am responsible for having such an inclination as leads to a wrong choice; responsible for my opinions and views which influence my feelings; responsible for my disposition, in so far as it is the result of causes within my own control.

Different Uses of the Term Power. — It ought to be clearly defined in all such discussions *what we mean* by the principal *terms* employed. In the present instance what we mean by the words *power*, *ability*, *can*, etc., ought to be distinctly stated. Now, there are two senses in which these words are used, and the question before us turns, in part, on this difference.

1. We may use the word power, *e. g.*, to denote all that is requisite or essential to the *actual doing* of a thing, whatever is so connected with the doing, that, if it be wanting, the thing will not be done.

Or, 2. In a more limited sense, to denote merely all that is requisite to the doing the thing, provided we please or choose to do it, all that is requisite in order to our doing what we *like* or wish.

The latter distinguishes between the *ability* and the *willingness* to do; the former includes them both in the idea of power. In order to the *actual doing* there must be both. But does the word *power* properly include both? In ordinary language, certainly, we distinguish the two. I *can* do a thing, and I wish to do it, are distinct propositions, and neither includes the other. It is only by a license of speech that we sometimes say I *cannot*, when we mean simply, I have no wish or disposition. If we make the distinction in question between power and disposition, then we *can* do what we have no wish to do. If we do not make it, but include in the term power the disposition to exert the power, then we *cannot* do what we have no disposition to do.

§ III. — Influence of Motives

I. Is the Will always as the greatest apparent Good?

The Answer depends on the Meaning of the Question. — If by this be meant simply whether the mind always wills as it is, on the whole, and under all the circumstances, disposed or inclined to will, I have already answered the question. If more than that be meant, if we mean to ask whether we always, in volition, act with reference to the one consideration of *advantage* or utility, the good that is to accrue, in some way, to ourselves or others from the given procedure — and this is what the question seems to imply — I deny that this is so. I have already shown, in presenting the psychological facts respecting the will, that our motives of action are from two grand and diverse sources: *desire* and *duty* — *self-love*, or, at most such love as involves mere natural emotion, and *sense of obligation;* that we do not always act in view merely of the agreeable, but also in view of the *right*, and that these two are not identical. Now the greatest apparent good is not always the right; nor even the *apparent* right. We are conscious of the difference, and of acting, now from the one, now from the other, of these motives. But to say that the will is always according to the greatest apparent good, is to resolve all volition into the pursuit of the agreeable, and all motives of action into self-love. It is to merge the feeling of obligation in the feeling of desire, and lose sight of it as in itself a distinct motive of action.

Defect in the Socratic Philosophy. — This was the capital defect in the ethical system of Socrates, who held that men always pursue what they think to be good, and, therefore, always do what they think is right, since the good and the right are identical; sometimes, indeed, mistaking an apparent good for a real one, but always doing as well as they know how; from which it is but a short step to the conclusion that sin is only so much ignorance, and virtue so much knowledge — a conclusion to which the modern advocates of the doctrines under discussion would by no means assent, but from which that shrewd thinker and most consistent logician saw no escape.

II. Is the Will determined by the strongest Motive?

The Term "strongest" as thus employed. — Much depends on what we mean by "strongest" in this connection, and what by the word "determined?" If we mean, by the strongest motive, the one which in a given case prevails, that in view of which the mind decides and acts, then the question amounts merely to this, Does the *prevalent* motive actually *prevail?* To say that it does, is much the same as to say, that a straight stick is a straight stick. And what else can you mean by strongest motive? What standard have you for measuring motives and guaging their strength, except simply to judge of them by the *effects* they produce? Or, who ever supposed that, of two motives, it was not the stronger but the weaker one that in a given case prevailed?

The Word "determined." — The question may be made, however, to turn upon the word *determined.* Is the will *determined* by that motive which prevails? Is it *determined* at all by *any* motive or by any thing? If by this word it be meant or implied that the motive, and not the mind itself, is the producing cause of the mind's own action, then I deny that the will *is, in any such sense,* determined, whether by the strongest motive, or any other. The will is simply the mind or the soul willing; its acts are determined by itself, and itself only. If you mean simply that the motive *influences* the will, prevails with it, becomes the *reason why* the will decides as it does, this I have already shown to be true, and in this sense, undoubtedly, the motive determines the volition, just as the fall of an apple from a tree is, in the first instance, produced or caused by the law of gravitation; but the particular direction which it takes in falling, depends on, and is determined by, adventitious circumstances as, *e. g.*, the obstacles it meets in its descent. Those obstacles, in one sense, determine the motion; they are the reason and explanation of the fact that it falls *just as* it does, and not otherwise; but they are not the producing cause of the motion itself.

III. Are Motives the Cause, and Volitions the Effect?

Incorrect Use of the Term Cause. — It is common, with a certain class of writers, to speak of motive as the *cause* of action or volition. This is, if at all correct and allowable, certainly not a fortunate use of terms. The agent is properly the *cause* of any act, and in volition the soul itself is the agent. It is the mind itself, which is, strictly, the efficient cause of its own acts. The motive is the *reason why* I act, and not the producer or cause of my act. In common speech, this distinction is not always observed. We say, I do such a thing *because* of this or that, meaning for such and such reasons. In philosophical discussion it is necessary to be more exact.

Liable to be misunderstood. — The use of the word, as now referred to, is particularly to be avoided as liable to mislead the incautious reader or hearer. It suggests the idea of physical necessity, of *irresistibility*. Given, the law of gravitation, *e. g.*, and a body unsupported *must* fall — no choice, no volition; whereas, the action of the mind in volition is, by its essential nature, *voluntary*, directly opposed to the idea of compulsion. Those who use the word in this manner are generally careful to disclaim, it is true, any such sense; but such are our associations with the word *cause*, as *ordinarily* employed, that it is difficult to avoid sliding, unawares, into the old and familiar idea of some sort of absolute physical necessity. It were better to say, therefore, that motives are the reasons why we act thus and thus. To go further than this, to call the motive the *cause* of the volition, is neither a correct nor a fortunate use of terms, since the idea is thereby conveyed, guard against it as you will, that, in some way, the influence was irresistible, the event unavoidable.

The Phrase "moral Necessity." — The same objections lie with still greater force against the phrase *moral necessity* as applied to this subject. Those who use it are careful, for the most part, to define their meaning, to explain that they do not mean necessity at all, but only the *certainty* of actions. The word itself, however, is constantly contradicting all such explanations, constantly suggesting another and much stronger meaning. That is necessary, properly speaking, which depends not on my will or pleasure, which cannot be avoided, but must be, and must be as it is. Now, to say of an act of the will, that it is necessary, in this sense, is little short of a contradiction in terms. The two ideas are utterly incongruous and incompatible.

A volition may be certain to take place; it may be the motive that makes it certain, but if this is all we mean, it is better to say just this, and no more. If this is all we mean, then we do not mean that volitions are necessary in any proper sense of that term. There is no need to use the word necessity, and then explain that we do not mean necessity, but only certainty. It is precisely on this unfortunate use of terms that the strongest objections are founded, against the true doctrine of the connection of motive with volition. Even Mill, one of the ablest modern necessitarians, objects to the use of this term, and urges its abandonment.

The true Connection. — *What, then, is the connection between Motive and Volition?* — I have all along admitted, that there is such a connection between volitions and motives, that the former never occur without the latter, that they stand related as antecedent and consequent, and that motives, while not the producing cause of volitions, are still the *reason why* the volitions are *as* they are, and not otherwise. They furnish the occasion of their existence, and the explanation of their character. So much as this, the psychology of the subject warrants — more than this it does not allow. More than this we seem to assert, however, when we insist on saying that motive is the cause, and volition the effect. We seem, however we may disclaim such intention, to make the mind a mere mechanical instrument, putting forth volitions only as it is impelled by motives, these, and not the mind, being the real producing cause, and the volitions following irresistibly, just as the knife or chisel is but the passive instrument in the hand of the architect, and not at all the producing cause of the effects which follow.

Difference of the two Cases. — Now there is a vast difference between these two cases. The impulse, communicated to the saw, produces the effect irresistibly; not so the motive. The saw is a passive instrument; not so the *mind.* There is, in either case, a fixed connection between the antecedent and the consequent, but the *nature* of the connection is widely different, and it is a difference of the greatest moment. It is precisely the difference indicated by the two words *cause* and *reason* — as applied to account for a given occurrence — the one applicable to material and mechanical powers and processes, the other to intelligent, rational, voluntary agents. There is a *cause* why the apple falls. It is gravitation. There is a *reason* why mind acts and wills as it does. It is motive.

But IS *the Mind the producing Cause of its own Volitions?* — This, the advocates of moral necessity deny. "If we should thus cause a volition," says Dr. Edwards, "we should doubtless cause it by a causal act. It is impossible that we cause any thing without a causal act. And as it is supposed that we cause it freely, the causal act must be a free act, *i. e.*, an act of the will, or volition. And as the supposition is, that all our volitions are caused by ourselves, the causal act must be caused by another, and so on infinitely, which is both impossible and inconceivable." That is, if the mind causes its own volitions, it can do it only by first acting to cause them, and that causative act is, itself, a volition, and requires another causative act to produce it, and so on ad infinitum.

The Dictum Necessitatis proves too much. — This celebrated argument has been called, not inappositely, the *dictum necessitatis.* It rests upon the assumption, that no cause can act, but by first acting to produce that act. Now this virtually shuts out *all* cause from the universe, or else involves us in the infinite series. Apply this reasoning to any cause whatever, and see if it be not so. Suppose, *e. g.*, that *motive*, and not the mind itself, is the producing cause of volition. Then, according to the dictum, motive cannot act, but by first acting in order to act, and for that previous causative act, there must have been an ulterior cause, and so on forever, in an endless succession of previous causative acts.

The Dictum as applicable to Mind. — But it may be said this dictum applies only to mind, or voluntary action. How, then, is it known, that mind cannot act without first acting in order to act? Would not this virtually shut out and extinguish all mental action? The mind thinks; must it first think, in order to think? It reasons, judges, conceives, imagines, must it first reason, judge, etc., *in order* to reason, and judge, and conceive, and imagine? If not, then why may it not *will* without first *willing* to will?

The Dictum as applicable to Deity. — If mind is not the cause of its own volitions, then how is it with the volitions of the infinite and eternal mind? Are they caused or uncaused? If caused, then by what? If by himself, then there is again the infinitely recurring series according to the dictum. If by something else, still we do not escape the series, for each causative act must have its prior cause. Are the volitions of Deity, then, *uncaused?* Then certainly there is no such thing as cause in the universe. Motives, then, are no longer to be called causes. Deity is not, in fact, the cause of any thing, since not the cause of those volitions by which alone all things are produced. If he is not the cause of these, then not the cause of their consequences and effects. In either case, you shut out all cause from the universe, whether the dictum be applied to mind or to motion, to man or to God; or else you are, in either case, involved in the vortex of this terrible infinitive series.

To give up the dictum, is to admit that mind may be the producing cause of its own volitions.

CHAPTER V.

THE DOCTRINE OF THE WILL VIEWED IN CONNECTION WITH CERTAIN TRUTHS OF RELIGION.

The Relation of Psychology to Theology.—The very close connection between the philosophy of the will, and the science of theology, has already been remarked. We have discussed the questions which have come before us thus far, on purely psychological grounds, without reference to their theological bearing. It would be manifest injustice to the matter in hand, however, were we to overlook entirely the relation of our philosophy to those higher truths which pertain to the domain of theological science.

The whole question respecting the freedom of the human will, especially, assumes a new importance, when viewed in connection with the truths of natural and revealed religion.

It ceases to be a speculative, and becomes an eminently practical question when thus viewed.

There are two points which require special attention, as regards that connection; the one, *God's power over man;* the other, *man's power over himself.*

§ I. — The Power which God Exerts over the Human Mind and Will.

Dependence of Man. — It seems to be the teaching of reason, no less than of religion, that man stands to the Creator in the relation of absolute dependence. The one is the subject, the other the sovereign. The control of Deity extends, not merely to the elements and forces of nature, which are by no means the chief and most important part of his works, but over all intelligent, rational beings. This is implied, not only in the fact that he is the Creator of all, but in the fact of moral government, and of a superintending providence. Manifestly, there could be no such thing as moral government, and no control over the affairs of the world, if the conduct of men, the minds and hearts of intelligent beings, were not subject to that control. This is not only the inference which reason draws from the acknowledged supremacy of the Creator, it is not only thus a tenet of natural religion, but it is also one of the plainest doctrines of revealed truth. In the most explicit and direct terms, the Scriptures ascribe to God the supreme control of human conduct, of the human mind and heart. This power over the thoughts and purposes of intelligent beings is the very highest power.

This Control unlimited. — This control, moreover, in order to be complete and effective, must reach beyond the present and passing moment, must take in the future, must sweep through the whole range of coming duration, and comprehend whatever is to be. Nothing must take place without his foreknowledge and permission. The minutest events, the falling of a sparrow, the number of the forest leaves, and of the hairs of our head, must be no exception to this general law.

Implies a Plan, and that Plan embraces human Conduct.—If we suppose the supreme Being to be, not only a Creator and Ruler, but a wise and intelligent one, then we must suppose him to have some *plan* of operations. The very idea of *providence*, indeed, implies this. And this plan must be supposed to extend to, and include, future events, all events, minute events; for the little and the great are linked together, the future and the present are linked together, and the plan and government that has to do with one, must have to do with all, and with human conduct among the rest. This, again, is not more clearly the doctrine of reason than of revelation.

The Difficulty stated.—Whatever freedom man has, then, it must be such a freedom as is consistent with God's complete control and government of him. Neither his present nor his future conduct, neither his thoughts, his feelings, nor his purposes, must be beyond the reach of the divine purpose and control. But how are these things to be reconciled—man's entire freedom, God's entire control and government of him?

Different Positions assumed.—Both are facts, and, therefore, true. Either, by itself, can be well enough conceived and comprehended, but, taken together, they appear inconsistent. Many do not hesitate to pronounce them so. Some, who accept them both as true, regard them as still inexplicable and incomprehensible. Others receive one and reject the other, or, at least, assume such a position as amounts to a virtual rejection of one of these truths. Thus the fatalist secures the supreme government of God, only at the expense of human freedom, and thus weakens, if not destroys, the foundation of human accountability. Others again, in their horror of fatalism, preserve the freedom and accountability of man, at the expense of the divine government and purposes, thus virtually placing man beyond the power and control of Deity.

Application of the preceding Psychology to this Question. — How, then, are these two great facts to be reconciled? If we mistake not, a true psychology, a correct view of the nature of the will, prepares the way for this. What have we found to be the process of the mind in volition? The several steps of the process are found to be these: In the first place, some object to be accomplished is presented, as such, to the understanding. This object, thus presented, appealing to the desires or to the sense of duty, influences or inclines the mind. This, again, leads to choice, choice to volition, volition to action.

Freedom lies where. — Now in this whole process, *where* does the element of freedom lie? Not in the final executive act — the doing as we will to do — for that is merely a bodily function, a physical and not a mental power; nor yet in the control of the motives which influence or incline us; for these are, for the most part, out of our power. Evidently freedom, so far as it pertains to the human will, lies in the power of forming and putting forth such volitions as we please, in other words, of choosing as we like, and willing as we choose, so that whatever our inclinations may be, we shall be at liberty to choose and to will accordingly. This is the highest practical freedom of which it is possible to conceive, and it is all the freedom which pertains to the human will.

How this may consist with the divine Control. — Let us see, now, if this be not a liberty perfectly compatible with the divine government and control over us. These volitions and choices of ours are by no means arbitrary or casual; there is a reason for them; a reason why we choose as we do. We choose thus and thus, because we are, on the whole, so disposed or *inclined;* and this inclination or disposition depends on a great variety of circumstances, on the nature and strength of the motive presented, our physical and mental constitution and habits, our power of self-control, the strength of our desires, as compared with our sense of duty, the presence or absence of the exciting object; in fine, on a great variety of predisposing causes and circumstances, all of which are to be taken into the account, when the question is, why do we choose thus, and not otherwise? Now, these circumstances which go to determine our inclinations, and so our choices and volitions, are, in a great measure, beyond our direct control. Our physical and mental constitution, our external condition, our state of mind, and circumstances at any given moment, whatever in the shape of motive or inducement may be present with moving power to the mind, inclining us this way or that, all this lies much more under divine control than under our own.

The Point of Connection. — Here, then, to speak reverently, lies the avenue of approach, through which Deity may come in and take possession of the human mind, and influence and shape its action, without infringing, in the least, on its perfect freedom. He has only to present such motives as shall seem to the mind weighty and sufficient, has only to touch the main-spring of human inclination, lying back of actual choice, has only to secure within us a disposition or liking to any given course, and our choice follows with certainty, and our volition, and our action; and that action and volition are *free* in the highest sense, because our choice was free. We acted just as we pleased, just as we were inclined.

The Influence of Man over his fellow Men an Illustration of the same Principle. — Now this is just what we, in a limited way, and to a small extent, are constantly doing with respect to our fellow men. We present motives, inducements, to a given course, we work upon their inclinations, we appeal to their sensibilities, their natural desires, their sense of duty, and in proportion as we gain access to their hearts, we are successful in shaping and controlling their conduct. The great and difficult art of governing men lies in this. We have only to suppose a *like* power, but complete and perfect, to be exercised by the supreme disposer and controller of events, so shaping and ordering circumstances as to determine the inclinations of men, gaining access, not in an uncertain and indirect manner, but by immediate approach to the human heart, all whose springs lie under his control, so that he can touch and command them as he will; we have only to conceive this, and we have, as it seems to me, a full and sufficient explanation of the fact that man acts freely, and just as he is inclined, while yet he is perfectly under the divine control.

Power which the Scriptures ascribe to God. — And this, if I mistake not, is precisely the sort of control and power over man which the Scriptures always ascribe to God, viz., power over the inclinations, affections, dispositions, from which proceed all our voluntary actions. In his hand are the *hearts* of men, and he can turn them as the rivers of water are turned.

The Theory does not suppose a divine Influence to Evil. — It is not necessary to suppose that God ever influences men to evil; the supposition is inconsistent with the divine character, with all we know and conceive of Deity. Nor is any such influence over man necessary in order to the accomplishment of evil, but, on the contrary, much is needed to restrain and prevent him from sin. Sufficient already are the motives and influences that incline him to go astray; feeble and inefficient, the inducements to a better life. Could we suppose, however, any influence of this sort to be exerted over man, inclining him to evil, we can still see how such influence might be perfectly consistent with his entire freedom. It is not the integrity of human freedom, but the integrity of the divine character, that forbids such a supposition.

Does not interfere with Responsibility. — Does such a power over human conduct, as that now attributed to the supreme Being, interfere with human *responsibility?* Not in the least. Responsibility rests with him who acts freely, and as he pleases, doing that which is right or wrong, of his own accord, knowing what he does, and because he has a mind to do it. And it is thus man acts, under whatever degree of divine influence we may suppose him placed.

§ II. — Man's Power over Himself.

Unjust to require what it is impossible to perform. — Have I power, in all cases, to do what the divine will requires; power to do *right?* It would seem to be the verdict of reason, and the common sense of mankind, that to require of any man what is literally and absolutely beyond his power, is unjust, and that such a requirement, if it were made, would impose no obligation, since obedience would be impossible. We cannot suppose God to be guilty of such manifest injustice. His commands are right. They carry with them the judgment and reason of men. Conscience approves them. Obligation attends them. They must, therefore, be such commands as it is possible for us to obey. It would be manifest injustice and wrong to require of me what it is actually and absolutely out of my power to do.

Supposed Disinclination. — But suppose I have really no inclination, no disposition, to do right. My affections and desires are all wrong, inclining me to evil, and my sense of duty or moral obligation is not strong enough to prevail against these natural desires and evil inclinations; suppose this, which, alas! is too often true, and what then becomes of my *power* to do right? Does it any longer exist? Have I any power to change those affections and inclinations; or, they remaining as they are, have I any power to go contrary to them? A question this, at once profoundly philosophical, and intensely practical.

Position of the Fatalist. — The fatalist has no hesitation in replying *no*, to these questions. Man has no power to change the current of his own inclinations, nor yet to go against that current. He is wholly under the influence of motives; they turn him this way and that. He has power to do as he wills, but no power over the *volitions* themselves. He has power to do only what he has a mind to do. He has no mind, no inclination to do right, therefore, no power to do so.

This Position at Variance with a true Psychology. — A correct psychology, as we have already seen, gives a different answer. It is not true, as a matter of fact in the philosophy of the human mind, that man has no *power* to do what he has no *disposition* to do; nor is it true that his inclinations and affections are wholly out of his power and control. In both respects, fatalism is at war, not more with the common sense of mankind, than with a sound and true philosophy.

Confounds Power with Inclination. — To say that man has no *power* to do what he is not *inclined* to do, is to confound power with inclination. They are distinct things. The one may exist without the other. I have power to do what I have no disposition to do; on the other hand, I may have the disposition to do what is not in my power. I have power to set fire to my own house, or to my neighbor's, or to cut off my right hand; power, but no disposition. Present a motive sufficiently weighty to change my mind, and incline me to the act, and you create, in that way, a new disposition, but no new power. This point has been fully discussed in the previous chapter, and I need not here repeat the argument. It was shown that in order to the actual doing of a thing, two things are requisite, namely, the *power* to do, and the inclination to *exert* that power; and that neither involves the other. Where the power alone exists, the thing *can be* done, but *will not be;* where both exist, it both *can* and *will* be done. It is not true, then, in any proper use of terms, that want of inclination is want of power.

Our Inclinations not wholly beyond our Control. — Equally incorrect is the position that our inclinations and affections are wholly out of our own control. Within certain limits it is in our power to change them. Inclination is not a fixed quantity. It may change. It ought to change. In many respects it is constantly changing. We take different views of things, and so our feelings and inclinations change. Circumstances change; the course of events changes; and our disposition is modified accordingly. So that while he affections and inclinations are certainly not under the *direct* and *immediate* control of the will, it is still, in a great measure, in our power to modify and control them. While they remain as they are, it is quite certain that we shall do as we do; but it is not *necessary* that they *should*, nor *certain* that they *will*, remain as they are.

The true Answer. — To the question, then, *can* the man whose inclinations are to evil, whose heart is wrong, do right? a true psychology answers *yes*. He *can* do what he is not inclined to do; nor is that evil inclination itself a fixed quantity; he can be, he may be, otherwise inclined.

Something else needed beside Power. — It must be admitted, however, that so long as the heart is wrong, so long as the evil disposition continues, so long the man *will* continue to do evil, notwithstanding all his *power* to the contrary. Left to himself, there is very little probability of his effecting any material change in himself for the better. In order to this, there is needed an influence from without, and from above; an influence that shall *incline* him to obedience, that shall make him *willing* to obey.

The Gospel meets this Necessity. — This is precisely the want of his nature which divine grace meets. It creates within him a *clean heart*, and renews within him a *right spirit*. This is the sublime mystery of regeneration. The soul that is thus born of God is made *willing* to do right. The inclinations are no longer to evil, but to good, and the man still doing that which he pleases, is pleased to do the will of God. The change is in the disposition; it is a change of the affections, of the *heart;* thus the Scriptures always represent it. This was all that was wanted to secure obedience, and this divine grace supplies.

It is not our province to discuss theological questions, as such. It has been our aim, simply, to show the relation of a true psychology to the system of truth revealed in the Scriptures. The perfect *coincidence* of the two is an argument in favor of each.

CHAPTER VI.

POWER OF WILL.

Differences in this respect. — There are great differences among men, as regards the strength and energy of this, as compared with the other departments of mental activity. The difference is, perhaps, as great in this respect, as in regard to the other mental faculties. Not all are gifted with equal power of imagination, not all with equal strength of memory, or of the reasoning faculty; not all with equal strength of the executive power of the mind. Some persons exhibit a weakness of will, a want of decision and firmness, an irresolution of character and purpose. They waver and hesitate in cases of doubt and emergency, requiring decision and energy. They are governed by no fixed purpose. The course which they adopt to-day, they abandon to-morrow for the opposite. They are controlled by circumstances. Opposition turns them from their course, difficulties discourage them. They are easily persuaded, easily led; ill fitted to be themselves leaders of men.

Others, again, are firm and inflexible as a rock. They choose their course, and pursue it, regardless of difficulties and consequences. Difficulties only arouse them to new effort. Opposition only strengthens their decision and purpose. They are hard to be persuaded, when once their minds are made up, and harder still to be driven. They take their stand, nothing daunted by opposing numbers, and, with Fitz-James, when suddenly confronted and surrounded by the hosts of Roderic Dhu, exclaim,

> "Come one, come all, this *rock* shall fly
> From its firm base, as soon as *I*."

Instances of Firmness. — Napoleon, fiery and impetuous as he was, possessed this energy and strength of will. Obstacles, difficulties, insurmountable to other men, established usages, institutions, armies, thrones, all were swept away before the irresistible energy of that mighty will, and that determined purpose, as the wave, driven before the storm, clears itself a path among the pebbles and shells that lie strewn upon the shore. In the character of his brother Joseph, King of Spain, we have an example of the opposite. Mild, cultivated, refined, amiable, of elegant tastes, a man of letters, loving retirement and leisure, he was lacking in that energy and decision of character which fit men for command in camps and courts. We have in the firm and terrible energy of Cromwell, as contrasted with the mildness and inefficiency of his son and successor Richard, the same difference illustrated. The Puritan leaders of the English Revolution were men of stern and determined energy of character. Among the Romans, Cæsar presents a notable example of that strength of will which fits men for great enterprises; while the great Roman orator, with all his acquisitions of varied learning, and all his philosophy, and all his eloquence, was deficient in firmness of purpose.

Often exhibited in military Leaders. — In general it may be remarked that great military commanders have usually been distinguished for this trait of character. It was by virtue of their energy, and decision, and firmness of purpose, that they accomplished what they did, succeeding where other men would have failed. Thus it was with Hannibal, with Frederic the Great, with Wellington, with our own Washington. They were, by nature, endowed with those qualities which fitted them for their important and difficult stations; while, at the same time, the work to which they were called, and the circumstances in which they were placed, tended greatly to develop and strengthen those peculiar traits and qualities, and this among the rest.

The same Trait exhibited in other Stations of Life. — Strength of will shows itself, however, in other relations and stations of life, as well as in the military commander. The leader of a great political party, as, for example, of the Administration, or of the Opposition, in the English Parliament, has abundant occasion for firmness and strength of purpose. It was not less strength of will, than of moral principle, in Socrates, that led him resolutely to withstand the popular clamor, and the opinions of his associate judges, and refuse to sentence the unsuccessful military commanders, on the day when the decision lay in his hands; the same trait showed itself in that retreat after the battle of Delius, so graphically described by Plato, when he walked alone and slowly from the field, where all was confusion and flight, with such coolness and such an air of calm self-reliance, that no enemy ventured to approach him; it was shown not less in his determined refusal to escape from prison, and the unjust sentence of death, notwithstanding all the entreaties and remonstrances of friends.

Strength of Will in the Orator. — The truly great orator, rising to repel the assaults of his antagonist, or to allay the prejudices and take command of the passions and opinions of a popular assembly, calm and collected, and conscious of his strength, master of his own emotions, and of all his powers, presents an illustration of the same principle. It was seen in Webster, when he rose in the Senate to reply to Hayne. The very aspect of the man conveyed to all beholders the idea of power — a strength, not merely of gigantic intellect, but of resolute will, *determined* to conquer.

Strength of Will as shown in the Endurance of Suffering. — The same principle is sometimes manifested in a different manner, and in different circumstances. If it leads to heroic *actions*, it leads also to heroic *endurance* and suffering. It was the firm and stubborn will of Regulus, that sent him back to Carthage, to endure all that the disappointed malice of his foes could invent. It was the firm will of Jerome of Prague, that kept him from recantation in the face of death; the firm will of Cranmer, that thrust his right hand into the flames, and kept it there till it was quite consumed. A like firmness of purpose has been exhibited in thousands of instances, both in the earlier and later annals of Christian martyrdom. Rather than renounce a principle, or abandon the deeply-cherished convictions of the soul, natures, the most frail and feeble, have calmly met and endured the greatest sufferings, with a firmness, and courage, and power of endurance, that nothing could shake or overcome.

How to be attained. — To multiply instances is needless. But how shall this strength of will, so desirable, so essential to true greatness and nobleness of character, be attained?

In part it is the gift of nature, doubtless — the result of that physical and mental constitution with which some are more fortunately endowed; in part it is an acquisition to be made, as any other mental or physical acquisition, by due care and training. It will be of service, especially, in any endeavor of this sort, to accustom ourselves to decide with promptness, and act with energy in the many smaller and less important affairs of life, and to carry out a purpose, once deliberately formed, with persistence, even in trivial matters. The habit thus formed, we may be able afterward, and gradually, to carry into higher departments of action, and into circumstances of greater embarrassment and difficulty. On the other hand, this must not be carried to the extreme of *obstinacy*, which is the refusal to correct a mistake, or acknowledge an error, or listen to the wiser and better counsels of others.

CHAPTER VII.

HISTORICAL SKETCH.—OUTLINE OF THE CONTROVERSY RESPECTING FREEDOM OF THE WILL.

Question early Discussed.—The question respecting human freedom, was very early a topic of inquiry and discussion. It enters prominently into the philosophy of all nations, so far as we know, among whom either philosophy or theology have found a place. It is by no means confined to Christian, or even to cultivated nations. It holds a prominent place in the theological systems and disputes of India and the East, at the present day. The missionary of the Christian faith meets with it, to his surprise, perhaps, in the remotest regions, and among tribes little cultivated. It is a question, at once so profound, and yet of such personal and practical moment, that it can hardly have escaped the attention of any thoughtful and reflecting mind, in any country, or in any age of the world.

The Greek Philosophy.—Among the Greeks, conflicting opinions respecting this matter prevailed in the different schools. The *Epicureans*, although asserting human liberty in opposition to the doctrine of universal and inexorable *fate*, were, nevertheless, *necessitarians*, if we may judge from the writings of Lucretius, whose idea of liberty, as Mr. Stewart has well shown, is compatible with the most perfect necessity, and renders man "as completely a piece of passive mechanism as he was supposed to be by Collins and Hobbes." This liberty is, itself, the *necessary effect of some cause*, and the reason assigned for this view is precisely that given by modern advocates of necessity, namely, that to suppose otherwise, is to suppose *an effect without a cause.*

On the other hand, the *Stoics*, while maintaining the doctrine of *fate*, held, nevertheless, to the utmost liberty of the will. With the consistency of these views, we are not now concerned. Epictetus is referred to by Mr. Stewart, as an example of this not unusual combination of fatalism and free-will.

The Jewish Sects.—Very similar was the relation of the two rival sects among the Jews, the Sadducees and the Pharisees, the former holding the doctrine of human freedom, the latter of such a degree, at least, of fatality, as is inconsistent with true liberty.

The Arabian Schools.—Among no people, perhaps, has this question been more eagerly and widely discussed, than by the Arabians, whose philosophy seems to have grown out of their theology. When that remarkable book, the Koran, first aroused the impulsive mind of the Arab from his idle dreams, and startled him into consciousness of higher truth, the very first topic of inquiry and speculation about which his philosophic thought employed itself, seems to have been this long-standing question of human ability and the freedom of the will. The Koran taught the doctrine of necessity and fate. A sect soon arose, called *Kadrites*, from the word *kadr*, power, freedom, holding the opposite doctrine, that man's actions, good and bad, are under the control of his own will. From this was gradually formed a large body of *dissenters*, as they styled themselves, and in maintaining these views on the one side, and opposing them on the other, the controversy became more and more one of philosophy, and for some three centuries, with varied learning and skill, Arabian scholars and philosophers disputed, warmly, this most difficult and abstruse of metaphysical questions. Fatalism seems ultimately to have prevailed, as, indeed, a doctrine so congenial to error, and to every false system of religious belief, would be quite likely to do, where any such system is established.

The Scholastics and the Reformers.—Among the scholastic divines of the middle ages, some held to the liberty of the will, while many allowed only what they called the liberty of *spontaneity*, *i. e.*, power to *do* as we will, in opposition to liberty of *indifference*, or power over the determinations of the will itself.

Among the moderns, the Reformers differed among themselves on the matter of liberty, the Lutherans, with Melancthon, opposing the scheme of necessity; Calvin and Bucer maintaining it, as the necessary consequence of their views of divine predestination.

Distinguished modern Advocates of Necessity.—Among the philosophical writers of the last and the present century, a very strong array of eminent names is on the side of necessity. Hobbes, Locke — who is claimed, however, by each side — Leibnitz, Collins, Edwards, Priestley, Belsham, Lord Kames, Hartley, Mill, advocate openly the doctrine of necessity.

Doctrine of Hobbes. — The views of *Hobbes* seem to have given shape to the opinions of subsequent advocates of this theory. The only liberty which he allows, is that of doing what one wills to do, or what the scholastics called the liberty of spontaneity. Water is free, and at liberty, when nothing prevents it from flowing down the stream. Liberty he defines, accordingly, to be "*the absence of all impediments to action that are not contained in the nature and intrinsical quality of the agent.*" A man whose hands are tied, is not at liberty to go; the impediment is not in him, but in his bands; while he who is sick or lame, is at liberty, because the obstacle is in himself. A free agent is one who can do as he wills.

This is essentially the view of freedom adopted by the later advocates of necessity, and almost in the same terms, it is the view of Collins, Priestley, and Edwards.

Doctrine of Locke. — It is, also, *Locke's* idea of freedom. Liberty, he says, is the power of any agent "to do or forbear any particular action, according to the determination or thought of the mind, whereby either of them is preferred to the other." This extends only to the carrying out our volitions when formed, and not to the matter of willing or preferring; power over the determinations of the will, itself, is not included in this definition.

Locke Inconsistent. — In this, Locke was inconsistent with himself, since, in his chapter on power, he seems to be maintaining the doctrine of human freedom. The liberty here intended, it has been justly remarked by Bledsoe, is not freedom of the will, or of the mind in willing, but only of the body; it refers to the motion of the body, not to the action of the mind.

Locke expressly says, "there may be *volition* where there is no liberty;" and gives, in illustration, the case of a man falling through a breaking bridge, who has volition or preference not to fall, but no liberty, since he cannot help falling. In this, again, Locke is inconsistent, since, elsewhere, he distinguishes between volition and desire or preference, while here he does not distinguish them.

There can be no doubt that Locke supposed himself an advocate of human freedom, for such is the spirit of his whole treatise, especially of his twenty-first chapter; at the same time, it must be confessed, his definitions are incomplete, and his language inconsistent and vacillating, so that there is some reason to class him, as Priestley does, with those who really adopt the scheme of necessity without knowing or intending it.

View of Leibnitz. — Leibnitz was led to adopt the doctrine of necessity from his general theory of the *sufficient reason*, that is, that nothing occurs without a *reason why* it should be so, and not otherwise. This principle he carries so far as to deny the power of Deity to create two things perfectly alike, and the power of either God or man to *choose* one of two things that are perfectly alike. This principle presents the mind as always determined by the greatest apparent good, and establishes, as its author supposed, by the certainty of demonstration, the absolute impossibility of free agency.

View of Collins. — Collins maintains the necessity of all human actions, from experience, from the impossibility of liberty, from the divine foreknowledge, from the nature of rewards and punishments, and the nature of morality. He takes pains to reconcile this doctrine with man's accountability and moral agency, and is careful to define his terms with great exactness. Thus the terms liberty and necessity are defined as follows: "First, though I deny *liberty* in a certain meaning of the word, yet I contend for *liberty* as it signifies a *power in man to do as he wills or pleases.* Secondly, when I affirm *necessity*, I contend only for *moral necessity*, meaning thereby that man, who is an intelligent and sensible being, is determined by his reason and his senses; and I deny man to be subject to such necessity as is in clocks and watches, and such other beings, which, for want of sensation and intelligence, are subject to an *absolute, physical*, or *mechanical necessity.*

Coincidence of Collins and Edwards. — The coincidence of these views and definitions, and, indeed, of the plan of argument, with the definitions and the arguments of Edwards, is remarkable. No two writers, probably, were ever further removed from each other in their general spirit and character, and in their system of religious belief; yet as regards this doctrine, the definitions and views of one were those of the other, and as Mr. Stewart has justly remarked, the coincidence is so perfect, that the outline given by the former, of the plan of his work, might have served with equal propriety as a preface to the latter.

Views of Edwards. — No writer has more ably discussed this question than the elder Edwards. He is universally conceded to be one of the ablest metaphysicians, as well as theologians, of modern times. His work on the Freedom of the Will is a masterpiece of reasoning. At the same time, as to the character and tendency of the system therein maintained, the greatest difference of opinion exists. By some he is regarded as a fatalist, by others he is claimed as an advocate of human freedom. There is some ground for this difference of opinion. No writer, from Plato downward, was ever perfectly self-consistent; it would be strange if Edwards were so. That the general scheme of necessity, maintained by Edwards, tends, in some respects, to fatalism, — that the ablest champions of fatalism, and even writers of atheistic, and immoral views, have held essentially the same doctrine, and maintained it by the same arguments — must be conceded; that such was not the design and spirit of his work, that such was not his own intention, is perfectly evident.

Main Positions of Edwards. — The definitions of Edwards, as we have already seen, are the same with those of Collins and Hobbes. He understands by liberty *merely a power to do as one wills.* The mind is always determined by the greatest apparent good. The motive determines the act, *causes* it. The mind acts, wills, chooses, etc., but the motive is the *cause* of its action. That the mind should be the cause of its own volitions, implies, he maintains, an act of will preceding the volition, that is a volition prior to volition, and so on forever in an infinite series. This argument, the famous *dictum necessitatis*, has been considered in a previous chapter. Now, to say that motive is the producing cause, and volition the effect, especially if the connection of the two is of the *same nature* as that between physical causes and effects, as Edwards affirms, is certainly to say that which looks very strongly toward fatalism.

Necessity, what. — Edwards maintains the doctrine of *necessity.* But what did he mean by *moral necessity?* The phrase is unfortunate, for reasons already suggested — it does convey the idea of irresistibility, of something which *must* and *will be* — in spite of all contrary will and endeavor. This, however, he is careful to disclaim. He means by moral and philosophical necessity simple CERTAINTY, "nothing different from certainty." "No opposition or contrary will and endeavor," he says, "is supposable in the case of moral necessity, which is a certainty of the inclination and will itself." Now we must allow him to put his own meaning upon the terms he uses; and to say that under given circumstances, there being given such and such motives, inclinations, and preferences, such and such volitions will *certainly* follow, is not to say that the will is not free in its action — is not to shut us up to absolute fate — is not, in fact, to say any thing more than is strictly and psychologically true. In defending himself from this very charge, he uses the following explicit language in a letter to a minister of the Church of Scotland: "On the contrary, *I have largely declared that the connection between antecedent things and consequent ones, which takes place with regard to the acts of men's wills, which is called moral necessity, is called by the name of necessity* improperly; and that such a necessity as attends the acts of men's wills is more properly called certainty than necessity; it being no other than the certain connection between the subject and predicate of the proposition which affirms their existence." "Nothing that I maintain supposes that men are at all hindered by any fatal necessity, from doing, and even willing and choosing as they please, with full freedom; free with the highest degree of liberty that ever was thought of, or that could possibly enter into the heart of man to conceive." This is explicit, and ought to satisfy us as to what Edwards himself thought of his own work, and meant by it. Still a man does not always understand himself, is not always the best judge of his own arguments, is not always consistent with himself, does not always express his own real opinions, nor do himself justice, in every part of his reasonings. This is certainly the case with Edwards. We are at a loss to reconcile some passages in his treatise with the foregoing extract, *e. g.*, *the dictum necessitatis;* also his declaration that the difference between natural and moral necessity "lies *not so much* IN THE NATURE of the connection as in the two terms connected." This is an unfortunate admission for those who would shield him from the charge of fatalism. If the necessity, by which a volition follows the given motive, is, after all, of the *same nature* with that by which a stone falls to the earth, or water freezes at a given temperature, it is all over with us as to any consistent, intelligible defence of the freedom of the will.

If, moreover, the doctrine of Edwards leaves man full power, as he says above, to *will and to choose as he pleases*, what becomes of the *dictum*, which makes it impossible for the mind to determine its own volitions?

Does not distinguish between the Affections and the Will. — It should be remembered that Edwards does not distinguish between the will and affections. This distinction had not, at that time, been clearly drawn by writers on the philosophy of the mind. The twofold division of mental powers, into understanding and will, was then prevalent; the affections, of course, were classed with the latter. Hence there is not that definiteness in the use of terms which modern psychology demands. Had Edwards distinguished between the affections and the will, it must have given a different cast to his entire work. Even Locke, whose philosophy Edwards follows in the main, had distinguished between *will* and *desire*, as we have already seen; but in this he is not followed by Edwards, who, while he does not regard them as "words of precisely the same signification," yet does not think them "so entirely distinct that they can ever be said to *run counter*."

Views of the later Necessitarians. — Of the views of the later advocates of necessity, Priestley, Belsham, Diderot, and others, of that school, we have already spoken in a previous chapter. They carry out the scheme, with the greatest boldness and consistency, to its legitimate consequences, fatalism, and the denial of free agency and accountability. God is the real and only responsible doer of whatever comes to pass, and man the passive instrument in his hand. Remorse, regret, repentance, are idle terms, and to praise or blame ourselves or others, for any thing that we or they have done, is merely absurd.

Advocates of the Opposite. — On the other hand, the doctrine of the freedom of the will has not wanted able advocates among the more recent philosophical writers. In general it may be remarked, that those who have treated of the powers of the human mind, as psychologists, have, for the most part, maintained the essential freedom of the will, while the advocates of the opposite view have been chiefly metaphysicians, rather than psychologists, and, in most cases, have viewed the matter from a theological rather than a philosophical point of view. Among the more recent and able advocates of the freedom of the will, are Cousin and Jouffroy, in France, Tappan and Bledsoe, in our own country. Previously, Mr. Stewart, in his appendix to his "Active and Moral Powers," had concisely, but very ably, handled the matter, and earlier still, Kant, in Germany, had conceded the liberty of the will as a matter of *consciousness*, while unable to reconcile it with the dictates of reason.

View of Hamilton. — Substantially the same view is taken by the late Sir William Hamilton, who, by general consent, stands at the head of modern philosophers, and who accepts the doctrine of liberty as a *fact*, an immediate dictum of consciousness, while, at the same time, he is unable to *conceive* of its possibility, since "to conceive a free act, is to conceive an act which, being a cause, is not, in itself, an effect; in other words, to conceive an absolute commencement;" and this he regards as impossible. At the same time, it is equally beyond our power, he thinks, to conceive the possibility of the opposite, the doctrine of necessity, since that supposes "an *infinite series of determined causes*," which cannot be conceived. But though inconceivable, freedom is not the less a fact given by consciousness; and is to be placed in the same category with many other facts among the phenomena of mind, "which we must admit as actual, but of whose possibility we are wholly unable to form a notion."

Remarks upon this View. — The difficulty here presented, — if I may venture a remark upon the opinions of so profound a thinker, and the same is true of Kant, — turns evidently on the peculiar idea of freedom entertained by those writers, namely, that in order to be free, an act of the will must be wholly undetermined, not itself an effect, but an absolute commencement. Any influence, from any source, going to determine or incline a man to will as he does, renders the act no longer free. Such freedom is certainly inconceivable; and what is more, impracticable; it exists as little among the possibilities of the actual world, as among the possibilities of thought. We never act, except under the influence of motive and inclination; and if acts thus performed are not free, then no acts that we perform are so.

View of Coleridge. — This eminent disciple of the earlier German philosophy, derives from Kant the view of freedom now explained, and carries it to the furthest extreme. All influence and inclination are inconsistent with freedom. The disposition to do a thing renders the will, and the act of the will, no longer free. A *nature*, of any kind, is inconsistent with freedom. This, of course, shuts out all freedom from the actual world. Nor is it possible to conceive how even the acts of Deity can be any more free than ours, on this supposition; nor how, if any such freedom as this were supposed to exist, an act thus performed, without any motive, or any disposition or inclination on the part of the agent, could be a *rational* or accountable act.

Views of Cousin, and Jouffroy. — Cousin and Jouffroy, while by no means denying the influence of motive upon the mind, place the fact of liberty in the power which the mind has of being itself a cause, and of putting forth volitions from its own proper power. The law of inertia, contends Jouffroy, which requires a moving force proportioned to the movement of a material body, does not apply to the human mind, and "to apply this law to the relation which subsists between the resolutions of my will and the motives which act upon it, is to suppose that my being, that I myself, am not a cause; for a cause is something which produces an act by its own proper power." Cousin, in like manner, places liberty in the absolute and undetermined power of the will to act as cause; and "this cause, in order to produce its effect, has need of no other theatre, and no other instrument than itself. It produces it directly, without any thing intermediate, and without condition; * * * being always able to do what it does not do, and able not to do what it does. Here, then, in all its plenitude, is the characteristic of liberty."

View of Tappan. — One of the ablest defenders of the freedom of the will in our own country, Mr. Tappan, in his review of Edwards, takes essentially the position just explained. All cause lies ultimately in the will. It is this which makes the nisus or effort that produces any event or phenomenon. Of this nisus the mind or will is itself the cause, and, as such, it is *self-moved.* It makes its nisus of itself, and of itself it forbears to make it, and within the sphere of its activity, and in relation to its objects, it has the power of selecting, by a mere arbitrary act, any particular object. It is a cause, all whose acts, as well as any particular act, considered as phenomena demanding a cause, are accounted for *in itself alone.*

Position of Bledsoe. — Similar is the position of Mr. Bledsoe, one of the most recent reviewers of Edwards, a writer of marked ability and candor. He denies, however, that volition is the *effect* of any thing, whether motive or mind, in the sense that motion of the arm is an effect. It is *activity, action, the cause of action,* but not *effect.* In distinction from most writers of the same theological views, he denies that the will is *self-determined,* or that it is *determined at all,* and by any thing. It is the *determiner,* but not the *determined.*

REFERENCES.

Among the authorities which have been consulted in the preparation of this work, the following may be referred to, with profit, by the reader who desires to pursue the subject further.

I. THE INTELLECT.

A. ON THE INTELLECTUAL FACULTIES IN GENERAL.

Locke. — Essays on the Human Understanding.
Reid. — Essays on the Intellectual Powers. Walker Ed.
" Works. — By *Hamilton*, with *notes and dissertations.*
Dugald Stewart. — Philosophy of the Human Mind. Bowen Ed.
" Philosophical Essays.
Brown. — Lectures on the Philosophy of the Mind.
The works of *Upham*, *Wayland*, *Winslow*, *Mahan*, may also be consulted with profit.
Cousin. — Cours de, 1828. Id., 1829.
" Fragments Philosophiques.
Jouffroy. — Mélanges Philosophiques. Nouvelles Mélanges.
" Esquisses de D. Stewart. Préface.
Descartes. — Méditations. Id., Discours de la Méthode.
Leibnitz. — Nouveaux Essais sur l'Entendement Humain.
Malebranche. — Recherche de la Vérité.
Royer Collard. — Œuvres de Reid. Fragments.
Damiron. — Cours de Philosophie.
Hegel. — Encyklopädie der Philosoph. Wissenchaft.
Rosenkrantz. — Psychologie.
Kant. — Anthropologie. Kritik Reiner Vernunft.
" Kritik der Urtheilskraft.
Aristotle. — Metaphysics.
" On the Soul.
Plato. — Republic.
Cicero. — Tusculanæ Questiones.

B. ON THE SPECIFIC FACULTIES.

I. SENSATION AND PERCEPTION.

Reid. — Intellectual Powers.
Hamilton. — Supplementary Dissertation, Note D.
O. Wight. — Philosophy of Sir W. Hamilton. Part II.
Stewart. — Philosophical Essays. Ess. II.
Brown. — Philosophy of Human Mind.
Mill. — Analysis of Human Mind.
A. Smith. — Essays on Philosophical Subjects. Of the External Senses.
Young. — Lectures on Intellectual Philosophy.
Comte. — Philosophy Positive.
Müller. — Elements of Physiology.
Tissot. — Anthropologie.
Maine de Biran. — Nouvelles Considerations sur les Rapports, etc.
Jouffroy. — Nouvelles Mélanges Philosophiques.
Royer Collard. — Fragments in Jouffroy's Œuvres de Reid.
Tortual. — Die Sinne des Menschen.
Buffier. — Traité des Premières Vérités.
Amédée Jacques. — Psychologie. Manuel de Phil. à l'usage des Coll.
Dictionnaire des Sciences Philosophiques. Art. Sens.
Aristotle. — De Anima. Parva Naturalia.
J. Barth. Saint Hilaire. — Psychologie de Aristotle. Notes and preface.

II. MEMORY.

Stewart. — Intellectual Philosophy.
Reid. — Intellectual Powers. (Walker.)
Brown. — Philosophy of Human Mind.
Mill. — Analysis of Human Mind.
Abercombie. — On Intellectual Powers.
Hume. — Treatise on Human Nature. Book I. Part I.
Aristotle. — Parva Naturalia.
Bartheleme Saint Hilaire. — Psychologie d'Aristotle. Part II.
Malebranche. — Recherche de la Vérité. Liv. II.
Rosenkrantz. — Psychologie.
Hegel. — Encycl. Phil. Wissench. Dritter Theil.

III. IMAGINATION.

Stewart. — Intellectual Philosophy.
Brown. — Philosophy of Human Mind.
Rauch. — Psychologie. Part II.
Sidney Smith. — Sketches of Philosophy.
Mill. — Analysis of Human Mind.
Amédée Jacques. — Manuel de Philosophie. Psychol. V.
Rosenkrantz. — Psychologie. *Die Einbildungskraft.*
Hegel. — Encyc. der Phil. Wissenchaft. Dritter Theil. *Die Einbildung.*

IV. ABSTRACTION AND GENERALIZATION.

Reid. — Intellectual Powers.
Brown. — Philosophy of Human Mind.
Stewart. — Intellectual Philosophy.
A. Smith. — Considerations on First Formation of Languages.
J. S. Mill. — System of Logic.
Whewell. — Philosophy of Inductive Sciences.
James Mill. — Analysis of Human Mind.
Thomson. — Laws of Thought.
Cousin. — Elements of Psychology. (Henry.)
Hume. — Treatise of Human Nature. Book I. Part I.

V. REASONING.

Hamilton. — Supplementary Dissertation, Note A.
Reid. — Intellectual Powers.
Stewart. — Intellectual Philosophy. Part II.
Locke. — On the Human Understanding. Book IV.
Whewell. — Philosophy of Inductive Sciences.
Buffier. — Premieres Vérités.
Brown. — Philosophy of Human Mind.
Mill. — System of Logic.
Hamilton.— Discussions on Philosophy. (Turnbull Ed.) Article IV, Logic also Appendix II. A and B.
Baynes.—New Analytic of Logical Forms.
Descartes. — Discours de la Méthode.
Condillac. — Art de Penser.
Dictionnaire des Sciences Philosophiques. Logique.
Pascal. — Pensées — de l'Art de Persuader.
Port-Royal. — Logique.
Aristotle. — Organon.

VI. INTUITIVE CONCEPTION.

FIRST PRINCIPLES.

Reid. — Intellectual Powers. Essay VI., cap. III.
Hamilton. — Dissertation A. §§ 3, 4, 5.
Stewart. — Intellectual Philosophy. Part II., cap. I.
Coleridge. — Aids to Reflection.
Mill. — System of Logic. Book II., caps. V. and VI.
Buffier. — Premières Vérités. Part I., cap. VII.

TIME, SPACE.

Cousin. — Cours de Philosophie. Tome II., Leçons XVII., XVIII.
" Idem. Elements of Psychologie. Henry. Cap. III.
Locke. — Essay on the Human Understanding. Book II., cap. XXVI.
Stewart. — Philosophical Essays. Essay II., cap. II.
Reid. — Intellectual Powers. Essay III., cap. II.
Mill. — Analysis of the Human Mind. Cap. XIV., § V.
Royer Collard. — Fragments, IX., X.
Kant. — Kritik rein. vernunft. Transcend. Æsthet. Part I., § II.
Dictionnaire des Sciences Philosophiques. Temps. Espace.
Hegel. — Encyclop. Philosoph. Wissench. Tsweiter Theil. Erst. Abschnitt.

IDENTITY.

Locke. — Essay, etc. Book II., cap. XXVII.
Cousin. — Review of do. as above. Eléments Psychologie, cap. III.
Reid. — Intellectual Powers. Essay III., cap. III.
Mill. — Analysis, etc., cap. XIV., § VII.
Whately. — Logic — Appendix. On Ambiguous Terms.
Butler. — Dissertation on Identity.

CASUALITY.

Mill. — System of Logic. Book III., cap. XXI.
Whewell. — Philosophy of Inductive Sciences. Part I. Book III.
Locke. — Essay. Book II., cap. XXVI.
Tappan. — On the Will. Cap. II. *Cause.*
Bowen. — Metaphysics and Ethics.
Maine de Biran. — Examples des Leçons de Philosophie de Laromiquière.
Cousin. — Œuvres de Maine Biran. Preface.
As above. El. Psychologie, cap. IV.

THE BEAUTIFUL.

Kames. — Elements of Criticism.
Alison. — On Taste.
McDermot. — On Taste.
Stewart. — Philosophical Essays. Part II.
Brown. — Philosophy of the Human Mind. *Emotions of Beauty.*
Jouffroy. — Cours d'Esthetique.
Cousin. — Philosophy of the Beautiful. (Daniel, Trans.)
Kant. — Kritik der Urtheilskraft.
Hegel. — Cours d'Esthetique. (Benard, Tr.)

THE RIGHT.

Stewart. — Active and Moral Powers. (Walker Ed.)
Brown. — Philosophy of the Human Mind. Ethical Science.
Butler. — Sermons.
Paley. — Moral Philosophy.
Adam Smith. — Theory of Moral Sentiments.
Upham. — Mental Philosophy. Vol. II.
Winslow. — Elements of Moral Philosophy.
Wayland. — Moral Philosophy.
Whewell. — Elements of Morality.
Jouffroy. — Introduction to Ethics. (Channing, Tr.)
" Cours de Droit Natural.
Emile Saisset. — Manuel de Philosophie à l'usage des Coll. *Morale.*
Descartes. — Lettres.
Cicero. — De Officiis.
Aristotle. — Nicom. Eth.
Plato. — Republic and Gorgias.

II. THE SENSIBILITIES.

Stewart. — Active and Moral Powers. (Walker Ed.)
Reid. — Faculties of the Human Mind. Essay III.
Brown. — Philosophy of the Human Mind. *Emotions.*
Upham. — Mental Philosophy. Vol. II.
Cogan. — On the Passions.
Descartes. — Les Passions de l'Âme.
Condillac. — Traité des Sensations.
Damiron — Cours de Philosophie. *De la Sensibilité.*

Jouffroy. — Mélanges Philosophiques. *De l'Amour de Soi.*
Aristotle. — On the Soul. Books II. and III.

III. THE WILL.

Edwards. — On the Will.
Tappan. — Review of do.
Day. — Review of do.
Bledsoe. — Examination of do.
I. Taylor. — Essay introductory to do.
Tappan. — On the Will, and do. on Moral Agency.
Mahan. —On the Will.
Upham. — On the Will.
Reid. — On the Faculties of the Human Soul. Essay IV.
Belsham. — Philosophy of the Human Mind.
Mill. — System of Logic. Book VI., cap. II.
Mill. — Analysis of the Human Mind. Cap. XXIV.
Cogan. — Ethical Questions. Question IV.
Stewart. — Active and Moral Powers. Cap. VI.
Reid. — Essays on Active Powers. Essay II.
Locke. — On the Human Understanding. Book II., cap. XXI.
Hamilton. — Philosophy of the Conditioned, cap. II., § 1. (O. W. Wight.)
Jouffroy. — Introduction to Ethics, § IV.
Leibnitz. — Essays de Théodicée.
Cousin. — Fragments Philosophiques. Preface.
Amédée Jacques. — Manuel de Phil. *Psychologie. Volonté.* XV. — XVII.
Maine de Biran. — Œuvres. Vol. IV.
" Controversy with Clarke.
Cousin. — Psychologie. (Henry, Tr.) Cap. X.
Damiron. — Psychologie. Liv. I., § II., cap. III.
Emile Saisset. — Dictionnaire des Sciences Philosophiques. Art. *Liberté.*

Valuable Works,

PUBLISHED BY

GOULD AND LINCOLN,

59 WASHINGTON STREET, BOSTON.

CHRISTIAN'S DAILY TREASURY: a Religious Exercise for every day in the year. By Rev. H. Temple. 12mo, cloth. $1.00.

WREATH AROUND THE CROSS; or, Scripture Truths Illustrated. By Rev. A. Morton Brown, D. D. 16mo, cloth. 60 cents.

SCHOOL OF CHRIST; or, Christianity Viewed in its Leading Aspects. By Rev A. R. L. Foote. 16mo, cloth. 50 cents.

THE CHRISTIAN LIFE, Social and Individual. By Peter Bayne, M. A. 12mo, cloth. $1.25.

THE PURITANS; or, The Church, Court, and Parliament of England. By Rev. Samuel Hopkins. In 3 vols., octavo. Vol. I., cloth, *ready.* $2.50.

MODERN ATHEISM; under its various forms. By James Buchanan, D.D. 12mo, cloth. $1.25.

THE MISSION OF THE COMFORTER; with copious Notes. By Julius Charles Hare. American edition; Notes translated. 12mo, cloth. $1.25.

GOD REVEALED IN NATURE AND IN CHRIST. By Rev. James B. Walker. 12mo, cloth $1.00.

PHILOSOPHY OF THE PLAN OF SALVATION. New, improved, and enlarged edition. 12mo, cloth. 75 cents.

YAHVEH CHRIST; or, The Memorial Name. By Alex'r MacWhorter. Introductory Letter by Nath'l W. Taylor, D.D. 12mo, cloth. 60 cents.

SALVATION BY CHRIST: Discourses on some of the most important Doctrines of the Gospel. By Francis Wayland, D.D. 12mo, cloth. $1.00.

THE SUFFERING SAVIOUR; or, Meditations on the Last Days of Christ. By Frederick W. Krummacher, D. D. 12mo, cloth. $1.25.

THE GREAT DAY OF ATONEMENT; or, Meditations and Prayers on the Sufferings and Death of our Lord. 75 cents.

EXTENT OF THE ATONEMENT IN ITS RELATION TO GOD AND THE UNIVERSE. By Thomas W. Jenkyn, D.D. 12mo, cloth. $1.00.

THE IMITATION OF CHRIST. By Thomas à Kempis. With a Life of à Kempis, by Dr. C. Ullmann. 12mo, cloth. 85 cents.

THE HARVEST AND THE REAPERS. Home Work for all, and how to do it. By Rev. Harvey Newcomb. 16mo, cloth. 68 cents.

(RELIGIOUS.)

LIMITS OF RELIGIOUS THOUGHT EXAMINED. By Henry L. Mansel, B. D. Notes translated for American ed. 12mo, cl. $.100.

THE CRUCIBLE; or, Tests of a Regenerate State. By Rev. J. A. Goodhue. Introduction by Dr. Kirk. 12mo, cloth. $1.00.

LEADERS OF THE REFORMATION. Luther — Calvin — Latimer — Knox. By John Tulloch, D. D. 12mo, cloth. $1.00.

BARON STOW. *Christian Brotherhood.* 16mo, cloth. 50 cents.

——— *First Things;* or, the Development of Church Life. 16mo, cloth. 60 cents.

JOHN ANGELL JAMES. *Church Member's Guide.* Cloth. 33 cts.

——— *Church in Earnest.* 18mo, cloth. 40 cts.

——— *Christian Progress.* Sequel to the Anxious Inquirer. 18mo, cloth. 31 cents.

THE GREAT CONCERN. By N. Adams, D. D. 12mo, cloth. 85 cents.

JOHN HARRIS'S WORKS. *The Great Teacher.* With an Introductory Essay by H. Humphrey, D. D. 12mo, cloth. 85 cents.

——— *The Great Commission.* With an Introductory Essay by William R. Williams, D. D. 12mo, cloth. $1.00.

——— *The Pre-Adamite Earth.* Contributions to Theological Science. 12mo, cloth. $1.00.

——— *Man Primeval:* Constitution and Primitive Condition of the Human Being. Portrait of Author. 12mo, cloth. $1.25.

——— *Patriarchy;* or, The Family, its Constitution and Probation. 12mo, cloth. $1.25.

——— *Sermons, Charges, Addresses, &c.* Two volumes, octavo, cloth. $1.00 each.

WILLIAM R. WILLIAMS. *Religious Progress.* 12mo, cloth. 85 cts.

——— *Lectures on the Lord's Prayer.* 12mo, cloth. 85 cents.

THE BETTER LAND. By Rev. A. C. Thompson. 12mo, cloth. 85 cents

EVENING OF LIFE; or, Light and Comfort amid the Shadows of Declining Years. By Jeremiah Chaplin, D. D. 12mo, cloth. $1.00.

HEAVEN. By James William Kimball. 12mo, cloth. $1.00.

THE SAINT'S EVERLASTING REST. Baxter. 16mo, cl. 50 cts.

Gould and Lincoln's Publications.

(RELIGIOUS.)

GOTTHOLD'S EMBLEMS; or, Invisible Things Understood by Things that are Made. By CHRISTIAN SCRIVER. Tr. from the 28th German Ed. by Rev. ROBERT MENZIES. 8vo, cloth, $1.00 Fine Edition, Tinted Paper, royal 8vo, cloth, $1.50.

THE STILL HOUR; or, Communion with God. By Prof. AUSTIN PHELPS, D. D., of Andover Theological Seminary. 16mo, cloth. 38 cents.

LESSONS AT THE CROSS; or, Spiritual Truths Familiarly Exhibited in their Relations to Christ. By SAMUEL HOPKINS, author of "The Puritans," etc. Introduction by GEORGE W. BLAGDEN, D. D. 16mo, cloth. 75 cents.

NEW ENGLAND THEOCRACY. From the German of Uhden's History of the Congregationalists of New England. Introduction by NEANDER. By Mrs. H. C. CONANT. 12mo, cloth. $1.00.

EVENINGS WITH THE DOCTRINES. By Rev. NEHEMIAH ADAMS, D. D. 12mo, cloth.

THE STATE OF THE IMPENITENT DEAD. By ALVAH HOVEY, D. D., Prof. of Christian Theology in Newton Theol. Inst. 16mo, cloth. 50 cents.

FOOTSTEPS OF OUR FOREFATHERS; what they Suffered and what they Sought. Describing Localities, Personages, and Events, in the Struggles for Religious Liberty. By JAMES G. MIALL. Illustrations. 12mo, cloth. $1.00.

MEMORIALS OF EARLY CHRISTIANITY. Presenting, in a graphic form, Memorable Events of Early Ecclesiastical History, etc. By Rev. J. G. MIALL. With Illustrations. 12mo, cloth. $1.00.

THE MISSIONARY ENTERPRISE. The most important Discourses in the language on Christian Missions, by distinguished American Authors. Edited by BARON STOW, D. D. 12mo, cloth. 85 cents.

THE RELIGIONS OF THE WORLD, and their Relations to Christianity. By FREDERICK DENISON MAURICE, Prof. of Divinity in King's Coll., London. 16mo, cloth. 60 cents.

THE CHRISTIAN WORLD UNMASKED. By JOHN BERRIDGE, A. M., Vicar of Everton, Bedfordshire. With a Life of the Author, by Rev. THOMAS GUTHRIE, D. D. 16mo, cloth. 50 cents.

THE EXCELLENT WOMAN, as described in the Book of Proverbs. With an Introduction by W. B. SPRAGUE, D. D. Twenty-four splendid Illustrations. 12mo, cloth. $1.00.

MOTHERS OF THE WISE AND GOOD. By JABEZ BURNS, D. D. 16mo, cloth. 75 cents.

THE SIGNET-RING, and its Heavenly Motto. From the German. Illustrated. 16mo, cloth, gilt. 31 cents.

THE MARRIAGE-RING; or, How to Make Home Happy. From the writings of JOHN ANGELL JAMES. Beautifully Illustrated edition. 16mo, cloth, gilt. 75 cents.

Gould and Lincoln's Publications.

(LITERARY.)

CYCLOPÆDIA OF ANECDOTES OF LITERATURE AND THE FINE ARTS. Containing a copious and choice Selection of Anecdotes of the various forms of Literature, of the Arts, of Architecture, Engravings, Music, Poetry, Painting, and Sculpture, and of the most celebrated Literary Characters and Artists of different Countries and Ages, etc. By KAZLITT ARVINE, A. M. Numerous Illustrations. Octavo, cl. $3.00.

This is unquestionably the choicest collection of *Anecdotes* ever published. It contains *three thousand and forty Anecdotes:* and such is the wonderful variety, that it will be found an almost inexhaustible fund of interest for every class of readers.

KNOWLEDGE IS POWER. A View of the Productive Forces and the Results of Labor, Capital, and Skill. By CHARLES KNIGHT. With numerous Illustrations. Revised by DAVID A. WELLS. 12mo, cloth. $1.25.

LANDING AT CAPE ANNE; or, The Charter of the First Permanent Colony on the Territory of the Massachusetts Company. By J. WINGATE THORNTON. 8vo, cloth. $1.50.

☞ "A rare contribution to the early history of New England."—*Mercantile Journal.*

THE CRUISE OF THE NORTH STAR. Excursion to England, Russia, Denmark, France, Spain, Italy, Malta, Turkey, Madeira, etc. By Rev. JOHN O. CHOULES, D. D. With Illustrations, etc. 12mo, cloth, gilt. $1.50.

PILGRIMAGE TO EGYPT. A Diary of Explorations on the Nile, the Manners, Customs, and Institutions of the People, the condition of the Antiquities and Ruins. By Hon. J. V. C. SMITH. Numerous Engravings. 12mo, cloth. $1.25.

VISITS TO EUROPEAN CELEBRITIES. Graphic and life-like Personal Sketches of the most distinguished men and women of Europe. By the Rev. WILLIAM B. SPRAGUE, D. D. 12mo, cloth. $1.00.

THOUGHTS ON THE PRESENT COLLEGIATE SYSTEM in the United States. By FRANCIS WAYLAND, D. D. 16mo, cloth. 50 cents.

SACRED RHETORIC; or, Composition and Delivery of Sermons. By H. J. RIPLEY, D. D. With Dr. WARE'S Hints on Extemporaneous Preaching. 12mo, cloth. 75 cents.

MANSEL'S MISCELLANIES; including "Prolegomina Logica," "Metaphysics," "Limits of Demonstrative Evidence," "Philosophy of Kant," etc. 12mo, cloth. *In preparation.*

MACAULAY ON SCOTLAND. A Critique, from HUGH MILLER'S "Edinburgh Witness." 16mo, flexible cloth. 25 cents.

NOTES ON THE UNITED STATES OF AMERICA. By T. H. GRAND PIERRE, D. D., Pastor of the Reformed Church, Paris. 16mo, cloth. 50 cts.

HISTORY OF CHURCH MUSIC IN AMERICA. Peculiarities; its legitimate use and its abuse; with notices of Composers, Teachers, Schools, Choirs, Societies, Conventions, Books, etc. By N. D. GOULD. 12mo, cloth. 75 cents.

THE CAPTIVE IN PATAGONIA; or, Life among the Giants. A Personal Narrative. By B. FRANKLIN BOURNE. With Illustrations. 12mo, cloth. 85 cents.

Gould and Lincoln's Publications.

(BIOGRAPHICAL.)

LIFE OF JOHN MILTON, in connection with the Political, Ecclesiastical, and Literary History of his time. By DAVID MASSON, M. A. 3 vols., 8vo. Vol. I., cloth. $2.75.

LIFE AND CORRESPONDENCE OF REV. DANIEL WILSON, D. D., late Bishop of Calcutta By Rev. JOSIAH BATEMAN. With portraits, map, and illustrations. One volume, royal octavo. $3.00.

LIFE AND CORRESPONDENCE OF THE LATE AMOS LAWRENCE. By W. R. LAWRENCE, M. D. 8vo, cloth. $1.50. 12mo, cloth. $1.00.

DR. GRANT AND THE MOUNTAIN NESTORIANS. By Rev. THOMAS LAURIE, his surviving associate. 12mo, cloth. $1.25.

MEMOIR OF THE LIFE AND TIMES OF ISAAC BACKUS. By ALVAH HOVEY, D. D. 12mo, cloth. $1.25.

LIFE OF JAMES MONTGOMERY. By Mrs. H. C. KNIGHT, Author of "Lady Huntington and her Friends" 12mo, cloth. $1.25.

MY MOTHER; or, Recollections of Maternal Influence. By a New England Clergyman. 12mo, cloth. 75 cents.

MEMOIR OF ROGER WILLIAMS. By Professor WILLIAM GAMMELL. 16mo, cloth. 75 cents.

LIFE AND CORRESPONDENCE OF JOHN FOSTER. By JOHN E. RYLAND. 2 vols. in one, 12mo, cloth. $1.25.

PHILIP DODDRIDGE. His Life and Labors. By JOHN STOUGHTON, D. D. 16mo, cloth. 60 cents.

MEMOIR OF ANN H. JUDSON. By Rev. J. D. KNOWLES. 18mo, cloth. 58 cents.

MEMOIR OF GEORGE D. BOARDMAN. By Rev. A. KING. Introduction by W. R. WILLIAMS, D. D. 12mo, cloth. 75 cents.

LIFE OF GODFREY WILLIAM VON LEIBNITZ. By JOHN. M. MACKIE. 16mo, cloth. 75 cents.

THE TEACHER'S LAST LESSON; A Memoir of MARTHA WHITING, of Charlestown Female Seminary. By C. N. BADGER. 12mo, cloth. $1.00.

MEMOIR OF HENRIETTA SHUCK, the first Female Missionary to China. By Rev. J. B. JETER, D. D. 18mo, cloth. 50 cents.

MEMOIR OF REV. WILLIAM G. CROCKER, Missionary to West Africa. By R. B. MEDBURY. 18mo, cloth. 63 cents.

THE KAREN APOSTLE; or, Memoir of KO-THAH-BYU, the first Karen Convert. By Rev. F. MASON, D. D. 18mo, cloth. 25 cents.

MEMORIES OF A GRANDMOTHER. By a Lady of Massachusetts 16mo cloth. 50 cents.

Gould and Lincoln's Publications.

(LITERARY.)

THE PURITANS; or, the Court, Church, and Parliament of England. By SAMUEL HOPKINS. 3 vols., 8vo, cloth. $2.00 per volume.

HISTORICAL EVIDENCES OF THE TRUTH OF THE SCRIPTURE RECORDS, STATED ANEW, with Special Reference to the Doubts and Discoveries of Modern Times. Bampton Lecture for 1859. By GEORGE RAWLINSON. 12mo, cloth. $1.00.

CHRIST IN HISTORY. By ROBERT TURNBULL, D. D. A New and Enlarged Edition. 12mo, cloth. $1.25.

THE CHRISTIAN LIFE; Social and Individual. By PETER BAYNE. 12mo, cloth. $1.25.

ESSAYS IN BIOGRAPHY AND CRITICISM. By PETER BAYNE. Arranged in two series, or parts. 2 vols., 12mo, cloth. $1.25 each.

THE GREYSON LETTERS. By HENRY ROGERS, Author of the "Eclipse of Faith." 12mo, cloth. $1.25.

CHAMBERS' WORKS. CYCLOPÆDIA OF ENGLISH LITERATURE. Selections from English Authors, from the earliest to the present time. 2 vols., 8vo, cloth. $5.00.

——————— *MISCELLANY OF USEFUL AND ENTERTAINING KNOWLEDGE.* 10 vols., 16mo, cloth. $7.50.

——————— *HOME BOOK;* or, Pocket Miscellany. 6 vols., 16mo, cloth. $3.00

THE PREACHER AND THE KING; or, Bourdaloue in the Court of Louis XIV. By L. F. BUNGENER. 12mo, cloth. $1.25.

THE PRIEST AND THE HUGUENOT; or, Persecution in the age of Louis XV. By L. F. BUNGENER. 2 vols, 12mo, cloth. $2.25.

MISCELLANIES. By WILLIAM R. WILLIAMS, D. D. 12mo, cloth. $1.25.

ANCIENT LITERATURE AND ART. Essays and Letters from Eminent Philologists. By Profs. SEARS, EDWARDS, and FELTON. 12mo, cloth. $1.25.

MODERN FRENCH LITERATURE. By L. RAYMOND DE VERICOUR. Revised, with Notes by W. S. CHASE. 12mo, cloth. $1.25.

BRITISH NOVELISTS AND THEIR STYLES. By DAVID MASSON, M. A., Author of Life of Milton. 16mo, cloth. 75 cents.

REPUBLICAN CHRISTIANITY; or, True Liberty, exhibited in the Life, Precepts, and early Disciples of the Redeemer. By E. L. MAGOON. 12mo, cloth. $1.25.

THE HALLIG; or, the Sheepfold in the Waters. Translated from the German of BIERNATSKI, by Mrs. GEORGE P. MARSH. 12mo, cloth. $1.00.

MANSEL'S MISCELLANIES; including "Prolegomina Logica," "Metaphysics," "Limits of Demonstrative Evidence," "Philosophy of Kant," etc 12mo. *In press.*

(SABBATH SCHOOL.)

POPULAR CYCLOPÆDIA OF BIBLICAL LITERATURE. Condensed, by JOHN KITTO, D. D. Numerous Illustrations. 8vo. $3.00.

THE HISTORY OF PALESTINE; with Chapters on its Geography and Natural History, its Customs and Institutions. By JOHN KITTO, D. D. With Illustrations. 12mo. $1.25.

ANALYTICAL CONCORDANCE TO THE HOLY SCRIPTURES; or, The Bible under Distinct and Classified Topics. By JOHN EADIE, D. D. 8vo. $3.00.

CRUDEN'S CONDENSED CONCORDANCE. By ALEX. CRUDEN. 8vo. Half boards, $1.25. Sheep, $1.50.

COMMENTARY ON THE ORIGINAL TEXT OF THE ACTS OF THE APOSTLES. By H. B. HACKETT, D. D. 8vo. $2.25.

ILLUSTRATIONS OF SCRIPTURE. Suggested by a tour through the Holy Land. With Illustrations. New, Enlarged Edition. By H. B. HACKETT, D. D. 12mo, cloth. $1.00.

PROF. H. J. RIPLEY'S NOTES.

——————— *ON THE GOSPELS.* For Teachers in Sabbath Schools, and as an Aid to Family Instruction. With Map of Canaan. Cloth, embossed. $1.25.

——————— *ON THE ACTS OF THE APOSTLES.* With Map of the Travels of the Apostle PAUL. 12mo, cloth, embossed. 75 cents.

——————— *ON THE EPISTLE OF PAUL TO THE ROMANS.* 12mo, cloth, embossed. 67 cents.

COMMENTARY ON THE EPISTLE TO THE EPHESIANS. Explanatory, Doctrinal, and Practical. By R. E. PATTISON, D. D. 12mo. 85 cents.

MALCOM'S NEW BIBLE DICTIONARY of Names, Objects, and Terms, found in the Holy Scriptures. By HOWARD MALCOM, D. D. 16mo, cloth. 60 cents.

HARMONY QUESTIONS ON THE FOUR GOSPELS, for the use of Sabbath Schools. By Rev. S. B. SWAIM, D. D. Vol. I. 18mo, cloth backs. 13 cents.

SABBATH-SCHOOL CLASS-BOOK. By E. LINCOLN. 13 cents.

LINCOLN'S SCRIPTURE QUESTIONS; with Answers. 8 cents.

THE SABBATH-SCHOOL HARMONY; with appropriate Hymns and Music for Sabbath Schools. By N. D. GOULD. 13 cents.

EVIDENCES OF CHRISTIANITY, as exhibited in the writings of its apologists, down to Augustine. By Prof. W. J. BOLTON, Cambridge, England. 12mo, cloth. 80 cents.

Gould and Lincoln's Publications.

(SCIENTIFIC.)

ANNUAL OF SCIENTIFIC DISCOVERY. 11 vols., from 1850—1860. By D. A. WELLS, A. M. With Portraits of distinguished men. 12mo. $1.25 each.

THE PLURALITY OF WORLDS; a new edition, with the author's reviews of his reviewers. 12mo. $1.00.

COMPARATIVE ANATOMY OF THE ANIMAL KINGDOM. By Profs. SIEBOLD and STANNIUS. Translated by W. I. BURNETT, M. D. 8vo. $3.00

HUGH MILLER'S WORKS. *TESTIMONY OF THE ROCKS.* With Illustrations. 12mo, cloth. $1.25.

—————— *FOOTPRINTS OF THE CREATOR.* With Illustrations. Memoir by LOUIS AGASSIZ. 12mo, cloth. $1.00.

—————— *THE OLD RED SANDSTONE.* With Illustrations, etc. 12mo, cloth. $1.25.

—————— *MY SCHOOLS AND SCHOOLMASTERS.* An Autobiography. Full-length Portrait of Author. 12mo, cloth. $1.25.

—————— *FIRST IMPRESSIONS OF ENGLAND AND ITS PEOPLE.* With fine Portrait. 12mo, cloth. $1.00.

—————— *CRUISE OF THE BETSEY.* A Ramble among the Fossiliferous Deposits of the Hebrides. 12mo, cloth. $1.25.

—————— *POPULAR GEOLOGY.* 12mo, cloth. $1.25.

HUGH MILLER'S WORKS, 7 vols., embossed cloth, with box, $8.25.

UNITED STATES EXPLORING EXPEDITION, under CHARLES WILKES. Vol. XII., Mollusca and Shells. By A. A. GOULD, M. D. 4to. $10.00.

LAKE SUPERIOR. Its Physical Character, Vegetation, and Animals. By L. AGASSIZ. 8vo. $3.50.

THE NATURAL HISTORY OF THE HUMAN SPECIES. By C. HAMILTON SMITH. With Elegant Illustrations. With Introduction, containing an abstract of the views of eminent writers on the subject, by S. KNEELAND, M. D. 12mo. $1.25.

THE CAMEL. His organization, habits, and uses, with reference to his introduction into the United States. By GEORGE P. MARSH. 12mo. 63 cents.

INFLUENCE OF THE HISTORY OF SCIENCE UPON INTELLECTUAL EDUCATION. By W. WHEWELL, D. D. 12mo. 25 cents.

SPIRITUALISM TESTED; or, the Facts of its History Classified, and their causes in Nature verified from Ancient and Modern Testimonies. By GEO. W. SAMSON, D. D. 16mo, cloth. 38 cents.

Gould and Lincoln's Publications.

(EDUCATIONAL.)

THESAURUS OF ENGLISH WORDS AND PHRASES; arranged to facilitate the expression of ideas. By PETER MARK ROGET. With additions by BARNAS SEARS, D. D. 12mo, cloth. $1.50.

THE CICERONIAN; or, the Prussian method of teaching the elements of the Latin Language, adapted to American Schools. By Prof. BARNAS SEARS. 18mo, half mor. 50 cents.

HALL'S GEOLOGICAL CHART; with a section of geological formations from the Atlantic to the Pacific Ocean. By Prof. JAMES HALL, Albany. Mounted. $9.50.

A KEY TO THE GEOLOGICAL CHART. By Professor JAMES HALL. 25 cents.

SERIES OF TEXT-BOOKS. By W. S. BARTON, A. M.

——————— *EASY LESSONS IN ENGLISH GRAMMAR.* For young beginners. 12mo, half morocco. 50 cents.

——————— *INTERMEDIATE GRAMMAR.* For the use of Schools and Academies. 12mo, half morocco. 75 cents.

——————— *HIGH SCHOOL GRAMMAR.* 12mo, half morocco. $1.00.

——————— *PRACTICAL EXERCISES IN ENGLISH COMPOSITION;* or, the Young Composer's Guide. 12mo. 75 cents.

——————— *RHETORIC.* In Press.

ROMAN ANTIQUITIES AND ANCIENT MYTHOLOGY. By C. K. DILLAWAY. Illustrated by elegant Engravings. Eighth edition, improved. 12mo, half morocco. 67 cents.

THE YOUNG LADIES' CLASS-BOOK. Lessons for reading in Prose and Verse. By EBENEZER BAILEY, A. M. Fifty-second edition. Cloth embossed. 84 cents.

BLAKE'S NATURAL PHILOSOPHY; with Notes, Questions, and a Dictionary of Philosophical Terms. 28 Steel Engravings. By J. L. BLAKE, D. D. Sheep. 67 cents.

BLAKE'S FIRST BOOK IN ASTRONOMY; for the use of Common Schools. Illustrated with steel-plate Engravings. By J. L. BLAKE, D. D. Cloth. 50 cents.

MEMORIA TECHNICA; or, the Art of Abbreviating those Studies which give the greatest labor to the memory. By L. D. JOHNSON. Half bound. 50 cts.

PROGRESSIVE PENMANSHIP, Plain and Ornamental, for the use of Schools. By N. D. GOULD, author of "Beauties of Writing," "Writing Master's Assistant," etc In five parts, each 13 cents.

Gould and Lincoln's Publications.

(EDUCATIONAL.)

LECTURES ON METAPHYSICS. By SIR WILLIAM HAMILTON. With Notes from original materials. 8vo, cloth. $3.00.

LECTURES ON LOGIC. By SIR WILLIAM HAMILTON. With an Appendix, containing the author's latest development of his new Logical theory. 8vo, cloth.

ELEMENTS OF MORAL SCIENCE. By FRANCIS WAYLAND, D. D., late President of Brown University. 12mo, cloth. $1.25.

THE SAME, Abridged for Schools and Academies, half morocco. 50 cents.

ELEMENTS OF POLITICAL ECONOMY. By FRANCIS WAYLAND, D. D. 12mo, cloth. $1.25.

THE SAME, Abridged for Schools and Academies, half morocco. 50 cents.

MENTAL PHILOSOPHY; including the Intellect, the Sensibilities, and the Will. By JOSEPH HAVEN, D. D. 12mo, cloth. $1.50.

MORAL PHILOSOPHY; including Theoretical and Practical Ethics. By JOSEPH HAVEN, D. D. 12mo, cloth. $1.25.

THE EARTH AND MAN; Lectures on Comparative Physical Geography in its relation to the History of Mankind. By ARNOLD GUYOT. 12mo, cloth. $1.25.

THE ELEMENTS OF GEOLOGY; adapted to Schools and Colleges. With numerous Illustrations. By J. R. LOOMIS, President of Lewisburg University. 12mo, cloth. 75 cents.

PRINCIPLES OF ZOÖLOGY; for the use of Schools and Colleges. With numerous Illustrations. By LOUIS AGASSIZ and AUGUSTUS A. GOULD, M. D. 12mo, cloth. $1.00.

PALEY'S NATURAL THEOLOGY. Illustrated by forty Plates. Edited by JOHN WARE, M. D. 12mo, cloth. $1.25.

GUYOT'S MURAL MAPS; A series of elegant colored maps, exhibiting the Physical Phenomena of the Globe.

MAP OF THE WORLD, mounted. $10.00

MAP OF NORTH AMERICA, mounted. $9.00.

MAP OF SOUTH AMERICA, mounted. $9.00.

MAP OF GEOGRAPHICAL ELEMENTS, mounted. $9.00.

GEOLOGICAL MAP OF THE UNITED STATES AND BRITISH PROVINCES; with Geological Sections and Fossil Plates. By JULES MARCOU. 2 vols., 8vo, cloth. $3.00.

www.ingramcontent.com/pod-product-compliance
Lightning Source LLC
LaVergne TN
LVHW021219110826
845150LV00002B/203

* 9 7 8 1 4 2 5 5 6 4 2 6 1 *